St. Louis Community College

Forest Park
Florissant Valley
Meramec

Instructional Resources
St. Louis, Missouri

GAYLORD

THE QUEST FOR
A LIVING WAGE

THE QUEST FOR A LIVING WAGE

The History of the Federal Minimum Wage Program

Willis J. Nordlund

Contributions in Labor Studies, Number 48

GREENWOOD PRESS
Westport, Connecticut • London

Library of Congress Cataloging-in-Publication Data

Nordlund, Willis J.
    The quest for a living wage : the history of the federal minimum
wage program / Willis J. Nordlund.
       p.   cm.—(Contributions in labor studies, ISSN 0886-8239 ;
no. 48)
    Includes bibliographical references and index.
    ISBN 0-313-26412-0 (alk. paper)
    1. Minimum wage—United States—History. 2. Minimum wage—Law and
legislation—United States—History. I. Title. II. Series.
HD4918.N67 1997
331.2'3—dc20   95-48354

British Library Cataloguing in Publication Data is available.

Library of Congress Catalog Card Number: 95-48354
ISBN: 0-313-26412-0
ISSN: 0886-8239

First published in 1997

Greenwood Press, 88 Post Road West, Westport, CT 06881
An imprint of Greenwood Publishing Group, Inc.

Printed in the United States of America

The paper used in this book complies with the
Permanent Paper Standard issued by the National
Information Standards Organization (Z39.48-1984).

10 9 8 7 6 5 4 3 2 1

To Kathy, Jeff, and John

Contents

Tables

APPENDIX

Preface

Minimum wage programs did not originate in the United States. The first contemporary programs have their roots in New Zealand and Australia, with intervening development in Britain and France. The precursors to all of these programs can be found as *maximum* wage proclamations dating back to the thirteenth century in England. While there is an interesting developmental process over the intervening centuries, it is beyond the scope of this book.

Minimum wage programs evolved in response to the inhumane problems of "sweating," which involved work at wages so low that they could not, and did not, support a socially acceptable level of wholesome family life. Out of this milieu came the desire to institute a level of compensation that became known as the "living wage." It was a wage rate that would permit average workers, working average hours to earn enough to sustain their famil:lies at a socially acceptable level of well-being. The concepts of sweating and a living wage were less-than-precise analytical devices, and many of those concerned about low wages and the consequences of low wages on individuals, families, and society crafted their own definitions. Politicians, the clergy, economists, social reformers, the courts, and others worried about these issues, and each group viewed solutions to the problem differently.

Considerable disagreement occurred because of the confusion between *individual* wages and *family* income. There was a general lack of clarity concerning the relationship between wages, hours of work, and income. There was a lack of clarity about worker productivity and appropriate wage rates. Nevertheless, those concerned about the deleterious effects of low wages on family well-being continued to press for legislative initiatives to resolve the problem. As this book shows, there were legislative responses, but they satisfied few proponents or opponents of minimum wage programs. In some cases, legislative activity was viewed as the cure-all for society's problems, and it necessarily fell short. In other cases, the legislation was poorly crafted and had no effect on the labor market or the problems of society it purported to address. These outcomes should not be surprising, but they demonstrate that minimum wage programs have historically taken on roles they cannot address and that they are political as well as economic devices.

Historically and today, few are neutral about minimum wage programs. There are those who attribute all of society's problems to these programs, while others see them as the mechanism to cure everything from low wages to poor income distribution to economic stagnation to low productivity. In reality, of course, both views of minimum wage programs are incorrect. These programs are one element in the fabric of the economy that affects the relationship between economic sectors and individual economic participants but whose impacts are large or small, depending on the character of the legislation, the state of the economy, the level of enforcement, and a host of other variables.

Since these programs are legislated, the courts have had an important effect on their structure and implementation. American courts were initially hostile toward these programs in the States, and the U.S. Supreme Court declared them unconstitutional. However, the problems these programs attempted to address did not disappear simply because the Court invalidated the legislation. In most cases, the problems intensified through time. Social and political leaders struggled to craft legislation that would address the Court's concerns while simultaneously addressing the economic and social problems. Importantly, most foreign programs did not have to stand constitutional challenges because they developed in countries with parliamentary forms of government. The courts in Australia, New Zealand, and Great Britain did not find problems with these programs as long as they met the legislative requirements of general government. In the U.S., however, the character of these programs bumped against the constitutional requirements of freedom of contract and due process of law early in their development.

This book begins with the development of the state programs and works its way through the enactment of the Fair Labor Standards Act (FLSA), its implementation, court challenges, and evolution into today's program. The FLSA was a central part of the New Deal legislation which included other major legislation familiar to most readers. The Davis–Bacon Act of 1931, the Wagner–Peyser Act of 1933, the National Labor Relations Act of 1935, the Social Security v Act of 1935, the Unemployment Insurance Act of 1935, and the National Apprenticeship Act of 1937 predated the FLSA but formed the basis of the federal legislative response to labor problems. In addition, there were major New Deal programs designed to stimulate the economy, such as those involving the Civilian Conservation Corps, the Public Works Administration, the Civil Works Administration, and the National Youth Administration. All of these programs had significant effects on the use of labor in the economy.

Throughout its evolution, the FLSA has been amended several times to expand coverage, raise the minimum wage, and initiate a variety of other programmatic changes. These amendments have not been without controversy. In its golden anniversary year, the FLSA is being considered for additional amendments. The character and impacts of these amendments are being debated in the Congress and the national press. What is clear is that there is little consensus about impacts or effects of changes in the program and, equally important, what role it should play in the economy. After fifty years of experience, one would presume that enough was known about the program to formulate a defensible analytical strategy depicting effects of program change. This is not the case. There is no more agreement about these effects today than there was at the program's inception fifty years ago. What this says about the program, other than that it is very complex, is not clear. However, it is a safe bet that we are unlikely to be much more successful in vithis assessment process during the seventy-fifth or one hundredth anniversary than we are today. This general observation may give some solace to those who support programs of this type for philosophical reasons, but it may also place the program in a difficult legislative position. If supporters cannot devise methods to unequivocally demonstrate the benefits and advantages of this program, it may at some point be the target for less sympathetic legislators.

The FLSA has identified hundreds of millions of dollars of back wages due to hundreds of thousands of American workers. It has identified child labor problems that begged for intervention. Whether the FLSA's response has been adequate in all cases is open for discussion. Program supporters still believe that there is much remaining to be done and that the FLSA can be an effective tool to address remaining issues and problems. Program critics seem to believe that the FLSA has outlived its usefulness, if it was ever useful, and that other mechanisms should be developed to address whatever issues and problems remain.

This captures the challenge for the reader: What have we learned about the FLSA and it effects through fifty years of experience? On balance, were these effects positive or negative in terms of addressing the concerns of low–wage workers? Is the federal minimum wage program the appropriate device for ensuring a living wage to the nation's lowest wage earners? Is the program structured today in a manner that will permit it to be an effective force in the next twenty–five to fifty years? If the answer is that it is not structured to effectively address future problems, what have we learned through the review of the program's history that will permit development of a more responsive program? These are the types of questions that make writing this book worthwhile. Of necessity, the focus of this book is on the federal program. There is an interesting story about the evolution of international minimum wage programs, from their birth in Australia to their presence in over 100 countries today. That story will not be told here.

There are minimum wage programs in the majority of states. Each state program is different in terms of wage levels, coverage, enforcement programs, and other standards. This fascinating story must also be left for future research.

This book is about the nation's *minimum wage* program. The FLSA also includes overtime standards and child labor protection. While the latter issues will be touched upon, they will not be fully developed here. Similarly, some parts of the minimum wage program—such as the industry committee structure, the Section 14 programs, and the quantitative evaluation of the program's effects—will be reviewed but not exhaustively developed. Each of these and other aspects of the federal program warrant full treatment in a separate study.

In short, this study addresses the legislative and programmatic dimensions of the federal minimum wage program but leaves several other interesting areas for further research and assessment.

THE QUEST FOR
A LIVING WAGE

Chapter 1

State Minimum Wage Legislation and Early Economic Conditions

Minimum wage programs emerged in the United States because sweating was a prevalent condition and the plight of low-wage workers, especially women and children, required attention. The early state laws focused their attention only on women, with occasional restrictions on child labor. Adult men were not afforded wage protection through legislation—except for Oklahoma—until passage of the Fair Labor Standards Act (FLSA) in 1938.

The evolution of minimum wage legislation in the United States started with the Massachusetts law in 1912 and the flood of state laws the following year. In many ways, the early legislation was different from state to state, and to understand the FLSA, it is important to understand these differences. For purposes of initial comparison, the laws of Massachusetts and Oregon will be examined—Massachusetts, because it enacted the first minimum wage law, and Oregon, because it withstood the first U.S. Supreme Court challenge.

While the primary focus of this discussion is the determination of wage rates, other conditions of employment were also important during the early period. At the turn of the century, work hours were long, and the use of children was commonplace in U.S. industry. Industrial accidents imposed high costs on workers, their families, and often society, generally. Both the miracle and the scourge of the Industrial Revolution in the United States were emerging during the first two decades of the twentieth century. Consequently, major changes in labor standards legislation occurred during this early period, much of it in nonwage areas.

The remainder of this chapter will focus on the economic conditions during the first three decades of the twentieth century. First, however, since the concept of "sweating" was the philosophical and economic basis underlying the protection of women and children, a brief review of that condition is required.

SWEATING

Rudolf Broda noted that "[a]s in Australia (1896) and in Great Britain (1909), minimum wage legislation in the United States (1912) sprang from anti-sweating agitation."[1] One of the earliest definitions of sweating was developed by the thoughtful critic M.B. Hammond. He observed that sweating is "the payment by an employer to his work people of a wage which is insufficient to purchase for them the necessaries of life."[2]

In this context, the "necessaries of life" are the minimum components of life-supporting systems—food, housing, clothing, and the like—needed to maintain life on a sustained basis. A somewhat more explicit definition of sweating is "the unfair exploitation by unscrupulous employers of the necessities of the poorer and more helpless class of workers by requiring them to work for wages inadequate to their needs or for excessive hours or under insanitary [sic] conditions."[3]

English economist Mrs. Sidney Webb (to whom the word *sweating* is often attributed) explained the origins and character of sweating in a capitalistic system. She noted that

experience has demonstrated, to the satisfaction of public opinion, as well as of economists, that to leave the determination of wages, in a capitalist organization or industry, to the unfettered operation of "individual bargaining" and the "higgling of the market" between individual employers and individual wage-earners, is to produce, in the community, a large area of "sweating"—defined by the House of Lords Committee of 1890 as "earnings barely sufficient to sustain existence."[4]

As Broda noted, the state programs evolved in response to sweated employment in the United States, too. The federal statute emerged from twenty-five years of economic development that had its primary roots in the 1920s. A brief overview of that decade and the early years of the Great Depression will provide the backdrop for understanding the character of the federal minimum wage law.

ECONOMIC CONDITIONS IN THE SECOND AND THIRD DECADES

Between 1923 and 1933, there was no important legislative or judicial activity related to the minimum wage, but several public interest groups such as the National Consumer's League continued their efforts to address low-wage problems. Editorials avoided the issue, and scholarly writing dwindled to nothing. However, the problems that precipitated earlier efforts did not go away. Studies in Connecticut and Pennsylvania in the early 1930s underscored the problem. For example, women in Pennsylvania working a full workweek earned weekly wages below the levels of two decades earlier. One half of the 5,342 women in the studies earned less than $6.37 per week, over 18 percent earned less than $4.00 per week, and 9 percent earned less than $3.00 per week.

Irene Andrews suggested, "Starvation wages have come to be so prevalent that an insistent demand has again arisen for minimum wage legislation to put a stop to such ruthless exploitation of women and children."[5] President Franklin Roosevelt, too, recognized the threats of falling wage rates. In April 1933, he noted that a persistently falling wage is "a serious form of unfair competition against other employers, reduces the purchasing power of the workers and threatens the stability of industry."[6] The president's message struck a responsive chord, and state legislatures began considering new minimum wage programs.

During the decade immediately preceding the Great Depression and the nine years prior to the passage of the Fair Labor Standards Act, the American economy went through a wrenching experience. Contrary to a widely held belief, the decade of the 1920s was *not* a period of exuberant economic growth that resulted in a higher standard of living for *all* Americans. The 1920s was a unique decade for many reasons, but widespread economic improvement was not one of them. Unemployment had been high throughout the decade of the 1920s, and the distribution of income was uneven. As Irving Bernstein noted in *The Lean Years*, "[T]he jobless constituted 13 percent of the labor force in 1924 and 1925, 11 percent in 1926, 12 percent in 1927, 13 percent in 1928, and 10 percent in 1929."[7] National income increased significantly throughout the decade, but wage earners enjoyed relatively few of the fruits of growth. In addition, "a paradox of the American economy in the twenties was that its glittering technical achievements gave birth to a dismal social failure" called technological unemployment.[8] The lure of the large city combined with the explosion of agricultural technology simultaneously pulled and pushed workers from the farm. The perceived glitter and glamour of large city life was transformed into despair and frustration for those unable to adjust to the rapidly changing skill requirements.

Corporations, as institutions, did well, but unions did not thrive in the 1920s. Even though the conditions in the economy suggested that union membership should have expanded, it did not. There were several conditions that seemed to frustrate union growth. President Calvin Coolidge set the tone for change in the 1920s by proclaiming that "the business of America is business." There was widespread support for the expansion of business activities, and unions were not viewed as integral to that process. The workforce was also changing in ways that made union expansion difficult. Women were entering the workforce in large numbers, there was a shift from manual to white-collar jobs, and "the Negro found the unwelcome mat laid out for him at the union door."[9]

During this era, the evolving structure of industry militated against unions and collective bargaining. The growth industries were less "craft" oriented and involved high levels of mechanization—chemicals, automobiles, rubber, and others. The great merger movement of this period resulted in conglomerates that vigorously opposed unionization—steel, tobacco, glass, and automobiles. The final event that relegated unions to mediocrity in the 1920s was the death of Samuel Gompers on December 13, 1924, and the selection of William Green as president of the American Federation of Labor on December 19, 1924. Green was viewed as ineffective, shallow, and predictable. He was honest and decent but impotent.

The rise of company unions, "welfare capitalism," the "American Plan," the belligerent attitude of firms, the antiunion attitude of the courts, and the inflexibility of craft unionism all contributed to union stagnation and impotence. Strikes and strike effectiveness both declined dramatically during this decade. Unions had lost sight of Samuel Gompers' credo of "More, more, more." However, this lapse was not particularly relevant because they had no mechanism for getting "more" anyway. Business failures and, in particular, bank failures began escalating early in the downturn. There were 22,909 commercial (nonbank) failures in 1929. The following year the number of commercial (nonbank) failures increased to 26,355 businesses. According to the Board of Governors of the Federal Reserve System, the number of bank suspensions escalated dramatically during the first four years of the Great Depression.

While it is well known that the stock market crash in October 1929 did not *cause* the Great Depression, this date in history is a convenient marker for the onset of a decade of economic and social trauma.

While the major impacts of social and economic change in the 1920s related to a large degree to workers and their families, employers, too, experienced ambiguity in how to adapt to the change process. Bernstein noted, "Employers were unsure whether to regard the worker as a displaceable cog in the productive machine or as an indispensable consumer of industry's rising output, his wage as a cost item to be kept low or as an income factor to be pushed high."[10]

After the stock market crash, conditions worsened every day. However, the dimensions of the calamity were not immediately recognized. As Bernstein observed:

Despite the fact of great and growing joblessness, many, if not most, Americans were hardly aware of the problem in the first year or two of the depression. In smaller communities and in parts of larger cities, unemployment could not be seen. Because no one really knew how many were out of work, it left a wide field for statistical juggling. The Hoover Administration exploited the whole mechanism of opinion-molding to minimize the gravity of the situation and to raise public hopes of speedy improvement.[11]

It took two full years for President Herbert Hoover to admit publicly that the United States was in deep economic trouble.

Nevertheless, as Denis W. Brogan observed, despite the troubles on Wall Street in 1929, "[w]hen Christmas came, the stores were as busy as ever, the worst seemed over, and it was reasonable to expect that in 1930 the short pull upwards would begin again."[12] Reasonable, indeed. Not only did the "short pull upwards" not begin in the new year, but the economic slide gained in momentum and size. A recurrent theme was that the option of returning to the "home place" vanished for these workers, and unemployment expanded. Double-digit unemployment throughout the decade symbolized the turmoil of the economic adjustment process.

The differentials between similarly situated men and women in the 1980s also existed in the 1920s. In occupation after occupation, men consistently earned 30 to 50 percent more than women in comparable jobs.[13]

Union-nonunion wage differentials were also large. The hourly wage rate in the predominantly union trades was 75 to 100 percent higher than in the nonunionized occupations. If anything, the differentials in the union–nonunion trades widened over the decade. The picture that these observations suggest is that the economy of the 1920s was characterized by wide differentials of various types that led to dislocation, frustration, and unbalanced growth. Extreme concentrations of wealth and unequal distribution of income—in 1929, the combined income of the top one tenth of 1 percent of the population equaled the combined income of the bottom 42 percent of the population—combined with similar distributions of stock ownership produced an unbalanced society destined for failure.

This was not a pretty picture, but it was the real one. As the nation moved into the decade of the 1930s, the patterns of change initiated in the 1920s intensified. One indicator of economic and social stress was the precipitous decline in weekly earnings between 1929 and 1933. Average weekly earnings for all manufacturing were $25.03 in 1929. In 1933, average weekly earnings in manufacturing were $16.73—a 33.2 percent decline.[14] Even larger declines occurred in agriculture. Total farm wages were $1.284 billion in 1929. By 1933, total farm wages had fallen to $512 million—a decrease of over 60 percent.[15] Average hired farmworker income in 1929 was $430.29 per year. In 1933, average annual farmworker income had decreased to $210.44 per year. While *income* was falling, an important dimension of the onset of the Great Depression that is not well known is the relative stability of *wage rates* during the early years of the downturn. Bernstein observed, "The stock market crash had little immediate impact upon wages. Wage rates, as distinguished from earnings, held firmly in the first year of the depression. A survey of union scales for May 1930 actually showed a rise over the spring of 1929."[16] The factor that was primarily responsible for the dramatic decrease in income was a reduction in work hours. Table 1.1 shows the annual averages of wage rates and weekly hours worked in manufacturing for selected years.

Another indicator of the severity of the economic decline in the initial years of the Great Depression was the fall in retail sales. In 1929, all retail sales totaled $48.459 billion. At the depth of the Great Depression, 1933, total retail sales were only $24.517 billion—a decrease of 49.4 percent. Sales of durable goods fared worse than nondurable goods. Between 1929 and 1933, durable retail sales fell over 65 percent, while nondurable retail sales fell about 43 percent.

Table 1.1
Average Hourly Wage Rates and Average Weekly Hours Worked, 1929-1933

Year	Hourly Wage Rates	Weekly Work Hours
1929	$.59	48.3
1930	.59	43.9
1931	.56	40.4
1932	.50	34.8
1933	.49	36.4

Source: M. Ada Beney, *Wages, Hours, and Employment in the United States, 1914-1936*, No. 229 (New York: National Industrial Conference Board, 1937), Table 2.

These changes suggest that consumers were delaying the purchasing of commodities not necessary for day-to-day living. Sales of automobiles also reflected this basic pattern. In the span of one year, between 1929 and 1930, the U.S. Department of Commerce showed a decline from 5,358,420 automobiles sold in 1929 to only 3,354,870 units sold in 1930—a decrease of 37.4 percent. By 1932, only 1,331,869 automobiles were sold. It took two decades for the sale of automobiles to return to the 1929 level.[17] The average weekly payroll in the automotive industry followed the pattern of decreases described above. In 1928, for example, in the year prior to the beginning of the Great Depression, average weekly payroll was about $14.4 million. In 1933, average weekly payroll had decreased to about $4.8 million—a decrease of about 67 percent.[18]

President Roosevelt assumed the duties of the presidency in March 1933. This event coincided with the lowest point in the Great Depression. The unemployment rate reached almost 25 percent in 1933. The new president had been elected to provide leadership in the resolution of the economic calamity facing the United States and the world. The president knew that the dislocations were pervasive and deep-seated and would have to be resolved through a variety of innovative legislative, executive, and private sector initiatives. As *The Economist* noted in 1936, "An encyclopedia is needed for an adequate description of the gigantic experiment that has been proceeding in America under President Roosevelt."[19] The centerpiece of the new administration's initiatives was a huge—by historical standards—public works program under the National Industrial Recovery Act (NIRA). The Congress appropriated over $3.3 billion for these activities. It was a pump-priming effort that was assumed to have a significant employment-generating effect.

There was concern that workers obtain jobs and income but, at the same time, that their rights were protected. After all, there was a belief that an important problem leading to and perpetuating the economic downturn was the exploitation of workers through low wages and long hours.

The events of this period and the acceptance of the departure from the

long-standing laissez-faire economic philosophy set the stage by creating a philosophical void in U.S. economic policy. Into this void flowed the New Deal
economic policies of extensive government intervention in the economy supported by or in some sense legitimized by John Maynard Keynes' *General
Theory of Employment, Interest, and Money* in 1936. The view of the
macroeconomy and, importantly, the role of the government in the economy
was forever changed.

As the nation struggled under the burden of major depression, economic
and political leaders recognized that more than rhetoric was needed to move
the economy forward. Of all the legislative initiatives of the Great Depression
era, the one that has come to symbolize this period is the NIRA. This legislation and the organization established to administer it—the National Recovery
Administration (NRA)—contained or created elements that were later to become the nucleus of important legislation or programs of independent standing.

No one quibbled with the notion that in the early 1930s something had to
be done as the Great Depression deepened. Business failures, rising unemployment, soup lines, and destroyed families were everyday events. The political
leaders had few historical precedents of this character from which guidance
could be sought. Therefore, they were forced into efforts to forge original measures to combat massive economic dislocations. The NIRA was the centerpiece
of these measures.

In an extensive analysis and appraisal in *The Economist* on October 3,
1936, the writer observed, "The NIRA, passed in May, 1933, probably collects
more divergent economic and social theories under the roof of a single enactment than any other piece of legislation ever known."[20] The deputy administrator of the NRA argued before the American Federation of Labor Annual
Convention in October 1933 that [t]he National Recovery Administration is
the Greatest experiment in practical idealism ever conceived in the minds of
human beings.[21] The NIRA was enacted with great expectations. There was
skepticism in abundance, but strong industry and union pressure was placed on
the legislators to construct a law that would achieve objectives in addition to
economic recovery. The need for immediate passage of a "recovery" measure
undoubtedly resulted in the inclusion of statutory provisions that should have
been dealt with elsewhere.

The two stated objectives of the NIRA were to stimulate economic recovery and to ensure justice to the American worker. The "good times" and "bad
times" of the 1920s had resulted in the accumulation of massive public and
private debts. As price levels fell, the burden of debt increased. The real thrust
of the NIRA recovery program was to bolster price levels for all groups in the
economy. Describing the NIRA, President Roosevelt explained in a March 5,
1934, speech, "Its aim was to increase the buying power of wage earners and
farmers so that industry, labor, and the public might benefit through building
up the market for farm and factory goods."[22]

It is significant that the National Association of Manufacturers (NAM) recognized early what the New Deal programs and policies were designed to accomplish. Writing in May 1933 for the NAM, Dr. Alfred Haake noted in his description of the NIRA:

It should be borne in mind that, while the immediate declared objective is to increase employment and to raise purchasing power through increased and wider spread wages, as well as to encourage improved conditions of employment, *the fundamental and real effect of the bill is not revealed in its emergency character.* Its eventual consequences are designed by its authors to be a better-balanced national economy, built on the premise that the welfare of all the people is a necessary condition of the welfare of the individual in contrast to the theory of laissez-faire, which exalts the individual, rather than the group of which he is a part. [Emphasis added] [23]

The Economist argued, "Perhaps the dominant theory in the genesis of the Act was the belief that industrial depression could be reduced by getting rid of 'wasteful, cut-throat competition.'"[24] The NRA charged ahead with an aggressive program of change. First administrator "General Johnson tore into action as if a war were to be won or lost in thirty days. He was practically unknown to the country. The fresh shock of his blunt manner and amazing energy had the effect of a hypodermic."[25] Even though the NRA was in existence less than two years, it approved over 546 "codes of fair competition" and 185 "supplemental" codes. The sheer volume and complexity of these codes doomed the efficient management of this program.

One of the most controversial parts of the NIRA was Section 7. This "labor" section fell when the entire act was declared unconstitutional in May 1935, but major parts of Section 7 found their way into subsequent statutes such as the Fair Labor Standards Act of 1938 and the National Labor Relations Act of 1935. Section 7(a)(3) of the NIRA provided "that employers shall comply with the maximum hours of labor, minimum rates of pay, and other conditions of employment approved or proscribed by the President."[26]

The designers and administrators of the new program knew that code implementation would not be immediate but that to capture interest and momentum, immediate direction was needed. President Roosevelt appealed to the nation for cooperation to initiate early changes in the economy. One element in this cooperative effort was the President's Reemployment Agreement (PRA). Every employer of two or more workers was asked to comply with the voluntary agreement until a code was adopted for their industry. Importantly for later initiatives, "The voluntary agreement prohibited child labor and profiteering. For white-collar workers it established a minimum wage of from $12 to $15 a week depending on the location, and a maximum forty-hour week. For factory workers it established a thirty-five-hour week and a minimum wage of 40 cents an hour, with some exceptions."[27] In conjunction with the initiation of the PRA, the NRA adopted the "Blue Eagle" as the official symbol given to employers operating under approved "codes" or who had signed an agreement.

The intent, of course, was to encourage patronage of firms cooperating in the recovery program. Over 2.3 million agreements were signed, covering over 16 million workers.[28]

On February 20, 1935, President Roosevelt asked the Congress to extend the NIRA for two more years. He pointed to the reemployment of over 4 million workers and the eradication of child labor, starvation wages, long hours, and sweated employment. He argued that "dishonorable" competition between employers was banned. Price controls were working and the nation was on the road to recovery. What he needed, he argued, was two more years to consolidate and expand the gains already in place.[29]

While the president painted the best face possible on the NRA experience, there were mixed reviews about early NRA success. Some felt its impacts were substantial, but most believed that the NIRA was not a program that worked well or that was generally accepted by Americans as a solution to the Great Depression's problems. Most believed that the NIRA was a morass of detailed codes that applied to business and resulted in serious dislocations and confusion. Therefore, few business, government, or for that matter, labor leaders in the mid-1930s were unhappy at the NIRA demise. As Brogan observed:

The legal killing of NIRA was received with more verbal than real indignation. Widespread relief was felt inside as well as outside Administration circles. The Labor provisions were salvaged by more effective legislation than had been provided by 7-A; the controls of wages and hours and limitations on child labor were salvaged, too, by fresh legislation; but the whole idea of "industrial self-government" was extinct, not much regretted either by the 22,000,000 workers or by the 5,000,000 employers who had tried to live under the codes.[30]

Therefore, while the NIRA was generally viewed as a failure even before the U.S. Supreme Court legally killed it on May 27, 1935, what it did accomplish was a breakthrough in the attitudes toward protective labor legislation. Brogan noted that the "NIRA can be credited with breaking down legal and political barriers to Federal action in the field of child labor, wages and hours legislation, and other later achievements of the New Deal."[31]

NOTES

1. Rudolf Broda, "Minimum Wage Legislation in the United States," *International Labour Review*, Vol. XVX, No. 10, January 1920, p. 24.

2. Matthew B. Hammond, "The Minimum Wage in Great Britain and Australia," *Annals*, Vol. XLVIII, July 1913, p. 26.

3. Dorothy W. Douglas, "American Minimum Wage Laws at Work," *American Economic Review*, Vol. IX, No. 4, December 1919, p. 710.

4. Mrs. Sidney [Beatrice] Webb, *The Wages of Men and Women: Should They Be Equal?* (London: Fabian Society, n.d.), p. 9.

5. Irene O. Andrews, "Minimum Wage Comes Back!" *American Labor Legislation Review*, Vol. XXIII, No. 2, June 1933, p. 103.

6. Ibid.

7. Irving Bernstein, *The Lean Years: A History of the American Worker, 1920–1933* (Boston: Houghton Mifflin Co., 1960), p. 88.

8. Ibid., p. 60.

9. Ibid., p. 68.

10. Ibid., p. 146.

11. Ibid., p. 257.

12. Denis W. Brogan, *The Era of Franklin D. Roosevelt: A Chronicle of the New Deal and Global War* (New Haven: Yale University Press, 1950), p. 7.

13. Bernstein, 1960, p. 59.

14. U.S. Department of Labor, Bureau of Labor Statistics, *Handbook of Labor Statistics* (Washington, D.C.: Government Printing Office, 1947), tables A-12 and C-12.

15. Ibid.

16. Bernstein, 1960, p. 259.

17. Chilton Company, *Automotive Industries*, Vol. 116, No. 6, March 1957, p. 85.

18. American Manufacturers Association, *Men, Methods, and Machines in Automobile Manufacturing*, adapted from a study by Andrew T. Court (New York: American Manufacturers Association 1939), p. 24.

19. "The New Deal: An Analysis and Appraisal," *The Economist* (London) October 3, 1936, p. 9.

20. Ibid., p. 8.

21. American Federation of Labor, *Report of Proceedings*, Fifty-third Annual Convention, Washington, D.C., October 2–13, 1933, p. 374.

22. Louis M. Hacker, *A Short History of the New Deal* (New York: F. S. Crofts and Company, 1934), pp. 27–28.

23. A.P. Haake, *A "Model Code" for Self-Governing Industries Under the National Industrial Recovery Act* (Now Pending in Congress) (Washington, D.C.: National Association of Manufacturers, May 31, 1933), p. 5.

24. *The New Deal*, 1936, p. 8.

25. Ernest K. Lindley, *The Roosevelt Revolution: Phase One* (New York: Viking Press, 1933), p. 233.

26. National Industrial Recovery Act, Public Law No. 67, 73rd Congress, Section 7(a)(3).

27. Lindley, 1933, p. 237.

28. Franklin D. Roosevelt, *The Year of Crisis, Public Papers and Addresses*, 1933 vol. (New York: Random House, 1938), pp. 308–312.

29. Franklin D. Roosevelt, *The Court Disapproves, Public Papers and Addresses*, 1935 vol. (New York: Random House, 1938), pp. 80–84.

30. Brogan, 1950, pp. 91–92.

31. Ibid., p. 92.

Chapter 2

Minimum Wage Programs Take Shape

THE MASSACHUSETTS LAW

The primary components of this 1912 law were (1) a *commission* to administer the program; (2) *tripartite wage boards* or conferences to recommend appropriate wage rates to the commission; (3) the principle for minimum wage determination to be a sum that is adequate to supply the necessary *cost of living* and maintain the worker in health; (4) consideration of the *financial condition of the industry* or occupation involved; (5) enforcement through "public opinion" rather than direct legal sanction; and, (6) protection of only *women and children*.

These components of the Massachusetts law reflected the caution legislators felt in crafting a path-breaking initiative. Part of the timidity flowed from the prospects of a legal challenge, part flowed from a basic uncertainty about the economic effects on Massachusetts employers and employees, and part was undoubtedly due to the perceived imprecision in the wage-setting process.

There was no experience in the United States to rely upon, and the Australian, New Zealand, and British programs were less than two decades old. The Massachusetts legislators did, of course, draw from the experiences of these foreign programs, but they realized that both the American Constitution and the U.S. economic system were different from their foreign counterparts. All major foreign programs covered both men and women, for example. American legislators believed that the U.S. Constitution would invalidate any legislation that interfered with the "freedom of contract" requirements of the "due process" provisions of the Fourteenth Amendment. However, they also believed that the unique characteristics of women and children in the workforce suggested that a narrowly drawn statute with a responsible administrative mechanism could meet a constitutional challenge. The state, through the exercise of its "police powers," can protect the rights and conditions of vulnerable groups. Thomas Reed Powell noted, "For a statute to be a proper exercise of the police power, it must tend to promote some end which is public and not private merely, and it must be a reasonable and not an arbitrary method of serving this end."[1] The test of this new minimum wage program rested on the concept of "reasonableness" as it related to the protection of women and children in the workplace. A question remained whether or not another vehicle or mechanism could be used to achieve a comparable end.

Of more than passing importance, the Massachusetts law was the only one that escaped intact from the Supreme Court's 1923 *Adkins* decision. The major reason it escaped was its "voluntary" enforcement provisions. While it can be argued that Massachusetts lawmakers were clever architects of the statute, in retrospect, "public opinion" was an ineffective mechanism to ensure compliance with wage orders issued by the Massachusetts Minimum Wage Commission. Public opinion required effective communications both in the formulation of the opinion and in the expression of support but required a pivotal event to coalesce the sentiment into a force for change.

The early minimum wage programs were not well understood by the public, employers were viewed as important community institutions that one dared not confront, communications within and outside the firm were imperfect at best, and workers, themselves, did not fully understand the rights and protection provided to them under the new law. Consequently, public opinion was an impotent enforcement mechanism for the Massachusetts law.

Resistance to the imposition of a minimum wage in Massachusetts began almost immediately. Firms resisted paying the recommended rate because the consequences of not doing so were small. Even the specter of adverse publicity was minimized. As Rudolf Broda observed, "The names of the firms refusing to comply with the law were not published. Instead of a 'black list,' a 'white list,' containing only the names of the firms *complying* with the law was published."[2] Since sanctions were small, there was widespread noncompliance with the recommended wage rates. When firms found it easy to comply, they did. When they found it easy to ignore the law, they did. For example, in Massachusetts, "[t]he women's clothing industries were covered in 1917. One-half of the firms refused to comply, but later on, as prices rose, there was no longer refusal to apply the minimum rates."[3]

Since the Massachusetts law had a dual criteria for wage determination, for example, the necessary cost of living *in conjunction with* financial conditions in the industry or occupation, as Emilie Hutchinson noted, "it is clear that when a wage ruling must take into consideration the 'financial condition of the business,' no effective enforcement of the law can be obtained if employers choose to oppose it."[4] Whatever the strengths or weaknesses of the Massachusetts law, its critics from both sides were vehement in their attacks. The practice of "white listing" irritated the program's critics who sought positive change. Whether the law meant anything will remain a debatable point. While it is true that few states developed legislation with provisions similar to the Massachusetts program, that may not be the important point. The Massachusetts law was weak in several important respects, but it established the principle of legislating minimum wage rates in the United States. The substantive differences between subsequent state programs and the Massachusetts program left the former vulnerable to constitutional challenge that was ultimately successful. Before we get to that point in history, however, it is important to note the upsurge of new state programs immediately after the Massachusetts program.

THE MOVEMENT GAINS MOMENTUM

On the one hand, the Massachusetts law was viewed as "path breaking," a major departure from established laissez-faire economic doctrine, innovative, and daring. On the other hand, some argued that it was timid, crude, weak, and disgraceful. It probably was some combination of the two. There was a problem of long duration and of substantial proportions—sweating—that demanded resolution.

The Massachusetts legislator moved first. While not denigrating their actions, if Massachusetts had not enacted a law in 1912, there is some evidence that other states would almost certainly have done so the following year. To demonstrate that an initiative of this type was known to the American people and viewed as a possible answer to the problem of sweating, the Ohio Constitutional Convention of 1912 submitted an amendment "authorizing the establishment of a minimum wage law." It "was ratified by the people of the state at an election in September, 1912, by a vote of 353,588 to 189,728."[5] However, even with constitutional authority, the Ohio state legislature did not enact a minimum wage law in the early years.

While the significance of the Massachusetts law should not be underrated, 1913 was the year of state minimum wage laws. Eight states enacted minimum wage statutes: "Utah (May 13), Oregon (June 2), Washington (June 13), Minnesota (June 26), Nebraska (July 17), Wisconsin (August 1), California (August 10), and Colorado (August 12). On March 25, 1915 a minimum-wage law went into effect in Arkansas, and on May 22, in Kansas."[6] Arizona passed a flat-rate minimum wage law (patterned after the "Utah" model) in 1917. The U.S. Congress enacted a minimum wage law for the District of Columbia in 1918. The following year, Texas, North Dakota, and Puerto Rico also passed minimum wage legislation.

The minimum wage laws enacted during the early years followed one of three "models." Since it was the first law, the Massachusetts statute became a standard against which other programs were judged. Only two other states—Nebraska and Colorado—adopted the Massachusetts model. As noted above, its primary attributes were voluntary compliance, the dual wage-setting criteria (e.g., the living wage and the financial condition of the employer), and the utilization of boards and commissions for rate determination. The second model was characterized as the "Oregon" model because of the prominent role Oregon played in the initiation of this version of the legislation. This model incorporated *only* the living wage criterion in wage setting and had *mandatory* enforcement procedures.

An interesting historical footnote is that "[t]he first minimum-wage orders promulgated in the United States were those of the Oregon Industrial Commission,"[7] rather than of the Massachusetts Minimum Wage Commission. The theory underlying the Oregon statute was "not that the employer must pay what the labor produces for him, but that he must pay what it costs to produce the labor," for example, the living wage.[8]

The third model is characterized as the "Utah model." While only adopted by Arkansas and Arizona during the early years, the Utah model is the precursor of the rate structure of the FLSA today. The unique feature of this model was that it established a flat-rate minimum wage *in the statute*. As Dorothy Douglas noted in 1919, "The flat-rate laws differ from both the earlier models in that they operate, not through commissions, but through direct fiat of the statute itself."[9] Therefore, analyzing the expansion of state programs for the decade following the Massachusetts law in 1912, "nine may be said roughly to copy the Oregon model, [two] the Massachusetts model, while three have to be put into a separate category of flat-rate laws."[10]

THE OREGON PROGRAM

The conditions of workers in Oregon, particularly women workers, were typical of those in other states. Judge Louis D. Brandeis observed in 1914, "It was found that in Oregon a large number of such women were ruining their health because they were not eating enough. Those that ate enough," he said, "roomed under conditions that were unwholesome, or they were insufficiently clothed." Further, he noted that the investigators "found that in a large number of cases, the insufficient wage was supplemented by contributions from 'gentlemen friends.' " [11]

It was believed that these conditions existed because of the weak bargaining position of women workers. Employers exploited women workers because of their general over-supply, because they had few labor market alternatives, and because they were unorganized. Consequently, development of minimum wage legislation in Oregon proceeded in two directions. First, the very purpose of the statutory restrictions was "to assure the parties [women and employers] an equal basis for bargaining, so that they may be free to bargain on the merits, and not under the compulsion of a crippling necessity."[12] Second, as suggested in the general conditions described above, "it was found that in the State of Oregon, whatever might be the case elsewhere, a majority of the women to whom the investigation extended, were working for a wage smaller than that required for decent living."[13]

Edwin V. O'Hara, chair of the Industrial Welfare Commission of the state of Oregon in 1916, outlined the results of submerging major segments of the population below decent standards of living. These results included (1) "economic evils . . . diminished power of production . . . diminished power of consumption . . . inefficient workers"; (2) "social evils . . . spread of infections and contagious diseases . . . lowering educational standards . . . deteriorating of public morals"; (3) "domestic evils . . . disintegration of family ties . . . diminution of parental control . . . growth of parental irresponsibility"; (4) "individual demoralization . . . undermining of individual ambition . . . inferior education . . . moral strain . . . deterioration of physique"; and (5) "national weakness . . . sapping and decay of patriotism . . . physical unfitting of citizens for national defense."[14]

Conditions of working women and the consequences of these conditions on society were so adverse that the Oregon legislature passed a law in which the sole criterion for setting the minimum wage was the determination of a living wage. No consideration was provided for the productivity of the individual worker. Rather, "[t]he statute says that, if he [the employer] chooses to take the benefit [output from the working woman], he must bear the burden."[15] In the arguments supporting the Oregon statute before the U.S. Supreme Court, Mary Hopkins, in 1917, articulated the same notion in a more descriptive context: "You [Stettler] shall not use all her [Simpson] working energy unless you pay her the cost of producing that energy." That, she said, "is why Stettler and not John D. Rockefeller should pay, because Stettler has the use of all her working power and John D. Rockefeller has not. Someone must pay the cost of her labor, and self-evidently it must be the man who profits by it."[16]

An important point raised about the Oregon statute that is often disregarded is that the minimum wage program did not compel the employer to hire any particular worker. It was argued that employers could and were expected to act in their best economic interest. However, if an employer decided to hire a particular worker, then he was required by law to pay that worker a living wage. It was assumed that the employer would not hire any worker at any wage rate if the worker's productivity did not justify hiring him or her. In short, "[t]hat the statute may deprive some employees of the opportunity to get what they are now getting is clear. An employer who is compelled to raise the wages of an employee or dismiss her may choose the latter alternative."[17]

Since the Oregon statute did not permit consideration of *industry* conditions in the wage-setting process, a collateral goal of the Oregon program was to protect the *individual employer* who wanted to pay his employees a fair wage. As Hopkins argued in defense of the Oregon statute, "[B]y fixing Simpson's [an employee's] wage the state . . . acts in the interest of the fair employer. The great testimony to the success of the system is the gradual but sure support of manufacturers in states and countries where it has been tried."[18]

The Oregon legislation differed materially from the Massachusetts statute.

The first difference involved the standards, factors, or basis for determining the minimum wage. The Massachusetts law incorporated the living wage concept but provided for consideration of the financial condition of the occupation, firm, or industry in which the individuals worked. Employers could avoid complying with the Massachusetts Minimum Wage Commission's published rates if adverse "financial conditions" existed or would result. The Oregon legislation was silent on the financial condition of the employing unit.

The second major difference between the Massachusetts and Oregon statutes was in the enforcement area. Massachusetts used "public opinion" as the driving force behind employer compliance. Oregon instituted fines and imprisonment for employers who did not comply.

The Oregon Industrial Welfare Commission (the administrative unit for the minimum wage program) attempted to conduct its rate setting through "informal conferences of employers." It hoped that compulsory wage orders would not be needed. The informal process failed. "After several weeks of fruitless efforts along this line," said O'Hara, "the Commission realized that suspicion of their competitors on the part of many employers and disinclination to cooperate with the Commission on the part of not a few, rendered the issuing of mandatory rulings the only practicable course to follow."[19] These two major differences—exclusion of employer impact considerations and method of enforcement—put the Oregon legislation in a different arena from the Massachusetts effort. There were "teeth" in the Oregon statute that permitted a reasonable expectation of providing a living wage for women and minor workers.

EARLY COURT DECISIONS AND THE LEGAL PRECEDENTS OF THE MINIMUM WAGE (1913–1937)

One of the most interesting aspects of the evolution of minimum wage programs in the United States is the shifting attitudes of the court system toward the legislation. The courts—especially the U.S. Supreme Court—are presumably mirrors of the social, political, and economic standards of the time. Judges become judges for a whole variety of reasons that include their standing in the community and judicial system, their perceived impartiality and fairness, and their political and economic beliefs, among others.

Americans believe strongly in self-sufficiency and individualism and have adhered to the concept of laissez–faire through much of the Industrial Revolution. However, as Judge Thomas Powell noted in 1917, "[N]either the doctrine of individualism nor of laissez faire is contained in the language of the constitution, [yet] they permeate many judicial opinions interpreting the constitution."[20] This is the reality that *opponents* of minimum wage programs so artfully exploited in the first three decades of U.S. minimum wage programs. To a large degree, the courts accepted these concepts as reflecting the values, standards, and morals of American society. To understand the rationale behind court decisions and, more important, how these decisions changed through time, one must understand that

[a]part from the alleged evils that it involves, thecontroversy between the advocates and opponents [of minimum wage programs] resolves itself into a conflict of social philosophy. The latter revert to the working of national law and the principle of competition; the former would extend the principles of state control to raise the plane of competition and to restrict its working in the interest of the common good.[21]

Rinehart Swenson argued even more persuasively in 1917 that the single-minded drive toward individualism in the United States had caused extreme polarization of society. "We have been so imbued with the individualistic philosophy," he said, "that we have permitted the lower stratum of laborers to degenerate into virtual serfs, rather than interfere with the individual's liberty to sell his labor in the market of his own choice, and on his own terms."[22]

The laissez-faire philosophy, the constitutional guarantee of liberty, the common good, the freedom of contract, and several other equally difficult concepts permit wide latitude in judicial decisions. Besides these complexities, "[j]udges cannot know as part of general knowledge the facts as to the actual conditions of employees in industry."[23] Therefore, they must rely on the character and quality of evidence and argument in formulating their decisions. Commenting on the U.S. Supreme Court *Adkins* decision in 1923 that effectively stymied state minimum wage programs for over a decade, Father John Ryan observed that

the Constitution does not explicitly pronounce sentence of death upon statutes of this kind. The constitutional provision upon which a bare majority of the Supreme Court have based their unfavorable decision prohibits minimum wage legislation only implicitly at most; and even the implicit prohibition is a matter of individual interpretation by the Justices. [24]

Therefore, it may be useful to describe the judicial process that began soon after enactment of the Massachusetts law in 1912 and ended twenty-five years later. Courts at every level of the judicial system had opportunities to review these statutes and to formulate decisions and opinions. There were reversals on appeal, and in several cases, the high state and federal courts sustained lower court rulings. It is fair to say that proponents and opponents of minimum wage legislation were frequently surprised as the courts changed their collective minds regarding the legality and constitutionality of these programs.

The judicial story begins in Multnomah County, Oregon, 3,000 miles from the site of the first state program. In November 1913, Judge Cleeton of the Circuit Court of Multnomah County dismissed the complaint of Mr. Frank Stettler by declaring the Oregon minimum wage law constitutional. Mr. Stettler had sought an injunction against enforcement of the law because (1) it violated the Fourteenth Amendment of the federal Constitution (it deprived "the employer of his proper right and his liberty of contract without due process of law and also denies him the equal protection of the law");[25] (2) it attempted to delegate legislative power to the conference and commission created to enforce the law; and (3) it violated Section 20 of Article I of the Oregon State Constitution, "which forbids the passing of any law granting to any citizen or class of citizens privileges or immunities which, upon the same terms, shall not equally belong to all citizens."[26]

Judge Cleeton, in dismissing the complaint, reached to the precedent established in other decisions concerning the conditions under which workers participate in the labor force. He "found that the objects of this law were identical with those to be accomplished by laws fixing maximum hours of employment of women and children, and since laws of this nature have been sustained by the courts of last resort of the States, and also by the Supreme Court of the United States, a basis was laid for the upholding of the present statute."[27]

Shortly after Judge Cleeton's decision, the next step in the judicial review process was set in motion. An employee of Stettler's, Ms. Elmira Simpson, brought suit in the same court, seeking to prevent enforcement of the law. The basis for her suit was that the law would cause her being denied employment because the legislated minimum wage would exceed her productive capacity. She argued that the $8 per week she received was as much as "she was able to obtain for any labor that she was capable of performing" and that by her current employment "she lived and maintained herself in health and comfort, that the employment was clean and healthful, and the surroundings good."[28]

Judge Cleeton similarly dismissed this complaint, and both plaintiffs appealed the decisions to the supreme court of the state of Oregon. In a unanimous decision, the state supreme court upheld the lower court with one caveat. The supreme court noted that the Fourteenth Amendment of the federal Constitution would invalidate the legislation unless "it could be justified as an exercise of the police power of the State for the protection and betterment of the public health and welfare and reasonably tending to that end."[29] After extensive review of conditions within the industry in the state of Oregon and how these conditions affected the employment of women and minors, the state supreme court concluded in its decision: "We think we should be bound by the judgment of the legislature that there is a necessity for this act, that it is within the police power of the State to provide for the protection of the health, morals, and welfare of women and children, and that the law should be upheld as constitutional."[30]

The appeal to the U.S. Supreme Court on a writ of error was argued before the High Court in December 1914. No decision was rendered by the Court, and a rehearing was scheduled for June 1916. Reargument occurred in January 1917, but only eight justices participated in the decision. The vote was equally divided, and therefore no opinion was rendered by the Court. Consequently, the decision of the Oregon Supreme Court stood, and the Oregon law remained constitutional and in full force.

The appeal to the U.S. Supreme Court was based solely on alleged infringement of Fourteenth Amendment protection. The decisions by the state court had resolved the several arguments related to state constitutional provisions. The U.S. Supreme Court challenge revolved around the question of whether a *compulsory* minimum wage statute of this type was warranted and within the police power of the state. The alleged conflicts with the protection of the Fourteenth Amendment were three in number: (1) that this legislation abridges "the privileges and immunities of these plaintiffs as guaranteed by" the Fourteenth Amendment; (2) "that by such action the plaintiffs are deprived of property and liberty without due process of law"; and (3) "that such statute denies of them the equal protection of the laws."[31]   The thrust, then, of the challenge focused on the character of the employment relationship in which the employer was *compelled* to pay a minimum wage rate based on the cost of supplying and maintaining labor in the production process rather than on the value of the contribution the worker made to output. It was argued that if there was no necessary relationship to the value of services rendered or output produced, then the employer could be compelled to contribute to the needs of other persons, which would amount to taking private property without appropriate compensation.

The arguments supporting the legislation took a different perspective. Judge Powell argued, "The purpose and result of minimum wage legislation is to insure that those who give a day's work receive a day's support in return. The purpose is a public purpose, because the evils which result from poverty and weakness and premature death are public evils."[32] This line of argument maintained that the state had the power to enact this legislation because of its purported positive effects on public health, public welfare, and public morals. In this context, the judgment of the legislature is paramount "unless the constitutional limitations have been palpably and beyond doubt overstepped by such action."[33] Judge Powell provided the most eloquent summary of this series of arguments when he said, "The theory of the legislation is that there is a public interest in having those who give their whole strength to an employer receive enough from that employer to maintain that strength, that there is a public interest in having an industry support itself instead of relying on outside subsidies."[34]

Concurrent with the Oregon legal challenge was a similar process in Minnesota. However, the steps in the Minnesota challenge resulted in the lower court (District Court of Ramsey County, Minnesota) declaring the Minnesota statute unconstitutional. The two major arguments underlying that decision were (1) the purported unconstitutionality of the law because it delegated legislative power to an appointive committee and (2) that it abridged the rights of individuals to enter into contracts. When Judge Catlin of the Ramsey County District Court had the Minnesota statute under review, he was inclined to delay issuing a decision. The Oregon case was before the U.S. Supreme Court, and Judge Catlin believed that the High Court decision would dispose of the issues and questions involved in the Minnesota legislation. While presumably in-clined to wait for the Oregon decision, Judge Catlin was compelled to issue a decision to resolve an administrative issue pending before his court. Plaintiff's counsel suggested that the Minnesota Minimum Wage Commission should sus-pend its wage orders until the U.S. Supreme Court had issued a decision. The commission refused to respond to this suggestion. Judge Catlin therefore de-clared the statute unconstitutional and resolved the immediate administrative problem. The circuit court decision was appealed to the Minnesota Supreme Court. This judicial body withheld its decision until the U.S. Supreme Court's equally divided vote sustained the constitutionality of the Oregon statute.

Because of the Oregon decision and a decision on appeal to the Arkansas Supreme Court that reversed a lower court ruling of unconstitutionality of the Arkansas statute, the Minnesota Supreme Court reversed Judge Catlin's order and declared the Minnesota statute constitutional. The Arkansas judicial re-view process noted above took a similar route to resolution as did the Minne-sota review. The Circuit Court of Sebastian County, Arkansas, found the state minimum wage statute unconstitutional. The state of Arkansas appealed the decision to the Arkansas Supreme Court. On June 4, 1917, the Arkansas Su-preme Court, with the Oregon case resolved, reversed the lower court decision and declared the statute constitutional.

The fourth test of minimum wage legislation occurred in the state of Wash-ington. The issues here were somewhat different from those in previous judi-cial challenges. The plaintiff brought suit to recover the *difference* between the wages the employer actually paid her and the wage rate established by the State Welfare Commission (the administrative organization for the state minimum wage statute). A lower court had ruled in favor of the plaintiff, and conse-quently her employer appealed to the state supreme court. The appeal sought to set aside the lower court decision and, in more general terms, sought to obtain a decision to invalidate the statute. The Washington Supreme Court relied on the Oregon decision to dismiss the constitutionality issue. Further, the court upheld the lower court decision requiring payment of the wage differ-ential. This case exposed for the first time an issue that was to surface fre-quently in subsequent judicial reviews. The court argued that an employer and an employee could *not* enter into a contract for a lower wage rate than the rates established under the statute. The court argued that the rates established by the statutory process are not solely for the individual wage earner's benefit but also protect the public as a whole. Therefore, the court decided that "any agreement to pay or receive a smaller sum unless the state had participated in the agree-ment, is voidable, if not void."[35]

The fifth challenge occurred in the state of Massachusetts. Six years after enactment of the statute and in light of several state supreme court decisions described above, the Supreme Court of Massachusetts declared the Massachu-setts statute constitutional. Here, too, the constitutional question arose from the refusal of employers to provide actual wage rates as determined by the State

Minimum Wage Commission. While the wage rates established by the commission were not compulsory, the commission had the authority to investigate the extent to which their recommendations were observed and, further, to publish the names of firms failing to pay the established rates. Firms in the laundry industry refused to provide actual wage rate information to the commission. To establish a basis for their ruling, the Supreme Court of Massachusetts considered the constitutionality issue. Since the statute provided for *voluntary* conformance with the commission-established rates, no invasion of freedom of contract occurred. Firms could pay lower rates if they could stand the public scrutiny of their actions. The court argued: "The guaranties of the Constitution as to liberty and freedom of contract do not go to the extent of protection against publicity respecting contracts with women and minors, which the consensus of opinion of the Commonwealth, as formulated in a statute requiring impartial investigation by a public board, declares wanting in affording to them necessary support."[36] Employers were ordered to provide the information to the commission.

Based on the consistent stream of state court decisions, there was optimism that minimum wage laws for women and minors had become an established part of protective labor legislation. It was confidently asserted in 1921 that the principle of laissez-faire no longer dominated the marketplace and that "disturbances to competition" and the operation of the laws of supply and demand were secondary to higher economic, social, and political goals. There were more challenges to the Minnesota and Washington statutes in 1919 and 1920 that caused further confirmation of the legislation. A challenge to the statute in the state of Texas in 1919 was set aside by the Texas Court of Appeals. A challenge to the issuance of certain wage orders by the North Dakota Workmen's Compensation Bureau was upheld by the state supreme court, but the constitutionality of the law remained untouched.

THE DEMISE OF STATE PROGRAMS

In what appeared to be yet another routine challenge to the constitutionality of minimum wage programs, the Supreme Court of the District of Columbia denied an application for an injunction to restrain the operation of the law on the ground that it was unconstitutional. Based on this decision, the case (*Children's Hospital v. Adkins*) was appealed to the court of appeals. The challenge to the statute was based "upon the ground that it authorizes an unconstitutional interference with the freedom of contract included within the guaranties of the due process clause of the Fifth Amendment."[37] Upon rehearing, the court of appeals found the act unconstitutional.

The court of appeals remanded the case to the trial court, which entered decrees consistent with the higher court's mandate and granted permanent injunctions against further enforcement of the statute. This decision was appealed to the U.S. Supreme Court. The U.S. Supreme Court decision to affirm the court of appeals decision shocked the nation and placed most of the state programs in jeopardy. Thus, it is important to review the issues and arguments in the *Adkins* case underlying the constitutionality question.

The issues are embedded in concepts such as "police power," "freedom of contract," "due process of law," "private right," "public necessity," "public welfare," "price-fixing," and so forth, which are sufficiently imprecise as to permit discretion by the Court. It is of some importance, perhaps, to note that the U.S. Supreme Court appeal involved two cases—one by an individual plaintiff and the other by an institution. The individual plaintiff, Ms. Willie A. Lyons, argued that the District of Columbia minimum wage statute caused her dismissal from employment because her services were insufficient to warrant a wage greater than the one she negotiated with her employer. Her position was very similar in substance to the position of Ms. Elmira Simpson in the initial Oregon case. Both individuals felt they were receiving as high a wage as their effort permitted, that the conditions of work were safe and wholesome, and they wanted to continue working at wages below the statutorily determined rate.

The institutional plaintiff was Children's Hospital in the District of Columbia. This corporation employed large numbers of women in numerous occupations and generally negotiated a mutually acceptable wage rate with them. Sometimes, this negotiated rate was less than the board-determined minimum wage rate.

Suit was initiated in the Supreme Court of the District of Columbia to "restrain the board from enforcing or attempting to enforce its order on the ground that the same was in contravention of the Constitution, and particularly the due process clause of the Fifth Amendment."[38] Thus, the appeal to the U.S. Supreme Court was on narrow grounds, for example, the constitutionality of the act. Francis Sayre suggested that "the precise question involved being whether the law violated the provisions of the Fifth Amendment to the Constitution which provides that no person shall 'be deprived of life, liberty or property without due process of law.'" [39]

In its opinion, the U.S. Supreme Court recognized the importance of the judicial review process. Writing for the Court, Justice Sutherland noted, "The judicial duty of passing upon the constitutionality of an act of Congress is one of great gravity and delicacy."[40] He further noted, "This Court, by an unbroken line of decisions from Chief Justice Marshall to the present day, has steadily adhered to the rule that every possible presumption is in favor of the validity of an act of Congress until overcome beyond rational doubt."[41] But he warned, "A congressional statute is the act of an agency of this sovereign authority and if it conflicts with the Constitution must fall; for that which is not supreme must yield to that which is."[42]

Justice Sutherland then restated the scope of judicial review. He observed:

The statute now under consideration is attacked upon the ground that it authorizes an unconstitutional interference with the freedom of contract included within the guaranties of the due process clause of the Fifth Amendment. That the right of contract about one's affairs is a part of liberty of the individual protected by this clause, is settled by the decisions of the Court and is no longer open to question. [43]

The constitutionality question then hinged on the interference or not of the freedom of contract. Justice Sutherland asserted:

There is . . . no such thing as absolute freedom of contract. It is subject to a great variety of restraints. But freedom of contract is, nevertheless, the general rule and restraint the exception; and the exercise of legislative authority to abridge it can be justified only by the existence of exceptional circumstances. Whether these circumstances exist in the present case constitutes the question to be answered.[44]

Through analogy and inference, the Court embarked on a line of reasoning that led inevitably to affirmation of the lower court decision. The majority opinion argued, "The feature of this statute which, perhaps more than any other, puts upon it the stamp of invalidity is that it exacts from the employer an arbitrary payment for a purpose and upon a basis having no causal connection with his business, or the contract or the work the employee engages to do."[45] Further, "It ignores the necessities of the employer by compelling him to pay not less than a certain sum, not only whether the employee is capable of earning it, but irrespective of the ability of his business to sustain the burden, generously leaving him, of course, the privilege of abandoning his business as an alternative for going on at a loss."[46] Finally:

A statute requiring an employer to pay in money, to pay at prescribed and regular intervals, to pay the value of the services rendered, even to pay with fair relation to the extent of the benefit obtained from the service, would be understandable. But a statute which prescribes payment without regard to any of these things and solely with relation to circumstances apart from the contract of employment, the business affected by it and the work done under it, is so clearly the product of a naked, arbitrary exercise of power that it cannot be allowed to stand under the Constitution of the United States.[47]

It is interesting that the voluminous studies, reports, testimony, and other evidence presented to the Court in overwhelming support of benefits flowing from minimum wage programs were dismissed by the Court as "interesting but only mildly persuasive."[48] The documented improvements in the wages of women were dismissed by the general assertion that the changes were "due to other causes."[49]

The Adkins decision evoked widespread criticism. Father Ryan suggested, "Not a few of those who have heard about the recent decision undoubtedly imagine that there is some form of words in the Constitution which clearly and unmistakably conflict with the provisions of the minimum wage law. Nothing could be further from the truth."[50] Governor George Hunt of Arizona asserted that "[with regard to] the decision of the Supreme Court in the minimum wage law, I think the reasoning with reference to the 'right of contract' comes close to bordering on the ridiculous."[51] Samuel Gompers, agreeing with Father Ryan, suggested, "The thought that Supreme Court decisions are written out of inflexible law is a pleasant fiction. Supreme Court decisions, especially in cases involving what is generally known as social legislation, are shaped largely by the trend of mind and philosophy which happens at the time to dominate the court."[52] Jett W. Lauck argued, "Broad, underlying, fundamental principles have not been invoked, but technical and indirect reasoning has been used to nullify sound and desirable legislation."[53] Irene Andrews noted, "This action came as a great shock to the supporters of minimum wage legislation everywhere, especially since the laws had previously been upheld by no less than seven state courts, and in three of these states, unanimous favorable decisions had been twice given."[54]

Most disturbing to the critics of the Court's decision was that the basis of the decision apparently resided in elements outside the legislation or the legal system. Father Ryan pointed out, "Anyone who reads the decision written by Justice Sutherland will realize that by far the greater part of his arguments have nothing at all to do with law or precedent. He thinks that the minimum wage law is unfair to the employer, is contrary to economic and business interests, and is bad public policy."[55] Gompers argued, "The brutality of the majority decision can beget nothing but wrath. It went as far as to unblushingly liken the purchase of the labor power of women and girls to the purchase of provisions in a grocery store, or meat in a butcher shop." [56]

The dissenting opinions by Chief Justice Taft and Justices Holmes and Sanford also raised serious questions about the wisdom of the decision. Chief Justice Taft asserted that "it is not the function of this Court to hold congressional acts invalid simply because they are passed to carry out economic views which the Court believes to be unwise or unsound."[57] The chief justice did not, of course, feel the economic views underlying minimum wage programs were unwise or unsound. Justice Holmes noted,"I do not understand the principle on which the power to fix a minimum for women can be denied by those who admit the power to fix a maximum for their hours of work."[58] He argued further, "This statute does not compel anybody to pay anything. It simply forbids employment at rates below those fixed as the minimum requirement of healthy and right living."[59] Judge Powell in 1917 established a similar proposition when he argued, "It is plain that the minimum wage legislation does not compel employers to make any contract that in their judgment is not remunerative."[60] In any case, the decision of the Supreme Court vetoed the legislation and declared it unconstitutional. Needless to say, legislators and administrators in other states with minimum wage programs recognized that all of these programs were at risk. The U.S. Supreme Court ruling related narrowly to the District of Columbia minimum wage law, but it was clear that virtually every other program that had a compulsory provision for wage setting and payment would undoubtedly be struck down if challenged.

In a prophetic insight, Henry Seager noted in 1923:

Judging from the present trend of opinion and teaching in the law schools of the country and from the gradual revival of progressive thinking, after the post-war reaction, in every section there is good ground for hoping that the next appointees to the Supreme Bench will share the enlightened views expressed by Justices Taft and Holmes on such issues rather than those of Justice Sutherland and his associates.[61]

Mary Anderson, director of the Labor Department's Women's Bureau, believed that public opinion would compel the beginning of effective minimum wage programs but that the process of accomplishing that objective must not jeopardize constitutional protections. She argued specifically:

It is too early to see what the next step is, but it seems to me that public opinion can be depended upon in the long run to decide that no employer has a moral right, even though the Supreme Court has decided that he has a legal right, to pay a woman less than a living wage, and there must be some way of making this public opinion effective without destroying the effectiveness of constitutional guarantees.[62]

Interestingly, while there was not a mass exodus from these programs, "[t]est cases under three State laws were subsequently taken to the courts, and all three were held unconstitutional on the precedent of the decision in the District of Columbia case."[63]

The system then settled into a holding pattern without additional challenges. One could have expected that there would be challenges in the other states with these programs, but nothing happened. Employers in states like North Dakota and California simply accepted the rates in place in 1923 as reasonable and did not resist them. Massachusetts had a "noncompulsory" law, which was believed to be outside the scope of the *Adkins* decision. Other states began to address the issues in more creative ways. In Wisconsin, for example, the statute language was changed to *prohibit* an "oppressive wage" instead of *establishing* a "minimum wage." Work continued throughout the late 1920s and early 1930s to develop alternative legislative strategies that would address the problem and overcome the legal obstacles.

Out of these efforts, the National Consumer's League sponsored a standard uniform bill in 1933 that approached the living wage from a different direction. Stimulated by the National Consumer's League work, the New York legislature developed a "new" statute in 1933 that relied upon a "fair wage" rather than a "living wage" as provided in the District of Columbia statute. The New York statute attempted to incorporate both a "fair" value for services provided provision and a cost-of-living provision into a fair wage concept. In a four-to-three decision, the New York Supreme Court "ruled, in 1936, that the 'new' state minimum wage law of 1933 . . . did not differ in principle from the District of Columbia law and was, therefore, like that law in conflict with the

Constitution."[64] The U.S. Supreme Court upheld the decision of the state court.

This decision in June 1936 sent another shock wave reverberating through the economy. Seven other states—Connecticut, Illinois, Massachusetts, New Hampshire, New Jersey, Ohio, and Rhode Island—had, since 1932, enacted minimum wage legislation similar in structure and provisions to the New York law. The "new" approach to minimum wage legislation was apparently not working, but the problems still existed—sweatshop conditions and miserably low wages. In any case, by 1935, fully one third of the states had mandatory minimum wage programs in force. Colorado, Minnesota, California, Washington, Oregon, North Dakota, South Dakota, and Wisconsin had statutes in effect that had been enacted prior to 1932. Between 1932 and 1935, primarily through the work of the National Consumer's League, eight more states—listed earlier—passed minimum wage legislation. While the U.S. Supreme Court decisions may have hampered the enthusiasm for these programs, efforts to address the problems continued.

JUDICIAL REVERSAL

Within the course of one year, the judicial climate took a complete reversal. The U.S. Supreme Court agreed to hear a minimum wage case, on appeal, from the state of Washington. The court decided that economic conditions had changed and, "in the light of which the reasonableness of the exercise of the protective power of the State must be considered, make it not only appropriate, but we think imperative, that in deciding the present case the subject should receive fresh consideration."[65] By a five-to-four vote, the Court's decision

was given on 29 March 1937. It declared the law of Washington to be a valid and proper exercise of the authority of that State, overruled the decision in the *Adkins* case, and in categorical terms declared minimum wage legislation compatible with the provisions of the Federal Constitution.[66]

The Washington case was initiated by an employee, Ms. Elsie Parrish, who sued her employer for the income difference between the income she actually received and that provided by state law. The defendant, West Coast Hotel Company, "challenged the act as repugnant to the due process clause of the Fourteenth Amendment of the Constitution of the United States."[67] The Washington State Supreme Court ruled that the minimum wage statute entitled "Minimum Wages for Women" was constitutional. The state supreme court "decided that the statute is a reasonable exercise of the police power of the State."[68] The Court questioned:

What can be closer to the public interest than the health of women and their protection from unscrupulous and overreaching employers? And if the protection of women is a legitimate end of the exercise of state power, how can it be said that the requirement of the payment of a minimum wage fairly fixed an admissible means to that end? [69]

The Court then revisited the social costs involved in a system in which the employees receive less than a living wage. The Court argued, "What these workers lose in wages the taxpayers are called upon to pay. The bare cost of living must be met."[70] Justice Sutherland wrote the dissenting opinion for the Court in which three other justices concurred. The arguments for reversal of the Washington State Supreme Court decision were along the lines argued in the majority decision in the *Adkins* case in 1923. In any event, the path was now open for the enforcement of state laws in existence, the enactment of statutes in states without them, and the vigorous pursuit of a federal minimum wage program. All of the avenues were lubricated by the *Parrish* decision, and the response by the several jurisdictions was now clear.

NOTES

1. Thomas Reed Powell, "The Oregon Minimum-Wage Cases," *Political Science Quarterly*, Vol. XXXII, No. 20, June 1917, p. 297.

2. Rudolf Broda, "Minimum Wage Legislation in the United States," *International Labour Review*, Vol. XVII, No. 1, January 1920, p. 34.

3. Ibid.

4. Emilie J. Hutchinson, *Women's Wages* (New York: Columbia University, Longmans, Green and Company, Agents, 1919), p. 75.

5. Bureau of Labor Statistics, *Minimum-Wage Laws of the United States: Construction and Operation* (Washington, D.C.: U.S. Government Printing Office, May 1921), p. 11.

6. Hutchinson, 1919, p. 68.

7. R.W. Bruere, "Meaning of the Minimum Wage," reprinted from *Harper's Magazine*, January 1916, p. 278.

8. Powell, 1917, p. 303.

9. Dorothy W. Douglas, "American Minimum Wage Laws at Work," *American Economic Review*, Vol. IX, No. 4, December 1919, p. 709.

10. Ibid.

11. Supreme Court of the United States, *Minimum Wage Cases*, October Term, 1914: No. 507, *Stettler v. O'Hara*, and No. 508, "*Simpson v. O'Hara*", Brief and Arguments for Plaintiffs in Error" (Minneapolis: Review Publishing Company, 1914), p. 7.

12. Powell, 1917, p. 308.

13. See Supreme Court of the United States, 1914, p. 7.

14. Edwin V. O'Hara, *A Living Wage by Legislation: The Oregon Experience* (Salem: State Printing Department, 1916), pp. iii–iv.

15. Powell, 1917, p. 305.

16. Mary D. Hopkins, "Do Wages Buy Health? The Oregon Minimum Wage Cases Re-Argued," reprinted from *The Survey*, February 3, 1917, p. 2.

17. Powell, 1917, p. 309.

18. Hopkins, 1917, p. 2.

19. O'Hara, 1916, p. xi.

20. Thomas Reed Powell, "The Constitutional Issue in Minimum-Wage Legislation," *Minnesota Law Review*, Vol. II, No. 1, December 1917, p. 13.

21. Hutchinson, 1919, p. 96.

22. Rinehart J. Swenson, *Public Regulation of the Rate of Wages* (New York: H.H. Wilson Company, 1917), p. 21.

23. Powell, 1917, p. 297.

24. John A. Ryan, *The Supreme Court and the Minimum Wage* (New York: Paulist Press, 1923), p. 4.

25. Bureau of Labor Statistics, May 1921, p. 33.

26. Ibid.

27. Ibid., p. 34.

28. Ibid., p. 35.

29. Ibid.

30. Ibid., p. 37.

31. Idib., p. 38.

32. Powell, *Minnesota Law Review*, op. cit., p. 19.

33. See Bureau of Labor Statistics, May 1921, p. 40.

34. Powell, *Minnesota Law Review*, op. cit., p. 18.

35. See Bureau of Labor Statistics, May 1921, p. 46.

36. Ibid., p. 47.

37. Supreme Court of the United States, October Term, 1922: Nos. 795 and 796, Justice Sutherland Writing for the Court, Affirmed Decision in *Adkins v. Children's Hospital*, April 9, 1923, p. 5.

38. Ibid., p. 3.

39. Frances Bowes Sayre, "The Minimum Wage Decision: How the Supreme Court Becomes Virtually a House of Lords," *The Survey*, Vol. L, No. 3, May 1, 1923, p. 150.

40. Supreme Court of the United States, Nos. 795 and 796, October Term: 1922, op. cit., p. 4.

41. Ibid., p. 5.

42. Ibid.

43. Ibid.

44. Ibid., p. 6.

45. Ibid., p. 15.

46. Ibid., p. 15.

47. Ibid., pp. 16–17.

48. Ibid., p. 17.

49. Ibid.

50. Ryan, 1923, pp. 4–5.

51. George W.P. Hunt, "Ridiculous Reasoning," *The Survey*, Vol. L, No. 4, May 15, 1923, p. 217.

52. Samuel Gompers, "Usurped Power," *The Survey*, Vol. L, No. 4, May 15, 1923, p. 221.

53. Jett W. Lauck, "Require a Two-thirds Vote," *The Survey*, Vol. L, No. 4, May 15, 1923, p. 261.

54. Irene O. Andrews, "Minimum Wage Comes Back!" *American Labor Legislation Review*, Vol. XXIII, No. 2, June 1933, p. 104.

55. Ryan, 1923, p. 7.

56. Gompers, 1923, p. 222.

57. Supreme Court of the United States, 1922, p. 2.

58. Ibid., p. 3.

59. Ibid.

60. Powell, 1917, p. 8.

61. Henry R. Seager, "The Minimum Wage—What Next?" *The Survey*, Vol. L, No. 4, May 15, 1923, p. 216.

62. Mary Anderson, "Get Back to the Facts," *The Survey*, Vol. L, No. 4, May 15, 1923, p. 236.

63. Alice S. Cheyney, "The Course of Minimum Wage Legislation in the United States," *International Labour Review*, Vol. XXXVIII, No. 1, July 1938, p. 28.

64. Ibid., p. 32.

65. Ibid., p. 35.

66. Ibid.

67. Supreme Court of the United States, October Term, 1936: No. 293, *West Coast Hotel Company v. Parrish*, March 29, 1937, p. 2.

68. Ibid., p. 3.

69. Ibid., p. 7.

70. Ibid., p. 8.

Chapter 3

Enactment of the Fair Labor Standards Act and Its Constitutionality

As the economy lurched into the "second" depression in 1937—unemployment approached 20 percent—the stage was set for new or "repackaged" legislation. The Roosevelt administration had initiated a variety of new programs throughout the mid-1930s to stimulate recovery, but New Deal policies did not meet expectations. They were hastily assembled, large and unwieldy, and sometimes conceptually flawed. However, as noted, there were elements embedded in these policies—particularly the NIRA—that became the nucleus for legislative initiatives in later years.

The problems the country faced were truly national in scope and impact. Consequently, as Father Ryan noted a decade earlier, "The only logical and effective method of dealing with a unified national problem is by a national statute."[1] Early in the depression there was great pressure to focus the recovery process at the state level. This effort did not work. The character and size of the problems transcended the disjointed, uncoordinated efforts of states to address them.

Nothing more clearly typifies the new approach than the work of Harry Hopkins and the Works Progress Administration (WPA) in which state control of depression elimination programs was usurped by the Roosevelt administration. This attitude was in sharp contrast to the "state's rights" philosophy of government in which problem resolution was focused at the state and substate levels. In addition, the conditions were so severe in the mid-1930s that business, too, realized that something had to be done and in fact would be done.

There was an administration in Washington committed to using the Federal government's power in the economy. E.D. Golding observed:

Many employers knew that Congress was committed to some kind of minimum wage legislation, and believed that it was therefore better tactics to advocate the method of minimum wage legislation which would have the least practical effect rather than to oppose minimum wage legislation in toto. A statutory flat minimum would be the method of wage fixation involving the least practical effect since a statutory minimum without differentials must be fixed at a sufficiently modest level to avoid drastic effect upon employment in any industry.[2]

Business viewed minimum wage legislation as a fait accompli, and they clearly wanted to influence its shape and form as it emerged.

The form the legislation ultimately took emerged from several seemingly unrelated factors. In the most general sense, "[t]he act was passed primarily because of the existence in our economy of (1) interstate markets, (2) monopolistic competition, and (3) unemployment."[3] None of these phenomena were new to the American economy, but it became increasingly apparent that there was some interplay between them that could not be resolved through laissez-faire economic policies and certainly not through the actions of individual state governments.

The single most important economic problem in the 1930s was, beyond all doubt, unemployment. Political leaders were increasingly concerned about the "social dynamite" of large numbers of unemployed people, particularly when they were congregated in large urban areas. Consequently, the "Congressional debates on the wage and hour bill reveal clearly that it was proposed in part as a means of reducing unemployment through a cutting of weekly hours."[4] To a large extent, the bill was designed as a vehicle to promote "job sharing" through the reduction in the length of the workday.

The second important observation about the motivation behind this law was that the fervent rhetoric about lowwages and morals that occurred during the debate of the prior five decades was absent from this debate. W.E. Boles pointed out, "The one motive which has long been recognized as a sound justification for wage and hour legislation, that of protecting the health and morals of workers, seemed not to have played a dominant part in the enactment of the Fair Labor Standards Act."[5] Rather, insuring that economic depression would not depress wages further was a primary concern of the Congress and the Roosevelt administration. The federal minimum wage program was designed to be a floor under wages in addition to an income enhancement and poverty reduction mechanism.

THE NATIONAL DEBATE ON MINIMUM WAGE LEGISLATION

There was a belief—strongly articulated by President Roosevelt—that employers' actions were to a large degree responsible for the existence and persistence of the economic problems of the Great Depression. Whether or not this belief was based on factual evidence will not be addressed here. Suffice it to say, this belief existed and consequently modified the role of employers in shaping the FLSA legislation. The *employee* associations had not done well in the 1920s and were further weakened by the economic calamity of the 1930s. In the 1920s and early 1930s, employee associations were viewed as underdogs in the economic struggle. Employers had done well—so well, in fact, that a backlash set in and was reflected in President Roosevelt's assessment of responsibility for the Great Depression. As Irving Bernstein noted in *The Lean Years*:

At no other period in the Twentieth century . . . were employers as a class so free of the countervailing restraints of a pluralistic society as during the twenties. Labor organizations were deplorably weak and government was dedicated to fostering the employer's freedom. The businessman rode high, his voice the decisive one in a business society dominated by business interests.[6]

However, as the political shift to the Left gained momentum in the 1930s, labor's interests took on new life. Political leaders listened, and the people of the nation listened. New ideas were needed to devise policies for economic recovery. One of these policies was, of course, a minimum wage, maximum hour, and child labor program.

While there was a continual debate on the merits and problems with a federal wage and hour law, it was not until the middle of 1937 that a neatly packaged legislative proposal emerged. The federal government had experimented with a minimum wage program in late 1933. The Civil Works Administration (CWA) embarked on a large-scale job creation program financed and administered by the federal government. The CWA was the predecessor of the better-known WPA and had as a primary purpose "to provide for individuals work as near as possible to their previous employment and to pay the prevailing wage in each category and region with a minimum of thirty cents an hour."[7]

The president was fully supportive of wage and hour legislation and expressed his feelings on many occasions. The NIRA codes and the president's Reemployment Agreements provided the basis for national labor standards related to minimum wages, maximum hours, and child labor. While the experience with the NIRA was brief—about two years—it nevertheless whet the appetite of social reformers and many employers for major changes in the federal role in labor standards legislation. The president, too, vigorously spoke out about the need to rescue the one third of the nation that was ill-fed, ill-clothed, and ill-housed. He convincingly argued the need to bring the force of the federal government against unscrupulous employers who exploited workers and to compel well-intentioned employers to follow suit.

While the statutory life of the NIRA was to end in June 1935, the U.S. Supreme Court found the law unconstitutional days before it was scheduled to die statutorily. The president had sought an extension of the NIRA for two more years, but the Court's decision made that request moot. Critics may argue that the Court's action was a fortunate event. It permitted the extraction of elements from a cumbersome, floundering law and program that were molded into several pieces of protective labor legislation that addressed specific problems and have stood the test of Court scrutiny. The National Labor Relations Act and the Fair Labor Standards Act are the major legislative initiatives extracted from the NIRA that formed the foundation for five decades of federal government involvement in the labor market.

Gains from the NRA "experiment" quickly began evaporating after the Court decision. Testimony before Congress identified numerous examples of individual firms and major industries reverting to pre-NRA practices. Leon Henderson, NRA Research and Planning director, testified, "In the steel industry . . . only a few employees were exceeding code hours in 1935, when the Schecter decision was handed down. By May 1936, more than two-thirds of the employees were working longer than code hours."[8] In a study by the Bureau of Labor Statistics of sixteen industries in the post-NRA period, "all 16 industries lengthened the workweek of employees instead of adding new employees taken from the ranks of the unemployed."[9]

Apparently, American industry would not police itself and adhere voluntarily to employment practices that most believed were in the best interests of the country. Therefore, public pressure mounted to enact some type of federal wage, hour, and child labor legislation. To demonstrate the depth of this sentiment, an organization called the Council for Industrial Progress (CIP) was formed in 1935. The significant dimension of the CIP was that it contained a cross-section of major American industry and "official representation of the entire organized labor movement in the United States." The CIP took a strong stand supporting "suitable" standards of minimum wages and maximum hours in conjunction with an effective collective bargaining process. The management spokesman for the CIP, John G. Paine, recognized the unique character of the council. He argued before Congress, "The record speaks for itself and reflects a unity of opinion as between labor and management which must appeal to you as being unique in the industrial history of America."[10]

While pressure continued to mount for concerted action, the U.S. Supreme Court again shocked the nation with another decision invalidating a state minimum wage initiative. In *Morehead v. Tipaldo*, the Court handed down a rejection of New York State's "revised" minimum wage law. The jubilation of those opposing wages and hours programs was short-lived. In fact, *Tipaldo* was the last adverse Supreme Court decision before the restructured Court opened the flood gates for state and federal initiatives after the 1937 *Parrish* decision.

Organized labor tried to develop and present a coherent and rational policy toward minimum wage initiatives, but it never seemed able to convincingly explain exactly where it stood. In the three or four decades before passage of the FLSA, organized labor's institutional attitude toward minimum wage legislation was very different from what it was in the 1930s. Samuel Gompers, first president of the American Federation of Labor, stated the position of the labor movement in 1914 as follows: "The American Federation of Labor is not in favor of fixing, by legal enactment, certain minimum wages. The attempts of the government to establish wages at which workmen may work, according to the teachings of history, will result in a long era of industrial slavery."[11]

As Bernstein noted, Gompers "had little stomach for social legislation, laws fixing minimum wages and maximum hours, except as they affected the weak and unorganized, like women and children. Gompers opposed state-sponsored unemployment and health insurance and was unenthusiastic about old age pensions."[12] Interestingly, his position, as stated in the *American Federationist* in 1914, was essentially the position of the U.S. Supreme Court in 1923 when the District of Columbia minimum wage program was declared unconstitutional. Describing minimum wage legislation, Gompers observed:

This species of effort to better human conditions does more credit to our hearts than to our heads. It secures immediate relief, perhaps, but in such a way as to hinder future initiative. Whatever is purchased at the expense of liberty of action and personal rights is purchased at a price too dear for any free people to afford. Freedom of personal contract is the one narrow distinction between the free worker and the unfree.[13]

This attitude and institutional opposition to minimum wage programs were not unique to the United States. As R. Bruere noted, "In 1896 there were many workers in Victoria [Australia] who feared that the minimum-wage act would disrupt the unions, and that the minimum wage would tend to become the maximum."[14] To understand this institutional position, it is important to note that unions, as institutions, have a variety of roles to play and goals to achieve. They represent members' interests specifically but all workers' interests generally. These two sets of interests do not always coincide.

When an initiative like the FLSA emerged, there was ambivalence by union leaders about it. There was a natural inclination to support it but carefully delimit its scope so that it did not impinge on the union's "turf." This ambivalence was noted by Rudolf Broda when he observed that "[t]he American Federation of Labor opposes minimum wage legislation for adult men, fearing that State protection might replace fighting tactics . . . . The American Federation of Labor favors, although without, great zeal, minimum wage legislation for women and minors; the present legislative status and its limitations are conditioned, to a large extent, by its policy."[15]

A more pointed assertion by E.T. Devine arrives at the same conclusion. He argued that in general "[o]fficial union leaders prefer that working men should be accustomed to rely on the unions rather than on the legislature or on wage commissions for protection, and apprehension is expressed that there will be a tendency for minimum wages to become standard and so eventually maximum wages."[16] It is important that there was apprehension by early American unions concerning protection for groups that could not protect themselves. Gompers argued, "In my judgment the proposal to establish by law a minimum wage for women, though well meant, is a curb upon the rights, the natural development, and the opportunity for development of the women employed in the industries of our country."[17]

It is not clear how Gompers expected women workers to "develop" in the economy. Very few women were organized, many had few options for other employment, many had few labor market skills, and there was a general over-supply of them. These conditions could hardly be expected to lead to improvements in the working conditions of women or, for that matter, the other groups mentioned above. Since "public sector" employees were not organized during the first three or four decades of this century, Gompers found it appropriate and acceptable to extend legislative protection to them. He observed in 1914 that "a minimum wage for governmental employees was justified as in that case the government was the employer, but workers in private employment must depend upon the intelligence, the energy, and the solidarity of the organization of wage-workers."[18]

Thus, it was believed early in the debate on the FLSA that American labor leaders universally opposed minimum wage and maximum hour legislation for the protection of *men*. Labor leaders believed that legislation of this type would threaten the existence of the labor movement because workers would seek improvements in wages and hours through elected public officials rather than through the collective bargaining process. In addition, it was believed that legislated *minimum* wages would become legislated *maximum* wages that would undercut organized labor's bargaining position.[19]

The AFL was not wildly enthusiastic about the NRA program, but there was a realization that they could not effectively resist the program. Probably the most important aspect of NRA activities was that organized labor learned a few important lessons about minimum wage and maximum hours programs that were to influence their position on the 1937 bill. Most important was the recognition that federal legislation including protection for men did not seriously threaten the institutional position of organized labor. Certainly, there remained the preference for excluding men from federal wage and hour labor legislation, but if the legislation were "appropriately" structured, it could coexist with active union programs.

Second, there was no evidence that the *minimum* wage rates provided under the NRA codes became the *maximum* wage rates. The turbulent economic conditions of the NRA years were probably not a good test environment for this presumed relationship, but the results were consistent with the experiences of foreign and several state programs and of sufficient importance to raise serious questions about the inevitability of the change process.

As a consequence of the NRA experience, the AFL lowered its institutional resistance to federal wage and hour legislation. The AFL began working with congressional allies with the expectation that an acceptable federal law could be developed. The AFL rationalized its institutional acceptance of the coverage of *men* by the proposed statute by making clear that the law applied only to low-wage workers earning less than $1,200 per year. This segment of the labor force was the unorganized segment. Green argued in his testimony on June 4, 1937, "The proposed act deals only with the fixing and regulation of wages of men, as well as women, in that very limited class of workers whose total annual income is less than $1,200 per year. There is no interference in the field covered by industries employing workers who earn in excess of $1,200 per year. That is exempt."[20] The inference was that because organized labor did not protect these workers, it was acceptable for the federal government to provide protection.

The Congress of Industrial Organizations had taken a more supportive institutional position from the early years of the Roosevelt administration, and therefore few changes were needed in its public position on the program.

As the nation moved toward a national minimum wage program, union apprehensions still existed, but it was more defensible to be on the "winning" side than to fight a losing battle. Some unions provided outright support for the legislation, while others registered "nonopposition." John L. Lewis, for example, forcefully supported the initiative by testifying before Congress that "the United Mine Workers [UMW] of America, and . . . the Committee for Industrials Organization, . . . pledge our general support to the principle of a minimum wage and maximum workweek."[21] He identified four elements underlying UMW-CIO support for the minimum wage: "It will increase purchasing power," "through reduction in hours of work, [it will] make way for the employment of hundreds of thousands of industrial workers who are now without work or on relief"; "it will bring a greater measure of leisure and economic well-being"; and "the pending measure will offer to these unfortunate victims of our existing economic system an opportunity to rise to industrial citizenship."[22] The CIO, composed of generally lower-paid industrial workers, undoubtedly viewed the force of federal law as a vehicle to raise these wage levels.

There is little question that organized labor—certainly the AFL—modified its institutional position on the desirability of wage and hour legislation during the 1930s. Given the choice, they preferred to exclude men from FLSA protection. But once they saw the scope of coverage and the levels of wages contemplated, they realized that the legislation was no real threat to their institutional roles or philosophical position.

All this institutional baggage was the framework within which the two most prominent labor leaders of the 1930s sparred. There was an intense and very acrimonious fight during this period between the AFL and the CIO. This fight involved the institutional position of the organizations in the U.S. economy and not the proposed wage and hour legislation. However, the leaders of the two organizations —William Green of the AFL and John L. Lewis of the CIO— used the wage and hour debate as a vehicle for exchanging strongly held views about each other. Green was particularly vehement in his attacks on Lewis. The CIO-supported Labor Non-Partisan League was referred to by Green as a "ventriloquist's dummy" for Lewis, and moreover he characterized Lewis as a "dictator."[23]

The acrimonious personal relationship between Green and Lewis was immersed in divergent institutional interests in their organizations. Both the AFL and the CIO wanted to claim responsibility for advocating and helping obtain passage of a federal minimum wage, maximum hour, and child labor program. However, each individual and organization wanted to participate on their terms. It was frequently difficult to determine precisely what those terms were, however, because of the mixed signals emerging in the heat of battle. Even in the last days of intense debate before passage of the bill, Green had difficulty keeping AFL components in line. As the final bill took shape, it was observed "If the building trade unions were to have their way Mr. Green would oppose the entire measure as these craftsmen see no benefit to them in the new act."[24]

Nevertheless, one cannot say with certainty that either the AFL or the CIO fully supported the 1937 bill. The AFL had attempted to influence the character of the initial bill by establishing several specific—fundamental—requirements. As reported at the 1938 AFL Annual Convention, "We proposed that a ceiling for hours and a foundation for wages be incorporated in the Act with no differentials; that wages and hours should not be determined by a board and that prosecution of violators should be by the Federal Department of Justice."[25] These views were well known by congressional leaders, but "during the long fight for the bill there were several occasions when members of Congress were at a loss to know where the AFL stood because of different statements made by some of its spokesmen."[26] Specific examples were given in which an AFL spokesman told one senator that the AFL favored one provision in the bill—a North-South differential—while another senator was led to believe precisely the opposite. Whatever position the AFL took on the bill, there is evidence that the CIO, as an institution, played a more significant role in structuring the initial administration bill and the compromise bill that became law in June 1938. The CIO's early role, excluding John L. Lewis, helps explain its reluctance to compromise on provisions of the bill that resulted in vigorous attacks by AFL's Green. A *New York Times* report observed, "The bill as it now stands [June 1938] comes close to covering all the chief features of a memorandum presented by Mr. Hillman [vice president of the CIO and general president of the Amalgamated Clothing Workers of America] to Frances Perkins in 1933 when it was apparent that she was about to be named Secretary of Labor."[27]

While the fireworks and acrobatics of the struggle between the AFL and CIO intrigued and amused those watching from the outside, other organizations and institutions expressed strong views about federal wage and hour legislation. There were several critical issues embedded in the legislative proposals about which there was vigorous disagreement. There was a strong argument, for example, that a federal statute was not needed because the regulation of wages and hours was not a proper federal function. President Roosevelt noted in early 1938 that part of the opposition to the proposed law stems from a sincere belief "that an effort thus to raise the purchasing power of lowest paid industrial workers is not the business of the federal Government."[28] Business leaders were particularly vehement in their belief that wage and hour laws were outside the purview of federal regulation. "Whatever else they may say about any such measure [the wage and hour bill], these two leading spokesmen [the U.S. Chamber of Commerce and the National Manufacturers Association] for organized business believe that the wages paid and hours required of industrial workers are not a proper field for Federal intervention."[29] Leo Wolman argued in a May 1938 editorial that "If we are to have minimum-wage legislation in this country, it is wiser policy to depend on State legislation, drafted and administered by persons close to the local situation and familiar with it problems."[30] These views in opposition to a federal program were articulated well and repeatedly. However, the impetus for the compelling need to engage the force of federal authority to ensure fair labor standards for all workers overwhelmed the opposition.

The president wanted a federal statute; his labor secretary, Frances Perkins, wanted a federal statute; the AFL and CIO urged federal legislation; several business associations such as the National Association of Cotton Manufacturers urged federal legislation; and private groups such as the National Consumers' League, the National League of Women Shoppers, and major national newspapers were in support of either a federal statute or a combined federal/state program. Therefore, though there was continual opposition to the federal government entering the wage and hour area, the administration and Congress pushed ahead with a proposed bill.

A major issue that seriously delayed passage of the bill concerned the adoption of a single federal minimum wage standard. This issue arose because of the wide geographic differences in wage rates and the role these differences played in the relative competitiveness of sectors of the country. Southern congressmen and business leaders viewed a uniform national minimum wage as destroying their ability to attract and maintain industry that relied on low wages to survive. Northern congressional and business leaders in conjunction with union leaders saw the proposed wage and hour legislation as a vehicle to recapture or retain a competitive edge.

Those arguing the "Southern Case" were opposed to wage and hour regulation in general but even more vehemently opposed to a uniform Federal minimum wage. The Southern Case rested on five propositions:

1. The proposal violates the historic political philosophy of the South.
2. It seeks to achieve a national economic parity for which the South, being a region of relatively recent industrial development, is not yet ready. A sounder policy would be to permit this parity to be approached through natural development.
3. It does not take into account the fact that there are climatic and other differences within the nation that are reflected in living and construction costs and the relative efficiency of labor.
4. It does not make due allowance for the freight-rate differential, which puts the South at a disadvantage when it comes with its products into the populous market of the "official freight territory"—roughly the area north of the Ohio and the Potomac and east of the Mississippi.

5.   Instead of raising the purchasing power of the South, it would increase unemployment through the closing of industries that would not be able to pay their employees the minimum wage.[31]

These arguments were viewed as interesting, but not compelling reasons for wage rate differentials. In an editorial in the *Charleston Gazette* (West Virginia), the southern position was taken to task in a blunt manner. The editor argued, "The South developed one economic system which was based upon a fallacious principle—slavery. It is now proposed to try to build another one on cheap wages. We state without fear of contradiction that no lasting prosperity, no real sound economic system can be built upon the foundation of low wages."[32] The *Charleston Gazette* argued further that "what the southern industrialists are doing by promising cheap wages is to furnish northern employers with a club to hold over the heads of their employees."[33] The viewpoint of southern congressmen did not fall on deaf ears. A Gallup Poll in June 1938 showed that "[p]ublic opinion, as measured in a nation-wide survey, overwhelmingly endorses the principle that any wage-hour legislation passed by Congress should provide for a wage differential among the various geographical sections."[34]

In the final months of legislative activity, President Roosevelt had apparently accepted the argument that a uniform national minimum wage was inappropriate. Regional wage differences were simply too great to permit the "shoe-horning" of states into one mold. In early 1938, there were specific minimum wage proposals attributed to the administration that contained a $13 per week minimum wage for the North and an $11 per week minimum wage for the South.[35]

In his 1938 message to Congress, President Roosevelt was explicit about the North-South differential. He said, in part, that

[n]o reasonable person seeks a complete uniformity in wages in every part of the United States; nor does any reasonable person seek an immediate and drastic change from the lowest pay to the highest pay. We are seeking, of course, only legislation to end starvation wages and intolerable hours; more desirable wages are and should continue to be the product of collective bargaining.[36]

While southern industry argued strongly for regional wage differentials, there were employer groups in the South supporting a uniform minimum wage rate program. The Association of Cotton Manufacturers, for example, advocated a federal minimum wage without regional differentials. The association's legislative chairman argued that "wiping out the regional differential would work no hardship on the efficient manufacturer in any section of the country."[37]

Claudius Murchison, president of the Cotton Textile Institute, argued that "it is no news that the cotton-textile industry endorses and advocates without qualification the desirability of a standard workweek of 40 hours for manufacturing industries . . . the complete elimination by legislative methods or otherwise of the employment of all persons in manufacturing industry under the age of 16" and "a minimum-wage floor below which no wage payment should go with the exception of wages paid to learners or to substandard workers."[38]

Testifying as an individual textile manufacturer, Austin T. Levy provided one of the most compelling arguments supporting a uniform and high minimum wage. "I have long championed the cause of short hours and high wages in American industry," he argued,

not entirely from considerations of a humanitarian nature, but also from the conviction that the technological developments of the past 30 years in all forms of endeavor leave us practically no choice; and it is my present belief that if we are to maintain the kind of civilization on which we are clearly embarked, we must have a general level of wages that is measurably higher than those that now obtain.[39]

Levy's beliefs were based on the basic Keynesian notion that spending drives the machine of industrial production and the main determinant of spending is income. Expand income through higher wages and the result will be expanded production, employment, and even higher income. He continued, "The common objection to high wages is the belief on the part of those who pay them that they cannot afford to pay more than they do, and that the things that are made cannot be sold if wages are advanced. I think the people who think these things are really quite sincere about it, but I think they are mistaken."[40] There was a tendency, in Levy's view, for employers to focus on labor cost changes and on dire consequences flowing from these changes. He observed that "everyone knows that people [employers] who choke over a 10-percent wage increase swallow a 30-percent rise in the cost of raw materials without a murmur."[41]

The importance of the testimony of Levy and other representatives in industry and, in particular, the textile industry was bolstered by the poignant testimony of John P. Davis, representing the National Negro Congress, before the U.S. Congress in 1937. Davis lamented the disparity between wages paid to blacks and those to nonblack workers throughout the nation. The codes established under the NRA furthered these disparities by considering "unique" economic conditions in different regions and different industries. Davis argued, however, that there may have been other motivation behind the creation of code differentials. "The geographical differentials established in practically every code bore no relationship to economic conditions in industry," he argued, "other than the relative predominance of unorganized Negro workers in the industry."[42] The National Negro Congress urgently supported the creation of a uniform minimum wage that would protect all workers equally. The National Negro Congress was particularly opposed to the proposed "Labor Standards Board" that would be charged with determining differential wage rates by occupation and not industry. In this instance, there would be even greater chance that occupations in which blacks were dominant would end up with a low wage structure. Davis concluded his testimony by urging, "The bill, rather than permitting differentials, should expressly declare as a part of its policy its opposition to any type of differential treatment so far as minimum wages are concerned."[43]

Another issue of major importance was the administrative location for the proposed wage and hour program. There were only two agencies seriously considered—the Departments of Labor and Justice. The AFL strongly supported placing the program in the Justice Department. In the 1938 *Proceedings* of the Fifty-eighth Annual Convention of the AFL, the fundamental principles supported by the AFL were outlined again. These principles included: "a ceiling for hours and a foundation for wages . . . with no differentials; that wages and hours should not be determined by a board and that prosecution of violators should be by the Federal Department of Justice."[44] The position of the AFL was motivated by Green's lack of support for Secretary Frances Perkins.

Among the several "firsts" that Secretary Perkins attained—the first woman in a presidential cabinet, the first woman chosen as secretary of labor—probably the most important to Green and the AFL was that she was the first labor secretary who did not emerge from the organized labor movement. Green and his associates sulked publicly after her appointment as labor secretary and were never quite able to accept her role as the workers' advocate.[45] In fact, in the final hours before passage of the FLSA (five years after her appointment as secretary), "[t]he Federation leaders opposed permitting Secretary Perkins to have any hand in the bill's administration."[46]

While the AFL was adamant in its opposition to Labor Department administration of the program, there was wide support for Labor Department administration in other sectors. The *New York Times* reported, "The federation's opposition to administration of the proposed law by a board or any other agency except the Department of Justice is said to have alienated several House votes from the measure killed in the special session last year."[47]

Elmer Andrews, to be designated first wage and hour administrator, wrote to Congressman Alfred F. Beiter on November 20, 1937, opposing regional differentials and supporting Labor Department administration of the program.[48] The National Consumer's League similarly supported Department of Labor administration. In a letter to Congressman Arthur D. Healey on December 9, 1937, the National Consumer's League supported Department of Labor administration but opposed *statutorily* determined minimum wage or maximum hour provisions.[49]

While President Roosevelt's personal preferences were not clearly known, there is compelling evidence that he supported Labor Department administration of the program. He enlisted Secretary Perkins as the administration's primary spokesperson before the Congress and in the public arena. It would have been difficult, indeed, for the president to yank the rug from under his labor secretary and place the program in another federal agency.

The fourth issue of major importance was enactment of a statutory minimum wage as opposed to the utilization of wage boards. Secretary Perkins favored the use of wage boards. In her testimony on June 4, 1937, she suggested that "conditions in different industries vary so much that I am not at all convinced of the wisdom of inserting any specific figure in the bill."[50]

To the surprise of no one, the AFL was vehemently opposed to the wage board method of rate determination and fought vigorously for a statutorily set wage level. In principle, the AFL was opposed to both regional differentials and the use of wage boards that could permit these differentials to emerge.

These were the four major issues that dominated the debate on the proposed bills. The positions and attitudes of the AFL and CIO on these issues were singularly important in the debate. Though less focused and usually less well articulated were the viewpoints of the public. Public attitudes and opinions will be summarized later, but first, the views of the business community deserve attention.

Equally important, but decidedly less interesting as compared to the vociferous bickering and fighting within the organized labor community, were the positions and views of the business community. It is axiomatic that employers in a laissez-faire economy—individually and through their associations—oppose the initiation and/or the expansion of minimum wage programs. These programs place constraints on the employer's freedom to take action, and consequently, these constraints are, in principle, resisted. An important question is whether the axiomatic presumption is true.

There was vigorous and uncompromising rejection of the overall idea by some employers. As H.R. Seager argued, "The proposal is opposed on the ground that it is contrary to the spirit of American institutions and that it leads logically to socialism."[51] And further, "That it involves a complete break with the laissez faire theory of government."[52] Whether it was "contrary to the spirit of American institutions" or "leads logically to socialism" are both open questions. E.J. Hutchinson said in 1919, "Again and again employers have contended before investigating commissions that wages are fixed by the natural law of supply and demand, which no legislation can abrogate."[53] Nevertheless, as with union attitudes, there was less than unanimity in the employer community about these programs. Importantly, "It may be recorded as a matter of interest," said E.V. O'Hara, "that the first real encouragement which the movement for wage legislation received in Oregon was a unanimous resolution of endorsement by the Board of Governors of the Portland Commercial Club."[54]

The minimum wage program has differential impacts on employers, and therefore their responses may reflect these differences. It is risky to generalize about "employers' views" concerning this program because for every employer who may show support for the program in private, one is likely to find an equal number who vigorously resist it in a public forum. However, what is intriguing about the questions raised above is that there are employers who support and encourage minimum wage programs. Some employers support them because "it makes good economic sense" to pay a living wage. It is not because of benevolence that they support the program. Rather, they believe that adequately paid workers are usually happier and more productive workers. Some employers are unaffected by minimum wage programs because most or all of their employees earn wages substantially above the mandated rate. Wearing their "social consciousness" hat, these employers may argue that higher wages expand purchasing power and therefore stimulate the economy for everyone's benefit.

Employers in some industries provide support because it places all employers on an "equal footing" concerning labor resource costs. In other words, all other things being equal, employers who want to pay higher wages are not at a competitive disadvantage in relation to low-wage employers.

To some degree, the various state minimum wage programs and particularly the early successes of these programs had the effect of desensitizing employers to these initiatives. As a practical matter, the wage rate was set low, and as a result, few employers were affected. Employers recognized the economic and social value of establishing a floor under wages to support purchasing power and to reduce pressures on other income maintenance programs. To some degree, these programs also compelled low-paying firms to bring wage rates to a more acceptable level. Importantly, however, perceptive employers noted that a statutory minimum wage could seriously disadvantage some employers in relation to their competitors if coverage was incomplete or enforcement was weak.

While there was ambivalence between employers, large and small, their lobbying associations have maintained more consistent opposition. There was rigid opposition to the FLSA by the U.S. Chamber of Commerce, the National Industrial Conference Board, the National Restaurant Association, and other employer associations. They suggested that firms would be destroyed, workers would be replaced by machines, prices would rise, exports would diminish, ad infinitum.

Finally, it is important to understand the feelings of the public toward these programs. Opinion polls in the first several decades of this century were not notoriously accurate, but they did capture a sense of the attitudes and changes in attitudes toward critical issues. In a public opinion poll in August–September 1934—near the depth of the Great Depression—about 60 percent of the respondents favored government fixing of wages and hours. During a period of low and declining wage rates, this is hardly surprising. The vast majority (70 percent) believed that only the federal government should institute the controls. More than 92 percent of those supporting controls favored only minimum wage controls.

Two years later (January–March 1936) the sentiment had changed. Slightly over 45 percent favored government control over minimum wage rates, and only 57 percent believed it should be initiated by the federal government. When asked in January 1939 whether they favored the new wage and hour law (FLSA), 71 percent answered in the affirmative. Interestingly, about two thirds of the respondents' thought there should be regional differentials in the minimum wage even though the legislation did not provide them. The respondents did not feel that a higher minimum wage *in their region of the country* would hurt business. For the most part, in January 1939, public respondents were satisfied with both the wages they received from their employers and the number of hours worked. About 79 percent thought they received a "fair wage," and 87 percent believed they were not required to work too many hours.

Emerging from ten years of depression, it is likely that people were happy to be working and were not inclined to be overly critical of wage levels and work hours. Therefore, these polls of public opinion provide anecdotal evidence that the public, in general, believed that minimum wage legislation was needed.

INTRODUCTION AND ENACTMENT OF THE BILL

To encourage states to develop these programs and to facilitate coordination and cooperation between the states and between the NIRA provisions and state programs, the Department of Labor established a long series of "Conferences on the Minimum Wage." The first two conferences were held in July and September 1933. The participants were state minimum wage administrators and organizations with interest in these programs. In the latter group were representatives of the National Consumers' League, the General Federation of Women's Clubs, the National Women's Trade Union League, the American Federation of Labor, the National League of Women Voters, and the National Young Women's Christian Association.

The early conferences were concerned with the enforcement of NRA codes and state minimum wage provisions when they were different. There was emphatic agreement that a "definite minimum" wage should be established under the NIRA and that no exemptions by type of work or geographic area should be permitted. Participants also agreed that home work should be eliminated and that overtime work should be compensated at "a rate of time and a half." There was some support for the payment of rates *higher* than the full-time minimum wage for workers employed on part-time schedules.[55]

In the November 25, 1935, conference, Secretary Perkins explained the importance of effective enforcement of minimum wage laws. This enforcement process performed an important "educative" function for citizens in the states, she argued, that showed the plight of low-wage workers. She suggested, "When members of a community become informed concerning these low standards, their whole-hearted support of minimum wage legislation is readily given."[56]

The sixth conference followed the *Tipaldo* decision that invalidated the New York minimum wage law. In spite of the depressing effects of the decision, Secretary Perkins told the participants, "Efforts to raise women's wages to a level of health and decency must go on. The gains in increased wages, in greater health and security, are social, as well as personal, and must be preserved and extended."[57] Conference participants were receptive to the secretary's pronouncements and in fact indicated that they were prepared to continue enforcement of their statutes until or unless specifically voided by the U.S. Supreme Court. These strong feelings were reflected in the conference report as follows: "The strong public support of minimum wage legislation testified to by the storm of protests which has arisen against the New York decision strengthened the administrators in their determination to preserve and extend the great social gains made under these laws."[58]

Since most states issued directory—nonmandatory—orders and relied heavily on public opinion for enforcement, the *Tipaldo* decision was believed to improve program administration. The conference report noted, "Public sentiment is so aroused by recent events, that administrators of these States felt that this form of enforcement [public opinion and not patronizing firms out of compliance with the law] will be more effective than ever before."[59]

The seventh conference convened on October 21, 1937, on a decidedly more upbeat note. Mary Anderson, director of the Women's Bureau, opened the conference with the observation that "you recall the black year of 1936, when we met under very difficult circumstances after the decision of the Supreme Court. Now we are meeting under very happy circumstances after another Supreme Court decision [*West Coast Hotel v. Parrish*], this time in favor of minimum wage legislation in the States."[60] Secretary Perkins expressed gratitude to the group for their commitment to these programs and encouraged them to work with their congressional representatives to support the new federal bill. She was careful to articulate the need for both state and federal efforts in this area and the importance of the state experience and expertise in administering a federal program.[61]

The importance of these conferences was that they were a vehicle through which the dialogue on these programs could be maintained during a decade of very difficult legal and economic events. The leadership role played by Secretary Perkins ensured that the interests of the Roosevelt administration were continually conveyed to a cross section of states attempting to enact and administer effective and responsive programs. These conferences were also a forum for discussing and resolving problems common to many state programs and, in that context, provided information for the structure and process of the federal statute.

Against the background of economic dislocation, Supreme Court decisions, and the development of state programs, President Roosevelt encouraged the Congress to enact a federal program. On May 24, 1937, he sent a message to the Congress that encouraged the enactment of a wages, hours, and child labor law. Some language in the president's message is particularly important because it sets the tone for the later discussion and explained the urgency of moving forward expeditiously. In his message, he made the observation, "One-third of our population, the overwhelming majority of which is in agriculture or industry, is ill-nourished, ill-clad, and ill-housed."[62] He observed that while well intentioned, the efforts of American industry operating under the guise of the laissez-faire system to advance economic and social progress had failed. He believed that only through the passage of federal legislation could there be real improvements in the deep-seated problems facing the nation.

This message also contained the often-quoted observation that "[a] self-supporting and self-respecting democracy can plead no justification for the existence of child labor, no economic reason for chiseling workers' wages or stretching workers' hours."[63] Further, "All but the hopelessly reactionary will agree that to conserve our primary resources of manpower, Government must have some control over maximum hours, minimum wages, the evil of child labor, and the exploitation of unorganized labor."[64] The president turned to the dissenting views of Chief Justice Holmes in *Hammer v. Dagenhart* that outlined the rationale for congressional prohibition of working conditions below "civilized social standards" involving shipments of goods in foreign and interstate commerce. After concurring with the chief justice's views on congressional powers to regulate interstate commerce, the president observed, "One of the primary purposes of the formation of our Federal Union was to do away with the trade barriers between the States. To the Congress, and not to the States, was given the power to regulate commerce among the several States."[65]

The president continued by asserting, "Goods produced under conditions which do not meet rudimentary standards of decency should be regarded as contraband and ought not be allowed to pollute the channels of interstate trade."[66] He recognized that these standards could not be assimilated in "one fell swoop" because of the large differences within a complex, advanced economic system. He observed further, "Most fair labor standards as a practical matter require some differentiation between different industries and localities. But there are a few rudimentary standards of which we may properly ask general and widespread observance."[67]

The president placed the responsibility on state governments to address labor standards issues involved with purely intrastate commerce. He argued, "No State is justified in sitting idly by and expecting the Federal Government to meet State responsibility for those labor conditions with which the State may effectively deal without fear of unneighborly competition from sister States. The proposed Federal legislation should be a stimulus and not a hindrance to State action."[68] The president ended his message by asserting, "Legislation can, I hope, be passed at this session of the Congress further to help those who toil in the factory and on the farm. We have promised it. We cannot stand still."[69]

On the same day that the president sent his message to Congress—May 24, 1937—Senator Black introduced the administration proposals as S.R. 2475. An identical bill was introduced on the same day by Congressman William J. Connery as H.R. 7200.

There was a shared interest to expedite the movement of these bills through

Congress. Therefore, joint hearings were conducted by the Senate Committee on Education and Labor and the House Committee on Labor between June 2 and June 22, 1937. Halfway through these hearings, Congressman Connery died. It is unclear what impact his death had on maintaining momentum for the bill in the House, but it took extraordinary parliamentary maneuvering to attain enactment. Congresswoman Mary T. Norton, who became chairperson of the House Labor Committee after Connery's death, had extensive learning to do to acquire the parliamentary acumen needed for this controversial legislative initiative.

The original bills—S.R. 2475 and H.R. 7200—provided, among other things, for (1) a five-member Fair Labor Standards Board; (2) a minimum wage of not more than $.80 an hour or $1,200 per year; (3) the general initiation of a $.40 per hour, forty-hour workweek except in exceptional circumstances; (4) the prohibition of interstate shipment of goods produced with "oppressive child labor"; (5) the exemption of agricultural workers and, executive, administrative, supervisory, and professional employees; and, (6) authorization of the Fair Labor Standards Board to appoint advisory committees to consider conditions in industries or occupations before establishing specific wage and hour standards.

These aspects of the original bills are important because they set the stage for a protracted series of legislative maneuvers. Senator Black had the most success in achieving passage of the bill. The Senate Committee on Education and Labor favorably reported the Fair Labor Standards Act of 1937, on July 8, 1937, with amendments. The major changes the committee sought to S.R. 2475 were (1) a single set of "fair" standards rather than a dubious distinction between "fair" labor standards and "oppressive" standards; (2) a mandatory requirement that industry committees be established; (3) the Fair Labor Standards Board could declare a minimum wage not to exceed $.40 per hour and a workweek of not less than forty hours; (4) the board could establish special standards for the employment of learners, disabled, retired, apprentices, and other specially situated workers; and (5) a modification of "oppressive child labor" to permit the employment of fourteen- and fifteen-year-olds if it did not adversely affect their education and was not detrimental to their health. Five days of Senate debate ended with passage of the bill on July 31, 1937, by a fifty-six to twenty-eight vote.

As S.R. 2475 moved through the Senate, it became clear that the legislative provisions acceptable to the AFL were not going to be incorporated into the bill. Therefore, the AFL decided that their next battleground was in the House Labor Committee. The AFL decided to ask the committee "to prepare a real bill that would be along the lines favored by the American Federation of Labor."[70]

The House Committee on Labor reported H.R. 7200 on August 6, 1937 with several important amendments: (1) the original child labor, provisions were retained; (2) the board had jurisdiction only if a collective bargaining agreement did not cover a "substantial" number of workers; (3) all provisions of the proposed bill applied to all workers regardless of sex; (4) the board was to establish the forty/forty conditions as soon as possible without adverse employment consequences; and (5) all board members had to be selected from civil service lists.

The House Rules Committee failed to adopt a rule permitting full House consideration of the bill. Virtually none of the AFL's legislative proposals were incorporated into the House bill, but little was lost because the first session ended without House passage. President Roosevelt convened a special session of the Congress in December 1937, to consider pending legislative initiatives. Among those initiatives was the proposed wage and hour bill.

During the congressional debate on the proposed legislation, there was a perceived concern that states may become discouraged and possibly abandon their programs or in some cases not initiate legislation. It was the view of the president that both federal and state programs were needed. He had discussed this issue at length in his May 24, 1937, message to Congress, but apparently states were uncertain about what would happen to their programs if a federal law was enacted. Secretary Perkins attempted to reassure the states by noting that a federal law could not provide protection to every worker, and therefore a role remained for state programs. With information provided by the Women's Bureau showing that over 1 million women would not be covered by the proposed wage and hour law, Secretary Perkins argued in late 1937 that "the need for State minimum wage laws to cover such cases will remain as great as ever even if a Federal Law is enacted."[71]

Because few of the AFL's proposals had been adopted, President Green urged every member of the House to vote to recommit the bill to the House Labor Committee "in order that proper amendments could be made to the bill."[72] On December 16, 1937, he argued, "Because the pending wage and hour bill is highly objectionable to membership of the American Federation of Labor, I respectfully request you to vote to recommit to the appropriate committee for revision, study and necessary changes in order to make it a practical and constructive measure."[73] Even though the CIO opposed recommittal, Green won the round because the House voted 216 to 198 to recommit the bill to the House Labor Committee.

In the special session of the Congress, the president urged favorable consideration of the bill. To overcome the Rules Committee blockage of the bill, the full House voted 285 to 113 to discharge the Rules Committee from further consideration of the bill. However, the floor debate resulted in numerous amendments being adopted. Due to the volume and complexity of the amendments, the bill was voted back into the House Labor Committee to consider the amendments, and the special session ended without House action.

As the legislative process unfolded in the Congress, the president took every opportunity to signal his unflagging support for minimum wage, maximum hour, and child labor legislation. For example, in his State of the Union

Message on January 3, 1938, he noted:

We have not only seen minimum wage and maximum hour provisions prove their worth economically and socially under government auspices in 1933, 1934 and 1935, but the people of this country, by an overwhelming vote, are in favor of having the Congress —this Congress—put a floor below which industrial wages shall not fall, and a ceiling beyond which the hours of industrial labor shall not rise.[74]

He graphically described the social and economic consequences of oppressive child labor, low wages, and long hours. He challenged the sincerity and wisdom of those who opposed these legislative initiatives by arguing that some opponents give "lip service" in support of the general objectives of the legislation but find reason for nonsupport on every specific proposal. He alluded to the notion of sweated employment by suggesting that some industries survive only because of "low wages and long hours."

In the third session of Congress, the president reiterated his support for the proposed legislation. Due to the number and complexity of the amendments, Chairwoman Norton appointed a seven-member subcommittee to revise the bill for full House consideration. Congressman Robert Ramspeck was designated chairperson of the ad hoc subcommittee. The Ramspeck subcommittee reported a revised bill that had the following provisions: (1) a five-member Board would be selected on a geographical basis; (2) the board would fix wages and hours to gradually reach the forty/forty position; and (3) minimum wage increases could not exceed $.05 per hour in any twelve-month period.

The House Labor Committee rejected the Ramspeck proposals and adopted a significantly different set of provisions. These provisions shaped the structure and content of the program for the next five decades. The major provisions were: (1) The Fair Labor Standards Board was replaced by a provision giving administrative control to the secretary of labor; (2) the minimum wage would be $.25 per hour in the first year with $.05 per hour increases each subsequent year to a limit of $.40 per hour; (3) maximum hours per week would be forty-four in the first year, forty-two in the second year, and forty in the third year; (4) overtime rates would be at 150 percent of the regular hourly rate; (5) the secretary of labor would determine industry coverage; (6) agricultural, fisheries, retail trade, and transportation were exempt; and, (7) industry committees would be established for each industry subject to the law.

A bill containing these provisions was reported by the House Labor Committee on April 21, 1938. The Rules Committee again refused to permit the bill to advance to the full House for debate. Frustration with the Rules Committee was beginning to show. Ms. Norton wrote a personal letter to President Roosevelt on April 29, 1938, seeking guidance or advice regarding the failure of the Rules Committee to permit full House consideration of the bill. The president wrote back the next day expressing concern and understanding, but did not suggest how to overcome the problem. He expressed confidence in the legislative process and the belief that the problems could be overcome.

A petition to circumvent the Rules Committee action was initiated in the House. This action resulted in a motion discharging the Rules Committee from further consideration of the bill being passed on May 23, 1938, by a vote of 322 to 73. The bill passed the House on May 24, 1938, by a vote of 314 to 97. Disagreeing with some of the House amendments, the Senate asked for a conference. After two weeks of debate, the conference agreed on the conference report, and it was returned to the House and Senate for consideration. The Senate passed the conference report without a recorded vote on June 13, 1938. The next day, the House passed the identical measure by a vote of 291 to 89.

In summary, the bill submitted to the president for signature included the following provisions: (1) it created a Wage and Hour Division in the Department of Labor; (2) it provided an administrator who would be appointed by the president, by and with the advice and consent of the Senate; (3) it provided an annual report to the Congress; (4) it required that the administrator appoint industry committees; (5) it mandated a $.25 minimum wage on October 25, 1938; a minimum wage not less than $.30 per hour by October 24, 1939; and $.40 per hour by October 24, 1945, and thereafter; (6) it mandated maximum work hours at forty-four per week on October 24, 1938; forty-two hours per week on October 24, 1939; and forty hours per week on October 24, 1940; (7) it established the overtime rate for hours in excess of the mandated number at one and one-half times the regular rate of pay; (8) it prohibited "oppressive child labor"; (9) it exempted a variety of employees including executive, administrative, professional, local retailing, and outside salesmen, seamen, most commercial fishing employees, employees in agriculture, among others; (10) it provided exemptions for learners, apprentices, and handicapped workers; and, (11) it established enforcement machinery including injunctions to restrain violations, fines, imprisonment, and double damages for unpaid wages.

The final bill was clearly a compromise involving several powerful forces within the Congress, the administration, the AFL and CIO, and the business community. Several provisions deserve note because of the strength of the debate related to them and at least one because of its absence in the bill. There were strong sentiment and support for regional differentials, and the president was known to support this provision. The final bill contained no regional differentials. Rather, it had a single national minimum wage and a mechanism, that is, industry committees, to address differences between industries, but not regional differences. The industry committees introduced a mechanism to establish an entire spectrum of minimum wage rates for different industries or industry segments and for the "offshore" areas. There are still remnants of the industry committee program existing in 1996, but for the most part, it served its purpose several decades ago.

Second, administration of the new law was given to the secretary of labor, and a wage and hour administrator was adopted rather than a wage and hour "board." Here, too, the industry committee mechanism provided some flexibility in the initial administrative process that proved useful in a smooth transition in a very large and complex economic setting. The industry committee mechanism permitted the department to escalate minimum wage rates throughout the economy at a more rapid pace than what would have occurred if the minimum wage was raised as provided for in the statute. In other words, while the FLSA provided for an increase in the minimum wage to $.40 per hour in 1945, in reality, recommendations made by industry committees and accepted by the wage and hour administrator resulted in virtually all segments of the economy covered with $.40 per hour wage levels well before 1945.

After enactment, the Department of Labor had 120 days to establish an administrative mechanism to implement the new law. The first wage and hour administrator was Elmer Andrews. Congress provided him a budget of about $400,000 for the first year's activities.

Even after the long and arduous legislative battle and ultimate political compromise, support for Secretary Perkins and the Department of Labor as the administrative organization by the AFL was absent. In fact, "[w]hen the Fair Labor Standards Act went into effect on October 24, 1938, President Green called on the Officers of the American Federation of Labor unions and especially on central labor unions and state federations of labor, emphasizing that the major responsibility for enforcement of the law rests upon organized labor" rather than the secretary of labor.[75]

LEGAL CHALLENGES TO THE FAIR LABOR STANDARDS ACT

As one would expect, the new law was in its early implementation stages when the legal challenges began. The U.S. Supreme Court in *Parrish* had established the constitutionality of state programs in 1937, but the FLSA was a federal statute that set national minimum wage, maximum hours, and child labor standards. The legal challenges took a somewhat different approach from what had been used in relation to the state programs.

Since this was a national law, little time was wasted in lower court proceedings. Everyone knew that the U.S. Supreme Court would have to consider this set of issues, and the process moved to this level quickly. Two U.S. Supreme Court cases formed the basis for the judicial challenges. The first case was *United States v. Darby*, 312 U.S.100 (hereafter *Darby*). The second case was *Opp Cotton Mills, Inc., et al. v. Administrator of the Wage and Hour Division of the United States Department of Labor,* 312 U.S. 126 (hereafter *Opp Cotton*).

Darby

The U.S. Supreme Court received this case on appeal from the District

Court of the United States from the Southern District of Georgia. The case was argued on December 19 and 20, 1940, and the decision was rendered on February 3, 1941. In a long opinion delivered by Justice Stone, two major questions stood before the Court for resolution. The first question was "whether Congress has constitutional power to prohibit the shipment in interstate commerce of lumber manufactured by employees whose wages are less than a prescribed minimum or whose weekly hours of labor at that wage are greater than a prescribed maximum."[76] The second question was "whether it has power to prohibit the employment of workmen in the production of goods 'for interstate commerce' at other than prescribed wages and hours."[77]

The district court had ruled that the FLSA was unconstitutional on the grounds that "manufacture" was not "interstate commerce," and consequently, the power of Congress to regulate interstate commerce did not apply to these activities.

There was a suggestion that the motives underlying the application of the FLSA were at variance with the stated purposes. Specifically, "under the guise of a regulation of interstate commerce, it undertakes to regulate wages and hours within the state contrary to the policy of the state which has elected to leave them unregulated."[78]

The Court refused to accept that interpretation of the act and argued, "Whatever their motive and purpose, regulations of commerce which do not infringe some constitutional prohibition are within the plenary power conferred on Congress by the Commerce Clause."[79] Consequently, the Court concluded that "the prohibition of the shipment in interstate commerce of goods produced under the forbidden substandard labor conditions is within the constitutional authority of Congress."[80]

To further clarify where the phrase "produced for interstate commerce" applies, the Court suggested, "The obvious purpose of the Act was not only to prevent the interstate transportation of the proscribed product, but to stop the initial step toward transportation, production with the purpose of so transporting it."[81]

The final aspect of the power of Congress to regulate interstate commerce relates to activities in intrastate commerce that impinge upon or are commingled with interstate activities. "The power of Congress over interstate commerce," said the Court, "is not confined to the regulation of commerce among the states. It extends to those activities intrastate which so affect interstate commerce or the exercise of the power of Congress over it as to make regulation of them appropriate means to the attainment of a legitimate end, the exercise of the granted power of Congress to regulate interstate commerce."[82] In addition:

The effect of the [District] Court's decision and judgment is thus to deny the power of Congress to prohibit shipment in interstate commerce of lumber produced for interstate commerce under the proscribed substandard labor conditions of wages and hours, its power to penalize the employer for his failure to conform to the wage and hour provisions in the case of employees engaged in the production of lumber which he intends thereafter to ship in interstate commerce in part or in whole according to the normal course of his business.[83]

Therefore, the Court reasoned, "[t]he power of Congress over interstate commerce 'is complete in itself, may be exercised to its utmost extent, and acknowledges no limitations other than are prescribed by the Constitution.'"[84] Finally, the Congress has the right to consider the impacts or consequences in *both* the sending and receiving states of the shipment of goods that may be injurious to public health, morals, or welfare even though neither state sought to regulate the use of these goods.[85] The Court argued that there were numerous examples of congressional regulation of intrastate activities that substantially affected interstate commerce. Specifically, the Court noted the National Labor Relations Act, the Sherman Act, the Clayton Act, and the Federal Trade Commission, among others. These acts, the Court argued, "are familiar examples of the exertion of the commerce power to prohibit or control activities wholly intrastate because of their effect on interstate commerce."[86]

The Court summarily dismissed several issues including the question of whether legislative minimum wage fixing is a denial of due process under the Fifth and Fourteenth Amendments. Based on *Parrish*, legislative wage fixing is not a denial of due process, nor is the legislative fixing of hours of work. Further, application of the statute equally to men and women is appropriate. Firms can also be required to maintain adequate records to permit a determination of their compliance with the law.

Overall, the Court was unable to find any basis for invalidating the law on constitutional grounds and therefore reversed the decision of the District Court of the United States for the Southern District of Georgia.

Opp Cotton

The companion legal challenge to *Darby* was that of *Opp Cotton*, which was argued on December 20, 1940, and decided on February 3, 1941. The issues in this case arose from four specific problems purported to emanate from the issuance of wage orders in the textile industry. The petitioner, Opp Cotton Mill, Inc., argued that the wage orders should be set aside because

(1) the Industry Committee was not constituted in accordance with the requirements of the Act; (2) the definition of the textile industry was not seasonably [sic] made in compliance with the Act; (3) the Committee did not proceed in accordance with the requirements of the Constitution and of the Act; and (4) the procedure followed by the Committee and the Administrator did not afford a full and fair hearing as required by due process of law.[87]

Justice Stone wrote the opinion for the U.S. Supreme Court. He summarily dispensed with several "constitutional" questions by asserting, "The objections that the sections of the Act imposing a minimum wage and maximum hours are not within the commerce power and infringe the Tenth and Fifth Amendments were discussed and disposed of in our opinion in *United States v. Darby, supra*. Since petitioners concede that they are engaged in the manufacture of cotton goods for interstate commerce it is unnecessary to consider these contentions further here."[88] What remained was the question of delegation of legislative power of the Congress to the administrator and the procedural issues related to the administrator's utilization of industry committees in the wage-setting process.

The Court argued that the constitutional mandate that all the legislative powers granted "shall be vested" in Congress did not preclude the use of administrative entities to assist the Congress in carrying out its "statutory command." Since the administrative entity conformed to congressionally determined standards and procedures, there was "no failure of performance of the legislative function." As the Court noted, "The essentials of the legislative function are the determination of the legislative policy and its formulation as a rule of conduct."[89] The Court was satisfied that the delegation of legislative power to an administrator under the FLSA satisfied its legislative function.

The procedural requirements embodied in the industry committee mechanism were also challenged. There were three basic issues in question: (1) "that the changes in definition of the textile industry made after the appointment of the Committee rendered the order of apportionment void"; (2) "that the order defining the industry is also invalid because the Administrator placed the woolen industry in a different industry under a different committee"; and, (3) "that the Committee was not properly constituted under the statute because the Administrator in selecting it did not give 'due regard' to the geographical regions in which the industry is carried on."[90]

On evidence provided at the hearing, the Court rejected all three procedural issues and affirmed the decision of the Circuit Court of Appeals for the Fifth Circuit. These two U.S. Supreme Court decisions laid to rest the constitutionality of the FLSA. It was clear that vigorous enforcement would be possible and that the administrator would find support in the court system. Therefore, after a somewhat slow start in the first fourteen months of the program, confidence surged in the program, and its activities began to accelerate.

NOTES

1. John A. Ryan, *The Supreme Court and the Minimum Wage* (New York: Paulist Press, 1923), p. 46.

2. Elroy. D. Golding, "The Industry Committee Provisions of the Fair Labor Standards Act," *Yale Law Journal*, Vol. 50, No. 7, May 1941, p. 1149.

3. Walter E. Boles, Jr., "Some Aspects of the Fair Labor Standards Act," *Southern*

Economic Journal, Vol. VI, No. 4, April 1940, p. 498.

4. Ibid., p. 499.

5. Ibid.

6. Irving Bernstein, *The Lean Years: A History of the American Worker, 1920–1933* (Boston: Houghton Mifflin Co., 1960), p. 144.

7. Robert E. Sherwood, *Roosevelt and Hopkins* (New York: Universal Library, Grosset and Dunlap, 1950), p. 53.

8. U.S. Congress, Senate Committee on Education and Labor and House Committee on Labor, *Fair Labor Standards Act of 1937*, Part 1, Joint Hearings on S. 2475 and H.R.7200, 75th Cong., 1st sess., June 2–5, 1937, p. 160.

9. Ibid., pp. 159–160.

10. Ibid., p. 128.

11. Samuel Gompers, *Labor and the Employer*, compiled and edited by Hayes Robbins (New York: E.P. Dutton and Company, 1920), p. 76.

12. Bernstein, 1960, p. 93.

13. Gompers, 1920, pp. 77–78.

14. Robert W. Bruere, "Meaning of the Minimum Wage," reprinted from *Harper's Magazine*, January 1916, p. 281.

15. Rudolf Broda, "Minimum Wage Legislation in the United States," *International Labour Review*, Vol. XVII, No. 1, January 1920, p. 27.

16. Edward T. Devine, "The Harm of Low Wages," reprinted from *The Survey*, October 2, 1915, p. 7.

17. Gompers, 1920, p. 76.

18. Ibid., p. 77.

19. American Federation of Labor, *Report of Proceedings*, Fifty-third Annual Convention, Washington, D.C., October 2–13, 1933), pp. 374–375.

20. U.S. Congress, June 2–5, 1937, p. 219.

21. U.S. Congress, Senate Committee on Education and Labor and House Committee on Labor, *Fair Labor Standards Act of 1937*, Part 2, Joint Hearings on S. 2475 and H.R. 7200, 75th Cong., 1st sess., June 7–15, 1937, p. 271.

22. Ibid., p. 272.

23. "Report Roosevelt Changing Strategy," *New York Times*, April 3, 1938, p. 2.

24. "Wage Bill Changes Sought by Labor," *New York Times*, June 16, 1938, p. 4.

25. American Federation of Labor, *Report of Proceedings*, Fifty-eighth Annual Convention, Houston, Texas, October 3–12, 1938, p. 153.

26. Irving Bernstein, "The Historical Significance of the CIO," *Labor Law Journal*, Vol. 36, No. 8, August 1985, p. 656.

27. *New York Times*, June 16, 1938, p. 4.

28. "Roosevelt's Message Opening the Second Regular Session of the 75th Congress: Declares People Favor Industrial Legislation," *New York Times*, January 4, 1938, p. 16.

29. "Roosevelt Program Is Facing Stiff Opposition," *New York Times*, January 9, 1938, p. 3–E.

30. *Congressional Record*, Vol. 83, Pt. 10, p. 2130.

31. Ibid., p. 2133.

32. Ibid., p. 2132.

33. Ibid.

34. George Gallup, "Pay Differential Favored in Survey," *New York Times*, June 1, 1938, p. 40.

35. George Gallup, "Trend Today Seen to Conservatism," *New York Times*, August 28, 1938, p. 11.

36. Felix Belair, Jr., "Roosevelt Favors Only Public Works that Pay Own Way," *New York Times*, February 2, 1938, p. 1.

37. Felix Belair, Jr., "Roosevelt Deal with South Wins Support of Wage Bill; Rail Rate Basis Is Involved," *New York Times*, January 8, 1938, p. 2.

38. "Uniform Pay Base Urged," *New York Times*, October 7, 1937, p. 8.

39. U.S. Congress, June 7–15, 1937, p. 808.

40. Ibid., p. 597.

41. Ibid., p. 598.

42. Ibid.

43. Ibid., p. 572.

44. American Federation of Labor, 1938, p. 153.

45. Ernest K. Lindley, *The Roosevelt Revolution: Phase One* (New York: Viking Press, 1933), p. 101.

46. *New York Times*, June 16, 1938, p. 4.

47. "Green Pledges Aid for the Wage Bill," *New York Times*, March 17, 1938, p. 4.

48. *Congressional Record*, Vol. 82, Pt. 3, p. 152.

49. Ibid., p. 405.

50. U.S. Congress, June 2–5, 1937, p. 178.

51. Henry R. Seager, "The Theory of the Minimum Wage," *American Labor Legislation Review*, Vol. III, 1913, p. 88.

52. Ibid.

53. Emilie J. Hutchinson, *Women's Wages* (New York: Columbia University, Longmans, Green and Company, Agents, 1919), p. 90.

54. Edwin V. O'Hara, *A Living Wage by Legislation: The Oregon Experience* (Salem: State Printing Department, 1916), p. xviii.

55. U.S. Department of Labor, Women's Bureau, "Preceedings of the Washington Conference of New Minimum Wage States" (Washington, D.C. July 19, 1933, mimeographed), p. 2.

56. U. S. Department of Labor, Women's Bureau, "Report of the Fifth Minimum Wage Conference" (Washington, D.C., November 25, 1935, mimeographed), p. 1.

57. U.S. Department of Labor, Women's Bureau, "Report of the Minimum Wage Conference Called by Secretary of Labor Frances Perkins," (Washington, D.C., June 16, 1936, mimeographed), p. 1.

58. Ibid., p. 3.

59. Ibid., p. 4.

60. U.S. Department of Labor, Women's Bureau, "Proceedings of the Seventh Minimum Wage Conference" (Washington, D.C., October 21–22, 1937, mimeographed), p. 1.

61. Ibid., pp. 2–4.

62. U.S. Department of Labor, Bureau of Labor Statistics, "Record of the Discussion Before the Congress of the United States on the Fair Labor Standards Act of 1938," Washington, D.C., October 1, 1938, mimeographed), p. 1.

63. Ibid., p. 2.

64. Ibid.

65. Ibid.

66. Ibid., p. 3.

67. Ibid.

68. Ibid.

69. Ibid.

70. American Federation of Labor, 1938, p. 153.

71. "Urge Budget Basis for Women's Wage," *New York Times*, October 22, 1937, p. 10.

72. Ibid.

73. *Congressional Record*, 82, pt. 3; 588.

74. Franklin D. Roosevelt, *The Court Disapproves, Public Papers and Addresses*, 1938 vol. (New York: The MacMillan Company, 1941), p. 5.

75. American Federation of Labor, *Report of Proceedings*, Fifty-ninth Annual Convention, Cincinnati, Ohio, October 2–13, 1939, p. 179.

76. *United States v. Darby* 312 U.S. 100 (1940), p. 108.

77. Ibid.

78. Ibid., p. 114.

79. Ibid., p. 115.

80. Ibid.

81. Ibid., p. 117.

82. Ibid., p. 118.

83. Ibid., p. 112.

84. Ibid., p. 114.

85. Ibid.

86. Ibid., p. 122.

87. *Opp Cotton Mills, Inc., et al. v. Administrator of the Wage and Hour Division of the United States Department of Labor*, 312 U.S. 126 (1940), pp. 129–130.

88. Ibid., p. 142.

89. Ibid., p. 145.

90. Ibid., pp. 146–147.

Chapter 4

The First Decade: The Fair Labor Standards Act Comes of Age

The first eleven years are a convenient period within which to describe and assess the initiation of this program but not a particularly "representative" one. During this period the nation participated in a world war, witnessed the demise of laissez-faire capitalism, emerged as the safe harbor for millions of immigrants, experienced one of the fastest real growth periods in the nation's history, and underwent many other economic and social changes that violated a "test tube" environment. However, the FLSA was set in place with little apparent economic disruption. Part of the reason for a smooth implementation may have been that the nation's interests were focused elsewhere. More probably, however, the program addressed the critical needs of the times.

ECONOMIC CONDITIONS DURING THE FIRST DECADE

The state of the economy and the labor market have been important factors in every change in the FLSA, as they were in the initiation of the program. However, while these forces are important in the economic framework within which the FLSA evolved, the singularly most important event that shaped the economic, social, and political climate of the program's first decade was World War II. Hitler's invasion of Poland in 1938 and the buildup of domestic military production between 1938 and 1941 provided economic stimulus leading to rising prices and low unemployment. The attack on Pearl Harbor escalated that process tenfold.

To provide perspective about the state of the economy during the early years of the program and how these conditions affected the program's implementation and performance, a variety of summary economic indicators can be used. Gross national product (GNP) increased from $192.9 billion in 1938 to $324.1 billion in 1949, measured in 1958 prices. Disposable personal income increased from $143.6 billion to over $230.8 billion over the same interval. Real per capita disposable personal income increased from $1,105 in 1938 to $1,547 in 1949. These aggregate income measures identified a robust, expanding economy in which real income experienced rapid growth.

Total wage and salary workers increased from 29.2 million in 1938 to about 43.8 million in 1949—a 50 percent increase in little more than a decade. Industrial change patterns suggested the beginning of major shifts in the composition of the productive sector. Wage and salary workers in manufacturing numbered 9.4 million in 1938, as compared to 14.4 million in 1949. Several other major industry groups changed as as shown in Table 4.1.

Table 4.1
Wage and Salary Workers in Nonagricultural
Establishments, 1938 and 1949 (in millions)

	1938	1949	% Change
Mining	.891	.931	4.4%
Contract Construction	1.055	2.165	105.2
Transportation and			
Public Utilities	2.863	4.001	39.7
Trade	6.179	9.264	49.9
Services	3.473	5.264	51.6
Government			
Federal	.829	1.908	130.2
State and local	3.054	3.948	29.3

Source: Economic Report of the President, transmitted to the Congress in February 1970 (Washington, D.C.: U.S. Government printing office, 1970), Table B-35, P. 273.

Each industrial change has its own story. It may be useful to note that the number of federal wage and salary workers increased from 996,000 in 1940 to 2,928,000 in 1944—a 194 percent increase—in response to the domestic needs related to the war effort. By 1947, the same category of workers had decreased to about 1,892,000 individuals. Wage and salary workers in the federal sector increased gradually to the 1944 level over the next four decades and remains at that level today.

Gross average hourly earnings in manufacturing were $.627 per hour in 1939, the first full year of FLSA activity. In 1949, they were $1.378 per hour in current dollars. The minimum wage increased from $.25 per hour in 1938 to $.30 per hour in 1939 to $.75 per hour in 1949. Comparing the minimum wage in 1939 and 1949 to gross average hourly earnings in manufacturing in the same years, the minimum wage was 48 and 54 percent, respectively, of this earnings measure.

Price changes during the first decade of the program reflected a substantial decline in the purchasing power of money. Based on 1958 = 100, the "all items" consumer price index (CPI) was 49.1 in 1938 and 83.0 in 1949. In real purchasing power, expressed in 1958 prices, the $.25 minimum wage in 1938 was worth about $.509. The $.75 per hour minimum wage in 1949 was worth about $.904.

The economic changes of the first decade were influenced by a variety of factors, but the war–dominated influences can be no more clearly captured than by the data series showing outstanding short- and intermediate-term consumer credit depicted in Table 4.2. The most dramatic changes affected automobile and other durable consumer credit. To a large degree, of course, Americans were prevented through rationing from acquiring these economic goods during the war years, and consequently, pent-up demand exploded in the latter years of the decade. Examining the outstanding credit for the years 1938 to 1949 provides a stark picture of the war's impact on the domestic economy.

Table 4.2
Short- and Intermediate-Term Consumer
Credit Outstanding, 1938–1949

Installment Credit (millions of dollars)				
			Other Consumer	
Year	*Total*	*Automobile*	*Goods*	*Other*
1938	3,686	1,099	1,442	1,145
1939	4,503	1,497	1,620	1,386
1940	5,514	2,071	1,827	1,616
1941	6,085	2,458	1,929	1,698
1942	3,166	742	1,195	1,229
1943	2,136	355	819	962
1944	2,176	397	791	988
1945	2,462	455	816	1,191
1946	4,172	981	1,290	1,901
1947	6,695	1,924	2,143	2,628
1948	8,996	3,018	2,901	3,077
1949	11,590	4,555	3,706	3,329

Source: Economic Report of the President, transmitted to the Congress in February 1970 (Washington, D.C.: U.S. Government Printing Office, 1970), Table C–56.

PROGRAM IMPLEMENTATION AND ADMINISTRATION

The first report on administration of the FLSA was submitted to the president and the Congress on January 14, 1939. The report covered a four-and-a-half-month period from August 15, 1938, to December 31, 1938.[1] The new Wage and Hour Division Administrator, Elmer Andrews, character- ized the report as an "informal interim report." Since the program was in its earliest developmental stages, the report focused on intent rather than accom- plishments. Andrews suggested that enforcement was of central importance: "Without compliance the purposes of the statute are merely pious wishes; and indeed the law may work real hardship on employers who comply if certain of their competitors do not."[2] The administrator described the structure of the division that was being established, the industry committee program, and a variety of administrative problems that arose while defining the scope or cover- age of the program. He suggested that early enforcement would be complaint driven. There was little need to worry about having enough work to do. Dur- ing the first two months of the program's operation—October 24 to December 31, 1938—the division received 5,294 complaints of violations of the statute. At year's end, the new Wage and Hour Division had 164 permanent and 92 temporary staff on board. The year ended with the basic framework of the new organization and core staff in place.

There was a sense of optimism that the task at hand could be accomplished. The first "official" *Annual Report* to the Congress for calendar year 1939 was transmitted to the Congress on January 3, 1940. One must be impressed by this accomplishment. Only three days into a new year was needed to write, edit, and print the first report. It was an extensive report encompassing 163 pages of text and tables that reflected every major aspect of the program. There was extensive discussion about the act and what it meant. The report examined the major provisions of the law, addressed questions of coverage and exemptions, and provided estimates of economic effects related to the program. In addition, there was extensive discussion of enforcement activity, the industry committee program, litigation activity, administrative problems, and several legislative proposals.

In a period of one year—December 1938 to December 1939—the personnel of the Wage and Hour Division increased from 264 to 1,147 employees. Dur- ing this interval, the "field" staff increased from 213 to 669 employees. Of the 1,147 employees in the division, 700 were in the Cooperation and Inspection Branch, that is, the enforcement branch. From the official initiation of the program in August 1938 to the end of 1939, a complex national enforcement program emerged. However, in spite of a rapidly expanding program, lack of resources created a major problem for the division in the early months of exist- ence. The administrator in 1939 noted, "By April . . . certain sections of indus- try that were anxious to avoid compliance with the act became aware that funds for the Division were extremely limited. Noncompliance began to spread, and it had become obvious that greatly increased appropriations were essential to prevent a complete break-down of enforcement."[3]

Because of the scope and complexity of the new program, the Wage and Hour Division relied heavily on other government agencies for assistance in implementing an effective enforcement strategy. In particular, the Women's Bureau, the Social Security Board, the Bureau of Labor Statistics, the Works Progress Administration, and the Treasury Department were helpful in lending needed personnel to the division, assisting in housing field staff, and training. In spite of the funding problems, the first year was highly successful. Additional resources were acquired for calendar year 1939 through a supplemental appropriation, widespread information dissemination occurred, nine industry committees were established, and inspection activity indicated that the program was going to have an impact on U.S. labor standards.

The second annual report to Congress shifted to a fiscal year (FY) reporting period. The second annual report covered July 1, 1939, to June 30, 1940. It overlapped, as a consequence, part of the period covered by the first report. One senses the acceleration in the pace of activities as investigators gained confidence in their roles and the public gained knowledge about their rights under the law. The pivotal event during fiscal year 1940 was the increase in the minimum wage to $.30 per hour and the establishment of the maximum workweek of forty-two hours. The administrator noted, "So far as the Division has been able to ascertain, the transition was made with little disturbance to industry and with no measurable loss in employment."[4]

The war in Europe was discussed extensively by the administrator. Of particular concern was the question of whether the FLSA would adversely affect the domestic military expansion program. Examination of this question by the administrator resulted in a letter to the president arguing that no adverse impact was detected and that few employer complaints had been received. To demonstrate his full support for a program he had fought hard to create, "the President declared that in preparing for defense the social and labor standards which had been written into law must not be relaxed."[5]

The 1940 *Annual Report* provided an extensive discussion of the relationship between hours of work, labor efficiency, and productivity. The administrator noted, "One of the important purposes of the Fair Labor Standards Act was to reduce the large volume of unemployment by discouraging overtime, thereby providing an incentive for employers to hire additional workers."[6] The *Report* contains an interesting comparison of British, French, German, and American efforts to reduce the length of the workday and workweek.

The enforcement program was pursued vigorously. While primarily a complaint-driven system, as knowledge was gained about where violations were concentrated, the administrator initiated a program of targeted enforcement as well. The first target of this program was the lumber industry. More than 100 inspections were directed "to concentrate on all lumber establishments, from the remote rural sawmill to the city concentration yard, in every State in the Union."[7] The effort was judged a success, and plans to extend it to other industries were initiated.

During the first twenty months of enforcement effort, the Wage and Hour Division received almost 50,000 complaints of alleged violations of the law.

About 36,000 establishments had complaints filed against them. The sources and character of these complaints suggested the nature of the program's impacts. About two-thirds of the complaints were in manufacturing industries. Within this category of establishments, the apparel industry experienced the largest number of complaints—4,683. Food and kindred products experienced 4,245 complaints, while lumber and basic timber products had 3,214. For all industries during this twenty-month period, the largest volume of complaints —5,793—came from the wholesale and retail trade industries. Almost three fourths of the complaints were made by employees, while unions were the source of 4.5 percent of the complaints.

Establishments that were the subject of complaints were charged with only minimum wage complaints in 12.4 percent of the cases, failure to pay overtime in 43.4 percent of the cases, and minimum wage violations in combination with failure to pay overtime in 43.3 percent of the cases. Overtime provisions were prevalent in that they appeared in almost 86 percent of the complaints received. Here, too, the same four industries were the major sources of alleged violations:

Wholesale and retail trade	3,352 overtime
Food and kindred products	2,331 overtime
Apparel	2,211 overtime
Lumber and timber basic products	1,897 overtime

The FLSA provided for the creation of industry committees to consider the unique conditions in an industry or industry segment and recommend wage rate changes to the administrator. By the end of FY1940, fourteen industry committees had been established. Committee deliberations had been completed and wage orders had been issued in nine industry groups covering about 2 million workers. About 500,000 workers were estimated to have received direct wage increases because of the issuance of wage orders.

It was estimated in the FY1941 *Annual Report* that due to the "application of material priorities," between 5,000 and 6,000 factories would be closed down, with over a million workers losing their jobs. In addition to the concern about unemployment, the impacts of inflation on the economy and the minimum wage program became evident. At the inflation rates experienced and those estimated to occur by June 1942, the administrator estimated that minimum wage levels of $.34 and $.46 were needed in 1942 to equate to the original levels of $.30 and $.40 provided in the 1938 statute. Importantly, the $.40 rate was not scheduled to go into effect until October 1945.

As the 1941 *Annual Report* was written, only two amendments to the original act had been enacted. The first amendment exempted telephone operators in small telephone exchanges from both the minimum wage and overtime provisions of the FLSA. The second amendment provided a separate industry committee structure for Puerto Rico and the Virgin Islands.

The industry committee program expanded rapidly during FY1941. Seventeen wage orders—twelve on the mainland and five in Puerto Rico—became effective in FY1941. In combination with the six earlier wage orders, over 700,000 workers received direct wage increases because of the industry committee program.

The attack on Pearl Harbor on December 7, 1941, changed the world, the nation, and the administration of the FLSA. Between 1939 and 1942, war-related production had increased to support U.S. Allies in Europe. However, the attack on Pearl Harbor thrust the nation into war, and domestic military production expanded dramatically. Consequently, military agencies needed more inspectors to ensure the quality and delivery of war materials. Since the Wage and Hour Division had developed an extensive field structure, it was enlisted as a major component of the war-related inspection program. Initially, there was an effort to combine FLSA enforcement with inspections for the war agencies. During FY1942, for example, "in addition to the 74,676 firms inspected for compliance with the provisions of the Act, 46,403 inspections were also made for the war agencies, to check records and inventories and determine whether or not firms were complying with price, conservation, and priority regulations."[8]

Because the war-related activities started late in the fiscal year, FY1942 was a year of high investigation activity. The division investigated and closed 54 percent more cases than in FY 1941—74,676 as compared to 48,449—and agreements to pay back wages were nearly double the level that occurred in FY1941.

This performance was particularly significant because of two "events" in 1942 that complicated program administration. First, in February 1942, the division was moved from Washington, D.C. to New York City. The move resulted in the loss of 55 percent of the division's national office staff. Extensive recruitment and training were needed to alleviate this problem. Second, the Wage and Hour Division was merged with the Public Contracts Division under a single administrator. The name of the organization thus became the Wage and Hour and Public Contracts Division. Since this combined organization still exists today, it has become customary to call it the Wage and Hour Division.

On October 3, 1942, the president issued Executive Order 9250, which froze wages in the economy at the level existing on September 15, 1942. The inspectors of the Wage and Hour Division were assigned the task of explaining, investigating, and enforcing the wage stabilization program. This program spawned hundreds of thousands of inquiries that the War Labor Board was unprepared to handle. The Wage and Hour Division responded to the challenge and "[b]y the end of June, 1943, . . . had acted on over 100,000 requests for rulings and handled about 900,000 informal inquiries relating to wage stabilization."[9]

The number of establishments inspected in FY1943 dropped to 61,356, as compared with 74,676 in FY1942. While division staff were used in the Executive Order 9250 program, equally important was the high turnover rate (due to Selective Services requirements) and the utilization of division staff by higher-priority war agencies.   Since the turnover rate was about 50 percent during FY1943, it was significant that the division could maintain a credible FLSA enforcement effort at all. If these limitations were not enough, the Congress cut the division's appropriations for FY1943 which required a 20 percent reduction in personnel for the regular work of the division.

As the war effort placed increasing pressure on women workers and young workers, child labor violations began to increase, but due to the war-related activities, the division did not have the resources to address this problem.

But the story does not end there. The division continued to address its statutory mandate of FLSA enforcement. The division conducted 54,431 inspections in FY1944, down 6,926 from the prior year. However, the value of restitutions increased in FY1944 to about $18.6 million, as compared with about $17.1 million the prior year. With substantially fewer inspections, but higher restitutions, it became apparent that FLSA enforcement was effectively targeting investigation activity in firms and industries with substantial compliance problems.

One important theme that the division would return to several times was that compliance with the law was a function of increased education. It was generally believed that as employers became aware of the law and its provisions, required enforcement effort would diminish. The administrator noted, however, that after five years of activity, "Such a view is not supported by experience."[10]

Historically, one of the most significant accomplishments of the division was the completion of the "industry committee" program for the U.S. mainland. About 1.6 million workers received direct wage increases because of the work of about 70 industry committees. Another 1.1 million workers received indirect wage increases as the wage order program took effect. The FY1945 report to Congress was entitled *Fair Labor Standards in the Final War Year*. The Wage and Hour Division's focus remained on the functions assigned by the War Labor Board, the War Manpower Commission, the War Production Board, and other military-related agencies. The division inspected less than 45,000 establishments in FY1945, but the level of restitutions remained high at about $15.8 million.

The administrator summarized the enforcement effort achievements of the program's first six and three-quarter years. He noted that about $85 million had been found due to about 2.5 million workers in more than 110,000 establishments. These accomplishments were achieved with reduced resource levels and a vastly expanded agenda of responsibilities.

The original designers of the program could not have seen the impacts of a world war on inflation. The mandated $.40 per hour minimum wage required in 1945 was reasonable in the context of economic conditions in 1938. However, war-induced inflation had been devastating throughout the first six years of the program and was destined to become worse. Consequently, an important issue relating to the minimum wage was the reduced purchasing power of the mandated wage rate. The administrator argued in 1946, "The 40 cents an hour minimum wage the act now provides is pitifully inadequate in the light of today's cost of living, and prompt amendment to bring the minimum wage up to at least 65 cents an hour is urgently necessary."[11] This was the first concrete recommendation by the administrator to change the statute to achieve a particular wage level above the level mandated in the 1938 act.

The division inspected about the same number of establishments in FY1946 as it did in FY1945. Importantly, 6,161 of these inspections were made under the provisions of the Public Contracts Act. Of the 6,161 inspections, the vast majority—6,107—were conducted concurrently with an FLSA inspection.

By middecade, the types of inspections had changed from the early years. Only 14 percent of the inspections—under both acts—were complaint driven, and about 19 percent were reinspections. The remainder were directed investigations in "high violation industries or areas." Apparently, the "targeting" process was effective because 85 percent of the establishments investigated were found to have one or more violations. Most of these violations—68 percent—were classified as "minor" because they involved record keeping, posting of notices, illegal discharge, or discrimination.

The enforcement effort in FY1946 produced $21.6 million in back wages due, of which $13.4 million was uncontested—firms agreed to pay. For the first eight years of the program's operation, the amount of restitution agreed or ordered to pay is shown in Table 4.3. By the end of FY1946, the Wage and Hour Division estimated that during the first eight years of the program 900,000 establishments had been subject to FLSA provisions at some time or other during this interval.

As the peacetime economy began gaining momentum, the configuration of the division's investigation process changed. On March 3, 1947, the Wage and Hour Division moved from New York City to the Labor Department Building in Washington, D.C. The onset of peace permitted the division to focus its attention away from war-related programs. Legislators and program administrators believed that it was now time to begin looking more closely at program activities and initiating legislative and program changes to address the basic mandate. The first problem was the $.40 per hour minimum wage. A strong push was started to raise the minimum wage to $.65 or $.70 per hour or higher. In fact, the administrator's recommendation to the Congress in the FY1946 *Report* was: "Raise the minimum wage to at least 65 cents an hour immediately and 70 and 75 cents an hour at stated intervals of not more than 2 years thereafter."[12] He also recommended the "industry committee" procedure to raise the minimum wage at a faster rate.

A second problem involved unfair competition between establishments that produced for interstate and intrastate markets. The administrator recommended that all "establishments and workers, engaged in activities 'affecting interstate commerce'" be subject to FLSA provisions. In addition, the administrator sought legislative change to strengthen child labor protection, extend the statute of limitations for lawsuits to recover back wages, narrow certain exemptions in agriculture, and grant the administrator authority to issue authoritative

Table 4.3
Restitution Agreed or Ordered to Pay, FY1939–1946

Fiscal Year	Restitution Ordered or Agreed to Pay	Average per Restitution Case	Average per Underpaid Employee
1939	$ 51,828	$322	$15
1940	1,714,494	746	24
1941	11,540,889	573	30
1942	20,920,956	724	36
1943	16,824,021	854	43
1944	18,620,369	903	35
1945	15,824,377	830	36
1946	13,360,826	782	49

Source: U.S. Department of Labor, Wage and Hour and Public Contracts Divisions, *Annual Report,* Fiscal Year 1946 (Washington, D.C.: Government Printing Office, 1947), p. 21.

Table 4.4
Investigation Activity, FY1941–1947

Fiscal Year	Number of Establishments of Inspected	Number of Establishments in Violation Minimum Wage Provisions	Percentage of Inspected Covered Establishments
1941	43,630	13,229	30%
1942	67,630	21,524	32
1943	56,826	9,580	17
1944	51,178	7,095	14
1945	42,613	6,264	15
1946	42,062	4,676	11
1947	38,622	3,633	9

Source: U.S. Department of Labor, Wage and Hour and Public Contracts Divisions, *Annual Report,* Fiscal Year 1947, transmitted to the Congress on January 2, 1948 (Washington, D.C.: Government Printing Office, 1948), p. 37.

definitions and regulations. These issues, identified early in the program's evolutionary process, became an important part of the agenda for the next several decades.

The division continued an investigation program in FY 1947 that produced smaller numbers of establishments in violation of the FLSA both relatively and absolutely. The pattern of change for the years 1941 to 1947 is shown in Table 4.4. The division attributed this change pattern to the learning process of employers that resulted in greater compliance with the law and to the upward movement of the wage structure so that fewer workers were at the minimum wage.

While minimum wage violations diminished significantly over the FY 1941 to FY 1947 period, violations of overtime provisions remained relatively stable. This pattern of stability is shown in Table 4.5.

Table 4.5
Inspections and Overtime Violations, FY1941–1947

Fiscal Year	Number of Covered Inspected Estimate	Estimated in Violation of Overtime Provisions	Percentage of Inspected Covered Estimate
1941	43,630	20,434	47%
1942	67,630	36,115	53
1943	56,826	24,157	43
1944	51,178	23,535	46
1945	42,613	21,095	50
1946	42,062	20,184	48
1947	38,622	19,086	49

Source: U. S. Department of Labor, *Annual Report*, Fiscal Year 1947, transmitted to the Congress on January 2, 1948 (Washington, D.C.: Government Printing Office, 1948), p. 9.

FY 1948 was the tenth anniversary of the FLSA. The administrator noted that the act had three relatively minor amendments over the ten-year interval. However, this low level of activity did not mean that the FLSA was addressing all the nation's fair labor standards problems or that other modifications were not appropriate. War-related events had consumed the energies of legislators and administrators.

On the tenth anniversary of the FLSA, about 22.6 million workers were subject to the minimum wage provisions of the law, and about 20 million were protected by overtime standards. About 638,000 establishments were covered by the law's provisions. The Wage and Hour Division was conducting its business through nine regional offices and 39 area offices and field stations. The division employed 1,132 employees—the bulk of whom were in field operations.

A significant aspect of the division's operations not discussed extensively earlier was the development of hazardous occupations (HOs) orders for workers under the age of eighteen. By the end of FY 1948, seven HOs had been established. These covered workers in the following industrial classifications: plants manufacturing explosives or articles containing explosives; motor-vehicle driver and helper; coalmine operations; logging occupations—including sawmill, lath mill, shingle mill, and cooperage-stock mill; power-driven woodworking machines; exposure to radioactive substances; and, elevators and other power-driven hoisting apparatus.[13]   In subsequent years, ten more HOs were developed as part of the child labor protection program.

The downward trend in the absolute and relative numbers of establishments inspected under the FLSA continued in FY 1948. The total number of inspections declined to 30,053 total investigations, of which 28,998 were inspected under FLSA provisions. Only 6 percent of the inspected, covered establishments had minimum wage violations, while 52 percent had overtime violations. The administrator argued, "this trend is not at all surprising. The average hourly earnings in covered employment are more than triple the 40-cent minimum hourly rate set by the Fair Labor Standards Act."[14]

The administrator judged the FLSA program a success on its tenth anniversary, though problems remained. He argued that "the Fair Labor Standards Act has proved basically efficient both in peace and war."[15]   In spite of its success, the pressure for changing the FLSA continued in FY1948. The first recommendation to the Congress was to increase the minimum wage to $.75 per hour, with additional increases determined by industry committees. In addition, the administrator recommended a variety of legislative changes to improve administration of the program.[16]

In response to these recommendations, one substantive amendment to the FLSA occurred in FY 1949. Enacted on July 20, 1949, Public Law 177 amended Section 7 of the FLSA to "clarify overtime compensation provisions of the Fair Labor Standards Act." The essence of the amendment was to remedy the "overtime on overtime" problem that had plagued the program for most of its existence. In the final year of the "first decade," investigations increased to 32,012, as compared with 30,027 in FY1948. Nevertheless, the proportion of establishments found in violation of minimum wage provisions continued to decline to 5 percent. Consistent with earlier years, about 53 percent of the establishments investigated had overtime violations.

The summary data for the first decade—about eleven years—produced several important observations. Between FY 1939 and FY1949, the division conducted 438,534 investigations. Almost half (49 percent) of the establishments were in violation of minimum wage and/or overtime provisions of the FLSA. About 77 percent (163,257) of the establishments in violation agreed to pay restitution of about $116.3 million.[17] While the aggregate numbers are impressive, there were several troublesome "trends" in the data that warrant discussion. First, the percentage of investigated establishments with minimum wage violations had declined monotonically from about 30 percent in 1941 to about 5 percent in 1949. Reasons for this decline were summarized earlier. Second, there was a sustained decrease in the absolute and relative number of firms with violations that agreed to pay restitution. About 96 percent agreed to pay restitution in 1940, while only 62 percent agreed in 1949. This change could have been due to a "learning effect" in which firms became more aware of the law and challenged more findings. It is also possible that the "hard core" cases were the first to be investigated, and therefore the less obvious cases of violation remained. Third, there appeared to be a persistent downward trend in the number of employees underpaid and the amount of back wages found due. These factors are partially explained by the smaller number of inspections.

THE 1949 AMENDMENTS TO THE FLSA

President Truman outlined an invigorated social agenda in his State of the Union Message in January 1949. Central to this agenda was minimum wage legislation that would bring the lowest-paid American workers into line with the wage and price structure that had evolved during and immediately after World War II. By mandate, all covered workers were required to be paid at least the $.40 per hour minimum wage by October 24, 1945, but in reality, most American industry had reached that level years earlier. The industry committee program had effectively responded to the urgent need for wage increases to offset inflationary increases. However, after the mandated increase in 1945 had taken effect, there was no requirement that employers increase wages further.

The inflationary spiral after World War II, the success of unions to obtain higher wage levels, and the general upward movement of the wage structure left the lowest-paid segment of the labor force further and further behind. Sixteen dollars per week could no longer buy the food, clothing, shelter, and other necessities that Americans believed were necessary to share in the American dream. Pressure began mounting to address the economic needs of America's lowest-paid workers.

Early in the debate, Congressman Lesinski identified six factors that provided the specific impetus for amending the FLSA. In a *Report* to accompany H.R. 3190, Fair Labor Standards Amendments of 1949, the Congressman observed that first, "as a result of the economic development of the country during the past 10 years, the 40-cents rate, inadequate when enacted, has long been outmoded as a measure of the amount required to yield a minimum standard of living for American workers." Second, there was confusion by employers and employees concerning coverage limits. Therefore, he said, "This limited application of the act has created intraplant inequities and has permitted some employers to gain an unfair competitive advantage." "Third, experience in the administration of the act for the past decade has shown that complex, overlapping, and in some cases, completely unworkable exemptions from the act's application have equally contributed to injustice, uncertainty, and undue competitive advantages."

Fourth, due to the failure of the act to define the term *regular rate*, to be applied in the calculation of overtime pay, the congressman argued, "Clarification must be sought by denoting the types of payment to be excluded in determining the 'regular rate' and by indicating the types of premium payments which are creditable against overtime pay required by the act." "Fifth, the child-labor provisions of the present act have been shown to be patently inadequate to effectuate fully the policy of restricting the employment of children." Sixth, the congressman was concerned about the division of responsibilities for administration and enforcement of the act between the Wage and Hour Division and the secretary of labor. Therefore, he said, "We believe that the Secretary of Labor . . . represents the most appropriate authority through whom may be coordinated the labor policies of the Government, both on a departmental basis and as to the executive branch as a whole."[18]

Importantly, the congressman observed that another problem in the administration of the act was "its failure to provide the administering officers with authority to supervise payment of back wages found owing as a result of violations. A significant tendency for wages to remain unpaid in these instances appears to the committee to impair the fundamental objective of the act to secure for workers the wages which they are required to be paid."[19] While supervision of the payment of back wages was provided to the administering agency, the issue of back wage payments remains with the FLSA on its fiftieth anniversary.

Early in the debate to amend the FLSA, experts and officials were asked by the Congress to give their opinion about what types of changes were needed. Wage and Hour administrator William McComb argued in December 1947, "I am convinced on the basis of past experience and the evidence on existing economic conditions that a 75-cent minimum is not only desirable from a humanitarian point of view but also that it is thoroughly practicable and realistic from the economic and business standpoint."[20] During strategy sessions by Democratic leaders, a second labor initiative kept diverting attention away from increasing the minimum wage. The Taft-Hartley Act, passed over President Truman's veto in 1947, was viewed by organized labor and the sympathetic elements in Congress as a frontal attack on American unionism. Elements in the Taft-Hartley Act softened the pro-union, pro-collective bargaining position of the National Labor Relations Act (Wagner Act). Therefore, emotional and political energy was focused on creating support to repeal the Taft-Hartley Act. Organized labor, while fully supportive of minimum wage increase legislation, had "bigger fish to fry" in obtaining repeal of the Taft-Hartley Act and therefore devoted less attention to the FLSA proposals. They believed that only one major piece of labor legislation was likely to move through the Congress quickly, and therefore the issue focused on which of the two initiatives should be surfaced first.

The Democratic leadership in the House was committed to moving the FLSA amendments first, but the Senate leadership was committed to repeal of the Taft-Hartley Act. Therefore, in mid-January 1949, when the House Democratic leadership tried to "move fast" to "raise the minimum wage from 40 cents to 75 cents an hour, as the first action toward enacting the President's social program, a decisive struggle opened at the same hour in the Senate over the place to be assigned on the calendar there for the Taft-Hartley Labor Act repealer."[21] Senator Claude Pepper was frustrated over the inability of the Senate to come to grips with the repeal issue and therefore planned to force Senate Labor Committee members to show their hands on repeal legislation by requiring a simple yes or no vote on the issue. Senate Labor Committee chairman Elbert Thomas wanted to avoid the trauma of repeal legislation until other elements in the president's social legislation agenda had moved through the Congress. Senator Thomas believed that the president's social agenda, including expanded support for education, the minimum wage increase, and others, would be derailed if the highly controversial repeal legislation was forced through the committee and onto the Senate floor.

The Truman administration proposed legislation early to increase the minimum wage to $.75 an hour, but the real goal was to raise the minimum wage even higher. In late January 1949, Secretary of Labor James Tobin, in his first congressional testimony as labor secretary, told the Congress that the administration wanted an immediate increase in the minimum wage to $.75 an hour but that it was hoped that the Congress would direct the industry committee structure to take the initiative to increase the minimum wage to $1.00 an hour as quickly as possible in industries that could manage this level of increase.[22]

Besides the wage increase, the administration also wanted to expand protection of American workers by removing exemptions for the food-processing industry and large retail stores. While the constitutional authority underlying the FLSA was found in the commerce clause, the administration wanted coverage expanded from those employees whose work was "in" interstate commerce to employees whose work "affected" interstate commerce.[23]

Congressional Democrats believed there was widespread support for an increase in the minimum wage and that the election of President Truman in November 1948 reflected this support. However, as the initiative gained momentum in the Congress, opposition to the increase became more vocal. The National Cotton Council argued, for example, that an increase to $.75 an hour would effectively ruin the domestic cotton industry by raising the price of cotton sufficiently high relative to other competing fibers that producers would switch to synthetics or wool for clothing production.[24] Hotels and the retail industry mounted vigorous attacks on the destructive power of any minimum wage increase. However, President Truman argued that opposition to the minimum wage increase are "making exactly the same speeches now against a 75-cent minimum wage that they made back in the Thirties against a 40-cent minimum wage—not a bit of difference."[25] He implied that the doomsday arguments of the 1930s were not persuasive, and similar arguments in the late 1940s were not persuasive either.

When it became apparent that the legislative process was going to produce a bill increasing the minimum wage, Republican opposition took a different approach. They argued that the minimum wage should only be increased to $.65 an hour and that a "flexible" minimum wage be enacted that would be tied to changes in the consumer price index. It is significant that the earliest initiative to "indexing" arose from the conservatives in the Congress because in future years they would oppose indexing of the minimum wage. Proponents of the indexing alternative, particularly Congressman Wingate Lucas of Texas, attempted to soften resistance by proposing that the change have three components: an increase to $.65 an hour in 1949, a tie in subsequent years to changes in the CPI, and an absolute floor of $.50 an hour despite movements in the CPI.

However, Republican opposition to the administration bill was not confined to an increase in the minimum wage. In fact, more insightful congressional leaders such as Representative Samuel McConnell, ranking member of the Labor Committee, argued "It should be clearly understood that the issues involved in this bill are the coverage provisions and not the minimum wage rate."[26] By its own admission, the proposed coverage changes in the Administration bill would bring a minimum of 5 million more workers under the act. The concerns of McConnell were the correct ones.

Embedded in the administration bill was another issue that brought strong resistance late in the debate. The bill provided that enforcement of the FLSA would contain provisions permitting the wage and hour administrator to sue employers on behalf of employees for back wages rather than employees being required to initiate and pursue lawsuits independently. The proposed bill would require the employee to petition the administrator to sue the employer, and the administrator would be empowered to seek only the amount of back wages that were legally due. Opponents of the bill viewed this intervention process as the first step to more aggressive enforcement in which the weight of the federal government was placed on the side of the employee.

The heat and humidity of Washington summers can soften even the most ardent resistance. House Republicans and southern Democrats supporting the Lucas bill grew weary of arguing what appeared to be a losing position. Therefore, in mid-August, a break in Republican ranks by Representative Velde of Illinois produced a trial balloon in which the Lucas bill would be changed to include a $.75 an hour increase in conjunction with indexing and other provisions. This tactical maneuver resulted in the opposition coalition taking charge of the legislative process in the House. The revised Lucas bill was brought to the House floor for a vote and passed by a significant margin—186 to 116. The administration bill was never brought to the floor for a vote, and therefore the provisions of the Lucas bill became the final House bill. There were efforts to amend the bill to eliminate or soften some of the provisions, but for the most part, these efforts failed. Most important was the administration bill provision expanding coverage to workers working in production "affecting" interstate commerce. The Lucas bill limited coverage to occupations "indispensable" or "closely related" to production.[27] The results of that provision were that coverage remained narrowly structured.

Secretary Tobin expressed approval of the $.75 minimum wage provision in the House bill but was disappointed in the coverage provisions. He observed that the "Senate had a good bill pending and if passed in its present form 'improvements' in the House bill can be made in conference."[28] The Wage and Hour Division estimated that the House bill removed coverage from about 1,160,000 workers and provided new coverage to about 155,000 workers, which left a net reduction of coverage of about 1,005,000 workers.[29] Democrats attempted to recommit the bill because of concerns about the coverage provisions. But there were not enough votes for recommittal, and the motion was rejected.

Organized labor immediately attacked the coverage provisions of the bill. John Edelman, speaking for the CIO, argued that while the increase in the minimum wage from $.40 an hour to $.75 an hour was a "historic step," "it was . . . incredible that Representatives who gave a higher statutory rate with one hand should with the other hand have snatched away the opportunity from many workers to enjoy that benefit. The CIO is convinced that the Senate bill will correct the injustices in the House Bill."[30]

The focus of legislative effort shifted to the Senate. Under the spectre of delaying the scheduled Senate recess, Senator Claude Pepper proposed a "stripped down" bill that in his view was devoid of controversy. The "new" Senate bill retreated on coverage provisions to those existing in the original legislation. The bill exempted small numbers of workers in narrow occupations such as newsboys, switch board operators in small exchanges, certain home workers, and young boys working in specified parts of the farm irrigation system. The Senate bill was estimated to remove from coverage a maximum of 200,000 workers.

Opponents of the legislation in the Senate, led by Senators Allen J. Ellender, William Fulbright, and McClellan, made a last-ditch effort to phase in the increase to $.75 an hour, but these efforts were defeated. Opposition senators proposed a variety of other amendments to "soften the blow" of the prospective changes, but for the most part, they, too, were rejected. The Senate bill was passed on August 31, 1949, and a conference of the House and Senate was scheduled for early October.

By mid-October, agreement was reached in Conference, and a bill was produced for final House and Senate passage. The Conference bill contained a $.75 an hour minimum wage, a reduction in coverage close to the Senate-passed bill, and a provision that the wage and hour administrator could sue an employer for back wages due to an employee if requested, in writing, by the employee; child labor provisions were made more stringent; small logging and sawmill operations and small newspaper organizations were exempted from coverage; annual wage plans were encouraged by delimiting overtime pay provisions; and the new law would take effect 120 days after enactment.

The Conference compromise bill was passed by the House and Senate, and President Truman signed it into law on October 26, 1949. It was estimated that 1.5 million wage earners received wage increases of $.05 to $.15 per hour when the amendments became effective on January 26, 1950. While heralded as a major step forward in the protection of the most vulnerable segments of the labor force, immediately after presidential signature, the drive for a $1.00 minimum wage began.

Thus, it took eleven years for the first substantive amendments to the FLSA. President Truman, in his signing statement, observed, "The act has proved to be wise and progressive remedial legislation for the welfare not only of our wage earners but of our whole economy."[31]   This assessment set the stage for a vigorous enforcement effort that carried the program into its second decade. The most noteworthy change brought forth in the 1949 amendments was the increase in the minimum wage from $.40 per hour to $.75 per hour. This 87.5 percent increase represented one of the largest relative increases in the history of the program. There was no phase-in of the increase, as has been the pattern in more recent decades.

The amendments prohibited the employment of child labor in hazardous occupations despite industry or family relationship of the worker. Firms were provided limited protection against prosecution if a "good-faith" effort was demonstrated to prevent the procurement (purchase) of goods (called "hot goods") that were produced with oppressive child labor. The coverage of the act was extended to include not only interstate commerce and outgoing foreign commerce but also incoming foreign commerce. Coverage was narrowed so that "activities" other than "actual production" were covered only if they were "directly related" and "directly essential" to production.

The amendments gave the administrator authority to bring suit to recover back wages if requested in writing by the employee. The two-year statute of limitations and a finding of good-faith effort were retained. The original act did not define "regular rate" of pay for use in the determination of overtime pay. This limitation was one of the most troublesome in efficient administration of the program and was one of the primary avenues for complaints. As noted earlier, the 1946 Amendments attempted to clarify the definition of *regular rate,* and some success was achieved. The 1949 amendments went further in delineating what categories of activities and compensation should underlie the determination of the regular rate. For all intents and purposes, this enumeration of the specific factors to consider resolved this issue.

The amendments expanded protection to several groups not previously covered, such as employees of airlines and employees of fish and seafood canneries. Coverage was restricted by exempting certain telegraph agencies, logging or forestry operations involving fewer than twelve employees, and employees of employers in taxicab operations. Finally, the amendments strengthened the restrictions on homework to safeguard the minimum wage provisions of the law. For the most part, these changes in the law were welcome additions to the program. They clarified several ambiguous areas and provided explicit direction on the operation of the program.

NOTES

1. U.S. Department of Labor, Wage and Hour and Public Contracts Divisions, *Interim Report to Congress*, transmitted to the Congress on January 14, 1939 (Washington, D.C.: Government Printing Office, 1939).

2. Ibid., p. VI.

3. U.S. Department of Labor, Wage and Hour and Public Contracts Divisions, *Annual Report*, Fiscal Year 1939, transmitted to the Congress on January 8, 1940 (Washington, D.C.: Government Printing Office, 1940), p. 123.

4. U.S. Department of Labor, Wage and Hour and Public Contracts Divisions, *Annual Report*, Fiscal Year 1940, transmitted to the Congress on January 2, 1941 (Washington, D.C.: Government Printing Office, 1941), p. X.

5. Ibid., p. 1.

6. Ibid., p. 2.

7. Ibid., p. 88.

8. U.S. Department of Labor, Wage and Hour and Public Contracts Divisions, *Annual Report*, Fiscal Year 1942, transmitted to the Congress on January 4, 1943, (Washington, D.C., 1943, mimeographed), p. 5.

9. U.S. Department of Labor, Wage and Hour and Public Contracts Divisions, *Annual Report*, Fiscal Year 1943, transmitted to the Congress on January 15, 1944 (Washington, D.C., 1944, mimeographed), p. 2.

10. U.S. Department of Labor, Wage and Hour and Public Contracts Divisions, *Annual Report*, Fiscal Year 1944, transmitted to the Congress on January 3, 1945 (Washington, D.C., 1945, mimeographed), p. 6.

11. U.S. Department of Labor, Wage and Hour and Public Contracts Divisions, *Annual Report*, Fiscal Year 1946, transmitted to the Congress on January 2, 1947 (Washington, D. C.: Government Printing Office, 1947), p. v.

12. Ibid., p. 46.

13. U.S. Department of Labor, Wage and Hour and Public Contracts Divisions, *Annual Report*, Fiscal Year 1948, transmitted to the Congress on January 3, 1949 (Washington, D.C.: Government Printing Office, 1949), p. 18.

14. Ibid., p. 31.

15. Ibid.

16. Ibid., pp. 56–57.

17. U.S. Department of Labor, Wage and Hour and Public Contracts Divisions, *Annual Report*, Fiscal Year 1949, transmitted to the Congress on January 3, 1950 (Washington, D.C.: Government Printing Office, 1950), p. 37.

18. U.S. Congress, *Report*, No. 267 (Washington, D.C.: Government Printing Office, March 16, 1949), pp. 13–14.

19. Ibid., p. 14.

20. U.S. Department of Labor, "Supplemental Statement of the Administrator of the Wage and Hour and Public Contracts Divisions, U.S. Department of Labor" (Washington, D.C., December 1947, mimeographed), p. 1.

21. William S. White, "75¢ Minimum Wage Set for House Vote," *New York Times*, January 19, 1949, p. 1.

22. "Tobin Pushes Plan to Raise Pay Scale," *New York Times*, January 28, 1949, p. 4.

23. Ibid.

24. "Wage Rise Opposed by Cotton Council," *New York Times*, February 8, 1949, p. 42.

25. "President Truman's Address to the Jefferson-Jackson Dinner," *New York Times*, February 25, 1949, p. 18.

26. "Minimum Wage Bill Debated in House," *New York Times*, August 9, 1949, p. 16.

27. Joseph Loftus, "75-Cent Pay Floor Is Voted by House," *New York Times*, August 11, 1949, p. 3.

28. Ibid.

29. Joseph Loftus, "75¢ Base Pay Voted by House, 361 to 35," *New York Times*, August 12, 1949, p. 1.

30. Ibid., p. 9.

31. Harry S Truman, *Public Papers of the Presidents of the United States*, January 1 to December 31, 1949 (Washington, D.C.: U.S. Government Printing Office, 1964), p. 530.

Chapter 5

The Second Decade: The Emphasis on Education

With the enactment of the 1949 amendments, the administrator observed in the FY 1950 *Annual Report* that "nearly every section of the original act was amended in the new law, and the task of initially interpreting, explaining, and applying these changed provisions has been almost as great as was the initial administration of the act of 1938."[1] The "second decade" began in peacetime, but was quickly consumed by the military buildup for the Korean War. This chapter will divide the decade into two parts—1950 to 1954 and 1955 to 1959— for purposes of discussion.

ECONOMIC CONDITIONS IN THE SECOND DECADE

There were no major economic dislocations during the decade of the 1950s, and in fact, GNP, expressed in 1958 dollars, increased monotonically from $355.3 billion in 1950 to $475.9 billion in 1959. There were a couple of slight "pauses" in 1954 and 1958, but for the most part, they were small in magnitude. The Korean War placed some stress on domestic economic production, but the conflict was confined enough to prevent major economic dislocations. These comments are not intended to denigrate the importance of the war effort or to reduce the contribution of those who served their country during that period. Rather, the effects of that action were, in domestic economic terms, easily absorbed in the macroeconomic change process.

Total unemployment hovered in the 4 to 5 percent range for much of the decade, with temporary increases in the 1954 and 1958 economic pauses. Hourly earnings in current dollars increased in a smooth progression from $1.33 an hour in 1950 to $2.02 in 1959. Average gross hourly earnings in manufacturing increased from $1.44 an hour in 1950 to $2.19 an hour at the end of the decade. Consumer prices increased from 83.9 in 1950 to 101.5 in 1959 on a base of 1958 = 100.

In 1932, the business failure rate was 154.1 businesses per 10,000 listed enterprises. In 1945, this rate had decreased to 4.2 failures per 10,000 listed enterprises. During the 1950s, the failure rate fluctuated between 30 and 50 failures per 10,000 listed enterprises. There was a tendency for the failure rate to move to the higher level near the end of the decade.

These aggregate economic changes suggest that the magnitude of change and the degree of economic dislocation were tolerated easily by the domestic economy. The historical "markers" that gave character to that decade were the Korean War, the merger of the AFL and the CIO, and the launching of *Sputnik*. The nation did, of course, have a popular two-term president who dominated the decade politically, but economic changes were not of great note. In terms of the FLSA, the event other than the 1955 amendments that had the major impact early in the decade was the Korean War. Much of what the Wage and Hour Division had learned from the experience of World War II was used during the Korean conflict.

WAGE AND SALARY STABILIZATION

In response to the U.S. involvement in the Korean War, wages and prices were frozen on January 25, 1951. On February 2, 1951, the Wage Stabilization Board designated the Wage and Hour Division as their agent in the Wage Stabilization Program. Wage and Hour Administrator McComb noted that the program was in full operation within three days.[2] The division was empowered to respond to inquiries and issue authoritative written rulings. The ease with which the division adapted to this new assignment was because over half of the personnel had experience with a similar process during World War II.

The division's responsibilities were, first, to disseminate information about the stabilization program and, second, to review required reports by employers to determine whether wage and salary increases were according to the board's regulations. In addition, employers seeking to give wage or salary increases that were larger than permitted by regulation could receive assistance from the division to prepare the appropriate petition. The volume of activity under the Wage Stabilization Program accelerated quickly. By the end of FY 1950, the division was handling more than 25,000 inquiries per week and issuing about 1,500 authoritative written rulings per week.

Just before FY 1951 ended—May 1951—a separate Salary Stabilization Board was established. This board was created to handle salary adjustments for "executives, administrative, or professional employees" and "outside salesmen" as defined by the FLSA. The division formulated investigation procedures that were being "tested" at the end of FY 1951.[3] During a twenty-three-month period—February 1951 to December 1952—the division processed 1,846,478 inquiries, assisted in the preparation of 47,675 applications for review of activities taken by the Wage and Salary Stabilization Boards, reviewed 112,830 reports from firms implementing self-reporting regulations, processed 87,525 petitions for wage or salary increases above the mandated level, and conducted 43,946 fact-finding investigations for the programs.

While these programs were of shorter duration than the War Labor Board activities during World War II, the level of effort during the twenty-three months was equally intense. Some additional staff were recruited for the programs, but the usual problems of training, high turnover, and postprogram conversion placed additional burdens on very limited resources. Overall, the division's efforts were rewarded by a smoothly functioning program that contributed to economic stability during wartime. The stabilization program had little effect on the program's primary enforcement program.

ENFORCEMENT IN THE FIRST HALF OF THE DECADE

Fiscal year 1950 was the low point for total investigations during the decade, with about 25,881 FLSA investigations. The number of investigations accelerated quickly to about 39,000 in FY 1952 and remained at that level between FY 1952 and FY 1955. However, the number of employees found underpaid and back wages owed both declined substantially during the four year period. The several categories of activity for the entire decade are shown in Table 5.1.

Table 5.1
Results of FLSA Investigations, FY 1950-1959

Fiscal Year	Number of Establishments Investigated	Number of Employees Subject to Minimum Wage (000)	Number of Employees	Under Payment Amount (000)	Payment Agreed to by Employer (000)
1950	25,881	1,515.6	140,872	$9,559.6	$4,081.2
1951	31,899	1,569.9	139,038	11,202.5	6,666.9
1952	39,109	2,125.1	208,078	15,663.9	8,467.7
1953	38,649	2,092.9	193,111	16,652.7	8,282.0
1954	39,430	2,019.6	141,368	n.a.	n.a.
1955	39,330	1,962.3	128,754	n.a.	n.a.
1956	33,148	1,581.6	112,710	11,085.9	6,051.9
1957	48,482	2,296.9	181,910	18,834.1	n.a.
1958	53,796	1,910.1	166,497	19,655.3	10,953.9
1959	54,916	1,630.3	177,908	22,403.1	12,885.9

Source: U.S. Department of Labor, Annual Report, Fiscal Year 1959 (Washington, D.C.: Government Printing Office, 1960), p. 16, n.a. = not available.

To some degree, the second decade was a period of experimentation combined with an effort to regularize enforcement of the law. One of the changes in the compliance effort that stabilized in the early 1950s was the impetus behind investigations. While the vast majority of investigations during the early years of the program were "complaint" driven, the division had transitioned by the early 1950s to primarily "targeted" or what were called "selected" investigations. In FY 1951, only about one fourth—27 percent—of the investigations were scheduled in response to a specific complaint. The pattern continued throughout most of the decade.

A second dimension of the program that received considerable attention was the noncovered segment of the workforce. In 1953, a special tabulation was provided of the industrial location of covered and noncovered wage and salary workers. Table 5.2 summarizes these data. Overall, 55 percent of wage and salary workers—excluding proprietors, self-employed, unpaid family members, government employees, and professional, administrative, and executive employees—were protected by the FLSA. In 1953, this represented about 24 million employees out of about 44 million wage and salary workers. It was clear where the emphasis for expanded coverage would be in the years ahead. More than 15 million workers in the lowest-paid jobs in retail trade, services, and agriculture were provided no protection by the FLSA.

Table 5.2
Workers Protected and Not Protected by the FLSA, 1953

Industry	Total Wage and Salary Workers	Protected (%)	Not Protected (%)
Total	43,954	55%	45%
Mining	768	97	3
Manufacturing	16,131	96	4
Transportation, communication, utilities	3,956	87	13
Wholesale trade	2,539	67	33
Finance, insurance, and real estate	1,792	59	41
Construction	2,565	24	76
Services not elsewhere classified	4,188	18	82
Retail trade	6,928	3	97
Agriculture	3,066	0	100
Domestic service	2,021	0	100

Source: U.S. Department of Labor, *Annual Report*, Fiscal year 1953 (Washington, D.C.: Government Printing Office, 1954), p. 46.

Table 5.3
FLSA Violations by Size of Firm, 1951

Number of Employees	Established Investment	Percentage in Violation	Violation of Minimum Wage	Violation of Overtime	Violation of Child Labor
1	655	49%	29%	30%	4%
2–3	2,336	49	24	37	5
4–7	5,980	49	18	37	8
8–19	9,443	55	18	43	10
20–49	7,509	59	18	46	10
50–99	3,456	61	20	49	8
100–199	2,241	67	21	55	9
200–499	1,325	65	15	55	8
500+	534	72	9	63	11

Source: U.S. Department of Labor, *Annual Report*, Fiscal year 1951 (Washington, D.C.: Government Printing Office, 1952), p. 16.

A third aspect of the investigation process involved an analysis of investigations in relation to firm size. One might hypothesize that firms with larger workforces would be more aware of the law, have a greater propensity to be unionized, and consequently have a lower probability of violating the law. Precisely the opposite was true. In FY 1951, for example, Table 5.3 shows the relative incidence of violations by number of employees. While larger firms had somewhat fewer minimum wage violations, they experienced substantially higher overtime and child labor violations. This general pattern occurred in every major industry group. Importantly, this pattern of relative violations did *not* change after firms were investigated. The relative incidence of FLSA violations was nearly identical regardless of whether the firm had previously been investigated or not. This observation raised questions about the frequent assertion that fewer violations were occurring due to enforcement efforts and the "learning process."

Administrator McComb observed in his FY 1953 *Annual Report*, "The Division's years of experience have demonstrated conclusively that the making of physical investigations is imperative to achieving compliance with the Fair Labor Standards Act."[4] However, he also believed "that employers as a usual rule want to comply with the law."[5] Consequently, the division developed an extensive education program to ensure that firms were given every opportunity to meet their legislated requirements. The belief that education and information dissemination would improve compliance led to the development of the Compliance Using Education (CUE) program fifteen years later. An unresolved question that still exists today is whether utilizing education and information dissemination in fact increases compliance.

In summary, the Wage and Hour Division was attempting to regularize the enforcement efforts through more targeted investigations and through an emphasis on education. The 1949 amendments provided further clarification and direction to the program and resolved several difficult problems. Investigation activity began to accelerate as the Wage and Salary Stabilization Program wound down in late 1952.

THE SECOND HALF OF THE DECADE

By mid-decade, the enforcement pattern was set. About 5 percent of covered establishments were physically investigated each year, the majority of investigations were "directed" or "targeted" rather than complaint driven, and education was stressed as an important compliance vehicle.

On August 12, 1955, the president signed Public Law 381. This action resulted in the culmination of an act entitled the Fair Labor Standards Amendments of 1955. These amendments provided for essentially one change: they raised the minimum wage from $.75 per hour to $1.00 per hour. There were no changes in coverage, exemption provisions, or overtime and child labor standards.[6] The amendments did change the procedures for minimum wage determination in Puerto Rico and the Virgin Islands. They also required that the Section 4(d) report contain an annual evaluation or assessment of the minimum wage and recommendations by the secretary for any changes needed in the law.

In comparative terms, the events leading up to the 1955 amendments to the FLSA were relatively unemotional and noncontroversial. Not long after the 1949 amendments, the rhetoric for another increase began. In 1952, the National Urban League argued, "The present minimum wage of 75 cents an hour is inadequate to meet the increased cost of living." Further, "Until the Federal standard is raised the states will not feel obligated to raise their sights."[7]

As the Truman administration came to an end in 1952, there was little discussion about minimum wage legislation. The country was emerging from the successful conclusion of the Korean War, and the political rhetoric focused on the upcoming election. Dwight Eisenhower defeated Adlai Stevenson for the presidency of the United States and inherited a number of problems related to the conversion of a wartime to a peacetime economy. Soon after taking office, the new president's labor secretary, Martin Durkin, proposed a higher minimum wage. However, since Secretary Durkin was only in office during the first year of the new administration, there was little opportunity for new legislation. After his resignation, Acting Secretary Mashburn recommended to the Budget Bureau that the president ask the Congress to increase the minimum wage to $1.00 an hour. The new administration was unready to advance a proposal of this type, and the existence of the Mashburn recommendation became a source of considerable embarrassment to the president and the in-coming secretary of labor, James Mitchell. Though the Mashburn recommen-dation was widely known to exist, in a press conference on October 28, 1953, President Eisenhower denied that a proposal of this type had ever been made to him. Rather, he characterized the situation as part of a general dialogue be-tween him and his advisers about the need for, and effects of, an increase in the minimum wage.[8]

Labor Secretary Mitchell did not take long to acquire the $1.00 per hour minimum wage fever. By the end of 1953, he was openly advocating the higher minimum wage, though the administration was attempting to be more tentative and circumspect. Secretary Mitchell was also an outspoken advocate of ex-tending coverage of the law to workers not enjoying its protection. When he became labor secretary, "he was shocked to discover that the law exempted more than 18,000,000 workers he had thought were covered; that the position of these workers was 'dangerously insecure,' and that the Administration was 'working hard to find ways and means to bring about an increase in the present 75-cent-an-hour minimum to a more realistic level.'"[9] The administration's more "realistic level" ultimately became $.90 an hour.

By the end of 1954, the president had come to the conclusion that both a wage and coverage increase were needed. His minimum wage proposal was $.90 an hour, but the dimensions of increases in coverage were less clear. Even before he had an opportunity to surface his proposals formally in the State of the Union Message on January 6, 1955, critics were attacking the paucity of the proposal. Senator James Murray argued that the president's proposal was a "very good move," but it didn't go far enough. George Meany, president of the American Federation of Labor, argued that the "President's proposal for in-creasing the minimum wage to $.90 an hour falls short of economic realities and the needs of low-income workers."[10]

The newly merged AFL and CIO immediately issued a joint statement encouraging a minimum wage of $1.25 an hour. The AFL–CIO argued for the increase because purchasing power was expanding and also because it improved the economic welfare of those directly receiving the increases. There was also concern that American enterprise was attempting to escape high-wage areas for low-wage areas, with the resultant disruption in workers' lives. A higher federal minimum wage would make such movement less profitable. While the AFL–CIO was seeking a $1.25 per hour increase, it was believed that some-thing less was probably realistic. The federation argued that a "substantial" increase in the minimum wage would have negligible impact on prices and unemployment.[11] These arguments were presented to President Eisenhower by a group of union leaders, and the president promised to consider their views seriously.

American labor was not the only segment of the economy struggling for improvement. Farmers, too, were pressing hard for a rigid price support pro-gram that would guarantee them higher prices for their commodities. The unions in the United States came out in support of the farm price subsidy program, much to the chagrin of administration officials. Since farm prices translate into higher commodity prices for American workers, this position seemed at variance with the goals of labor unions. However, the unions believed that low farm prices translated into fewer farm jobs. With fewer farm jobs, there would be migration of farm workers to the cities, where they would be in competition with urban labor for available jobs. While Walter Reuther denied that organized labor was seeking support by agricultural interests for the minimum wage legislation, there can be no question that a quid pro quo was wanted and expected.[12] In early May 1955, a major farm group, that is, the National Farmers Association, came out in support of the AFL–CIO position of a $1.25 per hour minimum wage.[13] The association was explicit in the rationale for providing support as the reciprocal support that had been provided by the AFL–CIO on farm price support legislation.

As the intensity of the debate gained momentum, supporters in the Congress for a minimum wage higher than $ .90 an hour grew. Senator William Purtell, Republican of Connecticut, noted, for example, that "he would not declare how high a figure he would support but it would be 'a great deal higher than 90 cents.'"[14] Within the administration, there was a growing consensus that *both* coverage expansion and a higher minimum wage were needed to bring American low-wage workers into parity with overall economic changes. The president was an outspoken advocate of both changes. He noted in the 1955 *Economic Report of the President*, "The coverage of the minimum wage is no less important than its amount. Only about 24 million of the 44 million workers of private firms are now subject to the Federal minimum wage, an additional 3.5 million being covered by the laws of 20 States."[15] The National Association of Manufacturers, however, took a diametrically opposed position. The NAM argued that coverage should be narrowed rather than broadened. In fact, the NAM position on the FLSA was that the entire wage and hour law should be repealed rather than modified through amendment.[16]

There was general agreement within the administration that expanded coverage was preferred to a higher minimum wage, though the conservatives in Congress were the primary opponents to expanding FLSA coverage less than a decade earlier. However, after the minimum wage was increased to $1.00 an hour in late 1955, the administration pushed further for an expansion of coverage. President Eisenhower noted in the 1957 *Economic Report of the President*, "It is again recommended that the Congress and the States extend the coverage of minimum wage legislation to additional workers needing this protection."[17] Coverage was to become a major area of controversy in the next several rounds of amendments to the FLSA.

ENFORCEMENT ACTIVITY IN THE SECOND HALF OF THE DECADE

Table 5.1 showed the overall enforcement statistics for the decade of the 1950s. During most of the decade, the number of investigations related to the FLSA were commingled with Public Contract Act (PCA) investigations. Therefore, there is some ambiguity in the exact change in FLSA investigations. However, what is clear is that the number of total investigations increased substantially from 25,881 in FY 1950 to 54,916 in FY 1959—a 112 percent rise. What is also clear is that the vast majority of investigations were conducted under the FLSA program, while very few were exclusively PCA investigations. As noted in the FY 1959 *Annual Report*, "Almost all investigations are made for compliance with the Fair Labor Standards Act; Public Contract Act investigations are usually made concurrent with investigations under the former law, since practically all establishments doing work for the Government under the Public Contracts Act are also covered by the Federal wage and hour law."[18]

In any case, changes throughout the decade were of sufficient magnitude to conclude that there had been substantial increases in investigations. In addition, the outcomes —back wages found due and employer agreements to pay— of these investigations were also of sufficient magnitude to suggest that real changes had occurred. A case could be made that the investigations were also becoming more efficient. In 1950, about 26,000 investigations produced $4.081 million in back wages that employers agreed to pay to 140,822 workers. This effort produced about $29 per employee due back wages. In 1959, about 55,000 investigations yielded $12.886 million in back pay to almost 178,000 workers. This activity produced about $72 in back pay to each deserving employee.

The division used the change in the law in 1955 to further expand the educational process. A basic descriptive circular with a poster, a form to elicit answers to specific questions, and a guide for determining the regular rate of pay for subject employees were sent to 800,000 covered establishments. In addition, articles were prepared for publication in trade journals; radio and television public information announcements were developed; and clinics, speeches, enclosures in contract solicitations, and other vehicles to disseminate information were utilized. By every measure, the flow of information was extensive and apparently well received by those needing authoritative guidance. The "education" process became so important in the compliance program that in the 1958 and 1959 annual reports, Administrator Clarence Lundquist included a section entitled "Compliance through Education" in addition to the standard section entitled "Enforcement by Investigation." The administrator viewed education as the most effective mechanism to provide appropriate information to employers who wanted to comply with the law. In addition, education would provide employees with tools for detecting and reporting employers not in compliance with the law. Education has been and continues to be an important element in the compliance program. What is not clear is what vehicles are most effective in the education process and what level of resources should be expended to educate employees and employers about their rights and responsibilities under the law.

ECONOMIC IMPACT OF THE MINIMUM WAGE

In addition to the basic purpose of the 1955 amendments to raise the minimum wage from $.75 per hour to $1.00 per hour, two other substantive changes are of interest. First, the 1955 amendments mandated a comprehensive evaluation program related to the FLSA; and second, they established procedures to expedite the wage order program in the Virgin Islands and Puerto Rico. Due to the evaluation criteria required in the 1955 amendments, a comprehensive program of data and information analysis was initiated. This program included a wage distribution survey, locality surveys, industry surveys, follow-up of complaints of adverse impact, and several other components.

The Bureau of Labor Statistics was asked to conduct most of the survey work, while Wage and Hour Division personnel conducted case studies and complaint follow-up activities. The results of these projects became the basis for an intensive review of the FLSA's effects and the identification of problems needing program changes. These data and information programs have remained important sources of information related specifically to the FLSA-covered segment of the work-force.

A large number of studies were prepared in response to the 1955 amendments, but several of the more important ones include the following. First, in September 1957, the division conducted the *Compliance Survey: Extent and Incidence of Noncompliance with the Fair Labor Standards Act*. This study, the first of several on this issue, attempted to "measure the degree to which establishments which come within the scope of the Fair Labor Standards Act are complying with the provisions of the Act, and the extent and nature of the violations problem presently confronting the enforcement staff of the Divisions."[19] It was the first comprehensive and systematic attempt to quantify the dimensions of noncompliance that would produce a more targeted enforcement program. As noted earlier, there were attempts to focus enforcement resources in industrial groups where noncompliance was either known to be high or there was reason to suspect that it was disproportionately high. This study pinpointed the precise extent and nature of the problem in the entire covered sector and in that sense permitted a more rationalized targeting program.

The survey methodology required a random sample of 12,406 establishments in the coverage universe except for construction, railroads, and business services sectors. About one third of the sample establishments were found to be out of business or did not have employees subject to the act and were therefore removed from the survey process. The findings summarized below were therefore based on a sample of 8,401 establishments. The sample was of sufficient size to yield "statistically sound" information for the covered establishments. The survey found about 21 million employees subject to the minimum wage provisions of the FLSA. About 2 million of these employees were paid less than the $1.00 minimum wage. These workers constituted the group with potential minimum wage violations. The survey found that during the profile workweek about 63,000 employees were in fact paid less than the legally due minimum wage. There was about an even split of employees in violation between manufacturing and nonmanufacturing industries. The South had about two thirds of the employees in violation. Small establishments with between one and nine employees had over half (53 percent) of the employees in violation. Nonmetropolitan areas had about two thirds of the violations. The average employee was underpaid about $6.00 during the profile workweek. The survey also collected data for the entire "investigation period" of two years. These data showed basically the same relative pattern of noncompliance.

The survey focused attention on the violations related to overtime work. Almost three times as many employees (194,000) were underpaid overtime compensation. While the FLSA is typically viewed as the nation's minimum wage statute, it actually has a much larger volume of overtime violations. This pattern has continued to the present. In relative terms, for the profile week, the patterns of minimum wage violations and overtime violations were quite different. As shown in Table 5.4, overtime violations were much more predominant in metropolitan areas than in nonmetropolitan areas.

While the wholesale trade industry had a disproportionate incidence of violations, coverage of retail trade and services was still limited, and therefore the compliance pattern today was not evident in the survey data. In 1988, approximately 75 percent of the violations are in retail trade and service industries.

The second major study was entitled *Studies of the Economic Effects of the $1 Minimum Wage*. Published in January 1959, it attempted to determine what impacts the $1.00 minimum wage had on twelve low-wage industry segments. This study built on an earlier study entitled *Results of the Minimum Wage Increase of 1950* that examined the short-term effects of the $.75 minimum wage. Onset of the Korean War in June 1950 obscured the longer-term effects of the 1950 minimum wage change.

In an effort to identify the effects of the $1.00 minimum wage, the twelve low-wage industry segments were subjected to several preincrease and postincrease surveys. In addition, the Wage and Hour Division conducted a series of follow-ups to complaints by firms concerning adverse effects of the increase in the minimum wage. The division also conducted a study of the adjustment processes in several individual plants to ascertain how they responded to the wage increase. Finally, through regularly published statistical series by the Bureau of Labor Statistics, the Bureau of the Census, and other statistical units, the Wage and Hour Division attempted to identify the overall macroeconomic effects of the minimum wage change.

The impact studies produced findings that formed the basis for both proponents' and opponents' arguments for the next three decades. The data were sufficiently "malleable" to permit those who believed the change produced unacceptably large impacts to make that claim and for those who thought the effects were relatively small to make that claim. The study found that there were no discernible impacts on the national economy in terms of changes in employment, unemployment, price levels, and other economic indicators. In addition, there were no proportional "ripple effects" on higher-income levels as a result of the increase in the minimum wage. However, there were some effects on specific commodity prices that "appeared" to be attributable to the minimum wage change. There was some specific job loss attributed to the higher minimum wage. There was a narrowing of wage differentials in some industries, but the study could not determine if these differentials persisted

Table 5.4

A Comparison of the Relative Incidence of FLSA
Violations for Minimum Wage and Overtime Work during the Profile Week

	Percent Distribution	
Economic Characteristic	*Minimum Wage Violations*	*Overtime Violations*
Industry		
Manufacturing	44%	45%
Nonmanufacturing	56	55
Region		
Northeast	10	25
South	68	36
Middle West	18	30
West	4	9
Size of establishment		
1-9 employees	53	32
10-19 employees	17	17
20-99 employees	21	29
100 or more	9	22
Area		
Metropolitan	35	64
Nonmetropolitan	65	36
Type of organization		
Single unit	88	75
Multiunit	12	25

Source: U.S. Department of Labor, Wage and Hour and Public Contracts Divisions, *Compliance Survey: Extent and Incidence of Noncompliance with the Fair Labor Standards Act* (Washington, D.C.: Government Printing Office, September 1957), Tables 1 and 5.

through time. A few employers indicated that they were more selective in hiring because of the minimum wage change. Finally, the higher minimum wage produced improved plant efficiency and in some cases increased automation.

A general observation flowing from the study was that

average hourly earnings of workers in selected low-wage industries generally subject to the Act have increased by a larger percentage that earnings from selected high wage industries or for all manufacturing workers combined. Earnings of workers in selected low-wage industries in which the Act is not generally applicable have lagged behind the other three groups, for the period 1938 to 1956 taken as a whole.[20]

A third important report during the late 1950s was entitled *Wage Order Program for Puerto Rico, the Virgin Islands and American Samoa*. This study and report examined the wage order program in the offshore territories in terms of industry committee activities and the effects of the minimum wage changes on the economy in these territories. Additional review of these programs will occur in a later section of this book when the industry committee program is discussed at length.

THE WAGE ORDER PROGRAM

The 1955 amendments substantially changed the wage order program in the Virgin Islands and Puerto Rico. The changes were designed to expedite the review of conditions in the offshore islands and remove the "second round" of public hearings by the secretary of labor. Specifically, the amendments required the review of minimum wage rates by industry committees at least once each fiscal year. The reports of the industry committees were submitted to the secretary of labor for publication in the *Federal Register* without a second round of public hearings. The committee recommendations were self-executing fifteen days after the secretary's *Federal Register* notice. Annual reviews required intensive attention to the economies in Puerto Rico and the Virgin Islands, which resulted in the expenditure of major travel and staff resources. It became apparent later that an annual review was not needed, and the program reverted to a biennial review process on August 25, 1958.

CONCLUSION

By the end of the 1950s, the program was a mature worker protection program with a national presence. It was perceived as an effective program that protected the rights of low-wage workers, a program that imparted stability in the economy, and reduced the level of poverty. It was, in short, achieving all or most of the original objectives of the program. However, there were shortfalls that required attention. Several of the lowest-wage industrial and occupational groups were not covered by the FLSA. The millions of workers most in need of its protection were beyond its legislative reach. There was concern that only 5 to 6 percent of the subject establishments were inspected each year. There was targeted enforcement that probably protected larger numbers of workers than the relatively small "penetration ratio" would suggest. However, employers were becoming less reluctant to exert their rights through challenges of investigative findings. Only about half the findings resulted in voluntary agreements to pay or court-ordered payment.

The education process, while good public relations, did not appear to produce greater compliance. However, the program was making its presence known, and the results of its enforcement activity affected every American industrial group. Of most significance was the candid discussion of not only accomplishments but problems faced by the program. There were problems related to staffing, training, and organizational efficiency, which plague every large organization. The first step in the improvement process is the recognition and clear statement of problems. There was no reluctance to explain to the Congress what needed to be done. The decade of the 1960s witnessed many of these changes.

NOTES

1. U.S. Department of Labor, Wage and Hour and Public Contracts Division, *Annual Report*, Fiscal year 1950, reprinted from the 38th *Annual Report of the Secretary of Labor* (Washington, D.C.: Government Printing Office, 1951), p. 194.

2. U.S. Department of Labor, Wage and Hour and Public Contracts Divisions, *Annual Report*, Fiscal year 1951, reprinted from the 39th *Annual Report of the Secretary of Labor* (Washington, D.C.: Government Printing Office, 1952), p. 1.

3. Ibid., p. 2.

4. U.S. Department of Labor, Wage and Hour and Public Contracts Divisions, *Annual Report*, Fiscal year 1953 (Washington, D.C.: Government Printing Office, 1954), p. 5.

5. Ibid., p. vii.

6. U.S. Department of Labor, Wage and Hour and Public Contracts Divisions, *Annual Report*, Fiscal year 1956, reprinted from the 1956, *Annual Report of the Secretary of Labor* (Washington, D.C.: Government Printing Office, 1957), p. 5.

7. Elie Abel, "Urban League Hits 'Politics' on Rights," New *York Times*, September 6, 1952, p. 14.

8. "The President's Press Conference on Foreign and Domestic Issues," *New York Times*, October 29, 1953, p. 26.

9. "Report Cautions on Minimum Wage," *New York Times*, January 29, 1954, p. 9.

10. Joseph A. Loftus, "Message Causes Labor to Frown," *New York Times*, January 7, 1955, p. 13.

11. "Eisenhower Hears Union Wage Plea," *New York Times*, March 8, 1955, p. 21.

12. Joseph A. Loftus, "Farm-Labor Bloc Upsets the G.O.P.," *New York Times*, April 11, 1955, p. 19.

13. "Farm Group Responds," *New York Times*, May 10, 1955, p. 59.

14. Joseph A. Loftus, "Union Heads Urge $1.25 Pay Minimum," *New York Times*, April 20, 1955, p. 26.

15. *Economic Report of the President*, January 20, 1955 (Washington, D.C.: U.S. Government Printing Office, 1955), p. 58.

16. Joseph A. Loftus, "Eisenhower Urges Wage Law Spread," *New York Times*, April 28, 1955, p. 23.

17. *Economic Report of the President*, January 23, 1957 (Washington, D.C.: U.S. Government Printing Office, 1958).

18. U.S. Department of Labor, Wage and Hour and Public Contracts Divisions, *Annual Report*, Fiscal Year 1959, reprinted from the 1959 *Annual Report of the Secretary of Labor* (Washington, D.C.: Government Printing Office, 1960), p. 217.

19. U.S. Department of Labor, Wage and Hour and Public Contracts Divisions, *Compliance Survey: Extent and Incidence of Noncompliance with the Fair Labor Standards Act* (Washington, D.C.: Government Printing Office, September 1957), p. I-1.

20. U.S. Department of Labor, Wage and Hour and Public Contracts Divisions, *Studies of the Economic Effects of the $1 Minimum Wage: Interim Report* (Washington, D.C.: Government Printing Office, March 1957), p. 5.

Chapter 6

The Third Decade: The Decade of Assessment

The third decade started with major amendments to the law, as did the second. On May 5, 1961, President John Kennedy signed a bill into law that, among other things, raised the minimum wage from $1.00 per hour to $1.25 per hour, expanded coverage to categories of workers previously without protection, strengthened the back wage recovery process, and required a variety of studies to determine the consequences of maintaining several exemptions to the law. Before the decade ended, the FLSA was amended again to provide for a second round of phased-in minimum wage increases. This chapter examines the third decade from the perspective of the economic climate, the continuation of an effective enforcement program, a review of several amendments during the decade, the Equal Pay Act, and the economic assessment program.

THE ECONOMIC SITUATION IN THE 1960s

Between 1960 and 1969, gross national product in the United States increased from $503.7 billion to $932.3 billion in current dollars. Real GNP growth over this period (based on 1958 = 100) went from $487.7 billion to $727.7 billion—a 49.3 percent increase.[1] The United States experienced a healthy expansion period during the 1960s.

Between 1960 and 1969, the number of wage and salary workers increased from 54,234,000 to 70,139,000—a 29.3 percent increase.[2] The average weekly hours of work in the private nonagricultural economy continued its decline from 38.6 hours per week in 1960 to 37.7 hours per week in 1969.[3] Average gross hourly earnings in the private nonagricultural economy increased from $2.09 per hour to $3.04 per hour over the decade.[4] On an index number basis, productivity—output per person-hour—increased from 105.0 in 1960 to 139.9 in 1969.[5] While the 1960–1961 recession reduced the expenditures of business on new plant and equipment, after the recession ended, there was a constant expansion in this category of expenditures throughout the remainder of the decade.

The overall consumer price index increased from 103.1 in 1960 to 127.7 in 1969. The unemployment rate was 5.5 percent in 1960, increased to 6.7 percent during the 1960–1961 recession, and then declined monotonically to 3.5 percent in 1969. Modest rates of price increase, declining unemployment, and expanding output and productivity suggested that the economy was in reasonably good shape throughout the 1960s.

The "good" economic conditions of the 1960s placed in stark relief a major problem in the U. S. economy—poverty. Not all Americans were enjoying the "good life." The benefits of the economic growth process were accruing to members of society in unequal ways. The total U.S. population in 1960 was 180.7 million people, of which 39.9 million were classified as poor—22.1 percent. One in five Americans lived and worked but were unable to extricate themselves from the ravages of poverty. Ten years later, major improvements had occurred. Total population exceeded 220 million people, of which 25.4 million were poor—11.5 percent.[6]

The decade of the 1960s is remembered by Americans for many reasons: the Vietnam War, the first person on the moon, the coming of age of the "Yuppie generation," and the assassinations of President John Kennedy, Dr. Martin Luther King, and Senator Robert Kennedy. In terms of the role of public policy and one of its most significant objectives, Secretary of Labor W. Willard Wirtz stated it most succinctly. He suggested in his 1968 *Annual Report* to Congress that "[t]he decade of the 6O's takes its particular character from the national determination to eliminate poverty in the United States."[7]

It is interesting and significant that as recently as 1969 the "living wage" was explicitly identified as an objective of the FLSA. In his discussion concerning the next appropriate steps to address the poverty issues, Secretary Wirtz urged that "the appropriate and feasible next step is to assure—through further amendment of the Fair Labor Standards Act—that every person who works in this country receives at least enough for his labor to maintain himself and his family decently."[8] Secretary Wirtz pointed out in the FY 1968 *Annual Report*, "There is significant coincidence today between the groups of people in this country who work at jobs not covered by the Fair Labor Standards Act and those who are still earning less than 'poverty level' incomes."[9]

As the nation's experience with the FLSA increased, the practical economic, political, social, and bureaucratic issues became more apparent. A "wage and hour" and "child labor" law seemed disarmingly simple. Establish a minimum level for wages, a maximum number of permissible work hours, and prevent the abuse of children in the workplace. What could be simpler? What was intuitively simple turned out to be gigantically complex when applied to a large, heterogeneous, complex society with a variety of competing economic, social, and political goals. The 1961 and 1966 amendments to FLSA clearly showed just how complex the law had become after two and one-half decades of operation.

THE 1961 AMENDMENTS TO THE FLSA

Even before the presidential ink was dried on the 1955 amendments to the FLSA, the rhetoric began for more changes. The genesis of the 1961 amendments occurred in the second half of the decade of the 1950s. At that point, President Dwight Eisenhower was pushing for expanded coverage without a further increase in the minimum wage rate. He was not specific about the dimensions of additional coverage in his budget message in early 1956, but he recommended "that the Congress extend the protection of the minimum wage law to additional workers."[10] In his economic report to Congress one week later, the president recommended that the country should "[p]roceed as far as is practical to extend coverage of the minimum wage."[11] Again, there were no specific coverage proposals forthcoming and the president placed the burden of suggesting the dimensions of coverage to the Congress. The AFL–CIO advocated an increase in the minimum wage to $1.25 an hour, with the extension of coverage to "millions" of additional workers. These coverage proposals, in early 1956, were similarly vague.

On March 1, 1956, the minimum wage increased from $.75 an hour to $1.00 an hour for covered workers. In anticipation of the increase, the Department of Labor engaged in a massive educational campaign to educate workers and employers about the nature of the changes and their respective rights and responsibilities. This effort was intended to minimize violations of the new law based on ignorance of the law. However, in the event that the educational process was not effective, the Wage and Hour Division added over 400 new staff, 300 of which were field investigators (compliance officers [COs]). Nevertheless, Newell Brown, wage and hour administrator, testified before Congress that "wage law violations almost doubled after the minimum was raised to $1 an hour last year."[12]

There was concerted attention needed as the new law went into effect. Correctly or incorrectly, some manufacturing groups believed that the higher minimum wage would have a major impact on costs and prices, and therefore the impetus for violating the law was present. The National Association of Hosiery Manufacturers, for example, argued that "the new wage level will raise manufacturing costs substantially in the hosiery industry."[13] The inference was that consumers could expect that prices of textile products would begin increasing in the near future.

Nevertheless, the attention in the second half of the decade was not on "old history." The 1955 amendments were the law of the land, and there was little industry or anyone else could do about them. Therefore, the opponents and proponents of changes in the FLSA began looking to the future. The president's support for an expansion of coverage was well known and was vigorously opposed by employer groups. The U.S. Chamber of Commerce and the National Association of Manufacturers argued strenuously against expansion of coverage and in particular the inclusion of retail and service establishments. These groups also opposed further increases in the minimum wage, but their main concern was the administration-supported expansion of coverage.

Interestingly, after the 1955 amendments had become law, everyone wanted to take credit for "helping the American worker." The primary area of disagreement was over who had been instrumental in obtaining the $1.00 an hour minimum wage. As noted earlier, the administration's solid position was for a $.90 an hour minimum wage with expanded coverage. The Democrats were supporting a $1.00 minimum wage, with the promise to study expanded coverage later. Adlai Stevenson, the soon-to-be Democratic presidential standard bearer, took exception with "Republican campaign speakers" when they attempted to take credit for the higher minimum wage. In fact, he argued that "the rise in the statutory wage floor had been made possible by a Democratic Congress acting over the objections of President Eisenhower" who had pressed hard for the $.90 level.[14] Regardless of who could rightly claim credit for the $1.00 minimum wage, the lines of battle quickly formed once again as the country moved toward another presidential election. The Democrats now had their position more clearly articulated with a strong push for a $1.25 an hour minimum wage and a significant expansion of coverage. The Democratic proposal would in the view of most experts bring about 9 to 10 million additional workers under the provisions of the wage and hour law.

George Meany, president of the AFL–CIO, was particularly critical of the administration proposal for coverage expansion. He argued that the dimensions of coverage proposed by the administration would bring about 2.5 million additional workers under the law but that only about one tenth of that number would in fact receive a wage increase. Meany characterized the administration's proposal as "narrow, restricted, and unrealistic."[15] He further accused Secretary Mitchell of adopting a "new and tricky definition of what constitutes interstate commerce," with the result that millions of deserving workers were precluded from FLSA protections.[16] Other union leaders similarly attacked the specific coverage proposals set forth by the administration. Some suggested that the administration had gained political mileage over the past several years by arguing for an extension of coverage but never being specific about the dimensions of the coverage change. Once the specific character of the coverage change were defined, it became clear that the effective coverage of new workers would be small indeed. William Schnitzler, secretary-treasurer of the AFL–CIO, argued, "To our mind, this is outrageous. First of all, by the Secretary's own admission, only 400,000 workers would get additional money in their pay envelopes, for most of the group he proposes to cover already has the minimum wage in fact if not in law."[17]

As the legislative year moved forward in 1957, the impetus behind a new minimum wage coverage bill evaporated. The main support for a new bill was in the Senate, but even there little concrete action was occurring. The blame was laid primarily on Senator John Kennedy, a sponsor of the bill, for not taking the leadership necessary to move the bill to the Senate floor. The Kennedy bill had been reported to the full Labor and Public Welfare Committee without recommendations, and it languished as the heat of summer descended on Washington. There was some support for the observation that many senators who would support the bill were frequently absent. Others believed the bill was dead and therefore didn't want to waste time fighting for its passage. By midsummer, Senator Kennedy was still hopeful but was becoming "increasingly discouraged" about the progress of the bill in the full committee. There was even less support for the bill in the House, and therefore there was no chance for passage in 1957.[18]

The new session of Congress starting in January 1958 brought a renewed effort to sponsor legislation to expand FLSA *coverage*. Senator Kennedy was again the major Senate proponent of this legislation and suggested that he would push hard for early consideration by the Labor and Public Welfare Committee. There was general interest in considering this legislation, but more support arose when both coverage and wage-level provisions were included. Consequently, late in 1958, the AFL–CIO offered its legislative plan that called for a $1.25 minimum wage.[19] Shortly after that, a major American manufacturer—J. Spencer Love, chairman and president of Burlington Industries, Inc.— argued for a higher minimum wage to improve competitive conditions in the textile industry and a "general uplifting of the overall economy of the industry."[20] Leon Keyserling, chairman of the Council of Economic Advisors under President Truman, began arguing for a $1.50 an hour minimum wage. His rationale was that the higher wage level was needed to raise consumption to levels needed to expand employment and full production.[21] In addition, the National Consumer's League publicly supported a $1.25 minimum wage and the expansion of protection by all states in which the federal statute did not apply.

In response to widespread interest in increasing the minimum wage and expanding coverage, the administration identified its position in the debate. Secretary Mitchell recommended to the Congress that the increase in the minimum wage be delayed but that coverage be extended to several millions of workers.

By the late 1950s, most states had enacted minimum wage laws. As the debate on various proposals proceeded, a "new" issue surfaced. Some congressman believed that care was needed to prevent the encroachment of federal prerogatives on state responsibilities and further that when states had effective programs related to minimum wage programs that the federal government should delegate administrative/enforcement duties to the states. Senator Ives proposed legislation in early 1957 that would have given the states enforcement responsibilities in situations where state laws were equal or better than the federal statute.[22]   Senator Allen J. Ellender feared that the new legislative proposals would intrude on state rights, and therefore care was needed to avoid undue interference in state matters.[23]

A new round of congressional hearings on several wage and hour bills began in early May 1959. George Meany, one of the first to testify on the proposed legislation, told the Senate Labor Committee, "The failure of Congress to take imaginative and courageous action on this matter has perpetuated the misery of sub-standard living conditions for millions of fellow Americans. It has weakened our domestic economy and damaged our prestige and the prestige of democracy itself—throughout the world."[24] The subsequent testimony broke no new ground. The Chamber of Commerce argued that a higher minimum wage and expanded coverage would be inflationary; representatives of the National Automobile Dealers Association argued that the proposed changes would lead to reduced service, higher prices, and the loss of jobs. Proponents of the legislation argued fairness, reduction of poverty, and equity. By a voice vote, on July 10, 1959, the Senate Labor Subcommittee voted for a $1.25 an hour minimum wage and expanded coverage.[25]

The wage increase was scheduled to increase in two steps over a fifteen-month period after enactment of the law. To further soften the impact of the proposal, the first in a long line of phased-in provisions in the bill contained different minimum wage levels for "newly covered" and "previously covered" workers. The 10 million newly covered workers would receive the current $1.00 an hour minimum wage, while presently covered workers would receive the phased-in increase. To further complicate the administration of the law, the newly covered workers were exempted from the overtime provisions of the law. Large retail and service establishments, that is, those with a sales volume exceeding $750,000 per year, would be phased in through a four-year progression of wage and hour changes.

The twin processes of "phasing in" and "exempting" injected massive complications into administration of the law. Proponents of the changes were attempting to make the proposals more palatable to the opposition. The necessity for these types of provisions also suggested that the implementation of changes in the FLSA had an effect on the economy. These effects were not well documented early in the program's history, but considerably more attention would be devoted to them over the subsequent two decades.

The year ended with the National Democratic Advisory Committee outlining its 1960 national platform. Couched in the fabric of the "shame of poverty in America," the committee argued, "At the bottom of the income scale are millions of families whose incomes are insufficient to provide even basic necessities of food, clothing, and shelter. It is a special shame upon the Republican Administration that it has turned its back upon these families who most need the help of their Government." Therefore, the committee argued, "Millions of persons work for poverty wages. For them, the minimum wage law should be extended in coverage, and the floor raised from $1 to $1.25 an hour."[26]

As the nation moved into an election year, the rhetoric relating to the minimum wage became more heated. Hubert H. Humphrey, vying for the Democratic presidential nomination, called poverty in the nation a scandal, and the vehicle for eliminating it was an increase in the minimum wage.[27] More important, the administration had staked out a conservative position that was so extreme that southern Democrats were favoring an increase in the minimum wage that went far beyond what the administration sought. The administration hung to the notion that only coverage should be extended, while the minimum wage remained constant. Southern Democrats were in full support of an increase in the wage level to at least $1.15 an hour and possibly $1.25 an hour in addition to extension in coverage. Unions, too, argued that the only real means of assisting large numbers of workers was to bring them under the law.[28]

It became clear to all that the administration's no-wage-increase position would not stand the political assault. Therefore, in late February 1960, Secretary Mitchell suggested that the administration might support an increase in the minimum wage above $1.00 an hour. The specifics of the increase were not publicized. This was the first time that the administration had deviated from its "coverage only" position.

While Senator Humphrey and many others argued the poverty reduction aspect of increases in coverage and in the minimum wage, another dimension of these changes was provided. New York City Welfare Commissioner James R. Dumpson argued that an increase in the federal *and* state minimum wage would save the State of New York at least $1 million each year in reduced welfare costs.[29]

Not to be outdone by the AFL-CIO's support of a $1.25 minimum wage, the Teamsters Union began a drive to increase the minimum wage to $1.50. Jimmy Hoffa purposely advocated a position exceeding that adopted by the AFL-CIO because the latter had expelled the Teamsters Union in 1957 for racketeering and corruption. Hoffa was under considerable pressure by the Congress and the courts to clean up the Teamsters Union, and the concern for the lowest-paid members of the labor force was undoubtedly an attempt to begin polishing the union's image. Hoffa used a Madison Square Garden rally as the stage to attack the "half-hearted" efforts by the AFL-CIO to improve the conditions for low-wage workers and to advance the Teamsters' position for the higher minimum wage.[30]

As the pace of congressional hearings gained momentum, a unique statement of support from a joint union-management group in support of the higher minimum wage occurred. Representatives from the men's clothing manufacturers and the Amalgamated Clothing Workers Union of America jointly testified before the House Labor Subcommittee that a higher minimum wage was needed to bolster purchasing power of industry workers and to prevent the ravages of low-wage cutthroat competition.[31]

As it became clear that the administration was going to support a higher minimum wage, pressure to substantiate that support intensified. Both Vice

President Richard Nixon and Secretary Mitchell were actively engaged in a consultation process with labor leaders and other public and private sector officials to determine where a compromise wage agreement could be reached. The vice president and secretary met with several major union leaders on April 7, 1960, to discuss what options there might have been for extended coverage and a higher wage level. Both sides came away from that meeting with a sense of commitment and tentative consensus about the Kennedy–Roosevelt bill.[32] In addition, the president indicated in his special message to Congress in early May, "The Secretary of Labor recently presented the Congress with information indicating that the minimum wage could be increased moderately without disruptive effects upon the economy."[33] What was left, of course, was to determine what that level should be and what coverage dimensions were appropriate.

Ironically, while it took months of intense public and private sector pressure on the administration to convince the president that some type of increase in the minimum wage was going to occur, the holdup in the process of legislative enactment came from the major sponsors of the bill. Senator Kennedy, a Democratic presidential candidate, had spent little time performing senatorial functions. Senator Everett Dirksen was critical of Kennedy's absence from Senate activity and the consequences of this absence on minimum wage legislation. Senator Dirksen complained that the legislation had been held up for over two months while Senator Kennedy had been campaigning. Dirksen observed that the presidential hopeful had "a perfect right to do that, of course, and I'm not complaining. But, it is a fact."[34] As the summer legislative calendar began bunching up, it became more and more difficult to schedule hearings. Though Senator Kennedy scheduled hearings on the bill in late May, Senator Barry Goldwater notified him that he would be unable to attend because of a conflicting schedule. A short postponement was arranged, but the Kennedy staff did arrange for hearings to begin on May 24, 1960, whether Senator Goldwater was available or not.

Kennedy's problems were not confined to members of the opposing political party. Senate majority leader Lyndon Johnson was battling with Kennedy for the Democratic presidential nomination. Senator Johnson, in his role as majority leader, controlled the hearing schedule for the full Senate. In an attempt to accommodate the customary meeting time of 12:00 noon, Senator Kennedy scheduled his subcommittee hearings at 10:00 A.M. On two occasions, May 24 and May 26, the majority leader called the Senate into "special session" at precisely 10:00 A.M. and thereby voided the subcommittee hearing process. There was evidence that the majority leader disliked the Kennedy bill and hoped that by delaying hearings he could substitute the House bill in its place. However, House action moved more slowly than Johnson had anticipated, and therefore he was compelled to permit the Kennedy subcommittee to convene hearings. The majority leader was criticized for delaying the hearings on the Kennedy bill, but—crafty politician that he was—Johnson obtained a statement from Kennedy in which Kennedy did not "blame" Johnson for the delay.[35] However, there were subsequent "early sessions" in the Senate that coincided with Kennedy subcommittee hearings that further delayed action on the bill.

House consideration moved ahead. On June 16, 1960, the Labor and Education Committee sent a bill to the House floor on a vote of 19 to 9 that extended coverage and gradually increased the minimum wage to $1.25 an hour. It took almost two weeks for the House Rules Committee to clear the bill for full House consideration. The Rules Committee did not strongly favor the bill but did move it to the House floor on the condition that other labor-supported legislation be abandoned.[36]

Before House action could occur on a bill similar to that proposed by Senator Kennedy, a coalition of conservative House members introduced and passed legislation more narrow in scope than what the administration proposed and what the labor-liberal party wanted. In the frantic throes of House debate, the liberals realized that the $1.25 minimum wage was in jeopardy. Therefore, they proposed a minimum wage of $1.15 an hour with wider coverage limits. Having the upper hand in the debate, House conservatives ignored the compromise proposals. The coalition bill became the legislation reported out of the House.

Senate consideration of the Kennedy bill proceeded at a snail's pace. Some conservative southern Democrats led by Senator Samuel Ervin tried to delay further Senate consideration of the Kennedy bill until after the election in November. Senate liberal leaders knew, however, that the aspiring presidential candidate needed a "victory" in the Senate as he moved into the fall election. Therefore, on August 18, the Senate passed legislation by a vote of 62 to 34 that provided for an extension of coverage and a minimum wage of $1.25 an hour. Democrats obtained the principle of coverage of retail and service employees, but they had to explicitly exempt employees of hotels, restaurants, automobile dealers, and farm implement dealers to gain sufficient support for bill passage.

The differences between the House and Senate bills required a conference before submission to the president for signature. The *New York Times* headlines on August 31, 1960, read: "Wage Conferees Clash and Quit; Bill Seems Dead." The House leadership was adamant that the only version that could successfully make it through the House on a vote was the House version. Senator Kennedy argued that the House version was not progress and that if necessary there should be a delay and reconsideration in January. The presidential aspirant did not want a stalemated conference, but the differences were too great. Congress adjourned in September with the bill still in the Conference Committee, and the legislation died.

In late September 1960, the two presidential contenders clashed in what has now become known as the first televised presidential debate that had a material impact on the public's perception of the candidates. During the debate, Senator Kennedy was pressed by news commentator Sander Vanocur about the senator's inability to push through minimum wage legislation even though the Democrats had firm control of both houses of Congress. The senator argued that the major difficulty was that the president opposed the legislation and that it was very difficult to pass legislation that the president flatly opposed and threatened to veto.[37] Whether the public connected the senator's leadership potential with his success in the Senate can only be judged by the results of the November election.

The year ended with a new president-elect and a new agenda for the nation's economic and social programs. President-elect Kennedy quickly reiterated his support for expanded coverage of the minimum wage and an increase to $1.25 an hour. He met with Representative Adam Clayton Powell, who as chairman of the House Education and Labor Committee had jurisdiction over minimum wage legislation. Both men agreed that the highest priority legislation was that involving the minimum wage and aid to American schools.[38] To regain the initiative on minimum wage legislation, Republican minority leader Everett Dirksen introduced a bill on January 9, 1961, that provided for a $1.10 minimum wage and "some" additional coverage.[39] The Senate minority leader knew that the Senate had approved the $1.25 an hour measure late in 1960 and that the House provision was $1.15 an hour. With a new president strongly supporting the $1.25 an hour bill, it was particularly surprising to see Dirksen's "low ball" proposal. However, Senator Ellender, a Louisiana Democrat, vowed to fight the new president on any increase in the minimum wage. Senator Ellender took the position that workers deserved a "fair wage" and that if they believed they were not receiving a fair wage, they could organize and seek wage increases through the collective bargaining mechanism.[40]

On February 2, President Kennedy submitted a wide-ranging economic recovery program that included a proposal to increase both the wage rate and coverage of the FLSA in line with the Senate-passed version of the legislation passed in 1960. His proposal provided for a two-step increase, with an immediate increase to $1.15 an hour and a subsequent increase within two years to $1.25 an hour. The coverage expansion provisions were primarily in retail trade and services. Since there was considerable controversy over what impact an increase in the minimum wage might have on U.S. trade competitiveness, the president pointed out that the new coverage provisions were generally in areas that did not affect foreign trade activity.[41] Concurrent with the president's statement, Representative Seymour Halpern, a New York Republican, introduced a bill in the House that would increase the minimum wage to $1.25 an hour and expand coverage by about 8 million workers.[42]

To support the Halpern bill and begin movement in the House, President Kennedy sent a letter to Sam Rayburn, Speaker of the House, noting that the proposed increase was primarily in line with cost-of-living changes and increases in worker productivity. The president argued, "Substandard wages lead necessarily to substandard living conditions, hardship and distress."[43] The specific administration proposal was embodied in a bill introduced by Representative James Roosevelt, a California Democrat. To reduce resistance to the wage increase provisions, the administration proposal was for a three-tier phase-in. The minimum wage would increase to $1.15 an hour the first year, $1.20 an hour the second year, and $1.25 the third year. Newly covered workers would experience a $1.00/$1.15/$1.25 an hour increase over the three-year period.

Recognizing that House support for the administration proposal was very close, Adam Clayton Powell, chairman of the House Education and Labor Committee, exercised his prerogatives to restructure leadership of several critical subcommittees. Importantly for the FLSA-proposed amendments, Representative Phil M. Landrum, a conservative Democrat from Georgia, was replaced by Representative James Roosevelt to head the Labor Standards Subcommittee. Congressman Roosevelt was known to support the administration proposal, and therefore Congressman Powell could be assured that timely hearings would occur on the bill.

Though the legislative machinery in the House was "well oiled" by House liberals, the administration proposal was quickly attacked not by Republicans but by House liberals and the AFL–CIO. Upon hearing the administration's specific proposals, Representative Powell vowed to fight to broaden its provisions. William F. Schnitzler, secretary-treasurer of the AFL–CIO, termed the proposal as "somewhat disappointing." In response to the criticism by individuals sympathetic to expansion of the FLSA protections, Labor Secretary Goldberg argued that the administration was striving for "the possible, the attainable, rather than the ideal."[44] Conservative opposition in the House began their attacks that the administration proposal would be inflationary, increase unemployment, and reduce the nation's international competitiveness.

Though House leaders wanted to expand the administration's proposal, what occurred was a delimiting of the coverage provisions and a reduction in the implementation schedule from three years to two years. The administration opposed both changes in the bill, but passage by the House Labor and Education Committee and the anticipation of a full House vote within a week placed the administration in a difficult bargaining position. More important, however, there was increasing sentiment in the House to amend the committee bill with even more restrictive language. When debate opened on the House floor, an amendment was proposed by Representatives William H. Ayes and Paul Kitchin to increase the minimum wage to $1.15 an hour and expand coverage to about 1.4 million additional workers. The Ayes–Kitchin amendment gained strong support in the House by Republicans and conservative Democrats. The administration realized that it was in deep trouble in the House and began a process of reducing coverage in the hopes of maintaining the proposed $1.25 minimum wage level. The president used a news conference to engender support for his proposal by calling the $1.25 minimum wage a "very minimum wage." In a further effort to salvage the proposal, Representative Carl Albert proposed an amendment that would have required, among other things, that service and retail enterprises doing $1 million or more business each year would have to have at least 25 percent of that business flowing in interstate commerce before they would be subject to the FLSA provisions. This amendment was defeated.

By March 24, 1961, the new president's honeymoon with the Congress was over. A one-vote margin—186 to 185—resulted in the approval by the House of the Ayes-Kitchin bill with the $1.15 minimum wage and expansion of coverage to about 1.4 million additional workers. The coalition of Republicans and southern Democrats had handed the president his first defeat on one of the major initiatives he had proposed in the 1960 campaign. The administration proposal's fate now rested in the hands of the Senate.

Senate leadership had purposely waited on the House bill. While Senate majority leader Mike Mansfield expressed guarded optimism that the Senate would pass a bill substantially in line with the administration proposal, many believed that the House defeat portended a weaker program. It was unlikely that the Senate would approve the extensive coverage expansion proposed by the administration that would weaken the bargaining position of the administration in the Senate-House Conference. However, Vice President Lyndon Johnson remained confident when he said that "we are going to enact a good minimum wage bill with a $1.25 figure" that after a Senate-House Conference "will be more in keeping with Kennedy's recommendations."[45]

On April 11, the Senate Labor and Public Works Committee passed a bill very close to the original administration proposal. However, there were several members of the committee who expressed displeasure with the bill and promised to offer amendments on the Senate floor. The Senate was in no mood to compromise on this critical legislation and after minimal debate rejected the amendments offered on the floor and passed the administration bill virtually intact by a vote of 65 to 28. Fourteen Republicans joined fifty-one Democrats in the final Senate vote.

There were expectations that the conference between the Senate and House would be hard-fought and long. To the surprise of everyone, neither prognostication came true. The conference was short, and what emerged was a bill very close to what the Senate had passed. Though Senator Dirksen lambasted his colleagues on the dire vagaries of passing the conference bill, it nonetheless passed by almost an identical vote to the original Senate bill—64 to 28. It took only an hour's debate in the House before the conference bill came up for a vote. It passed by a wider margin—230 to 196—than most had expected. Therefore, less than six weeks after the House had given the new president his first legislative defeat, the entire Congress gave him one of his sweetest victories. The president was expected to sign the bill into law immediately, and it would take effect just before Labor Day.

The 1961 FLSA amendments were decidedly more complicated than those of previous legislative changes. For workers covered prior to 1961, wages would increase to $1.15 an hour 120 days after the law was enacted. Two years later, this group of workers would receive minimum wage protection to $1.25 an hour. Newly covered workers, most of them in retail trade, services, and construction, would receive wage increases on a delayed schedule. The 3.6 million newly covered workers in retail establishments grossing more than $1 million in annual business of which 25 percent moved through interstate commerce, large gasoline companies, construction companies, and transit companies would receive $1.00 an hour minimum wage protection when the rates became effective in September 1961. Newly covered workers would be required to receive overtime pay for hours in excess of forty-four, two years after the law went into effect. One year later, these workers would receive an increase to $1.15 an hour and overtime rates applying after forty-two hours of work. Four years after the law went into effect, newly covered workers would receive $1.25 an hour and overtime after forty hours of work.

A variety of factors accounted for the change in voting patterns related to the conference bill. Of no small importance, administration strategists had obtained legislation that would result in a wage increase for several million workers in September 1964, two months before the next presidential election. In a more parochial sense, the Democratic leadership in the House enticed southern Democrats over to the administration side by eliminating laundry workers and cotton-gin employees from the compromise conference bill. This sweetner was enough to move about thirty southern Democratic votes from the opposition position.

Two days after congressional passage, President Kennedy signed the bill into law on May 5, 1961. While it gave him "great satisfaction," he observed that "this doesn't finish this job."[46] In his news conference on May 6, he was asked about the exclusion of laundry workers from the coverage provisions of the law. The president had made protection of these workers one of his campaign issues in the 1960 election. He expressed concern and regret that they had been dropped from the coverage provisions but observed that the political and economic realities had made coverage currently infeasible. However, he noted, "It's a hard fight, but I am hopeful that we'll come back to them [laundry workers] and get those groups covered."[47]

When the new provisions went into effect on September 3, 1961, the president had, by executive order, included federal workers in the covered category. State and local government employees were still exempt under statutory provisions. The president issued a statement on September 3 acknowledging the importance of this new law. He closed by stating:

I congratulate the Congress and all men of goodwill who worked so hard for this social gain. All fair employers know that a minimum wage does not harm the economy, but on the contrary helps eliminate unfair competition. In the months and years to come, I can see important gains for the whole economy resulting from this improvement to the living and working standards of our people.[48]

Thus, when the Fair Labor Standards Amendments of 1961 were approved by President Kennedy and became effective on September 3, 1961, they increased the $1.00 per hour minimum wage for workers covered by the law before September 3, 1961, to $1.15 per hour. The latter rate would apply until September 3, 1963, when a minimum wage of $1.25 per hour would apply. For the 3.6 million newly covered workers, a minimum wage of $1.00 per hour became effective on September 3, 1961. On September 3, 1964, the newly covered category minimum wage would increase to $1.15 per hour. One year later, the newly covered workers would receive a rate of $1.25 per hour.

The expansion of coverage—the first significant expansion since 1938—to about 3.6 million new workers was focused primarily in the retail trades and the service sector—2.2 million workers. However, the amendments added six new exemptions from both the overtime and minimum wage provisions in activities involved in the handling and processing of agricultural products. These six exemptions involved cotton ginning, shade-grown tobacco processing, small country elevators, livestock auction operations, transportation of fresh fruit and vegetables and fruit and vegetable harvesters, and homeworkers making holly wreaths.[49]

The 1961 amendments attempted to clarify the application of the FLSA to fishing operations and the seafood industry. The amendments extended minimum wage coverage to seamen on American vessels. However, the exemption for fishing operations was split in two. "Onshore" activities such as processing, marketing, distributing, and other handling activities were covered, while "offshore" activities were exempt.

The 1961 amendments provided for a 15 percent increase in wage order rates for Puerto Rico and the Virgin Islands, effective November 3, 1961, or one year after the most recent applicable wage order rate. There were other provisions concerning specific sections of the law relating to record keeping, redefinition of the term wage, adding "full-time students in retail and service establishments" to the Section 14 special minimum wage program, and the development of several special economic studies related to the effects of the 1961 amendments.

The 1961 amendments made no change in basic overtime provisions or child labor provisions. There was a phase-in of overtime hours requirements for newly covered workers. The phase-in was a three-year 44-42-40 reduction in which all newly covered workers would be covered by the forty-hour standard by September 3, 1965.

The 1961 amendments imposed new compliance problems on employers and enforcement problems on the Wage and Hour Division. The amendments were viewed as a major overhaul of the FLSA, but they turned out to be merely a prelude to the 1966 amendments. Before the Congress legislated new and higher minimum wages in 1966, another piece of legislation captured the attention of legislators.

THE EQUAL PAY ACT

There is a long history of interest and concern about pay equity that has been raised by the Women's Bureau and a variety of women's groups. Various pieces of legislation addressing this concern have been introduced in the Congress since 1945. Not until 1956, however, did a president explicitly say that legislation should be passed that addressed this issue. On January 5, 1956, President Eisenhower challenged the Congress to pass legislation by postulating that "legislation to apply the principle of equal pay for equal work without discrimination because of sex is a matter of simple justice."[50] He asked the Congress to enact legislation to accomplish this end. It would take the Congress seven years to bring this challenge to fruition.

While attention is focused primarily on the wage, hour, and child labor provisions of the FLSA, an important amendment to the FLSA in 1963 established the fundamental principle of pay equity. Entitled the Equal Pay Act, this amendment to the FLSA prohibited discrimination in pay based on the gender of the worker. The Wage and Hour Division began enforcing the Equal Pay Act on June 11, 1964. Firms with collective bargaining agreements were provided an additional year to come into conformity with the new law.

Though the philosophy underlying equal pay was widely accepted, the Equal Pay Act became a stepchild of the FLSA. It received some attention in the three annual Section 4(d) reports immediately after enactment in 1963 but then almost disappeared for several years. There is no mention of the enforcement activity related to the Equal Pay Act in the annual reports for FY 1966 through FY 1969. One can assume that compliance officers were conscious of equal pay requirements, but it is unclear what level of enforcement actually occurred.

Very early in the administration of the Equal Pay Act, field compliance staff were asked to forward to the national office information they obtained about implementation of the law. While they were encouraged to submit both positive and negative information, overall there were few submissions. What information was received was interesting but apparently inadequate to judge the effectiveness of the act in closing pay differentials. Anecdotal information was provided showing that sex-determined wage differentials were not atypical. There were clear examples of contract language in collective bargaining agreements after the additional time given for adjustment that put similarly situated men and women in different pay structures. Equal pay for equal work was now the law of the land. However, it was unclear what the new law did to rectify a long-standing problem of sex-based pay inequities. Over thirty years later, the situation remains as unsettled as it was in 1963.

THE 1966 FLSA AMENDMENTS

The phased-in increases in the federal minimum wage provided a respite for those who were opposed to expansions in this program. There was now a statute that would show periodic wage gains for covered segments of the workforce until at least 1964. Therefore, attention was focused away from this program to other items on the president's social and economic agenda. However, outside of Congress, there were those who believed the president when he said that the 1961 amendments did not "finish the job." Early in 1962, the AFL–CIO Executive Council strongly recommended an increase in the federal minimum wage to $1.50 an hour. If that increase was not possible, the council suggested that the timetable for increases provided for in the 1961 amendments be speeded up and that coverage to workers in the hotel, restaurant, and laundry industries be provided.

For the most part, these exhortations fell on politically deaf ears. The administration and the Congress were weary of the long battle over these issues, and there was little evidence that either one was prepared to propose new initiatives in this program. President Kennedy praised the Congress for the work they had done to increase the minimum wage and extend coverage as well as legislation related to reducing juvenile delinquency, assisting areas of high unemployment, improving the drug program, overhauling the welfare system, and so forth.[51] Part of the increases provided for in the 1961 amendments were needed before pressure would be felt to go even further.

The next major initiative in the minimum wage legislative process occurred in early 1964. Secretary of Labor W. Willard Wirtz urged, as part of President Johnson's War on Poverty, the extension of coverage to more than 2.6 million American workers. These workers were precisely the ones who had been denied protection in the 1961 amendments—hotel, restaurant, and laundry workers. The secretary argued that "special interest pressures" had resulted in the denial of protection to these workers and that now it was in the "national economic interest" to bring these workers under the law. He estimated that bringing these workers into coverage would provide over $80 million a year in increased spending power to the lowest-income groups in the economy.[52]

During this attempt to reopen the legislative process, Secretary Wirtz did not recommend further increases in the minimum wage. However, not to be outdone on its turf, the AFL–CIO quickly proposed not only extending coverage to more workers but increasing the minimum wage to $2.00 an hour.[53] Within three months, there was a House bill to increase the minimum wage. Representative William Ryan introduced a bill on May 12, 1964 that would increase the federal minimum wage to $1.50 an hour. The proposal was characterized as an effort to help reduce poverty.[54]

Early in 1965, Congressman Adam Clayton Powell, chairman of the House Education and Labor Committee, promised to introduce legislation to increase the minimum wage to $2.00 an hour. This promise was precisely aligned with the position of the AFL–CIO. However, in an attempt to go even further, Chairman Powell proposed that the standard workweek be reduced to thirty-two hours.

The AFL–CIO had urged a 35-hour workweek. In its winter meeting in Bal Harbour, Florida, the AFL–CIO staked out a four-part labor agenda including the $2.00 an hour minimum wage, the thirty-five hour standard workweek, extension of coverage to all workers in interstate commerce, and double time for overtime work. George Meany argued that the existing minimum wage of $1.25 an hour was below the government's self-proclaimed family poverty wage and therefore a higher minimum wage did not amount to "dreaming, being radical or unreasonable."[55]

The administration was not prepared to buy into the higher minimum wage proposal or the shorter workweek. However, Secretary Wirtz did indicate that the administration supported the extension of coverage—on a more limited basis—and the double time for overtime proposal. The first "break" in the administration's position came in a speech by Vice President Hubert Humphrey. He suggested on April 13 that "I am quite confident there will be an adjustment [in the minimum wage] and that it will be upward." He went on to argue that "minimum wage improvement is good for the country."[56] There could be little question that the vice president knew exactly what he was saying and what the public reaction would be to his remarks. Nevertheless, other administration sources quickly argued that the president had not made a commitment to increase the minimum wage and that the vice president's comments were "misinterpreted as a hint that a minimum wage increase was coming."[57]

The issue had now been broached, and it wasn't long before further corroboration of the administration's position occurred. Secretary Wirtz spoke to the International Ladies Garment Workers Union (ILGWV) on May 13 and argued that it was "part of his job . . . to seek improvements in the present minimum wage of $1.25 an hour."[58] To help the secretary advance a proposal for increasing the minimum wage, David Dubinsky, president of the ILGWU, provided Wirtz with a convention resolution supporting a $2.00 an hour federal minimum wage. Dubinsky challenged the secretary to be the union's "advocate" and carry this message to the president. Two days later, the secretary spoke to the Utility Workers Union Convention on the same issue. He argued that "the government is supporting an income level of $2,500 a year at the same time we are fighting a war on poverty where we define the family income as below $3,000." The secretary suggested parenthetically that "something is out of gear here."[59]

While this change in position was taking place, attention was diverted to the Taft–Hartley Act's Section 14(b) permitting states to enact right-to-work statutes. To repay his political debt to the labor movement for their support in the November 1964 election, the president attempted to accommodate their concerns by proposing repeal of Section 14(b). Since this issue was much closer to home for organized labor and directly affected their day-to-day activities, it monopolized their attention.

The president finally showed a part of his hand in his labor message to Congress on May 18, 1965. He did not propose a specific increase in the minimum wage but argued, "The question is not whether the minimum wage should be increased but when and by how much."[60] He then tossed the issue to the Congress and charged them with carefully considering the impacts of a higher minimum wage on various labor force groups, costs, and prices. The president did reaffirm his support for the expansion of coverage and the payment of double time for "excessive" overtime. The administration supported double time only for hours worked in excess of forty-eight per week.

It proved difficult to obtain a specific minimum wage proposal from the administration. Secretary Wirtz, testifying before the Senate Labor Committee in July, argued that the president wanted Congress to "study" the impacts of a change in the minimum wage and further that the administration had no position on an increase in the minimum wage "at this time." The secretary urged the Congress to extend coverage of the existing law. He argued that workers did not want or need public assistance or charity. These workers were perfectly capable of taking care of their affairs, but "[w]hat they need is a living wage for the head of the family."[61]

In early August, the first major congressional action occurred. A House Labor Subcommittee approved a bill to, among other things, increase the minimum wage to $1.75 an hour by 1968. In addition to the wage increase, the bill provided coverage, for the first time, to farmworkers including migrant laborers. A separate, lower wage scale would apply to these newly covered workers.

On August 12, the House Education and Labor Committee approved the extension of coverage to over 6 million additional workers. The administration proposal had provided coverage for about 4.6 million additional workers. This bill provided coverage for the several categories of workers that the late President Kennedy had hoped to bring under protection of the law, including laundry workers, hotel and motel employees, restaurant workers, seasonal employees in resorts, employees in motion picture theaters, among others. The full committee removed employees in seafood processing plants, fisheries, and small weekly newspapers who had been included in the subcommittee bill.

Committee Republicans opposed the bill and indicated that they planned to offer amendments to increase the minimum wage to $1.60 an hour. Republican opposition to the committee bill was summed up by Representative Acres, who called it "ridiculous." He expressed his sense of frustration and disagreement by suggesting that if the House passed the bill, he hoped that the Senate would exercise greater "wisdom." In a surprise move, the full committee rejected a provision introduced by Congressman James O'Hara to require double time for overtime hours in excess of forty-nine hours in a workweek. Employer groups testified that the provision would not accomplish the employment "spreading" objectives that supporters suggested but would increase labor costs. Committee members believed that before a provision of this type was enacted, a study of its effects was needed.

On August 18, the House Labor and Education Committee completed action on the bill and passed it on a voice vote. Since the bill's provisions went far beyond those supported by the administration, Chairman Powell noted with some sense of reticence, "This should show that we're not just a rubber stamp for the President."[62] Importantly, the AFL–CIO revised its position on the minimum wage, and George Meany indicated that he would work to seek passage of the $1.75 an hour level adopted by the House Committee. However, the committee bill was known to be too much for the administration to swallow, and therefore it was never taken up by the full House. The session ended without further consideration of the bill.

Early in January 1966, the House Committee began consideration of another bill that would be more responsive to the administration's position. In his State of the Union message, President Johnson again alluded to improving conditions "for those who labor" by expanding "minimum wage benefits." He did not provide any indication about the level of the minimum wage he would consider acceptable but, rather, indicated that the Congress should carefully consider the effects of higher minimum wage levels. One of those effects related to their impacts on prices. The administration had a series of wage "guideposts" in place to provide unions and industry with information about acceptable levels of wage increases. Secretary Wirtz noted that the $1.75 minimum wage level would exceed the guidepost standard but that a $1.50 an hour level would not be inflationary. This was clear evidence of the increase that the administration would consider acceptable.

To further complicate the policy development process, the Council of Economic Advisors (CEA) indicated support for an increase in the minimum wage to $1.40 immediately, with a further increase to $1.60 an hour in 1970. This position infuriated the AFL–CIO. The federation had retreated from its $2.00 an hour minimum wage and accepted the $1.75 an hour proposal by the House Committee. In addition, they had lost in the Senate on repeal of Taft–Hartley Section 14(b). Therefore, they felt they had compromised enough and the Council of Economic Advisors' position rubbed them the wrong way. In his traditional feisty fashion, George Meany threw down the gauntlet and indicated that he was prepared to fight the administration if the CEA position was adopted. He indicated that the AFL–CIO was not "looking for a war with anyone," but if "anybody wants a war with us, that's different."[63] The "war" turned out to be little more than the exchange of empty rhetoric. In less than two weeks, the Congress, the AFL–CIO, and the administration were in agreement that a two-step increase to $1.60 an hour would be acceptable if implemented over a twenty-three-month period. Moving quickly to capture the momentum of the moment, the House Labor Subcommittee passed a bill incorporating the wage and coverage provisions adopted by the AFL–CIO, the Congress, and the president. However, after full committee action, the House Rules Committee held the bill and refused to clear it for full House consideration. Finally, in mid-May, the Rules Committee voted the bill out, and full House consideration began.

On May 26, the House passed a bill expanding coverage, raising the minimum wage in two steps to $1.60 an hour in 1969. The House bill, while breaking some new ground, was viewed as a defeat for the administration and organized labor. While the bill extended coverage to farm labor for the first time, it also provided for a delay of one year in the attainment of the $1.60 an hour rate. The delay caught all observers in and out of Congress by surprise. There was solid expectation that the $1.60 an hour level would be reached in 1968 because all major participants had struck a bargain with this provision in it. However, in what was an apparent gaffe by Representative Powell, the delay was inserted in the bill.

Representative Thomas Morris offered an amendment to the House bill, postponing the increase from the agreed-upon February 1, 1968, to *two* years later, that is, 1970. In response to this proposed amendment, to everyone's surprise, Congressman Powell indicated that a one-year delay, might be considered, but not a two year delay. Representative Acres immediately offered an amendment for a one-year delay and it was passed by the House. The entire House leadership, including Speaker John McCormack, was stunned by the move and could not reverse a position taken by Congressman Powell, though there was apparent confusion about what the Morris amendment provided. Though Chairman Powell's actions gave tacit support for the one-year extension, he voted against it on the House floor. Opponents of the bill had extracted a concession from the House supporters that no one expected and in all likelihood was not needed for passage.

The action then moved to the Senate. Senate leaders saw the problem in the House bill and immediately reestablished February 1, 1968, as the date for the $1.60 level. A bill containing the exact provisions agreed upon by the administration and organized labor was passed by the Senate Labor and Public Welfare Subcommittee on July 15, 1966. A month later, the full committee passed a bill by a vote of 15 to 0 that kept intact the agreed-upon provisions. On August 26, the Senate passed a bill by a vote of 57 to 17 containing all the substantive provisions supported by the administration. The major difference between the Senate and House bills was the implementation date for the $1.60 an hour minimum wage.

Senate and House conferees began immediate consideration of the two bills. To no one's surprise, the Conference Committee produced a bill that contained most of the provisions of the administration's proposal. The effective date for the $1.60 an hour minimum wage was February 1, 1968. Coverage expansion to farmworkers, employees in hotels, motels, and restaurants, laundries, and retail establishments was provided in the compromise bill that resulted in initial protection to about 8 million workers.

President Johnson succeeded in getting everything he wanted in the Conference Committee bill. He wanted to sign the bill on Labor Day, 1966. However, House opponents of the bill were successful in denying the president this media event by delaying final House action until after Labor Day. With the Labor Day ceremony no longer possible, work in conference was delayed until September 1. On that day, conferees agreed on a completed bill and it was referred back to both houses of Congress for final passage.

House Republicans attempted to delay final approval of the bill by attempting to reestablish the 1969 implementation date for the $1.60 an hour level. It took strong administration pressure to squeak out a 20-vote victory defeating the "delay" proposal. With all other provisions essentially in agreement, the House passed the bill in a lopsided vote of 259 to 89. A week later, September 14, 1966, the Senate cleared the final bill by a vote of 55 to 38, and it was sent to the president for signature. With apparent personal pleasure, President Johnson signed the bill into law on September 23, 1966. During the signing ceremony, the president took the liberty of commenting on his beliefs about minimum wage programs. He noted that minimum wage legislation helps both workers and business. He argued, "The straight fact is that a fair minimum wage doesn't hurt business in any way. If a businessman can't do well with this minimum wage in our booming economy that we have today," he said, "perhaps he might not be just a good businessman."[64] Thus ended a legislative struggle that had started almost four years earlier.

In summary, the 1966 amendments to the FLSA increased the minimum wage to $1.40 per hour on February 1, 1967, and to $1.60 per hour one year later. When the $1.40 per hour rate became effective, an estimated 3.7 million previously covered workers received wage increases totaling $800 million annually. Newly covered workers—about 1 million—received $304 million additional wages annually.

Most significant in the 1966 amendments was the expansion of coverage. The amendments brought over 9 million additional workers into coverage. The amendments extended coverage beyond the private sector to include certain federal government workers—wage board employees and those paid from nonappropriated funds—and certain state and local government employees—local hospitals and educational institutions.

The 9.1 million newly covered workers were primarily located in public and private hospitals and nursing institutions—2.0 million; retail trade—1.7 million; and public and private educational institutions—1.3 million. The remaining 4 million were primarily in the construction industry, laundry workers, and federal government wage board and nonappropriated funds employees.[65]

In addition to the changes described above, the 1966 amendments mandated three significant studies. Section 605 of the 1966 amendments mandated a study of wage payments to handicapped clients in sheltered workshops. Section 603 examined the practices of overtime payments for work in excess of forty hours per week and the implications of these practices in relation to new job opportunities. The results of these studies were summarized in the 1968 *Annual Report* to Congress dated January 31, 1968.

The third study mandated by Section 606 directed the secretary to provide legislative recommendations to the Congress based on a study of the character of employment discrimination. The secretary's recommendations formed the basis for the Age Discrimination in Employment Act (ADEA) of 1967. The act is the basis for the federal government's increased interest in the relationships between a worker's age and his or her ability to perform work and the role of age in hiring and promotion decisions. In the early years, the Department of Labor had the enforcement responsibilities under the ADEA and submitted the annual report to Congress provided for in the statute. In 1979, these responsibilities were transferred to the Equal Employment Opportunity Commission (EEOC), where they reside today. The department did retain the Section 5 responsibilities related to a program of research under the act.

The Department of Labor conducted a wide range of impact studies related to the 1961 and 1966 amendments. There were wage bill impacts of relatively small size, but there were few, if any, disemployment effects identified in these studies. Invariably, the studies described the expansion of employment rather than the unemployment effects routinely described in studies during the 1970s and 1980s. In addition, the mandated studies found little, if any, generalized price impacts that could be attributed to the minimum wage program.

As with the 1961 amendments, the 1966 amendments phased in newly covered workers. Therefore, the last minimum wage increase resulting from the 1966 amendments was on February 1, 1970, when the last contingent of newly covered workers received a mandated increase. Importantly, this contingent of newly covered workers had a mandated minimum wage of $1.45 per hour, while previously covered workers received $1.60 per hour.

Within one decade, the basic minimum wage rose 60 percent—from $1.00 per hour to $1.60 per hour—and the number of covered workers increased from about 24 million workers to more than 40 million workers—a 67 percent increase. In addition, the decade of the 1960s ushered in the emphasis on assessment of impact. The studies, while extensive, lacked the rigor found in the studies of the 1970s.

MINIMUM WAGE IMPACT ASSESSMENT

Reading the literature, one gets the distinct impression that minimum wage programs are powerful tools for economic change. Opponents of these programs argue that minimum wage programs produce higher crime rates for youth, increase nepotism; destroy jobs; increase unemployment; reduce training opportunities; reduce international competitiveness; and cause a variety of other economic, social, and psychological maladies. Proponents argue that these programs improve the distribution of income, reduce poverty, impart equity to the workforce, stimulate economic growth, enhance technological change, and produce many other laudable achievements. One is struck by the scope and depth of these purported impacts of initiating or changing the minimum wage. How can a program that directly affects less than two percent of the population —about 4 percent of the workforce—have such pervasive impacts? Do increases in the minimum wage really increase nepotism? Does the minimum wage really reduce poverty? Some scholars and policy officials seem to think so and are prepared to testify in any forum one gives them that the impacts are real.

In some ways, it seems that more impacts are attributed to this program than could reasonably be expected—positive and negative. This is not to suggest that the program is innocuous, that it has no impacts, or that it can be ignored. But the perspective to be maintained is that it is *one* of a variety of market intervention strategies that is purported to, on balance, provide more economic and social benefits than economic and social costs.

If one were to date the beginning of the serious empirical investigation of minimum wage effects on employment and unemployment, it would be 1964. In that year, two prominent economists provided a direct frontal attack on the minimum wage program. The weight of their reputations and academic positions provided the spark needed by opponents to launch an attack that accelerated into the 1970s. Speaking at the National Industrial Conference Board, Jules Backman, research professor of economics at New York University, argued that "any increase in the minimum wage would increase joblessness by pricing out of the market workers at the 'lower end' of the wage pyramid where unemployment is heaviest."[66] Three weeks later, George Stigler, president of the American Economic Association and professor of economics and business at the University of Chicago, argued for "the removal of minimum wage rates for unskilled young workers—a group . . . [who] should be employed at beginning low salaries."[67] He further argued that "the basic method of decreasing discrimination in the market is to offer a class of workers at bargain rates."[68] The professional and academic weight of these two prominent economists began the process of examining these programs in a systematic manner. After all, economists of this stature could not be "wrong," and therefore all that was needed was a method of verifying empirically what was then "known" to be true.

The opposition to minimum wage programs vehemently argued that *any* change in the minimum wage would increase prices and unemployment. The specter of firms being forced out of business, shorter work hours and lower income levels, and a variety of similarly negative consequences were described. In most cases, there was little, if any, empirical support provided for these views, but the suggestion was that these outcomes were common knowledge, certain, and didn't need verification. Proponents of increases in the minimum wage had consistently argued the contrary positions with, in most cases, equally inadequate empirical support. However, after the 1961 FLSA amendments had increased the minimum wage to $1.15 an hour, Secretary Arthur Goldberg reported about six months after that increase had gone into effect that "last September's increases in the Federal minimum wage did not create unemployment or price rises as some opponents of the measure had feared."[69] On the contrary, he argued that unemployment had decreased subsequent to the September increase, and the modest price changes could not be linked to the minimum wage increase. He argued, "The principal measurable effect of the 1961 amendments was to increase wages for a substantial number of workers in certain relatively low-wage industries."[70]

Somewhat later, looking at four changes in the minimum wage between 1961 and 1965, Secretary Wirtz attempted to summarize the results of studies focusing on these changes and changes in earlier years. He concluded by arguing:

> There is no way of determining definitively what the employment and unemployment record would have been if there had been no changes in the Fair Labor Standards Act. A review, however, of all available evidence reveals no indication whatsoever that there would have been more jobs or that unemployment would have been reduced further if the coverage of the Act had not been extended as it was or if the statutory level had not been increased. This evidence points strongly, on the contrary, to the conclusion that these changes had no adverse effect on employment.[71]

The secretary also observed that every change in the minimum wage since 1938 was accompanied by increases in employment generally, and importantly, lower-paid occupations had even greater employment growth. What is left unsaid is whether employment would have increased even more had the FLSA provisions not existed. This aspect of the "quantitative debate" assumes greater importance in the next decade.

PROGRAM COMPLIANCE

Each year subsequent to 1956, the number of investigations conducted, the amounts of back wages found due, and the amounts of agreements to pay all increased. As the decade began, complaints became more important as the vehicle for determining investigations. In 1960, "[o]ver 40 percent of the time spent on all investigations this year was devoted to complaints alleging violations. While every fourth investigation was based on a complaint, over half the total monetary underpayments were found in complaint investigations. Complaints, therefore, were the most fruitful source of information pinpointing noncompliance."[72]

The number of investigations decreased in FY 1960—45,729 completed in 1960, as compared with 54,916 in FY 1959—but the findings were substantially higher. Back wages found due were $8,663,703 in FY 1960, as compared with $6,937,265 the previous year. Underpayments of overtime were $19,369,611 in FY 1960, as compared with $15,465,851 in FY 1959. In short, the decade started with a substantial increase in "results" that established the impetus for further increases.

The number of employees owed unpaid wages resulting from minimum wage violations was about 62,253 in 1960. About 155,746 employees were due back wages due to overtime compensation violations. The monetary amounts of underpayment were about $8.7 million and $19.4 million for minimum wage and overtime compensation violations, respectively. In general terms, each *compliance action* produced about $614 in monetary findings of unpaid wages.

By the end of the decade—1969—about 72,520 compliance actions yielded 207,234 employees due $27.5 million because of minimum wage violations. About 308,306 employees were due $55 million because of overtime compensation violations. The average compliance action produced about $1,138 in monetary findings. Each employee underpaid minimum wages in 1960 was found due about $139. In 1969, the average employee was owed unpaid wages of about $136. The average employee underpaid overtime compensation in 1960 was due about $124. In 1969, the same category of employee was found underpaid by about $178.

Unfortunately, the data relating to employer agreements to pay are not available for the period from 1965 to 1972. However, the data for the first five years of the 1960s may suggest the overall pattern for the decade. In 1960, employers agreed to pay about 119,373 employees about $13.9 million for minimum wage and overtime compensation violations. In 1964, employers agreed to pay about 189,048 employees over $22.7 million. These agreements to pay provided each underpaid employee between $115 and $120 in back wage compensation.

An important perspective to keep in mind about these data relates to the number of compliance officers conducting investigations. In 1960, there were about 656 budgeted COs in the Wage and Hour Division. In 1969, there were approximately twice as many COs. On the average, each CO found over $42,640 unpaid back wages due in 1960. In 1969, each CO found over $68,864 in unpaid back wages. Therefore, while the number of COs increased about 82 percent over the decade, compliance actions increased by 59 percent and unpaid back wages found due increased about 194 percent. These data suggest that a larger number of COs were able to complete higher-quality investigations that produced substantially higher back wages due both in the aggregate and on the basis of the average CO.[73]

CONCLUSION

The decade of the 1960s witnessed increasing pressure opposing the minimum wage program, in general, and increases in wage level or coverage, in particular. There was increasing concern about the impacts of changes in this program on the economy, whether the program was achieving its purported goals, and whether some "other" measure might be more effective in addressing the plight of low-wage workers. These concerns were only to intensify in the next two decades and form the focus of attention in the program's golden anniversary year. It is fair to conclude that much more is known about the program and its impacts than was known two or three decades ago, but it is also fair to conclude that there is wide disagreement about what all of the relationships and interrelationships mean. The next decade will attempt to address these issues in more empirical terms.

NOTES

1. *Economic Report of the President*, transmitted to the Congress in February 1970 (Washington, D.C.: U.S. Government Printing Office, 1970), Tables C-7 and C-8.

2. Ibid., table C-27.

3. Ibid., table C-28.

4. Ibid., table C-29.

5. Ibid., table C-34.

6. *Employment and Training Report of the President*, transmitted to the Congress in 1982 (Washington, D.C.: U.S. Government Printing Office, 1982), Table G-8.

7. U.S. Department of Labor, Wage and Hour and Public Contracts Divisions, *Annual Report*, Fiscal year 1969, Transmitted to the Congress on January 14, 1969, Washington, D.C.: Government Printing Office, 1969, p. 1.

8. Ibid.

9. U.S. Department of Labor, Wage and Hour and Public Contracts Divisions, *Annual Report*, Fiscal year 1968, transmitted to the Congress on January 3, 1968 (Washington, D.C.: Government Printing Office, 1968), p. 3.

10. "Labor and Manpower," *New York Times*, January 17, 1956, p. 18.

11. "Eisenhower's Economic Report to Congress," *New York Times*, January 25, 1956, p. 18.

12. "Wage Violations Mount," *New York Times*, March 18, 1957, p. 4.

13. *New York Times*, March 15, 1956, p. 46.

14. A.H. Raskin, "Steel Workers Back Stevenson," *New York Times*, September 20, 1956, p. 23.

15. "Meany Denounces Wage Floor Plan," *New York Times*, March 5, 1957, p. 25.

16. Ibid.

17. "Wage-Hour Plan of G.O.P. Scored," *New York Times*, March 16, 1957, p. 12.

18. "Wider Wage Bills Dying in Congress," *New York Times*, July 7, 1957, p. 32.

19. Joseph A. Loftus, "10-Point Legislative Plan Offered by A.F.L.–C.I.O.," *New York Times*, November 8, 1958, p. 1.

20. "Increase Urged in Minimum Pay," *New York Times*, December 3, 1958, p. 61.

21. Bess Furman, "Labor Urges Rise in Minimum Wage," *New York Times*, December 5, 1958, p. 36.

22. "Asks Labor Act Change," *New York Times*, March 9, 1957, p. 9.

23. "Ellender Cautious on Encroachments," *New York Times*, March 30, 1959, p. 33.

24. Joseph A. Loftus, "Labor Urges Rise in Minimum Wage," *New York Times*, May 8, 1959, p. 16.

25. Joseph A. Loftus, "$1.25 Wage Voted by Senate Group," *New York Times*, July 11, 1959, p. 1.

26. Leo Egan, "Democrats Give '60 Plan Scoring G.O.P. Fiscal Aim," *New York Times*, December 7, 1959, p. 39.

27. "Humphrey Asks Aid to Depressed Areas," *New York Times*, January 26, 1960, p. 24.

28. Joseph A. Loftus, "2 Disputes Likely on Minimum Wage," *New York Times*, February 6, 1960, p. 19.

29. Joseph A. Loftus, "Mitchell Favors Minimum-Pay Rise," *New York Times*, February 19, 1960, p. 14.

30. A.H. Raskin, "Hoffa Will Urge $1.50 Pay Floor," *New York Times*, March 13, 1960, p. 59.

31. "Executives Back Minimum-Pay Rise," *New York Times*, March 17, 1960, p. 24.

32. "Unionists and Nixon Discuss Pay Floor," *New York Times*, April 8, 1960, p. 62.

33. "Eisenhower's Message to Congress on His Programs," *New York Times*, May 4, 1960, p. 22.

34. "Dirksen Sees Delay on Minimum Wage," *New York Times*, May 15, 1960, p. 21.

35. Joseph A. Loftus, "Congress Nearing Action on Wages," *New York Times*, June 12, 1960, p. 57.

36. Russell Baker, "Democrats Call Congress Recess for Conventions," *New York Times*, June 30, 1960, p. 14.

37. Russell Baker, "Nixon and Kennedy Clash in TV Debate on Spending, Farms, and Social Issues," *New York Times*, September 9, 1960, p. 29.

38. John D. Morris, "Kennedy Will Press School Aid and Wages Bills, Powell Reports," *New York Times*, December 1, 1960, p. 23.

39. "G.O.P. Pay Bill Offered," *New York Times*, January 10, 1961, p. 21.

40. "Kennedy Plan Opposed," *New York Times*, January 29, 1961, p. 32.

41. "Wage-Price Policies," *New York Times*, February 3, 1961, p. 10.

42. "Wage Bill Reintroduced," *New York Times*, February 3, 1961, p. 12.

43. Felix Belair, Jr., "Kennedy Presses $1.25 Minimum Pay with Wider Scope," *New York Times*, February 8, 1961, p. 1.

44. "Jobless Aid Bill Pressed in House," *New York Times*, January 18, 1961, p. 6.

45. John D. Morris, "Wage Bill's Fate Lies with Senate," *New York Times*, March 26, 1961, p. 44.

46. John F. Kennedy, "Remarks Upon Signing the Minimum Wage Bill," *Public Papers of the Presidents of the United States*, January 20 to December 31, 1961 (Washington, D.C.: U.S. Government Printing Office, 1962), p. 353.

47. "Kennedy Signs Wage-Floor Bill, 3.6 Million More Get Coverage," *New York Times*, May 6, 1961, p. 14.

48. Kennedy, *Public Papers*, 1962, p. 587.

49. U.S. Department of Labor, Wage and Hour and Public Contracts Divisions, *Annual Report*, Fiscal year 1962, reprinted from the 1962 *Annual Report of the Secretary of Labor* (Washington, D.C.: Government Printing Office, 1963), pp. 224–225.

50. "Report Lists Farm Aid and 'Human Concerns' as Pressing Problems for the Season," *New York Times*, January 6, 1956, p. 11.

51. Marjorie Hunter, "Kennedy Praises Congress Record," *New York Times*, October 11, 1962, p. 31.

52. "Wirtz Asks Minimum Wage for 2.6 Million Workers," *New York Times*, February 8, 1964, p. 13.

53. "Meany Sees Room for Big Wage Gain," *New York Times*, February 21, 1964,

p. 16.

54. Marjorie Hunter, "G.O.P. Fails to Bar New Poverty Unit," *New York Times*, May 13, 1964, p. 26.

55. Damon Stetson, "A.F.L.–C.I.O. To Seek $2 Minimum Wage and 35-Hour Week," *New York Times*, February 21, 1965, p. 1.

56. "Rise in Minimum Wage Hinted by Humphrey," *New York Times*, April 14, 1965, p. 4.

57. "Commitment Denied," *New York Times*, April 16, 1965, p. 14.

58. Damon Stetson, "I.L.G.W.U. Urges Repeal of Law," *New York Times*, May 14, 1965, p. 15.

59. "Wirtz Says Young Face a Job Crisis," *New York Times*, May 16, 1965, p. 71.

60. John D. Pomfret, "President Urges Congress to Kill Union Shop Curb," *New York Times*, May 19, 1965, p. 19.

61. "Wider Wage Law Backed by Wirtz," *New York Times*, July 7, 1965, p. 44.

62. "House Unit Votes $1.75 Pay Base and Adds 7.2 Million to Rolls, *New York Times*, August 19, 1965, p. 31.

63. Marjorie Hunter, "Johnson's Plan to Delay $1.60 Base Wage Till '68 Gains in House; Meany Vows Fight," *New York Times*, February 25, 1966, p. 15.

64. Max Frankel, "President Signs Minimum Pay Bill," *New York Times*, September 24, 1966, p. 8.

65. U.S. Department of Labor, Wage and Hour and Public Contracts Divisions, *Annual Report*, Fiscal year 1970, transmitted to the Congress on January 30, 1970 (Washington, D.C.: Government Printing Office, 1970), p. 3.

66. "Joblessness Tied to Economic Gain," *New York Times*, May 23, 1964, p. 29.

67. "A Lower Wage Base Urged for Unskilled," *New York Times*, June 12, 1964, p. 25.

68. Ibid.

69. "Goldberg Hails Raise," *New York Times*, February 3, 1962, p. 9.

70. Ibid.

71. U.S. Department of Labor, Wage and Hour and Public Contracts Divisions, *Annual Report*, Fiscal year 1966, ransmitted to the Congress on January 31, 1966 (Washington, D.C.: Government Printing Office, 1966, p. 7.

72. U. S. Department of Labor, Wage and Hour and Public Contracts Divisions, *Annual Report*, Fiscal year 1960, reprinted from the 1960 *Annual Report of the Secretary of Labor* (Washington, D.C.: Government Printing Office, 1961), p. 233.

73. U.S. Department of Labor, Wage and Hour and Public Contracts Divisions, *Annual Report*, Fiscal year 1970, p. 21.

Chapter 7

The Fourth Decade: The Decade of Empiricism

The minimum wage increased to $1.60 per hour in February 1968 and remained at that level for over six years. However, once increases began in May 1974, there were a series of subsequent increases every remaining year of the decade—except 1977—and the first two years of the 1980s. The minimum wage was $1.60 on January 1, 1970, and $2.90 on December 31, 1979. This 81 percent increase in a ten-year period was both the largest absolute and relative increase in the federal minimum wage in the program's history. The decade of the 1970s is interesting in that while the escalation of the minimum wage was rapid, it was also the decade of the most sophisticated and persistent attacks on the program.

Economists developed untold numbers of economic models that purported to resolve definitively the effects of the minimum wage program on the economy. No one can fault the economics discipline for not putting forth maximum effort and extravagant ingenuity in both the attacks on and defense of the minimum wage program. It may be fair to conclude that the decade ended with the debate at a stalemate in an intellectual sense, but there can be little question that the forces in support of this program won the legislative battle.

This chapter will examine the following: the state of the economy in the 1970s, program legislation, the decade of empiricism, and program activities. While it has been referred to periodically throughout the earlier discussion, the FLSA industry committee program drew to a substantial close during the 1970s. There were only industry committees in the offshore territories after the mid-1940s. The only remnant left in the fiftieth year of the program is in American Samoa. However, this program provided an extremely important mechanism that permitted a smooth phase-in of the program. The lessons learned from this experience are important to understand, and therefore a summary review of the industry committee program under the FLSA is provided.

THE STATE OF THE ECONOMY

The 1960s were an unheralded economic success story. After the short 1960–1961 recession, the economy grew steadily during the remaining nine years. The decade of the 1970s was different. The average number of workers unemployed in 1969 was 2.8 million. In 1970, the average number unemployed rose to 4.1 million. By 1975, almost 8 million workers were unemployed, and the unemployment rate was 8.5 percent. The annual average unemployed never fell below 6 million workers for the remainder of the decade, and the unemployment rate never fell below 5.8 percent.

In addition to high unemployment, consumer prices began to escalate. The consumer price index stood at 116.3—on a base of 1967 = 100—in 1970. By 1979, the CPI had increased to 217.4. In each of two years—1975 and 1979—the index increased 11 percent or more. The economic and political vagaries of "stagflation" were rampant. The population in the 16 to 19-year-old age group was 15,289,000 in 1970, reached a high point of 17,288,000 in 1978, and began a slow decline into the 1980s.[1] This increase of almost 2 million youth provided the fuel for expanding youth unemployment.

There were other weaknesses in the economy throughout the 1970s that narrowed the policy choices while simultaneously requiring increased intervention. For example, real average gross weekly earnings in the private nonagricultural sector declined in four of the ten years of the decade. Only twice in the prior twenty-five years had real earnings declined. The United States experienced problems related to worker productivity, too. Output per hour of all persons had not experienced a negative change from 1948 to 1970. However, twice in the decade of the 1970s, this nation experienced negative productivity changes.

This summary description of the "state of the economy" during the 1970s suggests two things: First, the economy was in almost every dimension worse off than in the prior decade; and second, these economic and social difficulties were the driving force behind public policy intervention. The wage and price controls initiated under the Economic Stabilization Act remained in operation through most of the first half of the decade. The 1974 *Economic Report of the President* acknowledged however, "The controls have not recently been very effective in restraining inflation,"[2] and therefore a decontrol process was initiated. The Organization of Petroleum Exporting Countries (OPEC) oil embargo in October 1973 set in motion a series of wrenching domestic and foreign economic adjustment processes. The dislocations in the aftermath of the oil embargo were important throughout the 1970s, and some are currently affecting policy development.

LEGISLATION IN THE FOURTH DECADE

Soon after the 1966 amendments became law, pressure began to raise the federal minimum wage to an even higher level and to expand coverage. The last mandated increase to $1.60 an hour on February 1, 1968, also provided an increase to $1.15 an hour for newly covered workers. Long before this increase took place, there was pressure from the AFL–CIO, the National Association for the Advancement of Colored People (NAACP), the National Consumers' League, and many other organizations to increase the minimum wage to $2.00 or $2.50 an hour. The nation was moving into a presidential election year, and that event assured plenty of rhetoric concerning the importance of helping the lowest-paid American workers. The Democratic Platform Committee adopted a provision to increase the minimum wage "to assure those at the bottom of the economic scale a fairer share in rising living standards" and to extend FLSA protection to all workers.[3] The committee was careful to avoid a specific minimum wage rate because there was disagreement within the Democratic Party about the appropriate level.

Senator Humphrey, the Democratic presidential candidate, advocated a higher minimum wage as a poverty eradication measure. Opponents of an increase argued that these efforts increased poverty by producing unemployment for the very group that was most in need of higher income. Therefore, they argued, efforts of this type were singularly self-defeating and should be resisted. Some opponents, such as James Buckley, senatorial candidate from New York, argued for exemptions from minimum wage laws for those "who suffer the most from them—teenagers, the aged and the handicapped."[4]

The last significant issue related to the federal minimum wage program in 1968 was the proposal by the Department of Labor to require that all foreigners entering the United States to work be paid at least the prevailing minimum wage. Secretary Wirtz suggested that the department would deny work permits not containing wage rates at or above the statutory minimum. The secretary recognized that the initiative probably would raise the wage levels in occupations employing large numbers of foreign workers, but the need to maintain basic labor standards and reduce poverty made the change compelling.

George Schultz replaced Willard Wirtz as labor secretary early in the second Nixon administration. The new secretary was immediately confronted by the proponents of an increase in the minimum wage. He adopted a somewhat less aggressive stance than his predecessor when Wirtz argued that "all American workers should get a minimum wage of $2 an hour."[5] Secretary Schultz adopted a more cautious position arguing that the minimum wage was a "useful" device for poverty eradication but that increases had been occurring too fast. He argued, "A pause is called for and we should not push it too far."[6]

Late in 1969, the seminal study by John Peterson, administrator of the Arkansas Employment Security Division, raised serious questions about the "real" impacts of changes in the minimum wage. He argued that the Department of Labor studies were in error when they concluded that changes in the minimum wage had produced no adverse employment effects. He argued further that claims that increases in the minimum wage helped the poor were also misdirected. He noted that while employment seemed to increase during periods in which the minimum wage increased, there were sharp jumps "in teen-age and Negro unemployment, relative to white adult unemployment, every time minimum wages are raised."[7] This study, more than any other, provided fuel for the impact debate and provided support for "further study" of this issue by the administration. While a "youth differential" proposal had been discussed periodically from the early years of the FLSA, it was at this point in the late 1960s that the discussion of this issue started in earnest.

Not surprising, it was during the decade of the 1960s that youth unemployment—particularly black youth unemployment—became a critical social and economic issue. As shown in Table 7.1, unemployment rates for "Negro and Other Races" were about twice the overall rate during the late 1940s and 1950s. The youth segment of total "Negro and Other Races" unemployment was four or five times the overall unemployment rate. The overall unemployment rate rose in the late 1950s and early 1960s and declined into the mid and late 1960s. The "Negro and Other Races" unemployment rate followed the same pattern. However, the "Negro and Other Races" youth unemployment increased dramatically in the mid- and late 1950s and remained at a high level thereafter.

Shortly after the Peterson study was released, commerce secretary Maurice Stans announced that the administration was considering a proposal to lower the statutory minimum wage to about $1.25 an hour for teenagers. The commerce secretary made the announcement rather than the labor secretary, but Secretary Stans indicated that Secretary Schultz was "studying the proposal and was expected to have a report on it by next month."[8] Ten days later, Secretary Schultz announced that he was opposed to the proposal for a "special youth minimum wage below $1.60 an hour."[9] Furthermore, Secretary Schultz wrote to George Meany of the AFL–CIO and assured him that there was no study under way regarding a special minimum wage for youth. The only study under way in the Labor Department at that point was one examining "to what extent, if at all, the minimum wage is responsible for the high rates of unemployment among youths."[10] Always a pragmatist, Secretary Schultz observed that the lower minimum wage for youth was "not a saleable idea" without an increase in the regular minimum wage. He was quick to point out, however, that an increase in the federal minimum wage "was not yet favored by the administration."[11]

This announcement by Secretary Stans was the beginning point of public policy statements supporting a youth minimum wage. This issue became a part of every discussion of changes in the minimum wage for the next two decades. The problem—high and rising youth unemployment—that purportedly was the driving force behind this initiative began evaporating in response to demographic changes in the 1970s. However, those advocating a separate, lower minimum wage for youth never relented in their pursuit of this change. To demonstrate clearly that persistence ultimately prevails, in late 1989, a new minimum wage was passed and signed by the president that contained a youth differential.

Table 7.1
Unemployment Rates by Age and Race, 1948–1970 (in percent)

Year	Total Age 16+	Unemployment Rate Negro and Other Races				
		Total Age 16+	Male 16-17	Male 18-19	Female 16-17	Female 18-19
1948	3.8	5.9	9.4	10.5	11.8	14.6
1949	5.9	8.9	15.8	17.1	20.3	15.9
1950	5.3	9.0	12.1	17.7	17.6	14.1
1951	3.3	5.3	8.7	9.6	13.0	15.1
1952	3.0	5.4	8.0	10.0	6.3	16.8
1953	2.9	4.5	8.3	8.1	10.3	9.9
1954	5.5	9.9	13.4	14.7	19.1	21.6
1955	4.4	8.7	14.8	12.9	15.4	21.4
1956	4.1	8.3	15.7	14.9	22.0	23.4
1957	4.3	7.9	16.3	20.0	18.3	21.3
1958	6.8	12.6	27.1	26.7	25.4	30.0
1959	5.5	10.7	22.3	27.2	25.8	29.9
1960	5.5	10.2	22.7	25.1	25.7	24.5
1961	6.7	12.4	31.0	23.9	31.1	28.2
1962	5.5	10.9	21.9	21.8	27.8	31.2
1963	5.7	10.8	27.0	27.4	40.1	31.9
1964	5.2	9.6	25.9	23.1	36.5	29.2
1965	4.5	8.1	27.1	20.2	37.8	27.8
1966	3.8	7.3	22.5	20.5	34.8	29.2
1967	3.8	7.4	28.9	20.1	32.0	28.3
1968	3.6	6.7	26.6	19.0	33.7	26.2
1969	3.5	6.4	24.7	19.0	31.2	25.7
1970	4.9	8.2	27.8	23.1	36.9	32.9

Source: Bureau of Labor Statistics, *Handbook of Labor Statistics* (Washington D.C.: U.S. Government Printing Office, 1971), Tables 60 and 63.

The protracted tussling over the "special youth minimum wage" in the early 1970s temporarily diverted attention away from debate on the "bigger issue," that is, the minimum wage level. In July 1970, George Meany refocused the debate by urging Congress to increase the federal minimum wage from $1.60 an hour to $2.00 an hour. Meany's rationale was tied to poverty eradication. He observed, "It is time to realize that if we want to get rid of the bulk of poverty in the United States, the way to do it is to get rid of substandard wages."[12] Shortly after Meany's statement, the AFL–CIO Executive Council made a parallel recommendation and expanded the agenda by asking for an extension of coverage to 17 million additional workers, seeking a double time for overtime rate, paying overtime for hours in excess of eight hours in one day, and shortening the workweek or work year.[13] The overtime and workweek or work year proposals were initiated to encourage employment sharing during periods of high unemployment.

In both the Senate and House, there was interest in the proposed legislation for other than worker protection reasons. Senator Russell Long, chairman of the Senate Finance Committee, sought a linkage between pending welfare reform and the minimum wage proposal. He accepted the Meany prognosis that poverty and substandard wages were intimately interconnected. Therefore, Senator Long suggested that increasing the minimum wage would "reduce the Federal investment in welfare."[14] The Senator argued with simple math that the proposed Family Assistance Plan (FAP) would provide $300 a year to a worker and his family working at $1.60 an hour, while a $2.00 an hour minimum wage would raise the worker and his family over the poverty threshold and thereby save the government $300 a year. Thus, the FAP proposal would be a drain on federal revenues, while a minimum wage increase could raise incomes and produce additional revenue inflows. No crafty budgeteer could miss the irrefutable connection between these two public policy measures.

Secretary James Hodgson didn't think much of the idea. He recognized and acknowledged that a higher minimum wage may raise some workers and their families above the poverty line. However, there was, in his view, a high probability that the higher minimum wage would produce more unemployment and therefore exacerbate the welfare problem. Consequently, the secretary concluded that he was "not of a mind to believe raising the minimum wage is the answer to the welfare problem."[15]

Entering 1971, the AFL–CIO began pressing its legislative agenda with greater vigor. Foremost on the agenda was a national health plan. The second item was an increase in the minimum wage to $2.00 an hour. Carl Albert, Speaker of the House, included a provision in the House's antirecession program to "increase the minimum wage, now $1.60 an hour to $2."[16] Not to be outdone by his colleagues, Wilbur Mills, chairman of the House Ways and Means Committee, called for a $2.00 an hour minimum wage in February 1972, a year earlier than the legislative provision endorsed by Speaker Albert. Representative Mills adopted the same tie between welfare reform legislation and the minimum wage that Senator Long has argued six months earlier. An editorial in the *New York Times* suggested that the Mills's proposal was a fundamental change in the public regulation of wages. The editorial noted, "A calculated

Congressional decision to raise the minimum wage as a companion to welfare reform would represent at least tacit acceptance of the concept of a 'social wage'—one in which family need becomes a specific determinant in government wage regulation."[17] The "social wage" bore striking similarities to a living wage.

Having been on the defensive for most of the debate, the Nixon administration proposed an increase in the minimum wage to $1.80 an hour in January 1972, with a two-year delay in the increase to $2.00 an hour. Central to the proposal was the Administration's support for the lower minimum wage for youth. Secretary Hodgson reiterated the prospects of lost employment and inflationary impacts of the proposals for an earlier implementation of a $2.00 an hour rate and no youth differential.

Typical of the types of proposals being surfaced by proponents were those involving a federal minimum wage substantially above $2.00 an hour and for speeding up the implementation schedule. The International Ladies Garment Workers Union proposed a $2.50 an hour minimum wage. Senator Harrison Williams introduced legislation to increase the minimum wage to $2.25 an hour. Presidential aspirant Senator Humphrey called for an immediate, but unspecified, increase in the minimum wage.

The House was the first to act. After extended debate, the House Education and Labor Committee passed a bill on a vote of 26 to 7 that incorporated a $2.00 an hour minimum wage. The bill provided for an initial increase in January 1972 to $1.80 an hour, with a subsequent increase to $2.00 an hour one year later. Coverage was expanded to about 5 million additional workers, and a provision permitting the employment of college and high school students at less than the prevailing minimum wage was provided. Importantly, the committee bill did *not* include a provision for a generalized youth minimum wage as proposed by the White House. The session ended with no action by the full House on the bill.

Moving toward an election year, both Democrats and Republicans realized that prudence required enactment of a minimum wage bill of "some sort." Early in January 1972, House Republican leader Gerald Ford predicted that a minimum wage increase would be enacted in the next session of Congress. The carryover minimum wage bill from the first session of this Congress—1971—permitted quick attention. However, a move by Representative William Colmer, chairman of the House Rules Committee, to bottle up the bill suggested that House action could be delayed. House Democrats, led by Representative Richard Bolling, said they were going to challenge the aging Rules Committee chairman and force the bill out of the Rules Committee by a floor vote. To forestall this action by members of his party and the probable embarrassment of having the agenda for the Rules Committee removed from his control, Congressman Colmer announced plans to hold hearings on the minimum wage bill.[18] Having deflected a floor vote, the Rules Committee chairman delayed consideration of the bill for another month.

In parallel action in the Senate, a Senate Labor subcommittee and the full Senate Labor and Public Welfare Committee quickly passed a bill providing for a two-step increase in the minimum wage to $2.20 an hour and expansion of coverage to about 6 million more workers. The largest groups with new coverage were an estimated 3.2 million state and local government employees, 2 million retail store employees, 1 million domestic workers, and 150,000 farm workers.[19] The Nixon administration strongly opposed any expansion of coverage and supported an increase to $2.00 an hour after a two-year interval. In addition, the Senate bill contained no provisions for a "youth wage differential."

Over about one decade, opponents of minimum wage programs had shifted their position on coverage from strongly supportive of coverage expansion —President Eisenhower—to strongly opposed—President Nixon.

After Rules Committee hearings in the House, a bill was approved for floor consideration. However, the resistance of Chairman Colmer was apparent again when the Rules Committee sent the bill to the House floor under a parliamentary procedure rule that permitted the introduction of substitute bills. The Rules Committee procedure permitted the introduction of a Republican-supported bill that was more in line with the administration agenda. The substitute would contain a youth differential and a $2.00 an hour minimum wage after a two-year interval.

As expected, a White House-supported substitute bill was introduced on the House floor by Representative John Erlenborn and quickly passed by a vote of 218 to 192. Democrats in the House were upset with this defeat and vowed to rectify the "problem" in the Senate-House Conference. Representative John Dent said, "In conference we will write the kind of legislation that will provide the greatest good for the greatest number." This comment came back to haunt liberals during final consideration of the House bill.

After a two-week recess, the Senate began hearings on the Labor and Public Welfare Committee bill. Senators Peter Dominick and Robert Taft, Jr., attempted to head off the sentiment for quick Senate passage of the committee bill by proposing a substitute bill that was essentially equivalent to the recently passed House bill. The Senate rejected other compromise bills and the administration's bill and voted directly on the Committee bill. In what some thought was going to be a close vote, the Senate approved the committee bill by better than a two-to-one margin. In earlier voting, the administration bill had failed by a narrow vote of forty-seven to forty-six.

Passage of the Senate bill set the stage for one of the most unusual events in the Congress. Though the House bill was in line with the administration's minimum wage proposals, the House voted 198 to 190 not to send the bill to the Senate-House Conference. The motion to send a bill to conference is generally considered routine, and the House Parliamentarian's Office noted that the August 1, 1972, vote was "the first time such a motion had ever been defeated."[20] Representative Erlenborn, sponsor of the successful House bill, led the fight to prevent the bill from being sent to conference. The congressman knew that when a conference bill was reported out, the House would be required to vote either for or against it and could not send it back to Conference for further revision. He also knew that all the House Democratic conferees were individuals who had voted against the White House–supported bill and were therefore likely to acquiesce easily to their colleagues in the Senate. The earlier comments by Representative John Dent, a member of the House Conference Committee, were used as support for Erlenborn's actions. It was hoped by House Republicans that this action would force Congressmen Carl Perkins and Carl Albert to appoint fewer liberal Democratic members to the Conference Committee. They refused to do so.

Weeks of negotiations between House Democratic and Republican leaders didn't change the position of either side. On October 3, 1972, Congressman Perkins sought and obtained a House vote to send the bill to conference. Again, by a vote of 196 to 188, the House refused to advance the bill. Representative Erlenborn reiterated his concerns: "We can almost anticipate with certainty that the position of the members of the House will not be adequately represented" by the House conferees.[21] With the second rebuff by the House, Congressman Perkins declared the bill dead. However, Congressman Albert Quie suggested that Perkins was just playing on election-year concerns and bluffing. Quie argued that the bill was "too important to the Democrats for them to let it die," and therefore, "I just can't help but think that Carl Perkins is bluffing."[22]

The problem with the tactics used by Republicans was that time was running out. The presidential election was approaching, and the Democrats needed issues for a struggling McGovern campaign. It was no longer important to have an increase just to have an increase. The Democrats believed that it was better to hold out for a stronger bill and use the Republican rejection of their bill as a campaign issue than accede to the wishes of Representatives Erlenborn and Quie. While refusing to support George McGovern for president, the AFL–CIO agreed with the Democratic position, and the prospects for a 1972 minimum wage increase quickly faded.

Representative Perkins had been right on his prognosis of the bill's chances after the second House rejection. However, it did not become the major campaign issue the Democrats had hoped and it didn't help George McGovern's presidential bid. President Nixon won a landslide victory, and the nation temporarily forgot the plight of the low-wage worker.

A bipartisan bill was introduced in the House on January 24, 1973, but it received little attention. Most of the attention was outside the Congress. Academicians and politicians expounded on minimum wage impacts, but little new light was shed on this complex issue. Herbert Stein, chairman of President Nixon's Council of Economic Advisors, attributed high youth unemployment to, among other things, the minimum wage. He observed, "Certainly, we have made it [youth unemployment] worse, rather than better, by setting a minimum wage below which people cannot be hired."[23] Andrew Brimmer, a prominent black economist and member of the Board of Governors of the Federal Reserve System, believed that chronic high joblessness among youth was "aggravated" by the federal minimum wage, and as a consequence, he favored a lower minimum wage for young workers.[24]

George Meany softened his rhetoric toward the recently reelected president and began a process of accommodation to achieve as much of the labor agenda as possible. As the AFL–CIO president attempted to find some common ground on this set of issues, the administration reestablished its position on the inflammatory youth differential. The new labor secretary, Peter Brennan, fresh out of the New York Building and Construction Trades Council, testified in April in support of the lower minimum wage for youth. George Meany immediately attacked the labor secretary and accused him of abandoning "trade union principles he [Brennan] espoused for all of his life before coming to Washington."[25] This position was directly at variance with testimony the labor secretary had given at his confirmation hearings several months earlier. At that point, the labor secretary designate had strongly insisted that if youth performed the same work as adults, there was no reason to pay them different wage rates. In an attempt to deflect the barrage of criticism, the labor secretary suggested that he was not enamored with the youth subminimum wage but had to compromise on this issue to obtain administration support for the critically needed increase in the overall minimum wage.[26]

Secretary Brennan testified against expanding coverage to state and local workers and to domestic workers. The secretary argued that coverage of state and local employees would place federal control too close to decision making at the state and local levels. Covering domestics would, in his view, place the federal government directly into the kitchens of millions of American homes.

The brief honeymoon of the labor secretary was over, and the euphoria many in the labor movement felt when one of their own entered the Nixon cabinet quickly dissipated. The labor agenda that had seemed so firmly controllable with a sympathetic labor secretary in charge now seemed tenuous at best. The disappointment and "shock" related to "Pete's performance" was displayed by George Meany at every occasion. Even President Nixon came to the labor secretary's defense by alluding to the hard fight he (Mr. Brennan) had put up opposing the youth differential provision but had lost.

However, apparently feeling betrayed and having lost the voice they thought resided in the labor secretary, the AFL–CIO turned its attention back to the Congress as the source of support for its agenda. On May 2, 1973, the Subcommittee on Labor of the House Education and Labor Committee adopted a bill to raise the minimum wage to $2.20 an hour, to restrict the youth subminimum to students, and to permit a tax deduction for wages paid to domestic workers. On May 15, 1973, the House Education and Labor Committee passed essentially the same bill by a vote of 23 to 13 and sent it to the full House for consideration. Based on the reception a similar bill received in the House in late 1972, conventional wisdom gave the new bill little chance on the House floor. However, by a lopsided vote of 287 to 130, on June 6, 1973, the full House passed a bill substantially incorporating the provisions in the Labor Committee bill.

There were many supporters of the bill in the House, but by all accounts, Representative Shirley Chisholm stood above all of them. The first black woman in the House, she united a coalition of labor, women, and black groups in support of the bill. In addition, she strongly advocated the inclusion of coverage for domestic workers as a special group with urgent needs. She knew what it meant to work as a domestic. Her mother had worked as a domestic, and consequently, Representative Chisholm spoke from direct experience about low wages and long hours. Evelyn Dubrow, legislative representative for the International Ladies Garment Workers Union, gave tribute to Shirley Chisholm as the "front-runner in the fight to cover domestics because she above all understood what it meant to give them a minimum wage."[27]

The House bill provided for two increases—$2.00 in 1973 and $2.20 in 1974. Coverage was expanded to 1 million domestic workers, 1.7 million federal workers, 3.3 million state and local employees, and several other smaller workforce segments. Representative John Anderson proposed the administration-backed youth differential, but it was voted down and did not become part of the House bill.

Serious action started in the Senate on June 21, 1973, when the Senate Labor Subcommittee approved a bill to increase the minimum wage in steps similar to those provided in the House bill. Coverage provisions were similarly in line with the House bill except that the Senate went somewhat further in the coverage of small retail and service employees, and more agricultural employees would be protected than provided for in the House measure. In addition, the subcommittee voted to exclude children under the age of twelve years from working in agriculture except on family-owned farms.

One week later, the Senate Labor Committee approved a bill that was essentially identical with the subcommittee bill. While administration officials argued that the bill would be inflationary and cause unemployment for low-wage workers, the most objectionable aspect of the bill to the administration was the absence of the youth differential provision. Republican Senate leaders argued that the bill was unacceptable to the president and that he would veto it. However, the sentiment in the Senate was to ignore the veto threat and pass a bill that would address the needs of low-wage workers. Senate Republicans attempted to introduce compromise bills on the Senate floor, but they were overwhelmingly defeated. A bill introduced by Senators John Tower and Paul Fannin that provided for a $2.05 an hour increase in place of the $2.20 an hour provision was defeated by a vote of seventy-eight to nineteen. The principal sponsor of the Senate bill, Senator Harrison Williams, called the Tower–Fannin bill "cruel, harsh and unfeeling" and argued that the Williams–Javits bill would "restore a measure of dignity to the working poor."[28]

As Senate debate continued, other substitute bills were introduced by Senators Peter Dominick and Robert Taft, Jr., but all fell to defeat. When it became apparent that the Williams–Javits bill was going to become the Senate bill, Senator Taft argued that the bill "is about as certain to be vetoed as any I've seen."[29] Nevertheless, the Senate passed the bill by a vote of sixty-four to thirty–three (one less than needed for sustaining a presidential veto).

Work in the Conference Committee was quick and predictable. The two bills were very similar in every major respect. In addition, while the House and Senate votes had been close to what was needed to override a presidential veto, Labor Secretary Brennan publicly supported the main provisions of the bill. When asked on public television whether he supported the bill, the secretary responded that he had been "in favor of a minimum wage increase all along and so has the president, as well as the administration." He quickly added that he could not speak for the president, but he (Brennan) did not feel the proposed $2.20 an hour minimum wage was out of line and would urge the president to sign the bill.[30]

After resolving minor differences, the Conference Committee approved the bill on July 26, 1973, and sent it back to the House and Senate for final approval. After repeated assurance by Secretary Brennan that he supported the bill and would urge the president to sign it, Senator Javits personally called the labor secretary before the Senate's final vote and was told, "I'll recommend to the President that he sign the bill. I have no assurance or commitment that he will do so."[31] With uncertainty about the reception the bill would get from the President, the Senate approved the Conference Committee bill by a vote of 62 to 28 (2 more than needed for a presidential veto override). The following day, August 3, 1973, the House approved the bill by a vote of 253 to 152 (substantially fewer votes than needed to override a presidential veto).

The stage was now set for the Congress-executive showdown on a piece of legislation that had strong support in principle from both branches of government but wide differences of opinion on specific provisions. Congressional leaders wanted the president to address this issue directly. However, the Congress was going into recess for about thirty days, and therefore, the president would have an opportunity for a pocket veto if the bill was sent forward prior to the recess. Senate leaders decided to retain the bill until after the recess so that they would have a chance to override a veto if it occurred. While the House vote was seventeen votes short of the two-thirds vote needed for an override, it was felt nonetheless that a good chance for an override existed.

On September 5, 1973, President Nixon confirmed the prediction of Senate leaders by saying that he would veto the minimum wage bill. He expressed "very deep regret" in having to return the bill to Congress, but he believed that the increase in the minimum wage would give "an enormous boost to inflation" and have a substantial disemployment effect on unskilled workers and teenage workers.[32]

The reaction to the president's action was immediate and vigorous. To no one's surprise, George Meany denounced the decision as a "callous, cruel blow" that made "the poor of this nation the front-line troops in the war against inflation."[33] A *New York Times* editorial argued, "The extent of the gap that has opened up in the earnings of those at the bottom of the economic ladder makes it topsy-turvy to suggest, as Mr. Nixon did in his news conference, that the catch-up approved by Congress would give 'an enormous boost to inflation.'"[34] I.W. Abel, president of the United Steel Workers of America, called the president's action "the most cold-hearted, cold-blooded legislative action taken by the president since he assumed office in 1969."[35] The president, himself, in his veto message agreed that an increase in the minimum wage was needed but argued that the bill before him contained provisions that "would unfortunately do far more harm than good."[36]

In preparation for an attempt to override the president's veto in the House, George Meany vehemently attacked every argument the president had used in justifying the veto action. Meany provided statistical detail from official Bureau of Labor Statistics data that showed economic responses to earlier changes in the minimum wage to be precisely the opposite from what the president had suggested. The president of the AFL–CIO charged President Nixon with perpetuating myths about the nation's poor. But the uproar from organized labor, congressmen, and the media did not turn the tide for proponents of the bill. The House sustained the president's veto on September 19, 1973, by a vote of 259 to 164. Minimum wage legislation was a dead issue for the remainder of 1973.

Editorials continued to condemn the veto action, but other issues, not the least of which was the Watergate fiasco, began to dominate the political debate and the public's attention. The level of frustration with everyone in this initiative was apparent in a *New York Times* editorial on September 22, 1973. The editor discussed the ravages of inflation on the purchasing power of the minimum wage. A minimum wage of $2.12 was needed just to maintain the level of purchasing power provided for when the minimum wage was increased to $1.60 an hour. However, the editor placed the blame squarely on the shoulders of not only the administration but organized labor as well. The editor argued:

It is inexcusable on the part of both the Administration and organized labor that an ideological difference over one phase of the bill—whether or not to set a lower minimum to encourage the employment of teenagers—threatens for the second year to keep millions of workers at the bottom of the wage scale from getting the higher minimum that means a measure of adequacy for their family budgets.[37]

In early 1974, Congress began reconsideration of minimum wage legislation. By this point, Watergate had blossomed into the political story of the Century. Many Watergate conspirators had been indicted—John Ehrichman, Egil Krogh, G. Gordon Liddy, among others—and the president was under siege to explain his role in the burglary and subsequent cover-up effort. This area of concern led the Congress to believe that the weakened president would be much more receptive to a minimum wage bill containing the provisions in the bill vetoed in September 1973. Five days later, the Senate Labor Committee approved a bill to raise the minimum wage to $2.20 an hour in several stages and to extend coverage to about 7 million additional workers. The Senate bill did not contain a provision for a youth differential.

While editorials suggested that the youth differential was a "marginal aspect" of the entire minimum wage bill and another delay based on this issue would be "inexcusable," George Meany made it clear early in the 1974 debate that he was inflexible on this issue. At the Bal Harbour, Florida, AFL–CIO Executive Council meeting on February 21, Meany said that "the labor federation would accept no compromise bill that included a subminimum wage for youth of the kind that was advocated by the President."[38]

The president recognized early in the legislative session that a minimum wage bill was inevitable and that the position he advocated was unlikely to be maintained. He wrote a conciliatory letter to congressional leaders and Labor Secretary Brennan publicly stating that compromise was possible on key issues in the bill. The labor secretary noted that the youth differential was one provision that may be subject to compromise by the president. The president told the Congress that he wanted a "responsible bill" but did not suggest a possible veto if key provisions were not included in the bill. The labor secretary would not deny that a veto was possible, but he argued, "My position is I want to get the bill passed. I don't want it shelved for any nonsense."[39] These words of positive support were important signals from the administration. The Watergate fiasco was taking its toll on presidential influence, and there was a belief by leaders of both parties that he could not tolerate another veto of this popular bill.

During Senate debate on the Labor Committee bill, Senators Dominick and Taft again tried to limit coverage expansion and slow down the implementation process. Both proposals were overwhelmingly rejected by the full Senate. Failing on these two efforts, Senator Dominick attempted to limit the application of the bill's provisions to domestics who worked more than twenty-four hours a week. The senator was concerned that families using maids would be forced to dismiss them and therefore lead to disemployment. The Senate rejected this proposal by a vote of fifty-eight to thirty-seven. On March 7, 1974, the Senate passed the minimum wage bill by a vote of sixty-nine to twenty-two. The bill raised the minimum wage from $1.60 to $2.00 upon enactment of the law and to $2.20 a year later. Over 6 million additional workers were brought into coverage status. The largest groups of newly covered workers were State and local government employees and domestic workers. With the extension of coverage to state and local government employees, the sticky issue of overtime protection for police and firefighters arose.

After minimal debate, the House passed a bill on March 20, 1974, that provided for an increase in the minimum wage to $2.30 an hour. By an overwhelming vote of 375 to 37, the House bill contained almost identical provisions to the recently passed Senate bill. Minor differences related to overtime exemptions, the level and timing of the wage increases, and the manner in which to compensate newly covered police and firefighting employees. With one day of conference discussion, all issues had been resolved except for overtime for police and firefighters. The conference bill contained a minimum wage increase to $2.30 an hour, expansion of coverage to over 6 million additional workers, a full-time student "subminimum wage," and delimitations of coverage for domestic workers working minimal hours each month.

On March 26, 1974, conferees had agreed on a compromise bill, and it was sent to the House and Senate for final approval. By votes of 345 to 50 in the House and 71 to 29 in the Senate, a bill was sent to the president for signature. The size of the majority votes in each chamber signaled the president that a veto could not be sustained. Political leaders in both parties agreed that with the possibility of impeachment hanging over his head, the embattled president could not risk a veto override. Therefore, putting the best face on it that he could, with "some reservations," the president signed the bill into law on April 8, 1974. In his signing ceremony, the president suggested that "raising the minimum wage is now a matter of justice that can no longer be delayed."[40]

The complex implementation schedule of the 1974 amendments was shown in Secretary Brennan's 1974 *Annual Report* to the Congress. Table 7.2 shows the sequence of changes. The 1974 amendments introduced a major change in the concept of FLSA coverage. Before 1974, coverage was defined by the firm's involvement in the production of goods for interstate commerce. The 1974 amendments modified the concept by covering domestic service workers employed eight or more hours in a workweek or whose compensation constituted wages as defined in the Social Security Act—generally, the receipt of at least $50 in cash wages in a calendar quarter.

Table 7.2
Implementation Schedule for the 1974 Amendments

	Nonfarm Workers Covered		
Effective Date	Prior to the 1966 Admendments	By and Subsequent to the 1966 Amendments	Farmworkers
Prior to May 1, 1974	$1.60	$1.60	$1.30
May 1, 1974	2.00	1.90	1.60
January 1, 1975	2.10	2.00	1.80
January 1, 1976	2.30	2.20	2.00
January 1, 1977	—	2.30	2.20
January 1, 1978	—	—	2.30

Source: U.S. Department of Labor, *Annual Report*, Fiscal year 1974 (Washington, D.C: Government Printing Office, 1975), p. 5.

The 1974 amendments mandated the secretary of labor to report biennially "to explore methods to prevent the curtailment of employment opportunities of disadvantaged manpower groups which have had historically high unemployment rates."[41] Secretary Dunlop transmitted the first Section 4(d)(3) report to the Congress on May 5, 1975.

Finally, the 1974 amendments restricted the employer tip credit by permitting the offset only if the employee received and retained the tip income. To qualify for the tip credit, employers were required to inform employees of the tip provisions of the law.

As was the case in prior amendments to the FLSA, the dust had not begun to settle before proponents were advocating another increase in the minimum wage level and expansion of coverage. In the Bal Harbour AFL–CIO Executive Council meetings in February 1975, George Meany called for a $3.00 an hour federal minimum wage. The AFL–CIO Convention in San Francisco in October 1975 formally adopted a recommendation that confirmed the position taken at the Bal Harbour meeting. Unknown to policy and program officials, the nation was approaching the last round of minimum wage increases in the first half century of the program's existence. The 1977 amendments to the FLSA would provide for four increases in the level of the minimum wage, and there would be no further increases until after 1988.

The political debate leading to the 1977 amendments reintroduced a new element in the framework of the FLSA. In mid-1976, Congressman John Dent introduced the concept of "indexation" as a method of preventing low-wage workers from experiencing a disproportionate impact from inflation. William Usery, the new labor secretary, supported indexing as a viable tool for minimum wage change. However, other administration officials such as Alan Greenspan, chairman of the Council of Economic Advisors, were generally opposed to indexing. Opponents feared that indexation would provide "built-in inflation" in the wage structure and therefore should not be a part of the law. A provision for indexing the minimum wage to either a price or wage series quickly became part of the debate. While in the minority, some House Republicans such as Albert Quie found indexing an acceptable part of the law if it was structured as a "catch-up" mechanism for those at the bottom of the wage structure and not a "push-up" mechanism for those at the top. In one of the rare congressional alliances related to the FLSA in the House, Representatives Dent and Quie hoped to "sell indexation to Congress as a way to avoid a grinding minimum wage bill battle every two, three or four years—as a way to escape being lobbied by the low-paid on one side and small business on the other."[42]

Conservative members of the Congress generally opposed indexing and they received support from the U.S. Chamber of Commerce and other business organizations. Much to the delight of congressional Democrats, however, unsuspecting support for indexing arose from the grave. Legislators with good memories or effective staff surfaced testimony by Senator Robert A. Taft, affectionately known as "Mr. Republican" by a generation of conservatives, that proposed indexing of the FLSA in 1949. He had proposed a scheme in which the minimum wage would be indexed at 60 percent of average hourly earnings in manufacturing. The Democrats gleefully surfaced the provision of one of the nation's most prominent conservatives as convincing support for the current members of Congress.

As the congressional debate began heating up for further amendments to the FLSA, an important Supreme Court decision struck a serious blow to earlier extensions of FLSA coverage. In a five to four decision, the U.S. Supreme Court invalidated the provisions of the law that extended coverage to state and local government employees. Twenty-one states, the National League of Cities, the National Governors Conference, and other interest groups challenged the extension of the 1974 amendments to the "traditional functions" of state and local government. Three states, the federal government, and many public employee associations argued the case for state and local coverage. The latter groups argued that the fiscal impacts of coverage were exaggerated and, more important, "public employees were entitled to a living wage."[43]

However, in the *National League of Cities* decision[44] the High Court reaffirmed the sovereignty of state and local government in matters essential to state sovereignty. The question decided by the Court was whether wages paid to state and local employees represented a function essential to state sovereignty. Overturning a 1968 High Court decision, the 1976 Court ruled that wages paid to state and local employees were an essential function of state sovereignty. About 7 million American workers were removed from the provisions of the FLSA.

The proponents of a higher minimum wage, indexing, and expanded coverage were not without opposition. Arthur Burns, chairman of the Federal Reserve Board, suggested that part of President Jimmy Carter's economic recovery program should be using the federal government as the "employer of last resort" paying participants less than the minimum wage. A *New York Times* editorial on March 21, 1977, directly attacked the minimum wage program as an antiquated relic of a bygone era. The editorial suggested that organized labor had ulterior motives in its support for this legislation that were different from its stated concerns for low-wage workers. The editorial rejected the youth differential as a proposal resulting in "dubious social benefit."[45]

The diversity of opinion in the press and the Congress was also present in the new Democratic administration. The division within the administration on a variety of major FLSA issues was so deep that it led to a rift with the AFL–CIO. President Carter had made promises to the labor movement during the campaign that resulted in strong labor support for his candidacy. The labor movement could, and did, expect that 1977 was going to be "labor's year" in the area of sympathetic legislation. However, within two days, the labor movement suffered two setbacks on its legislative agenda that produced an acrimonious exchange between labor leaders and officials in the administration. The Congress didn't pass legislation permitting "situs picketing," which would have increased the effectiveness of labor picketing activity. The AFL–CIO had identified this legislation as its number-one legislative priority because it was felt that passage by the Congress was assured. President Carter did not exert appreciable pressure to pass the bill, and the labor movement did relatively little lobbying in support of the bill. A comparable measure had passed in an earlier session of Congress, and there was reasonable expectation that no trouble would be encountered the second time around.

On March 24, 1977, Labor Secretary F. Ray Marshall presented a plan to Congress that would increase the minimum wage to $2.50 an hour. The AFL–CIO had been pressing hard for a $3.00 an hour wage rate and was bitterly disappointed in the administration proposal. George Meany called the proposal "shameful," while other labor leaders termed it "incredible." The AFL–CIO president argued that the administration proposal was "a bitter disappointment to everyone who looked to this Administration for economic justice for the poor."[46] The specific proposal advanced by the administration was to raise the minimum wage to $2.50 an hour in July 1977 and then index it to 50 percent of the average wage in manufacturing in July 1978. The AFL–CIO saw the proposal in terms of the absolute monetary increase and sought to index the minimum wage to 60 percent of the average wage in manufacturing.

While the administration was quarreling with the labor movement over the minimum wage issue, an interesting departure from previous rhetoric emerged from the U.S. Chamber of Commerce. In an interview with the Chamber's chief economist, Jack Carlson, concerning the position of the Chamber on the minimum wage, Carlson responded, "We are opposed to any excessive increases in the minimum wage. Clearly inflation has reduced the effective nature of the minimum wage, and Congress may well want to increase the amount. If it were modest, the Chamber of Commerce would not object strenuously."[47] This moderate position on an increase in the minimum wage by an organization that had vigorously resisted not only increases in the wage rate but the existence of the program was welcomed by proponents of change.

George Meany charged the new president with a lot of rhetoric but little action. Therefore, the federation adopted another approach. The Reverend Theodore Hesburgh, president of Notre Dame University, Clarence Mitchell, chairman of the Leadership Conference on Civil Rights, and Dorothy Heigh, president of the National Council of Negro Women, joined Meany in a "Coalition for a Fair Minimum Wage." The coalition's objectives were simple and clear. Mitchell said their objectives were to enact a minimum wage that would be "sufficient to lift America's lowest-paid workers out of poverty and keep them off the street."[48]

The March 21, 1977, editorial in the *New York Times* entitled "The Minimally Useful Minimum Wage" drew a number of responses from the academic community and the labor unions. The editorial attempted to argue that the minimum wage, as a policy tool, no longer made economic sense. If an increase in the minimum wage occurs, there would be general disemployment effects, there would be North-South competitive shifts, and, the editorial continued, an increase would not address the vagaries of poverty. In addition, the editor labeled indexing as a "gimmick" that will not work to improve the conditions of low-wage workers. The editorial did not support the youth differential because of its substitution effects and because many of its purported beneficiaries were members of middle-class families rather than impoverished youth.[49]

One of the most insightful objections to the editorial was made by Michael Piore of the Massachusetts Institute of Technology. He argued that the editorial was wrong in its assertion about the job-creating capacity of lower minimum wages. Piore's argument was based on what he believed were the factors motivating low-wage workers. He criticized the assumption that the low-wage segment of the labor market operates similarly to commodity markets. The assumption is that at low wages more jobs are available, and at high wages, fewer jobs arise. He criticized this assumption as "very dubious." In Piore's view, low-wage workers are what he termed "target earners." In other words, most low-wage earners work to generate income to meet a certain "target." He argued:

A large proportion of low-wage workers are target earners: youth working to finance Saturday night; women trying to purchase specific durable goods; migrants accumulating an investment fund and then going home. When the wage falls, it takes these people a longer time to meet their target; they work more and, as a consequence, there are actually fewer employment opportunities for others.[50]

The question is essentially an empirical one but an extremely important one. Whether they are target earners as Piore asserted is an issue that has never been thoroughly explored.

By early summer, the AFL–CIO had reassessed its legislative agenda and its feelings about President Carter. George Meany indicated disappointment in the performance of the new president in several critical economic areas. The two legislative defeats in March had severely dampened enthusiasm for the administration. Therefore, the AFL–CIO shifted its priorities and made an increase in the minimum wage number one on its legislative agenda. A viable but unacceptable minimum wage proposal was in the Congress, and with enough pressure, there was reasonable expectation that it could be molded into an acceptable bill.

To the surprise of many, a quasi-celebrity during the 1970s, Billy Carter, the president's brother, was adopted as a spokesperson for small American business. *Nation's Business* interviewed Billy Carter about the frustrations he experienced as a small businessman. In characteristic form, he expounded at length about the vagaries of the "Washington bureaucracy" including problems he experienced with welfare programs, environmental protection, occupational safety and health, the Internal Revenue Service, among others. To the delight of conservatives, he also chose to describe how he, as a small businessman, responded to changes in the minimum wage. He observed, "Every time the minimum wage goes up, we have to lay off a few more people. A lot of people simply aren't worth the minimum wage."[51] Congressional representatives such as Congressman Robert Michel and Senator Herman Talmadge exalted the observations of this "common-sense businessman" who provided the nation with "gems of wisdom" in its search for policy direction.

The bitter rift between the AFL–CIO and President Carter was softened by a compromise engineered by Speaker of the House Thomas P. O'Neill, Jr. The Speaker worked out a scheme that would increase the minimum wage to $2.65 an hour in the first year but then index it on an increasing scale to 53 percent of the average wage in manufacturing in 1980. Based on projected increases in the manufacturing wage and the poverty level, it was agreed that the proposed indexing scheme would raise minimum wage workers above the poverty level. This realization provided the basis for AFL–CIO support of the proposal. George Meany "applauded" President Carter's support for the $2.65 an hour minimum wage because it demonstrated the president's "concern for the working poor."

With the positions now known, the House Education and Labor Committee quickly drafted and passed a bill incorporating the consensus provisions. On July 19, 1977, the committee approved a bill by a vote of twenty-nine to seven to raise the minimum wage to $2.65 an hour in January 1978, to index the minimum wage at 53 percent of the average wage in manufacturing, to bring agricultural workers on large farms up to the same wage rate as the non-farm sector and provide agricultural workers overtime protection, and to scale back the tip credit provisions.

Action in the Senate began heating up as the summer wore on. Senator Harrison Williams predicted that the Senate would pass a bill similar to the House bill because there was less resistance to an increase in the minimum wage than had existed earlier. Senator Richard Schwieker introduced a bill in the Senate Human Resources Committee to permit the payment of a subminimum wage to workers under twenty years of age. The committee rejected the Schwieker proposal by a vote of ten to four and simultaneously adopted a bill increasing the minimum wage to $2.65 an hour.

Many believed that these actions were setting the stage for an easy path for these bills through the Congress. However, the House, on September 15, 1977, defeated the indexing provision of the committee bill by a vote of 233 to 193. In addition, the House rejected the lowering of the tip credit and increased the gross receipts level for defining coverage for small business from the then-current $250,000 per year to $500,000 per year. In a dramatic roll-call vote, the Speaker of the House had to defeat a proposal for a youth subminimum wage by casting a tie-breaking vote. The measure was defeated by a vote of 211 to 210. The House then adopted increases in the minimum wage that were somewhat lower in the second and third years than provided in the committee bill. The House bill would increase the minimum wage to $3.05 an hour by 1980.

The White House immediately abandoned support for the indexing measure. To ameliorate this action, the president placed his support behind a Senate provision that would increase the minimum wage substantially higher than provided for in the House bill. The president supported the extension of the increases from three years to four years, with the last increase moving the wage level to $3.40 an hour. The Senate passed a bill on October 6, 1977 incorporating these provisions. By a vote of eighty-one to seven, the Senate approved a measure to reduce the tip credit.

The Senate and House versions of the bill contained several differences, but the most contentious was the exemption of small business through the gross annual sales test. The House bill doubled the sales test to $500,000 per year, while the Senate raised the exemption to $325,000 per year. In conference, after intense debate, conferees settled on a sales volume of $362,500 per year by the end of 1981.

The final conference bill contained four increases in the minimum wage that ended with a $3.35 an hour wage on January 1, 1981, a reduction in the tip credit in two steps to 40 percent by 1980, a sales volume test for small business of $362,500 per year by the end of 1981, and the expansion to six full-time students the number that business may hire at 85 percent of the minimum wage.

Three days after approval of the conference bill, the Senate approved the bill by a voice vote with no debate. The following day, October 20, 1977, the House approved the bill by a vote of 236 to 187 and sent the bill to the president for signature. Arguing that the bill was "a step in the right direction," the president signed it into law on November 1, 1977.

In his signing statement, President Carter noted, "Each time that we have tried to boost the lower level of salary for the most underpaid workers, there have been predictions of catastrophe, . . . but each time, in my opinion, . . . the change has helped our Nation and its economic strength."[52] In addition to the increases in the minimum wage, the 1977 amendments also contained several other important provisions. Among the most important of these was the creation of the Minimum Wage Study Commission (MWSC). The commission members were sworn in on May 24, 1978.

THE DECADE OF EMPIRICISM

While the 1960s produced the first serious FLSA assessment effort, the fourth decade—the 1970s—was the period of maximum examination of the quantitative dimensions of the FLSA. There were two basic categories of study: impacts and effectiveness. The impact studies focused on the changes in the FLSA in relation to unemployment, inflation, income distribution, and a host of other purported economic relationships. Effectiveness examined compliance, coverage, and related issues. The decade ended with an extensive examination under way by the congressionally created commission. The Minimum Wage Study Commission was charged with a comprehensive examination of the FLSA.

As the 1970s began, the studies of the FLSA were far advanced. While the level of effort and attention was substantial, it is fair to conclude that few definitive, unambiguous "answers" were formulated. The decade started in a condition of uncertainty and ended in a similar condition. What was perceived to be a relatively simple set of analytical tasks ended as a complex set of relationships and interrelationships that analysts were ill-prepared to address. However, as the study results poured out of the process, there was an understandable tendency to engage in great leaps from study findings to proposed policy or program changes. It was during the 1970s that it became "known" that every economist of any standing would agree that higher minimum wage rates resulted, inevitably, in fewer job opportunities. There are serious questions about this "inevitable" relationship.

The Minimum Wage Study Commission prepared voluminous studies in its seven-volume report. These studies examined virtually every important aspect of the minimum wage. Those interested in a complete overview of minimum wage effects can usefully consult the commission findings and recommendations. For the purposes of this examination of the FLSA, only two primary areas of possible minimum wage effects will be discussed.

EMPLOYMENT AND THE MINIMUM WAGE

For the last thirty years, there was much made of the notion that increases in the minimum wage usually coincided with increases in employment. Of course, it was also known, but not often stated, that most increases in the minimum wage coincided with expanding economic activity, that is, output and employment growth. A reasonable question is whether employment would have grown *even more* if an increase in the minimum wage (level or coverage, or both) had not occurred. While the "employment impact" literature is voluminous, several more prominent studies will be reviewed here.

The arguments can usefully be segmented into "general" employment impacts and the impacts on specific groups—most notably youth. Even within these two categories there are purported differential impacts. Therefore, care must be taken to ensure that the full character of employment impacts is considered.

This discussion will consider two aspects of the minimum wage/employment relationship: first, the minimum wage impacts on specific segments of the workforce; second, the impacts of minimum wage changes on other aspects of the employment relationship, for example, labor force participation rates, wage emulation, and labor mobility. These aspects of the employment/minimum wage relationship are not unrelated to one another. The literature has generally considered each dimension separately, and there is some understanding gained by maintaining the dichotomy.

If the demand schedule for low-wage, generally unskilled workers is elastic and due to their general substitutability it undoubtedly is then, *ceteris paribus*, that higher minimum wages will work to their detriment. In the short run, the employer of this category of labor has several choices. One choice is to discontinue the production activity that leads directly to increased unemployment or lower employment. A second choice is to replace the lower-skilled worker with a higher-skilled worker, that is, substitution. A third option is to raise the low-wage, low-skilled worker's productivity through training, job modification, incentive production (piece rate), or other related output enhancement processes. The fourth option may be to replace the low-wage worker with a machine.

Each of these options is likely to produce a different "employment effect." In some cases, employment simply falls, and unemployment rises. In other cases, some workers lose their jobs, while other workers expand their employment. There is also the possible outcome that the "stimulative effect" of increases in the minimum wage causes productivity and output expansion that benefits the individual worker and the economy. This may occur with the expansion of aggregate demand resulting from higher income levels. If the minimum wage increases in a tight labor market, that is, low unemployment, the firm may have few short-term options other than to expand output with its existing workforce or go out of business.

As Thomas Moore noted in 1971, since the demand for low-skilled or inexperienced workers is presumed to be elastic, "[t]heory would suggest that when the minimum wage is raised, the impact would be felt more strongly by the unskilled, the inexperienced, and those facing discrimination."[53] In addition, "[a] rise in the minimum wage relative to other wages should have an increasing impact over time. It takes time to substitute capital for labor. Employers prefer to reduce their work force by attrition rather than firing workers."[54]

Obscured in Moore's characterization of the change process is the critically important notion of "relative wages." The increase in any "price" relative to other prices will set in motion a process of substitution of the lower-priced good for the higher-priced good if they are substitutes. Labor of differing skill levels is generally substitutable, particularly in the low-wage, low-skilled segment of the employment queue. If all wages stay the same while the mandated minimum wage increases, the relative "price" of low-skilled workers will increase. The firm will attempt to set in motion a substitution process.

Wages generally increase despite changes in the minimum wage. Therefore, it is not clear that an increase in the minimum wage, except at the moment of increase, produces a "relative wage" problem. If the minimum wage change follows overall wage and price changes, then the increase in the minimum wage simply brings it back into line with the overall wage structure. Therefore, Moore's assertion that there should be an "increasing impact over time" in response to changes in the minimum wage relates directly to the relative wage issue. We know that the minimum wage today is about 33 percent of the average wage in the private, nonagricultural sector. It has historically been in the range of 45 to 55 percent. Therefore, minimum wage workers are "relatively" cheaper from the perspective of the firm. If an increase in the minimum wage simply restores the historical relationship, the relative wage argument loses some, but not necessarily all, of its force.

Douglas Adie examined the employment impacts from a theoretical perspective by noting, "Economic theory suggests that the quantity of labor demanded will decrease and the quantity of labor supplied increase if a minimum wage is set above the market clearing wage."[55] What is unknown, of course, is the level of the market-clearing wage. A minimum wage set below the market-clearing wage simply truncates the labor supply function at the minimum wage level without necessarily changing either the market-clearing wage rate or employment level. Whether employment would be higher or lower after an increase in the minimum wage is an important empirical question. However, it may not be the most important employment question about changes in the minimum wage.

What became clear early in the analytical process was that the employment impacts were relatively uninteresting. As more detailed data became available, the differential impacts on several labor market groups became the focus of theoretical and empirical examination. There are many reasons why increases in the minimum wage should affect different demographic groups differently. Wages are simply prices of factor inputs. These factor inputs are valuable to the producer because of their contribution to the production of output. Not all factors contribute equally to output, and therefore the producer selects the most productive units that will work for a given wage rate. The less productive a factor input, the less valuable it is to the producer and the less the producer will pay for it. Young workers with little education, few productive skills, and little labor market discipline are unlikely to be attractive to the employer. If the minimum wage is set higher than the productive potential of young workers, the employer will not employ them.

This was the notion that James Ragan had in mind when he noted, "Minimum wage legislation reduces youth employment; males, especially nonwhite males, are the hardest hit."[56] Robert Goldfarb noted in 1975 that "the studies consistently indicate that white teenagers suffer unemployment losses from minimum wages, but black teenagers do not."[57] It is important to observe that legislation that reduces employment is not the same as increasing unemployment. It is possible to have employment and unemployment moving in the same or opposite directions, depending on how the group's members are responding to conditions in the labor market and the economy. As Marvin Kosters and Finis Welch observed in 1972, "[A]s a result of increased minimum wages, teenagers are able to obtain fewer jobs during periods of normal employment growth and their jobs are less secure in the face of short-term employment changes."[58] If teenagers become discouraged and leave the labor force, fewer jobs will be obtained by them—employment will decrease—at the same time their unemployment rate falls.

The empirical evidence generated during the 1970s forged a strong tie between changes in the minimum wage and youth employment and unemployment. In a 1976 study, Jacob Mincer argued, "The greatest disemployment effects are observed for nonwhite teenagers, followed by nonwhite males (20–24), white teenagers, and white males (20–24)."[59] Not only did these groups experience the largest disemployment, for example, job loss; according to Mincer, "The largest increase in the unemployment rate is observed for nonwhite males (20–24), followed by nonwhite teenagers, white males (20–24) and white teenagers."[60] Apparently, members of these demographic groups were losing their jobs but were not leaving the labor force.

In the same year—1976—Edward Gramlich identified another dimension of the youth labor market experience related to increases in the minimum wage. Not only did teenagers lose jobs, but "high minimum wages reduce full-time employment of teenagers substantially, forcing many of them into part-time employment."[61] Therefore, many of those fortunate enough to retain employment status probably experienced reduced income flows because of shorter work hours.

The debate in the 1970s increasingly focused not on the question of whether increases in the minimum wage caused teenage disemployment but rather on the magnitude of the changes. Finis Welch and James Cunningham found in a 1978 study, "At the national mean, we estimate that as of 1970, minimum wages had reduced employment of 14- to 15-year-olds by 46%, by 27% for those 16–17, and by 15% for the 18- to 19-year-old group."[62] Other researchers such as Hyman Kaitz and Malcolm Lovell found that changes in minimum wage rates lacked significant disemployment effects. However, in Edward Gramlich's extensive review in 1976, he captured the prevalent sentiment of the research community when he suggested that

the most reasonable verdict is that teenagers have more to lose than to gain from higher minimum wages: they appear to be forced out of better jobs, denied full-time work, and paid lower hourly wage rates, and all these developments are probably detrimental to their income prospects in both the short and long run. If one of the goals of minimum wage legislation is to eliminate sweatshop low-wage jobs for teenagers the law appears to be counterproductive.[63]

Yale Brozen's 1969 study suggested, "The minimum wage has affected employment opportunities more for nonwhite teenagers than for teenagers in general."[64] However, in an extensive summary of the impact literature in 1975, Goldfarb reached the opposite conclusion. He maintained that "the studies consistently indicate that white teenagers suffer unemployment losses from minimum wages, but black teenagers do not."[65]

The Goldfarb summary is important from the perspective of minimum wage policy development. If black teenagers are not adversely impacted by minimum wage programs, there may be less impetus for initiation of a youth minimum wage program. Thomas Moore's 1971 study postulated, among other things, that "[h]igher unemployment may lead to workers or potential workers withdrawing from the labor force. There is some evidence that this has happened in the teenage market."[66] The results of Jacob Mincer's 1976 study were consistent with Moore's findings. Mincer argued, "The net minimum wage effects on labor force participation appear to be negative for most of the groups."[67] However, a later study by James Ragan found evidence suggesting that "[t]he minimum wage has little effect on labor force participation."[68]

The impacts of minimum wage changes on labor force participation may be of greater importance than the immediate disemployment effects. Workers choosing to leave the labor force lose work experience, skills, discipline, and self-esteem that may adversely affect them for the remainder of their working lives. Another consequence of changes in the minimum wage is the shift between and within the labor markets. Jacob Mincer noted, "The theoretical analysis indicates that minimum wages generate socially wasteful labor mobility between the 'covered' and not-covered sectors and between the labor market and the nonmarket."[69] Those workers remaining in the higher-wage covered sector may experience higher income levels—assuming they remain on full-time schedules. Workers in the not-covered sector may experience depressed wages or, at a minimum, less rapidly increasing wages due to the influx of displaced workers from the covered sector.

Finally, a major issue discussed with every initiative to increase the minimum wage or expand coverage concerns the "ripple" or "emulation" effects of these changes. There is less than unanimity on this issue, but Gramlich's work suggests that " substantial emulation effects are not long delayed, which seems plausible because increases in the minimum wage are well-advertised in advance."[70]

The impression one gets from the summary of the employment impacts literature of the 1970s is that the consequences of raising the minimum wage are uncertain, at best. If there is an adverse impact, it almost certainly is not uniformly felt by all labor force participants. Gramlich's observation may be the best that can be said about these programs. After extensive study, he concluded that "the minimum [wage] is simply less of a force for good or evil than people have believed."[71]

INFLATION, INCOME DISTRIBUTION, AND THE MINIMUM WAGE

Wages are the prices of labor resources. Wages are an important component of production costs and consequently are reflected in product prices. In this context, increases in wages should result in increases in product prices, for example, inflation, all other things being equal. To estimate the inflationary impacts of minimum wage changes, it is important to note that the wage bill impacts of minimum wage changes are unevenly distributed throughout the economy. Industries with large numbers of low-wage workers and industries with labor-intensive production processes are more likely to experience inflationary impacts than high-wage, capital-intensive industries. Historically, annual wage bill increases attributable to minimum wage increases have been in the aggregate in the one half of 1 percent to 1 percent range. Since labor costs are typically 30 to 35 percent of production costs, it would be surprising to see large price increases in response to minimum wage increases.

In addition to the relatively small aggregate wage bill impacts of minimum wage changes, there are several other complications. First, since wages are prices, as noted earlier, employers will attempt to substitute lower-priced factor inputs for higher-priced inputs. An increase in the minimum wage, *ceterius paribus*, should set in motion a process of factor substitution. To the extent this substitution process is successful, output may expand, and downward pressure on prices may occur.

Second, producers are likely to have varying capability for passing increased labor costs through to consumers, depending on the price elasticity of demand for the product or service. The more elastic the demand, the less success the producer will have in passing through wage increases.

Third, it is known that worker productivity increases, at least in the short term, in response to higher wage rates. Since increased productivity, for example, expanded output, places downward pressure on price levels, it is less compelling to argue that minimum wage increases will inevitably lead to increasing inflation.

However, even with these potentially offsetting forces, one of the traditional arguments opposing increases in the minimum wage was the "inflationary" argument. Opponents suggested that increasing the minimum wage was a self-defeating process. They argued that increasing the minimum wage inevitably leads to increases in inflation that left the low-wage worker in the same relative real position. The fallacy in this argument is derived from the fact that low-wage workers can come out ahead in *real* terms for two reasons. First, a 10 percent increase in money wages will not result in a 10 percent increase in inflation. Research shows that a 10 percent increase in the minimum wage leads to about a one tenth of 1 percent increase in inflation. Second, the goods produced by minimum wage workers—that presumably increase in price—are different from the goods they consume. In short, the wage gains accrue to a relatively small number of workers, but the price effects, large or small, are spread over the universe of consumers.

Numerous analysts examined the inflationary effects during the 1970s, and in general, they found a positive but relatively small effect. Robert Falconer noted that the 1978 increase in the minimum wage from $2.30 per hour to $2.65 per hour—a 15.2 percent increase—resulted in a *one third of 1 percent* increase in the level of prices.[72] It is conceivable that the total impact—direct and indirect—may have been twice the above estimate, but even then, it would be difficult to argue that the inflationary effect was large.

Some have argued that the minimum wage program is in reality a device for the redistribution of income. As Gramlich noted in 1976, "Although the minimum wage is favored or opposed for a wide variety of reasons, it appears to be basically an attempt to alter the distribution of income."[73] If this is true, the prognosis for this objective is dim. Steven Zell argued, "Economic theory and virtually all studies of the issue are in agreement that, at best, the minimum wage is a highly inefficient tool for redistributing income."[74] Part of what causes the weak redistributive effect is the demographic distribution of minimum wage workers. Most minimum wage earners are from middle- to upper-income families. This observation led Gramlich to argue, "The generally loose correlation between wages and family incomes implies that minimum wages will never have strong redistributive effects."[75]

To demonstrate the impotence of minimum wage programs in relation to income distribution, Gramlich suggested, "The inflationary potential of large increases in the minimum wage is likely to become serious long before the redistributive potential becomes significant."[76] Since, as noted above, the inflationary effects are relatively small, in their own right, the income redistributive effects are likely to be small.

The general impression one gets by examining these research and theoretical efforts is that the minimum wage clearly has some impact on the labor force and the economy but that the impacts are small and not easily identified. Part of the reason for the size and character of the effects involves the relatively small number of workers working at or near the minimum wage. With between 2 and 3 percent of the total labor force working at or near the minimum wage, one could hardly expect major wage bill or price consequences because of changes in the minimum wage.

It is important, however, to point out that the minimum wage program does not have uniform impacts across the economy. Specific industry segments and labor force groups are undoubtedly more directly affected than the impacts on the economy. The state of the economy within which an increase or expansion of coverage takes place is likely to materially alter the impacts or effects of the change. The interval within which each change is "phased in" will determine to some degree what the impacts will be on individual workers and the economy. In light of these complex interrelationships, it is a safe bet that no one will be clever enough to concoct an analytical methodology that will definitively reveal the impacts and consequences of these programs to everyone's satisfaction.

PROGRAM ADMINISTRATION

In spite of or possibly in response to extensive empirical examination of the minimum wage program, there were continued administrative changes initiated to improve the operation of the program. The early 1970s was a period of awakening about the real role of the minimum wage. It was acknowledged that it was not a panacea for all the nation's economic and social problems. In 1972, Secretary James Hodgson expounded at length about the philosophical and practical role of the minimum wage in American society. He observed in 1972, "In itself the minimum wage cannot guarantee a minimum but adequate family income."[77] Rather, "the minimum wage is a social norm which sets a floor below which no covered worker should be paid even if it means foreclosing employment opportunities to some very low productivity workers."[78] He further argued, "Too much has been asked of the minimum wage in the past. From the beginning it was unrealistic to expect that the minimum wage could assure a minimum but adequate level of living for wage earners regardless of family size."[79] Rather, the secretary argued that the minimum wage was one tool in the range of social policies to attack the problems of low wages and poverty.

The Wage and Hour Division emphasized an enforcement strategy of "worst first" in FY 1973. Due to the persistent large volume of complaints, there was increased use of conciliation and "limited investigation" techniques. In addition, Secretary Hodgson gave the Compliance Utilizing Education program high marks for improved compliance through a self-monitoring process by large firms. Started in 1969, the CUE program was a voluntary program that permitted firms to examine their compliance posture and correct deficiencies before Wage and Hour inspections were conducted. However, Secretary Hodgson noted, "Although the success of the program has led to its expansion, the Wage and Hour Division has not abandoned its responsibility to enforce applicable laws in the case of firms participating in the CUE program where such action is indicated."[80] There are still a few firms under CUE agreements in 1988, though the primary initiative was eliminated over a decade ago.

In response to the many changes in the minimum wage during the decade, FLSA investigations found increasing numbers of workers not being paid the minimum wage. In 1970, about 207,881 employees were underpaid about $29.4 million. By the end of the decade, in 1979, more than 426,000 employees were underpaid over $54 million. Both the number of employees in the underpaid category and the amount of underpayment reached their maximums in 1979 and decreased monotonically throughout the next eight years.

The numbers of employees underpaid overtime compensation has been a much more stable component of investigative activity. In 1970, more than 284,542 employees were underpaid about $54 million. In 1978, the comparable estimates were 264,000 employees underpaid about $51.7 million. In 1979, however, an estimated 287,000 employees were underpaid about $70 million. In years after 1979, the numbers of employees underpaid overtime compensation has fluctuated in a fairly narrow band between 260,000 and

330,000. However, the amounts of overtime compensation underpayment have increased steadily to almost $100 million per year in the fiftieth year of the program. Consequently, Wage and Hour Division investigations now find about $3 of overtime underpayment for each $1 of minimum wage underpayment.

While the overall investigative program developed in an orderly fashion, the early years of the decade were riddled with new ideas, new procedures, and new program emphasis. There was increasing awareness that an effective enforcement program required more than adding larger and larger numbers of compliance officers. An example of program emphasis was enforcement of the Equal Pay Act (EPA). While initially implemented in FY 1965, enforcement of the EPA gained significant momentum in FY 1969 and FY 1970. The first four years of its existence were marked by relatively few investigations that revealed few employees not paid equally as required by Section 6 of the FLSA. This upward momentum continued so that in 1976 nearly $18 million was found due to more than 24,610 workers. Investigations related to the Equal Pay Act through the end of FY 1978 had found more than 272,000 employees due over $163 million.[81] Then, under President Carter's Reorganization Plan No. 1 of 1978, the enforcement responsibilities of the Equal Pay Act were transferred to the Equal Employment Opportunities Commission on July 1, 1979.[82] Section 5 responsibilities related to research activities were retained by the Department of Labor.

In the next two years, however, changes by the executive branch of government altered the program in several substantial ways. First, to ensure that there were no sex-based differences in fringe benefits, the Wage and Hour Division issued an Interpretive Bulletin in 1978 that made "clear that employee benefits are 'wages' within the meaning of the equal pay provisions" of the FLSA.[83]

Second, Administrative Order No. 654, issued by the secretary of labor in 1978, indefinitely suspended industry committees in Puerto Rico and the Virgin Islands "since the automatic increases exceeded such increases recommended by the special industry committees."[84] The industry review program remained in effect in American Samoa.

INDUSTRY COMMITTEES UNDER THE ACT

By the late 1970s, industry committees had fulfilled their role and were substantially eliminated from the program. A brief summary of this part of the program will show the importance of industry committees in the evolution of the FLSA. Passed in 1938, the FLSA stipulated that the minimum wage would be at least $ .25 per hour from the date of initial enforcement—October 24, 1938—with two increases to $ .30 per hour and $ .40 per hour. The former was to become effective on October 24, 1939. Employers had until October 24, 1945, to reach the $ .40 per hour minimum wage. The wage and hour administrator had the authority to modify—accelerate—this schedule by adopting the recommendations of legislatively provided "industry committees." Elmer Andrews, the first wage and hour administrator, noted, "The Act requires the Administrator to appoint industry committees as soon as possible to recommend minimum wages for various industries which would be higher than the statutory rates but not exceed forty cents an hour."[85]

The concept behind the creation of industry committees was that there were significant differences within and between industries concerning their abilities to absorb minimum wage increases without substantial curtailment of employment. As Walter Boles noted in 1940, "In providing for the industry committee machinery, the framers of the act were utilizing a principle of minimum wage law administration which experience with state legislation of this nature indicated was superior to the rigid provision of minima within a statute."[86] All covered industries were brought to the $ .25 per hour rate in 1938 unless specifically exempted. Industry committees were intended to review the transition from the $ .25 rate to the higher rates. The relationship that drove the committee's actions was to find the highest minimum wage rate that could be adopted without substantial curtailment of employment. However, the statute provided that no minimum wage rate could be determined solely geographically and further that there would be no minimum wage classifications made on the basis of sex or age.

In the initial three years—October 24, 1938, to June 30, 1941—thirty-seven industry committees were appointed by the wage and hour administrator. The formation of a committee was preceded by an internal review by the Administrator in which three questions were addressed: (1) "Which industry should be selected for study and recommendations?" (2) "How shall the industry be defined?" and (3) "Who shall be appointed to serve on the committee?"[87] These questions, while basic, were the primary determinants of whether specific groups of workers would receive wage increases. Consequently, some attention is needed concerning the thought process that answered these questions. In terms of the selection of an industry for study, "[t]he Administrator's policy has been to select those industries in which prospects of improving the economic status of large numbers of wage earners are believed to be good."[88]

This general policy statement did little to delimit the industry selection process because the number of workers could be increased or decreased by simply changing the boundaries of the "industry." Therefore, industry definitions became critically important. As Elroy Golding noted, the industry classifications for rate determination were to consider "competitive conditions as affected by transportation, living and production costs; wages established for work of like character by collective agreements; . . . wages paid for work of like character by employers who, 'voluntarily' maintain fair labor standards"; and "other relevant factors."[89]

To understand the parameters of the industry configuration existing in the late 1930s, the Wage and Hour Division grouped industries into three categories: (1) those already paying $ .40 per hour or more; (2) those paying less than

$ .40 per hour, but believed to be capable of absorbing wage increases without serious dislocations; and (3) those paying less than $ .40 per hour but that would be severely impacted by wage increases.[90]

The depressed wage structure existing in 1937–1938 was very different from the conditions three years later. One might speculate whether the "success" of the industry committees would have been as easy without the rapidly expanding economy of the early 1940s. In any event, defining the scope or boundary of an industry became a difficult problem for the Wage and Hour Division.[91] There were several existing sources of industry definitions—Bureau of the Census, National Industrial Recovery Act definitions, among others—but none were determined acceptable to the requirements of the FLSA. As a result, before an industry committee could be appointed, the Wage and Hour Division was required to conduct "extensive original investigations involving in many cases extensive research into and investigations of manufacturing establishments, and conferences with manufacturers, trade associations, labor organizations, and other Government agencies."[92]

There was pressure by narrow industry groupings to have industry committees appointed for their "unique" industry conditions if it was believed advantageous to them. The research conducted early in this process resulted in collapsing many of these "unique" industry elements into much larger industry segments. Through research and negotiations with the full range of interested parties, industry boundaries were set. In some cases, after a generic industry committee was established, to accommodate the "narrow industry" interests, a subgroup or closely related industrial category would be separated out for a separate committee. For example, "[t]he appointment of a committee for the making of paper was followed by a committee for converted paper products to take in articles made of paper."[93]

The Wage and Hour Division realized that this was an imperfect process, that overlaps and gaps would occur, and that some misclassifications would result. Nevertheless, with extensive consultation and involvement of all interested parties in the information collection process, an industry classification scheme was adopted with minimal dissension. This process also generated large bodies of data and information that became important to the individual committees in subsequent deliberative processes.

The last step in the three-part process involved the selection of the committee personnel. The act required that committee membership be equally representative of public members and employers and employees in the industry. A public member had to be designated to chair each committee. During the period from October 24, 1938, to June 30, 1941, 193 public members were appointed to industry committees. The distribution by occupation gives an interesting insight into the character of these committees. Nearly half —ninety-seven—were educators. The second largest group—twenty-two— were law professors who were also presumably educators. Twenty business executives served on the committees as did thirteen labor mediators and ten newspaper executives. There were only nine practicing attorneys appointed to committees during this period. The total distribution of members is shown below:[94]

Business executives	20
Consumer organizations	3
Educators	97
Labor mediators	13
Law professors	22
Newspaper executives	10
Engineers	4
Practicing attorneys	9
Industrial organizations	4
Social workers	5
Judges	4
Clergymen	2

It would appear that the committees were not highly legalistic but were composed of individuals with stature and impartiality in a wide range of disciplines and occupations. The operation of the committees conformed to well-established norms for consensus decision making.

The administrator created each committee by official order in the *Federal Register*. A date was established to begin the proceedings, and interested parties were notified. The early committees generally met in Washington, D.C., with the exception of committee meetings in Puerto Rico. After an initial executive session to consider material provided by the Wage and Hour Division and other agencies, the committees went into public session. Information was provided through direct testimony or written briefs, or both. After these deliberations ended, an executive session was convened. The recommended minimum wage was determined by majority vote. All concurring members signed the recommendation that was sent to the administrator. Upon accepting the committee's recommendation, the administrator dissolved the committee.

The administrator was required to hold public hearings on the recommendations. Based on the outcome of these hearings, the administrator adopted in total the committee's recommended rates or rejected them—he could not modify them. If accepted, the rates were ordered, by wage order, into effect. If rejected, the administrator could reconvene the committee to engage in a reconsideration or establish another committee. There were established appeals procedures through the Circuit Court of Appeals or the Court of Appeals of the District of Columbia. Appeals to wage orders could reach the U.S. Supreme Court.

The above describes the general character and operations of the industry committees provided for in the original act. While there was optimism and a general feeling that these committees would work, soon after passage of the FLSA various industries in the Commonwealth of Puerto Rico requested an exemption from the mandated minimum wage. The governor of the Commonwealth established a committee to examine the effects of the FLSA on Puerto Rico's economy. The committee report, submitted in October 1939, painted a grim picture for the needlework industry and the tobacco industry if the $.25 minimum wage was enforced.

In addition, it was suggested that the canneries on the island would discontinue operation, which would in turn impact negatively on the agricultural sector. In response to these documented problems, industry committee activity for Puerto Rico, the Virgin Islands, and American Samoa was provided for by an amendment to the FLSA. As Fred Holly noted, "Once Congress determined that it would not be feasible to legislate fixed minima for Puerto Rico it decided to adopt a flexible approach under which industry committees would determine the minimum wage rate for an industry and classification therein under certain enumerated constraints."[95]   The FLSA amendment was enacted by the Congress in June and signed by the president on June 26, 1940. It authorized the administrator to appoint industry committees to "recommend minimum wages for employees in Puerto Rico and the Virgin Islands engaged in interstate commerce or in the production of goods for interstate commerce."[96]

In response to this legislation, the first industry committee for Puerto Rico was appointed on August 1, 1940. While the problems were of a similar nature, "[t]he first industry committee for the Virgin Islands was not convened until 1944."[97] The industry committee program on the mainland existed for about five years.

As Harry Weiss observed, "The last committee was appointed on 28 September 1943 and met on 22 October, just two days before the fifth anniversary of the effective date of the Fair Labor Standards Act."[98] When the last committee recommendation was provided to the wage and hour administrator in 1944, it effectively ended the mainland industry committee program. Industry committee activity in the three territories was to continue for several decades and, in fact, still exists today on American Samoa.

What started out as a deceptively simple notion evolved into a difficult economic and political issue. Progress was made by the industry committees, and by the end of 1947, all industries in Puerto Rico had been reviewed. While many industries in Puerto Rico had achieved parity with the mainland rates, some still lagged behind. The 1949 amendments to the FLSA raised the minimum wage to $.75 an hour for covered mainland workers, but the Congress left the wage order program in Puerto Rico intact. Some congressmen were concerned about the progress that had been made in Puerto Rico under the special industry committee program. As a consequence, a special committee of the House Committee on Education and Labor was created to study the minimum wage program in Puerto Rico. The committee's findings suggested that while progress had been made on the island through the special industry committee program, more progress toward achievement of the $.40 an hour standard could have been made with more frequent industry reviews. In response to the House special committee report recommending reviews of all industries on a two-year cycle, the wage order program was accelerated. During the six-year period be-tween 1949 and 1955, additional progress was made in approaching the statu-tory level of $.75 an hour through the special industry committees.

In the 1955 FLSA amendments, the mainland minimum wage was in-creased to $1.00 an hour, and the procedures for issuing wage orders changed in several important ways. First, beginning on July 1, 1956, the Department of Labor had to provide for review of minimum wage rates in Puerto Rico once each year. Second, the administrative review and authority to disapprove rates recommended by the special industry committees was eliminated. Third, upon receipt of facts and recommendations from the special industry committees, the secretary was required to publish the recommendations in the *Federal Register* without modification. The amendments required the secretary to issue an or-der stating that the rates in the *Federal Register* entry would become effective fifteen days from the date of publication. The review of wage orders was shifted to the courts of appeals.

In response to the expedited review process, large numbers of industries and industry segments were reviewed during 1957 and 1958. These reviews resulted in a wide range of rates from $.24 an hour in some parts of the fabric and leather glove industry to $1.00 an hour in several major industries. Even in an economy the size of Puerto Rico, annual industry reviews were time and resource consuming. Therefore, based on its review of the expedited review process over a two-year period, the U.S. Department of Labor—with support by labor, management, and the Commonwealth of Puerto Rico—recommended a biennial rather than an annual review process. The Congress amended the FLSA in 1958, incorporating a provision for biennial reviews with the proviso that the secretary could initiate additional reviews of particular rates if it was deemed necessary. While the special industry committee program in the terri-tories provided relief from the application of mainland rates, problems began to emerge. The industries of the three economies had access to mainland markets—some argued unfair access. While the industry committees function-ing in these areas were making some progress in increasing the legislated mini-mum rates, it was not clear that the rates would achieve parity with U.S. main-land rates any time in the foreseeable future. As a consequence, "[t]he pres-sures were great for the elimination of Puerto Rican wage discrimination. The first significant step in this direction was made in 1961 when Congress amended the wage provisions of the FLSA with respect to Puerto Rico."[99] The 1961 amendments "provided for a two-step automatic increase in existing wage or-der rates in Puerto Rico."[100] There was concern by Puerto Rican authorities that the pace of economic change would not permit the assimilation of the automatic increases. To ensure that Puerto Rico was treated fairly, the 1961 amendments

provided for two types of committees: (1)the industry committee, and (2) the special review committee. Both committees were given identical procedures, but their pur-

poses or objectives were different. The industry committee had the function of determining a minimum wage rate. . . . The special review committees were to hear hardship
cases arising from the percentage increases invoked in 1961."[101]

The industry committees of both types met almost continuously for more than a
decade. The automatic increases began bringing the wage structure into line
with the mainland rates.

By the early 1970s, industry committees in Puerto Rico and the Virgin
Islands had served their purposes. In fact, "[t]he 1974 FLSA amendments
made drastic alterations in the industry committee setup. The industry committee has expired, and the pre-existing authority for hardship review by special
industry committee has been discontinued."[102] While the industry committee
program in Puerto Rico and the Virgin Islands effectively ended in 1974, the
program continued in American Samoa. There are still industry committee
activities in that territory.

AN ASSESSMENT OF THE INDUSTRY COMMITTEE PROGRAM

The use of industry committees has been an accepted feature of foreign
minimum wage programs, many early state programs, and of course, the FLSA.
This assessment focuses on the FLSA experience. The seventy mainland committees brought 113 recommendations to the wage and hour administrator for
consideration. Importantly, "[o]f the 113 recommendations, . . . only six recommendations, part of the work of two committees, were disapproved by the
Administrator after consideration of the evidence."[103] This record suggests
that the committees were very effective in the development and presentation of
evidence to support their recommendations. It is important to note, however,
that

the Administrator is under strong pressure to affirm. If he failed to affirm, he would be
accused of unreasonable delay in administration, of incompetence in selecting the personnel of industry committees, of wasting funds provided for Wage and Hour Administration, and of failing to foster that cooperation between private groups and the Wage
and Hour Administration which is essential if the Fair Labor Standards Act is to be
adequately enforced.[104]

While "[t]he Act describes the committee's functions primarily in
fact-finding terms,"[105] it was in reality a commingling of economic and political forces that put considerable pressure on the administrator to accept the
recommended rate structure. The published rates could be, and in several instances were, challenged in the Courts, but "[i]t is a significant fact that not a
single wage order has been successfully challenged in the courts."[106] In some

ways, the outcome of the legal review process is not surprising. The experience of the committees showed remarkable consensus by all representatives on the recommended rates. As Weiss observed in 1945, while "[u]nder the law a majority vote of the entire committee is all that is required for approval, . . . it is very uncommon to find the voting sharply divided."[107] The wage and hour administrator reported in 1944 that "[m]ore than half the 113 recommendations were reached by a unanimous vote of employer, employee and public representatives."[108]

With this record of consensus, one would not be surprised that the courts were generally responsive to the rates recommended to the administrator. In spite of the broad consensus on specific rate structures, there were nevertheless problems in both the mainland and offshore programs. A difficult problem, described briefly above, was the delineation of the "industry." Observers compared the process used by the wage and hour administrator in the perspective of the National Recovery Act (NRA) of a decade earlier. As Weiss noted, "The success of the Wage and Hour Division in avoiding the experience of the NRA is strikingly brought out by the fact that through a total of about 55 industry definitions, coverage over an industrial field employing about 21 million workers was achieved; the NRA required some 550 codes to cover approximately equivalent employment."[109]

There were hundreds of requests by industry representatives to convene committees for narrow industrial classifications. The strategy of these industry leaders was to control the wage change process that would give them the best competitive advantage. Industries were concerned that by being commingled with their competitors they would be pulled into a process over which they had little influence or control. To some degree, these concerns were addressed through "subcommittees" of the industry committees, but these, too, were limited in number. There were forces pulling the administrator in both directions in the classification of industries. The unwieldy NRA experience argued strongly for fewer industry classifications involving larger numbers of possibly dissimilar components. On the other hand, a practical disadvantage of a broad definition of an industry is that "industry committees must be of limited size to be workable and therefore the composition of a committee for a comprehensive industry can seldom reflect with even a fair degree of accuracy the different groups subject to the jurisdiction of the committee."[110]

To a large degree, the public representatives were selected from universities, law firms, churches, and other institutions perceived to be impartial. However, the "employee" representatives were decidedly more difficult to identify. Some industry components had employees represented by unions, while others were open shop operations. The question focused on who represents the views of workers best and how could the administrator identify these representatives. There were few problems in unionized components because the unions designated knowledgeable candidates. One problem that did arise involved situations in which two or more unions represented workers in the industry sector.

The general approach was to designate representatives on a "proportion of work force represented" basis, and the process worked satisfactorily.

It was less clear how to identify open shop representatives who would have the knowledge necessary to represent a wide spectrum of workers. As Golding concluded, serious difficulties arose "from the Administrator's ruling that union officials are proper representatives of unorganized labor because they have sworn to maintain the interests of all classes of labor. By failing to secure participation of unorganized labor on industry committees, the Wage and Hour Administrator has established a procedure which is potentially unfair."[111] Fair or unfair, union representatives were selected to represent employees on the committees.

Importantly, reviewing the structure of the mainland committees, Golding observed, "In selecting employer representatives, the practice has been to obtain nominations from trade associations. . . . This seems to be subject to the same objection as the parallel practice of determining employee representatives by consulting unions. In the present state of industrial organization, however, no other course seem practical."[112]

A more fundamental problem with the committee participants was the level of expertise brought to the process. There had been no precedent for analyses of this scope and complexity that had to be made in compressed time periods. Alluding to this situation, Boles, in 1940, argued that "the difficult nature of the questions facing the economic laymen on the industry committees renders doubtful the soundness of their wage recommendations."[113] In retrospect, Boles's concerns may have been premature and largely off target. There was compelling evidence that the committees made sound, reasoned recommendations that were generally accepted by unions, employers, and the public. As Weiss observed, "The universal minimum wage of 40 cents an hour was achieved almost two years before the date it would have become effective automatically, and, for many industries, was established at a much earlier date."[114]

When one considers the enormity of the task facing the Wage and Hour Division in late 1938, one cannot help being impressed with the apparent speed and efficiency of the industry committee recommendation formulation process. Certainly, the mainland program achieved its objectives, and while taking longer and probably causing more dislocations, the Puerto Rican and Virgin Island efforts were generally considered successes as well.

CONCLUSION

This chapter focused on the FLSA's operation in the 1970s. The industry committee program played a major role in the early years of the program. Its history and impacts were described in the last part of this chapter. The decade ended with a congressionally mandated Minimum Wage Study Commission examining the full range of minimum wage issues and activities. It was anticipated that the commission's report and recommendations would establish the agenda for substantial improvements in the nation's minimum wage program. "Improvements" did not mean simply increases in the minimum wage. Anticipations were that coverage would be expanded and possibly there would be initiatives to improve enforcement. The seven-volume report did not meet those expectations.

NOTES

1. *Economic Report of the President*, transmitted to the Congress in February 1986 (Washington, D.C.: Government Printing Office, 1986), p. 287.

2. Ibid., p. 290.

3. "Employment Standards," *New York Times*, August 27, 1968, p. 26.

4. Will Lissner, "3 Candidates for Senator Give Prescriptions to Cure Poverty," *New York Times*, October 27, 1968, p. 75.

5. "Associated Press Note," *New York Times*, January 17, 1969, p. 16.

6. *New York Times*, February 21, 1969, p. 17.

7. Paul Delaney, "Minimum Wage Cut for Youths Studied," *New York Times*, September 8, 1969, p. 558.

8. Edwin L. Dale, Jr., "Researchers Conclude that Raising the Wage Floor Causes Loss of Jobs," *New York Times*, November 8, 1969, p. 1.

9. Paul Delaney, "Shultz Opposes a Youth Wage Rate," *New York Times*, November 18, 1969, p. 2.

10. Ibid.

11. *New York Times*, November 22, 1969, p. 51.

12. "Meany Seeks Rise to $2 in Pay Floor," *New York Times*, July 30, 1970, p. 15.

13. *New York Times*, August 5, 1970, p. 24.

14. Warren Weaver, Jr., "Long Is Rebuffed on Welfare Idea," *New York Times*, August 7, 1970, p. 14.

15. Ibid.

16. Eileen Shanahan, "Albert Bids Democrat Lead a Drive to End Slump," *New York Times*, April 9, 1971, p. 16.

17. *New York Times*, April 26, 1971, p. 34.

18. Marjorie Hunter, "Colmer to Allow Wage Bill Action," *New York Times*, March 15, 1972, p. 30.

19. "Washington: For the Record," *New York Times*, April 12, 1972, p. 13.

20. David Rosenbaum, "House Holds Up Wage Base Rise," *New York Times*, August 2, 1972, p. 12.

21. David Rosenbaum, "House Bars Move on Minimum Wage," *New York Times*, October 4, 1972, p. 1.

22. Ibid.

23. Edwin L. Dale, "Economic Aide to Nixon Scores Sentimentality and Prejudice on Major Issues," *New York Times*, February 15, 1973, p. 27.

24. Paul Delaney, "Rise in Black's Income Is Easing," *New York Times*, March 3, 1973, p. 39.

25. Philip Shabecoff, "$2.30 Wage Base by '76 Proposed," *New York Times*, April 11, 1973, p. 1.

26. *New York Times*, April 11, 1973, p. 18.

27. Martin Tolchin, "Mrs. Chisholm Led Fight for Domestics Base Pay," *New York Times*, June 21, 1973, p. 45.

28. Richard L. Madden, "Republicans Fail to Cut Wage Bill," *New York Times*, July 18, 1973, p. 19.

29. "Senate Rejects Substitute for Wage Bill," *New York Times*, July 19, 1973, p. 15.

30. "Nixon Aide Is Sure of Phase 4 Stability," *New York Times*, July 23, 1973, p. 16.

31. "Wage-Floor Bill Passed in Senate by 62-to-28 Vote," *Wall Street Journal*, August 3, 1973, p. 2.

32. James M. Naughton, "Nixon, in Challenge to Congress, Will Submit 'Bipartisan' Plans; He Will Veto Minimum-Wage Bill," *New York Times*, September 6, 1973, p. 1.

33. Ibid.

34. "Wrong End Squeeze," *New York Times*, September 7, 1973, p. 34.

35. Philip Shabecoff, "Labor and the Minimum Wage," *New York Times*, September 16, 1973, Sec. III, p. 4.

36. John Herbers, "Clash between President and Congress Intensifies," *New York Times*, September 7, 1973, p. 23.

37. "Ceiling Unlimited," *New York Times*, September 22, 1973, p. 30.

38. Philip Shabecoff, "Meany Says Labor Will Need 10% Pay Increase This Year," *New York Times*, February 21, 1974, p. 53.

39. Philip Shabecoff, "Compromise Seen on Minimum Wage," *New York Times*, February 28, 1974, p. 19.

40. R.W. Apple, "President Signs Rise in Pay Base to $2.30 an Hour," *New York Times*, April 9, 1974, p. 1.

41. U.S. Department of Labor, *First Section 4(d)(3) Report to Congress* (Washington, D.C.: Government Printing Office, 1975), p. 3.

42. Edward Cowan, "Washington and Business: Battle Looms on Minimum Wage 'Indexation,'" *New York Times*, May 7, 1976, p. IV-1.

43. Lesley Oelsner, "High Court Frees States and Cities from U.S. Pay Laws," *New York Times*, June 25, 1976, p. D-13.

44. *National League of Cities v. Usery*, 426 U.S. 833 (1976).

45. "The Minimally Useful Minimum Wage," *New York Times*, March 21, 1977, p. 26.

46. Philip Shabecoff, "$2.30 Minimum Wage Proposed by Carter in Setback to Labor," *New York Times*, March 25, 1977, p. D-13.

47. *New York Times*, March 25, 1977, p. C-9.

48. "Unemployment Rate Off to 7.3% in March," *New York Times*, April 2, 1977, p. 12.

49. "The Minimally Useful Minimum Wage," p. 26.

50. Michael J. Piore, "Of 'Target Earners,' Aliens, and Wages," *New York Times*, April 4, 1977, p. 28.

51. Marjorie Hunter, "Plains, Ga., Farmer Puts His Feelings in Nutshell," *New York Times*, May 18, 1977, p. 18.

52. U.S. Department of Labor, Employment Standards Administration, *Minimum Wage and Maximum Hours Standards under the Fair Labor Standards Act*, transmitted to the Congress on August 15, 1979 (Washington, D.C.: Government Printing Office,

1979), p. 11.

53. Thomas Gale Moore, "The Effect of Minimum Wages on Teenage Unemployment Rates," *Journal of Political Economy*, Vol. 79, No. 4, July-August 1971, p. 898.

54. Ibid.

55. Douglas K. Adie, "Teen-Age Unemployment and Real Federal Minimum Wages," *Journal of Political Economy*, Vol. 81, No. 2, Part 1, March-April 1973, p. 436.

56. James F. Ragan, Jr., "Minimum Wages and the Youth Labor Market," *Review of Economics and Statistics*, Vol. LIX, No. 2, May 1977, p. 135.

57. Robert S. Goldfarb, "Quantitative Research on the Minimum Wage," *Monthly Labor Review*, Vol. 98, No. 4, April 1975, p. 46.

58. Marvin Kosters and Finis Welch, "The Effects of Minimum Wages on the Distribution of Changes in Aggregate Employment," *American Economic Review*, Vol. LXII, No. 3, June 1972, p. 330.

59. Jacob Mincer, "Unemployment Effects of Minimum Wages," *The Journal of Political Economy*, Vol. 84, No. 4, Part 2, August 1976, p. S103.

60. Ibid.

61. Edward M. Gramlich, "Impact of Minimum Wages on Other Wages, Employment and Family Income," *Brookings Papers on Economic Activity*, Vol. 2, 1976, p. 442.

62. Finis Welch and James Cunningham, "Effects of Minimum Wages on the Level and Age Composition of Youth Employment," *Review of Economics and Statistics*, Vol. LX, No. 2, February 1978, p. 144.

63. Gramlich, 1976, p. 443.

64. Yale Brozen, "The Effect of Statutory Minimum Wage Increases on Teen-Age Employment," *Journal of Law and Economics*, Vol. XII, No. 1, April 1969, p. 117.

65. Goldfarb, 1975, p. 46.

66. Moore, 1971, p. S100.

67. Ibid.

68. Ragan, 1977, p. 135.

69. Mincer, 1976, p. 587.

70. Gramlich, 1976, p. 427.

71. Ibid., p. 426.

72. Robert T. Falconer, "The Minimum Wage: A Perspective," *Quarterly Review*, Federal Reserve Bank of New York, Vol. 3, No. 3, Autumn 1978, p. 6.

73. Ibid., p. 410.

74. Steven P. Zell, "The Minimum Wage and Youth Unemployment," *Economic Review*, Federal Reserve Bank of Kansas City, January 1978, p.15.

75. Gramlich, 1976, p. 445.

76. Ibid., p. 449.

77. U.S. Department of Labor, Employment Standards Administration, *Minimum Wage and Maximum Hours Standards under the Fair Labor Standards Act*, transmitted to the Congress on January 31, 1972 (Washington, D.C.: Government Printing Office, 1972), p. 2.

78. Ibid., p. 3.

79. Ibid., p. 2.

80. Ibid., p. 18.

81. U.S. Department of Labor, Employment Standards Administration, *Minimum Wage and Maximum Hours Standards under the Fair Labor Standards Act*, 1979, p. 2.

82. Ibid., p. 3.

83. Ibid., p. 36.

84. Ibid., p. 13.

85. Elmer F. Andrews, "Tribulations of a Wage-Hour Administrator," *Public Opinion Quarterly*, Vol. 4, No. 1, March 1946, p. 27.

86. Walter E. Boles, Jr., "Some Aspects of the Fair Labor Standards Act," *Southern Economic Journal*, Vol. VI, No. 4, April 1940, p. 500.

87. U.S. Department of Labor, Wage and Hour and Public Contracts Divisions, *Annual Report, 1942*, transmitted to the Congress on January 4, 1943 (Washington, D.C., 1943, mimeographed), p.1.

88. Ibid.

89. Elroy D. Golding, "The Industry Committee Provisions of the Fair Labor Standards Act," *Yale Law Review*, Vol. 50, No. 7, May 1941, p. 1143.

90. U.S. Department of Labor, 1942, p. 2.

91. Ibid., p. 3.

92. Ibid., p. 3.

93. Ibid., p. 4.

94. Ibid., p. 4.

95. Fred Holly, "Federal Minimum Wage Determinations in Puerto Rico" (Washington, D.C., n.d., mimeographed), p. 3.

96. U.S. Department of Labor, Wage and Hour and Public Contracts Divisions, *Annual Report*, Fiscal year 1959, reprinted from the Secretary of Labor's *Annual Report for 1959* (Washington, D.C.: Government Printing Office, 1961), p. 4.

97. Ibid., p. 12.

98. Harry Weiss, "Minimum Wage Fixing under the United States Fair Labor Standards Act," *International Labour Review*, Vol. LI, No. 1, January 1945, p. 23.

99. Holly, n.d., p. 4.

100. Ibid., p. 7.

101. Ibid., pp. 4–5.

102. Ibid., p. 6.

103. U.S. Department of Labor, Wage and Hour and Public Contracts Divisions, *Annual Report*, Fiscal year 1944, transmitted to the Congress on January 3, 1945, Washington, D.C., mimeographed, p. 22.

104. Golding, 1941, p. 1177n.

105. Weiss, 1945, p. 18.

106. Ibid., p. 40.

107. Ibid., p. 36.

108. U.S. Department of Labor, 1944, p. 22.

109. Weiss, 1945, p. 24.

110. Golding, 1941, p. 1153.

111. Ibid., p. 1157.

112. Ibid., p. 1158.

113. Boles, 1940, p. 510.

114. Weiss, 1945, p. 18.

Chapter 8

The Decade of the 1980s: Stalemate

During the decade of the 1980s, while the real minimum wage fell to historic lows, all efforts to raise the federal minimum wage fell short. With the large absolute and relative gains in the minimum wage in the 1970s, one could argue that the decade of the 1970s was a "tough act to follow." While few would have expected the decade of the 1980s to repeat or improve upon the experience of the 1970s, equally few would have thought that the decade would have been without substantial changes. There have been major changes in the economy that affected the minimum wage program, but to date, most of these changes have gone unchallenged. This chapter will complete the description of the program by describing the economic conditions in the 1980s and summarizing program and legislative activities in the 1980s. In addition, three important aspects of the FLSA that warrant special attention will be described. These elements are child labor provisions, Section 14 activities, and program staffing.

ECONOMIC CONDITIONS IN THE 1980s

The 1980s can be characterized in two ways: first, a period of sustained economic growth lasting over six years and, second, a period containing the deepest recession in the post–Great Depression era. These seemingly inconsistent or contradictory descriptions attest to the nature of the economic variability in the last eight years. The decade started with high rates of inflation, moderate unemployment, high interest rates, and decreasing productivity. Business failure rates began escalating in 1980 and continued to increase to a historical high of 115 failures in every 10,000 enterprises in 1985. During the three prior decades—1950 to 1979—the failure rate averaged 40 to 50 failures in every 10,000 enterprises.[1]

The economic problems at the beginning of the 1980s were pervasive and serious. While all the problems noted above were important, the one that was most troubling was the high rate of inflation. It was observed that even when the minimum wage increased from $2.90 to $3.10 on January 1, 1980, that "[t]he latest 6.9 percent increase is little more than half the nation's current inflation rate of 13 percent per year and is less than the 8.1 percent increase in the average wage over the past 12 months."[2] There were two rapid accelerations of price change during the 1970s and early 1980s. In two years, 1979 and 1980, the consumer price index increased over 25 percent. There were no periods during the post–World War II period that inflation approached increases of this size. The consuming public was bound up in inflation psychology, which led Dr. Alice Rivlin, director of the Congressional Budget Office, to observe that the primary cause of inflation was inflation.

The American public was alarmed by the dramatic reduction in the real value of their income and historically high unemployment rates. The defeat of President Carter can probably be traced to these economic events and the unresolved hostage situation in Iran.

By contrast, unemployment rates of 5.8 percent in 1979 and 7.1 percent in 1980 were moderate by contemporary standards, though viewed as high in a historical context. In an effort to bring inflation under control, restrained monetary and fiscal policies pushed the unemployment rate into double digits. The civilian unemployment rate of 10.7 percent in both November and December 1982 were the first double-digit levels since the Great Depression. During November and December 1982, slightly less than 10.2 million American workers were without jobs. These levels compared to the average of 6.1 million and 7.6 million in 1979 and 1980, respectively.

The anti inflation policies worked. The policies were not painless, but they broke the upward price spiral that threatened the domestic and international economic systems. In 1982, the inflation rate had decelerated to 3.9 percent per year. The percentage increase in prices remained near the 4 percent per year level until 1986, when it dropped to only 1.1 percent per year. This was the lowest percentage increase in prices in over twenty-five years.

While several primary economic indicators began to improve during the early 1980s, other trouble spots began to emerge. In FY 1979, the federal debt was $833.8 billion, and the federal deficit was $40.2 billion. The federal deficit began accelerating in the early 1980s and reached a high of about $212 billion in 1985. The deficit averaged in excess of $150 billion per year in the first half of the 1980s. By FY 1985, the federal debt had increased to $1.8 trillion. By the end of FY 1988, the federal debt was about $2.6 trillion. In 1979, exports of merchandise exceeded imports of merchandise by $27.5 billion. By 1986, imports exceeded exports by over $144 billion. The "twin deficits" began to occupy the attention of economic policy officials and the political leadership. It was generally believed that the two deficits of approximately $150 billion each could not be sustained over long periods of time.

However, the resilience of the U.S. economy and its ability to accommodate economic dislocations were clearly demonstrated by the existence and persistence of these deficits throughout the first eight years of the decade.

After the low point of a 1.1 percent increase in the CPI in 1986, the inflation rate began escalating again. The unemployment rate continued to decline into mid-1988, which was a good sign for federal policy officials. The American dollar had been weakening relative to other currencies for over two years, and fears were now expressed that it had weakened too much. These complex, interrelated economic problems were the environment within which those advocating increases in the minimum wage found themselves. For those opposed to increasing the minimum wage, arguments could be made that price stability had been achieved, and therefore there was no need to increase the statutory minimum wage. In addition, some argued that increasing the minimum wage would increase production costs and therefore contribute to inflation. Proponents argued that the real minimum wage had declined considerably and an increase was warranted. The state of the economy, the nature of the problems confronting policymakers, and the nature of the political process gave opponents and advocates of change in the minimum wage plenty of ammunition to argue their case.

THE 1981 MINIMUM WAGE STUDY COMMISSION

The 1977 amendments to the FLSA created the MWSC and provided it with a "charter" to study twelve specific topics relating to the "effects," "impacts," "consequences," "relationships," and "characteristics" of the program. The MWSC spent three years in its investigative process, which resulted in a seven-volume report to the Congress and the president concerning its findings and recommendations.

The general charter found in Section 2(e)2 of the 1977 amendments directed the commission to investigate the "social, political, and economic ramifications of the minimum wage, overtime, and other requirements of the Fair Labor Standards Act of 1938." The twelve specific topics the commission was directed to investigate were the following:

A) The beneficial effects of the minimum wage, including its effect in ameliorating poverty among working citizens; B) The inflationary impact (if any) of increases in the minimum wage prescribed by the Fair Labor Standards Act; C) The effect (if any) such increases have on wages paid employees at a rate in excess of the rate prescribed by that Act; D) The economic consequences (if any) of authorizing an automatic increase in the rate prescribed in that Act on the basis of an increase in a wage, price, or other index; E) The employment and unemployment effects (if any) of providing a different minimum wage rate for youth, and the employment and unemployment effects (if any) on handicapped and aged individuals of an increase in such rate and of providing a different minimum wage rate for such individuals; F) The effect (if any) of the full-time student certification program on employment and unemployment; G) The employment and unemployment effects (if any) of the minimum wage; H) The exemptions from the minimum wage and overtime requirements of that Act; I) The relationship (if any) between the federal minimum wage rates and public assistance programs, including the extent to which employees at such rates are also eligible to receive food stamps and other public assistance; J) The level of noncompliance with the Act; K) The demographic profile of minimum wage workers; and, L) The extent to which the exemptions from the minimum wage and overtime requirements of the Act may apply to employees of conglomerates.[3]

The congressional mandate was based on the belief that an independent study commission was needed to investigate and presumably resolve the myriad questions about this program's operation and impacts. There were extensive research studies on every aspect of the minimum wage and maximum hour program, but, as noted in the previous chapter, the only generalization that could be made was that there was no consensus within the research community on the questions of effects and impacts. The commission was composed of eight members who were nominated by four federal agencies —Labor, Health and Human Services, Commerce, and Agriculture. The eight members selected a chairperson to preside over their deliberations.

To facilitate the commission's work, the twelve specific study topics were grouped into six study areas. A senior commission economist was assigned to oversee each study area to ensure that a comprehensive investigation occurred. While commission staff conducted many investigations themselves, there was extensive use of external experts and consultants who prepared dozens of reports for the commission's consideration. The commission's chair, James G. O'Hara, described in his transmittal letters to President Ronald Reagan, Speaker Thomas P. O'Neill, and president of the Senate, George Bush, the scope of the inquiry. O'Hara indicated, "We have conducted the most exhaustive inquiry ever undertaken into the issues surrounding the Act —FLSA— since its inception. . . . We have sought to examine and balance the interests of business, labor, consumers, agriculture, and the working men and women of our country as a whole."[4]

This inquiry produced a series of conclusions and recommendations that sparked as many questions and evoked as much controversy as they were supposed to prevent. The commission's recommendations were based on a majority vote of the eight commissioners. Commissioners with minority viewpoints were given the opportunity to express them in the *Final Report*.[5] The commission's recommendations are detailed, numerous, and comprehensive. The interested reader can obtain a complete listing of these recommendations, the supporting viewpoints, and the minority comments by reading Volume I of the *Final Report*. For the purposes of this study, only the recommendations relating to several of the more controversial and well-known issues will be discussed.

The major commission recommendations were the following:

1. *Youth subminimum wage (youth differential)*. The question was whether or not the Congress should mandate a two-tier minimum wage—one for adult workers and a lower one for youth. The commission voted six to two to adopt the motion: "The commission recommends to the Congress that a uniform national youth differential not be enacted."[6] The motion to permit "local experimentation" with a youth subminimum wage was defeated by a five-to-one vote, with two abstentions.

2. *Minimum wage indexing*. The question was whether to adopt an indexing scheme for adjusting the minimum wage or continue the current process of periodic consideration by the Congress. The commission adopted a motion to recommend an indexing scheme on a five-to-two vote with one member not voting.[7]

3. *Exemptions*. The commission reviewed something in excess of forty categories of exemptions from the FLSA. While many of the exemption categories are very specific and narrowly defined, several have significant coverage impacts. In addition, several categories are controversial because of the character of the workers or organizations affected by them. The exemptions and the commission's recommendations that will be discussed here include:

   - 7(k) —Federal law enforcement and fire protection employees
   - 13(a)(1)—Executives, administrators, and professionals; and, outside sales workers
   - 13(a)(2)—Small retail trade and service establishments
   - 13(a)(6)—Small farm employers
   - 13(b)(12)—Agricultural employees and irrigation workers
   - 13(b)(27)—Motion picture theaters
   - 13(d)—Delivery of newspapers to the consumer

The FLSA requires overtime compensation of at least one and one-half times the straight-time hourly rate for covered employees working more than 40 hours per week. The 7(k) exemption provides for the modification of the maximum hours standard under the FLSA as they relate to federal firefighters and law enforcement personnel. Federal law enforcement personnel receive at least time and one-half for all work hours over 186 per twenty-eight-day work period. Firefighters must receive overtime pay for hours in excess of 216 per twenty-eight-day work period.

A study conducted in 1975 by the U.S. Department of Labor showed that law enforcement personnel worked an average of 186 hours per twenty-eight-day work period, while federal firefighters averaged 282 hours for the same work period. The unique work schedules involved with these two occupations suggested that the overtime hours requirements required modification. The initial hours standards for law enforcement and federal firefighters were, as noted above, 186 and 216, respectively. However, these standards were based on a survey of federal agency practices that the organizations representing these workers argued was too restrictive or not representative of the occupations. A court challenge to the hours standards ensued, and they were revised to 171 hours for law enforcement personnel and 212 hours for federal firefighters. These standards remain in effect today. When the MWSC reviewed this exemption, they adopted a motion by voice vote to "retain the exemption and continue efforts to reconcile FLSA provisions with those contained in the General Schedule."[8]

The Section 13(a)(1) exemption for executives, administrators, and professionals; and outside sales workers exempts these employees from both minimum wage and maximum hours provisions of the FLSA. The idea behind the exemption embraces the notion that some employees have the ability to fend for themselves if they occupy bona fide executive, administrative, and professional positions. Outside sales workers were difficult to monitor and were therefore exempt for administrative convenience. To be exempt under Section 13(a)(1), the employee must meet several "tests." To be considered exempt, the employee must earn a salary above an administratively prescribed test threshold. This level is currently $155 per week for executives and administrators and $170 per week for professionals. The second test is a "duties" test. These employees must perform activities administratively determined that are suitable for employees in these types of occupations. The third test limits the amount of time these employees can devote to nonexempt work (20 percent, generally; 40 percent in retail and service positions) and still retain the exemption. Approximately 20 million employees met the criteria for the executive, administrative, and professional exemption in 1987. About 2.5 million workers were exempt under the outside sales worker provisions of the FLSA. The commission recommended that this exemption be retained and that the test levels described above be revised upward to reflect conditions in the current economy.[9]

The Section 13(a)(2) exemption relates to the exempting of small businesses from the FLSA provisions. Currently, if an establishment in the retail trade or service industries has annual gross sales below $362,500, they are exempt under the Section 13(a)(2) provisions. This exemption removes the largest component of nonsupervisory workers from FLSA projections. There are about 1 million firms exempted that employ between 4 and 5 million workers. The commission's review of this exemption indicated that "three fourths of the exempt employees already earn at or above the minimum and about half of the exempt employers will not experience wage-bill increases."[10] These observations resulted in the commission's recommendation to eliminate the Section 13(a)(2) exemption.

The small agricultural employer exemption under Section 13(a)(6) applies to both the minimum wage and maximum hours provisions of the FLSA. The exemption is provided to small agricultural employers that used 500 man-days of labor or less in the peak calendar quarter of the previous year. About 350,000 employers employing something less than 800,000 workers are exempt under Section 13(a)(6). In addition, specific groups of workers in agriculture are exempt under these provisions. These are (1) immediate family members of the farm operator; (2) workers engaged in the range production of livestock; (3) local hand-harvest piece-rate workers employed fewer than thirteen weeks as farmworkers during the previous calendar year; and (4) children of migrant

agricultural workers employed as piece-rate harvest workers on farms employing their parents provided they receive the same piece rate as other employees.[11] The commission reviewed potential employment and wage bill impacts
of changing all or parts of the Section 13(a)(6) exemption. Their review resulted in a complex set of recommendations to retain, modify, and eliminate
various provisions of the exemption. The first recommendation was to lower
the 500 man-day test to 300 man-days in two steps. The second recommendation was to eliminate the minimum wage exemption—Section 13(a)(6)(c)—for
local hand-harvest piece-rate workers. The third recommendation related to
Section 13(a)(6) was to eliminate the exemption for migrant worker children
employed as hand-harvest piece-rate workers—Section 13(a)(6)(D). The fourth
recommendation was to retain the exemption for employees primarily engaged
in the range production of livestock. These employees would be subject to
minimum wage projections in agricultural employment other than range production of livestock if the employer met the man-day test.

The exemption relating to large agricultural employing units—Section
13(b)(12)—provides minimum wage protection, but not hours protection, in
farms hiring more than 500 man-days of labor in the peak employment quarter
of the previous calendar year. The specific group exemptions discussed in
Section 13(a)(6) also apply here. The 13(b)(12) exemption also applies to about
700 agricultural irrigation districts. The commission recommended that this
exemption be retained in its present form.

Section 13(b)(27) exempts motion picture theaters from the maximum hours
provisions of the FLSA. The commission reported that fewer than 5 percent
(about 6,000 workers) of exempt employers in this industry work more than
forty hours per week. Over 60 percent of these employees worked fewer than
twenty-five hours per week. As a consequence, the commission recommended
that the exemption be eliminated. Their rationale for this recommendation
was that the small amount of overtime work would have minimal wage-bill
impact. In fact, they suggested that the expansion in employment may totally
negate the wage bill impact.[12]

The last exemption discussed here relates to the home delivery of newspapers. The Section 13(d) exemption covers all three areas of the FLSA—minimum
wage, overtime, and child labor—because the vast majority of the employees
are eighteen years of age and under. The commission recognized that the traditional door-to-door process results in wages below the statutory minimum.
Nevertheless, this type of work has become an accepted part of Americana,
and its elimination would disrupt the introduction to responsible work experienced by millions of young people. In addition, the commission noted the
significant enforcement problems due to the difficulty in determining actual
"hours worked." As a result, the commission recommended continuation of
this exemption.[13]

As noted above, the commission considered a wide variety of existing
exemptions—about forty—and made recommendations for retention, modifica-

tion, or repeal.   Many of the exemptions relate to very narrow slices of an industry and to very small numbers of workers. This situation in itself does not make retention or repeal important or not important. There are arguments for both positions in virtually every instance. Rather, several exemptions were discussed here because of their contemporary interest and the controversy they generate. The interested reader will find a careful review of the full range of exemption issues summarized in Volume I of the commission's *Final Report*.[14]

DISPOSITION OF THE COMMISSION'S REPORT

Submission of the *Final Report* of the Minimum Wage Study Commission to the president and the Congress on May 24, 1981, brought the inquiry into this important set of issues to an official end. One might have thought that the *Final Report* would have spawned some intense debate, the generation of academic journal articles, and congressional oversight hearings. Nothing could be further from the truth. The *Final Report* was transmitted without fanfare, and the subsequent silence has been awesome. Several commission economists published follow-up articles in professional journals, but they have been few in number and broke no new ground.

Throughout this report, many issues—some of long standing—were addressed by the commission. In most cases the commission suggested one or more courses of action. It is a fair assessment to suggest that few, if any, of these recommended courses of action have been pursued.

PROGRAM ACTIVITIES IN THE 1980S

As the decade of the 1970s ended, an issue that had surfaced occasionally in the past gained importance: undocumented workers. These workers, referred to in earlier periods as "illegal aliens," were flooding into the American labor force. They were absorbing American jobs that many believed was enough reason to restrict the inflow. Because these workers were "undocumented," no one knew how many there were in the United States. Estimates between 2 and 12 million workers were commonly suggested. Besides the direct labor force impacts, the problem of worker exploitation arose. Due to their illegal status, these workers were susceptible to extreme employer abuse. Secretary Marshall suggested that these individuals "work hard and scared" without the protection of even rudimentary labor standards. In response to these conditions, the Wage and Hour Division began the undocumented worker enforcement program in June 1978. Several successful "strike force" enforcement efforts in New York City, northern New Jersey, and Houston, Texas, resulted in the identification of thousands of employees paid in violation of FLSA provisions. While these actions were great press, there is little evidence that they were of sufficient impact to materially address the problem.

In addition to the problem of undocumented workers, one of the most dif-ficult issues of the early 1980s was the employment of children in agriculture. The 1977 FLSA amendments established a waiver procedure for the employ-ment of ten- and eleven-year-old children in short-season, hand-harvested crops, for example, blueberries, strawberries, and potatoes. One criterion in the waiver process dealt with exposure of these children to pesticides or other chemicals used in the production process. The secretary had to determine, among other things, that these pesticides or chemicals would not have an "adverse effect" on the well-being or health of young workers. The department wrestled with the development of acceptable procedures for protecting young agricultural work-ers.

Most of these efforts were for naught because the U.S. Court of Appeals for the District of Columbia in *National Association of Farmworker Organiza-tions v. Marshall* established a standard of "zero risk" or absolute safety for ten- and eleven-year-olds before the secretary could issue an employment waiver. This test precluded the issuance of waivers for almost a decade. As Secretary Marshall noted in 1981, "[T]he Department's current position is to issue waiv-ers only to growers who state that no pesticides were used on the crop to be harvested or to those who provide objective data which can be used by the Secretary of Labor to establish safe reentry times."[15]

The department signed an interagency agreement with the Environmental Protection Agency in March 1980 to study the effects of pesticides and chemi-cals on workers under the age of fifteen years. This five-year agreement re-mained in place, and extensive research was conducted in field studies and in the use of laboratory animals. While a large body of scientific research find-ings was prepared under the agreement, the complex impacts of chemicals on young workers and the long latency periods for the manifestation of chemical effects have precluded the final publication of a compendium of "safe" chemi-cals and pesticides.

Another controversial issue that was to carry forward during the 1980s concerned the protection of homeworkers. Regulations in the early 1980s re-stricted the employment of homeworkers in seven industries: women's apparel, jewelry manufacturing, knitted outerwear, gloves and mittens, button and buckle manufacturing, handkerchief manufacturing, and embroideries. Enterprises seeking to use homeworkers were required to obtain a certificate that delin-eated the nature and scope of work and the types of record keeping needed to monitor the activity.   Based on a review of the homeworker regulations, the department implemented regulations on November 9, 1981, that removed the restrictions on knitted outerwear but continued the restrictions in the other six industries.[16]

While there were a variety of important issues during the 1980s, the single issue that dominated the debate was the youth subminimum wage. The *1982 Report* to the Congress was particularly significant because of its emphasis on youth. Secretary Raymond Donovan focused his "Statement of the Secretary" on the issue of a youth differential. He noted that the recently completed Minimum Wage Study Commission had recommended against adoption of a youth differential, and he called the recommendation "regrettable."[17] There were administration proposals every year in the first half of the 1980s to initiate a youth minimum wage, but none were successful in the Congress.

The next major "event" that affected the FLSA occurred in a U.S. Supreme Court decision in *Garcia v. San Antonio Metropolitan Transit Authority.* On February 19, 1985, the U.S. Supreme Court overturned the *National League of Cities* decision and returned about 7.5 million state and local government employees to FLSA minimum wage coverage. About 6.8 million state and local employees were returned to the FLSA overtime provisions. This decision affected about 83,000 units of state and local government. An excellent summary of the judicial considerations of FLSA coverage of state and local government employees can be found in the 1986 *Annual Report* to the Congress on pages 8–11. The *Garcia* decision was met with extensive protests of adverse impact. State and local officials argued that the overtime provisions of the FLSA would be "budget-busters" causing major disruption of the delivery of public services. A small number of state and local employees would require wage increases to meet the minimum wage provisions, but the largest fiscal impact resided on the overtime requirements of one and one-half times the regular rate of pay for hours in excess of forty in a workweek.

In the 1986 *Annual Report* to the Congress, Secretary William Brock provided the summary impact estimates shown in Table 8.1. The estimated adverse fiscal impacts resulted in the enactment of legislation on November 13, 1985, that provided relief to state and local government units. The substance of that legislation is discussed in the next sections.

One of the most recent FLSA-related activities of significance was the elimination of a waiver provision that permitted sixteen- and seventeen-year-old students to drive school buses. Hazardous Occupations Order No. 2 (hereafter HO2) established an eighteen-year-old minimum age for employment as a motor vehicle driver or helper.

However, the FLSA provisions did not apply to school systems until enactment of the 1966 amendments. HO2 was amended in 1968 to provide the secretary of labor with authority to approve exemptions Permitting the continuation of the employment of sixteen- and seventeen-year-old school bus drivers. For almost two decades, exemptions were approved by the secretary based on submissions provided by state governors. In some years, as many as fourteen states applied for and received exemptions for young drivers. In more recent years, the number of states seeking exemption has decreased to five or six.

Due to increasing public concern about the safety of young drivers, the department began a process to review the driving and safety records more carefully. In October 1987, a "Study of Sixteen and Seventeen Year-Old School

Table 8.1
Estimates of Economic Impact of the *Garcia* Decision

FLSA Provision	State and Local Government	
	Employees Affected (000)	Annual Cost of Complying ($ millions)
Minimum wage	260	$ 396
Premium overtime pay	364	733
Total	(not additive)	$1,129

Source: U.S. Department of Labor, *Minimum Wage and Maximum Hours Standards Under the Fair Labor Standards Act,* 1986 Report, transimitted to the Congress on April 17, 1986 (Washington, D.C.: U.S. Government Printing Office, 1986), p. 11.

Bus Drivers" was completed. The study verified that sixteen- and seventeen-year-old school bus drivers have much higher accident rates, but the data did not show that they were involved in more serious and fatal accidents. However, states were given notice that exemption approval was being terminated on April 1, 1988. State governors sought and obtained congressional approval to continue the use of sixteen-and seventeen-year-old drivers until the end of the 1987–1988 school year.

In 1987, Secretary Brock established a Child Labor Advisory Committee (CLAC) to study the employment of children. The CLAC Charter, signed by Secretary Brock on August 5, 1987, identified the committee's objectives and scope of activity as follows: "Provide advice and recommendations which will assist the Wage and Hour Division in effectively administering the child labor provisions of the Fair Labor Standards Act." The committee was composed of twenty-one members and was scheduled to cease functioning two years from the date of initiation. The first meeting of the CLAC occurred on March 9 and 10, 1988. Three subcommittees were formed at the March meeting. The three subcommittees were charged with examining HO2 and HO10 and Child Labor Regulation No. 3.(Reg. 3) The CLAC's activities included a review of research work recently completed on HO2 and Reg. 3. The only new area of inquiry was HO10, involving work in slaughterhouses and meat packing facilities.

LEGISLATIVE INITIATIVES IN THE 1980S

The election results in November 1980 were still officially being tabulated when the rhetoric for changing the minimum wage began. Since Republicans gained a majority in the Senate in the 1980 election, Utah's Senator Orrin Hatch was in line for the chairmanship of the Senate Labor and Human Resources Committee. He let everyone know that soon after the election he planned to introduce legislation to create a youth differential. Hatch exuded confidence that a bill would sail through the Republican-controlled Senate and the weakened House early in 1981. The senator recognized that "big labor" would be unhappy with the proposal but that he was willing to work with labor leaders to "reach an accommodation on the issue." There was little real chance for reasonable discussion between the incoming chairman and organized labor, however, because the senator had been instrumental in the defeat of the labor law reform package in 1978, which had strong union backing.

The mood of the nation reflected in the November 1980 election strongly suggested that proposals for raising the minimum wage were unlikely to be taken seriously. Several key legislators, including Representative Edward Beard of Rhode Island, who supported increasing the minimum wage, had been defeated. Republican control of the Senate and a weakened Democratic House were unlikely to be receptive to initiatives to further increase the minimum wage. All of the initiatives focused on precisely the opposite change, that is, reducing the minimum wage for certain parts of the labor force.

The legislative proposals of the new Senate Labor and Education Committee set the tone for initiatives through the remainder of the decade. As he had promised, the proposals by Senator Hatch contained a youth differential at 75 percent of the adult minimum wage. In addition, his proposal would apply only to work occurring during the first six months of an individual's employment or until the worker reached age twenty, whichever came first. To elicit labor support, the senator suggested that if the unions were willing to cooperate on a compromise bill, he would be receptive to a "trial period" for the differential rather than a permanent program from initial passage.

A second part of the senator's agenda involved a stipend or subsidy for employers who hired hard-core unemployed workers at the minimum wage. The stipend program was a much shorter term initiative and would be phased out over a three-year period. The senator knew that he had little chance of forging an alliance with organized labor on any of these items, but it appeared that the absence of support from the unions would do little to hinder his progress. The Utah Republican had finally ascended to one of the most influential chairmanships in the Senate, and he fully planned to put it to best use.

While they were never seriously considered by the Congress, a variety of initiatives including those proposed by Senator Hatch formed a focal point of discussion in the early part of the decade. The first initiative would have increased the overtime rate to twice the regular rate of pay and reduced the workweek to thirty-five hours over a two-year period. The second initiative was designed to extend FLSA protection to legislative branch employees. There was also legislation proposed to delay the implementation of the January 1, 1980, and January 1, 1981, increases in the minimum wage, to ensure that blind or sight-impaired employees received at least the statutory minimum wage, to liberalize the waiver process for the employment of children in agriculture, to restrict the importation of foreign goods produced under adverse labor standards conditions, to develop labor standards requirements for specified prisoners in federal government and District of Columbia correctional institutions, and to create a National Employment Relocation Administration in the Department of Labor.

Holding to the new agenda, in 1981 and 1982, there were numerous bills introduced to establish a youth differential, relax restrictions on the employment of youth, increase the tip credit, shorten the workweek, increase the overtime rate of pay to twice the regular rate of pay, remove undocumented workers from FLSA coverage, and outright repeal of the minimum wage provisions of the FLSA. Many of these proposals were "carried over" from prior years, and most of them would carry forward to subsequent years, but again, none of them became law in the early part of the decade.

By all accounts, though, the issue of the 1980s was the youth differential. With youth unemployment hovering around 20 percent overall and central city youth unemployment twice that level, the rhetoric supporting a youth differential escalated quickly. No one could deny that youth unemployment was a social travesty that required direct attention, but there was considerable disagreement about what caused the problem and, more important, what role, if any, the minimum wage played. Walter Williams, a prominent black economist at Temple University, was a strong advocate of FLSA repeal as a first step in addressing youth unemployment. Williams found some formidable opposition within the black community but throughout the decade stuck to his position. Herrington Bryce, consultant to the NAACP, called the youth differential an "unintriguing stupidity." He believed that the reasons for youth unemployment resided outside the minimum wage program, and therefore the solutions to these problems required something other than repeal of the law or, as some proposed, a youth differential. Bryce argued that there had to be some relationship between what people pay for goods and services and the wages they are paid. He strongly favored a tax credit program for employers that would offset the additional costs employers experienced hiring youth. The Hatch proposal would address some of Bryce's concerns.

Columnist William Raspberry observed, "If you buy Sen. Orrin Hatch's assumption that the rising minimum wage has priced teenagers out of the labor market, then it's hard to resist his solution."[18] Raspberry argued that the assumption was wrong and therefore the Hatch prescription was wrong. Raspberry suggested that it was not a "productivity" issue but, rather, a "job location" issue, that is, jobs in the suburbs and youth in the central cities, and that many employers just didn't want black, central city youth around. There was some evidence supporting both of Raspberry's assertions, but what was missing was what could be done to improve the situation.

While Senator Hatch pushed doggedly ahead and scheduled hearings on the youth differential, the administration remained more circumspect and cautious. Due to the believed windfall gain to the fast-food industry that would result from a youth differential, the opponents of the proposal dubbed it the "McDonald's Differential" or, in the words of Sol Chaikin, president of the International Ladies Garment Workers Union, the "McDonald's Windfall Gifts Amendment." Within the administration, there were those who saw that organized labor was not going to concede on this issue and that virulent opposition could carry over into other economic issues on which labor's help was needed.

David Stockman, director of the Office of Management and Budget, strongly recommended that the president resist antagonizing organized labor on this issue early in the administration because this controversy could undermine the budget reduction program. Stockman also recommended that the president obtain an agreement from congressional conservatives that they would not surface the subminimum wage proposal early in the legislative year. Either no agreement was sought or the president was unsuccessful in convincing Senator Hatch to keep the initiative on the back burner.

Much to most observers' surprise, the administration's position was bolstered by the most unlikely of allies. Those close to the legislative process realized that there may be tactical prudence in letting sleeping dogs lie. The fear was that if the FLSA was opened up to insert the youth differential provision, congressional supporters would attempt and probably succeed in obtaining an increase in the minimum wage. Therefore, the U.S. Chamber of Commerce issued a fact sheet in early 1981 that focused on holding a firm line on increasing the minimum wage rather than initiating a youth differential. The strength of the Chamber's argument was evident in the absence of several fast-food firms including McDonald's and Burger King from the Senate Labor Committee's hearings. In a cynical statement by Mark de Bernardo, a lobbyist for the Chamber of Commerce, he suggested, "If you hold the line on the minimum wage and inflation continues, it has the net effect of a rollback."[19] In other words, what the Chamber could not get through legislation, it hoped to achieve through the vagaries of the economic process. The 13 percent inflation rate gave the Chamber great hope that significant "advances" would occur.

Senator Hatch proceeded with his agenda, but as the year unfolded, the odds for legislation vanished. On the Labor Committee were two liberal Republicans, Senators Lowell Weicker and James Stafford, who were opposed to a youth subminimum, and therefore it was an uphill battle for the chairman to report out a bill. In testimony before the Senate Labor Standards Subcommittee, Secretary Donovan expressed uncertainty about the probable role a youth subminimum would play in eradicating the youth unemployment problem. The administration's position was that there was support for the youth differential in principle, but it was not prepared to endorse a specific legislative proposal. Subcommittee chairman Senator Don Nickles argued that the "opportunity wage" (phraseology adopted to place the youth subminimum wage concept in a more positive light) was needed to attack the unparalleled problem of youth unemployment. Senator Ted Kennedy argued that those who supported the youth differential carried a heavy burden of proof to show that the initiative would help young workers find jobs without hurting older workers.[20] To ensure that the Chamber of Commerce concerns expressed in its fact sheet earlier in the year were not forgotten, Senator Kennedy observed that any study of the minimum wage related to the youth differential must include a study related to raising the minimum wage to at least $3.75 an hour.

Senator Hatch's two-day hearings ended with little narrowing of disagreement between the polar factions but with a clear sense that the youth differential initiative would not move forward in either the Senate or the House. Secretary Donovan's call for "more study," the absence of support by the Chamber of Commerce and several major fast-food firms, and the strong objections by the AFL–CIO sealed the fate of the legislative proposal for 1981. In addition, in May 1981, the Minimum Wage Study Commission released its report to the Congress. As noted earlier, the commission recommended against enactment of a youth differential. Secretary Donovan indicated that the administration wanted to review the commission's findings and recommendations before formulating its final position on the issue. The commission report provided little flexibility for the administration to strongly endorse Senator Hatch's proposal, and it did not do so. The labor unions had won the first skirmish in this campaign, but the fight was not over.

The budget reduction process that David Stockman was so concerned about moved ahead with amazing speed. The president was given essentially everything he asked for in the Congress. The new president was experiencing a "honeymoon" with the Congress that had few historical precedents. With the budget legislation through the Congress in 1981, it was time to move to other issues.

The president's position on the minimum wage in general and the youth subminimum wage specifically were well known. In an early campaign speech in West Orange, New Jersey, the president said, "The minimum wage has caused more misery and unemployment than anything since the Great Depression."[21] Two years later, he argued that it had been a mistake to apply the minimum wage to youth seeking summer and after-school employment, and therefore the "right thing to do" would be to remove them from coverage. Knowing that those opposing the youth differential would have even greater problems with this idea, the president's fall-back position was with a lower minimum wage for youth.

While Secretary Donovan expressed reservations and proposed further study in 1981, the administration's position on the youth differential was no longer ambiguous by the end of 1983. On March 11, 1983, President Ronald Reagan transmitted a message to Congress that, among other things, sought to amend the FLSA "to establish a youth employment opportunity wage of $2.50 an hour or 75 percent of the otherwise applicable minimum wage, whichever is less, from May 1 through September 30, for persons under 22 years of age."[22] A bill incorporating these provisions was introduced in both the House and Senate, as were other bills containing slightly different age and wage rate levels. No action on these proposals occurred during FY 1983. Congressman Paul introduced a bill that "would repeal all Federal laws requiring private employers to pay a minimum wage."[23]

Besides the youth differential bill, there was the usual menu of other bills during 1983 to expand, contract, or otherwise modify the FLSA. Congressman Moris Biaggi introduced the first bill subsequent to the 1977 amendments to raise the minimum wage from $3.35 an hour to $4.15 an hour. Senator Hatch introduced a bill in 1983 that would have restricted the secretary's authority to prohibit industrial homework if the homeworker received the minimum wage and overtime pay required by the act.[24] Late in 1983, the president reiterated his strong feelings about the impacts of the federal minimum wage and in particular the need for a youth subminimum wage. He argued that "a lot of our ills are due to the minimum wage . . . [and therefore] the very least we should do is . . . have a lower minimum wage today for young people who are entering the job market for the first time."[25]

Since Congress did not act on the proposed legislation in his message of March 11, 1983, the president proposed, on May 17, 1984, the enactment of the "Youth Employment Opportunity Wage Act of 1984." The provisions of this bill were identical with those contained in his earlier message. While several hearings occurred related to this proposal, no committee votes or floor action occurred in either the Senate or the House. Representatives of organized labor attacked the proposal. Rex Hardesty of the AFL–CIO termed the proposal the "hamburger amendment" and alleged that it was discriminatory and an "idiotic idea." Michael Wachter, a University of Pennsylvania economist who had favored the conservative agenda while a member of the MWSC, sided with the opponents to the youth differential. He raised the rhetorical question, "Do you really want to have jobs that youths can hold and adults can't?"[26] Editorials hammered on the vagaries of the "McDonald's Bill" leading to age discrimination, restricting older workers from certain jobs, and providing a windfall of $.31 per share of McDonald's stock. The president's persistence on this issue was beginning to genuinely anger the opposition, and they began coming out of the proverbial woodwork. The time for a youth differential had not arrived.

Throughout this entire period from roughly 1980 to 1985, there was a peripheral fringe to the debate on the youth differential that in some respects seemed out of place. Andrew Brimmer, Walter Williams, Thomas Sowell, the National Conference of Black Mayors, Mayor Marion Barry, Reverend Leon Sullivan, and others supported the president's proposal. The basic rationale was that the problem of youth unemployment, and in particular central city black youth unemployment, was so severe that anything plausible was worth trying. Even Mary F. Berry, an outspoken critic of the president's policies on racial equality, believed that the president's youth differential proposal did not go far enough. She went directly to the heart of the matter and argued, "If the Administration were serious, they would understand that you don't get money to black youth by enacting generalized programs. I would support the idea if they would propose a program to pay the subminimum to black youths only. That's where the problem is, and that's where the legislation ought to be targeted."[27] All the peripheral support for the administration's proposal was not enough, however, to overcome the entrenched opposition.

Though the president's proposed youth wage did not receive favorable action in the Congress, other action did occur. In response to the Supreme Court's *Garcia* decision and the resulting protestations of fiscal disaster by state and local officials, the Congress passed, and the president signed, legislation to provide limited relief. With almost unanimous House and Senate support, a conference report was passed on November 7, 1985. The president signed the legislation into law on November 13, 1985, as Public Law 99-150.[28] The major provisions of the legislation provided for the accrual of compensatory time off in lieu of cash overtime pay. Compensatory time off would accrue at the rate of one and one-half hours for each overtime hour worked. Employees could accrue a maximum of 480 hours before cash overtime payments were required. The legislation also clarified the term "volunteers" for FLSA purposes.

Since the Congress did not act in either 1983 or 1984, the president again proposed a draft bill entitled the "Youth Employment Opportunity Wage Act of 1985." It contained the same provisions as his previous two proposals. The president now had a new labor secretary, William Brock, who appeared more receptive and understanding of the opposition's concerns. The secretary indicated that he understood the concerns of organized labor and other opposition groups and admitted frankly, "I have my reservations [about the subminimum wage]" and "These are concerns I share."[29] However, he felt that a "limited trial" of the youth differential should occur.

In addition, a similar set of proposals to amend the FLSA that had surfaced in earlier years was presented to the Congress in 1985. One major addition was the proposal of "The Employment Polygraph Protection Act of 1985." The bill's purpose was to "prevent the denial of employment opportunities by prohibiting the use of lie detectors on employees by employers involved in or affecting interstate commerce."[30]

Early in the year, editorials began appearing in support of an increase in the minimum wage. While generally sympathetic to the opposition to a youth differential, the editorials argued that economic conditions warranted a further increase in the overall minimum even if a youth differential was not part of the package. There were to be no changes in either the overall minimum wage or the initiation of a youth differential in 1986, but three other legislative changes directly affected the FLSA. They were relatively narrow in scope and content but important in relation to the aspects of the program they addressed. The first amendment was to Section 14(c), which required that handicapped workers be paid wages based on individual productivity. Employees paid a subminimum wage could petition the secretary for a review of their wage rate in a formal hearing before an administrative law judge. The second amendment voided the minimum wage rates for American Samoa that were established by the Industry Committee process. Employees in American Samoa were to be compensated at rates in effect on July 1, 1986, until a new Industry Committee establishes new rates. The third issue involved a study of the use of batboys and batgirls in organized baseball. The secretary was directed to study and submit a report and recommendations to Congress "as to whether a change in the permissible hours of employment for baseball batboys and batgirls under the FLSA child labor regulations would be detrimental to the well-being of these young people."[31] A study was conducted by the Department of Labor relating to the employment of batboys and batgirls in organized American baseball. The study concluded that, among other things, there was little evidence of adverse educational, health, social, or other consequences from the participation of young people in the functions identified above. Information and data obtained from parents, teachers, students, team officials, and so forth, generally supported the positive impacts of batboy and batgirl activity. The department did not recommend changes in the FLSA or the regulations in relation to these activities.

While Secretary Brock "shared the concerns" with organized labor about the probable impacts of a youth subminimum wage, he made it known early in 1987 that the administration opposed any increase in the minimum wage. However, both the House and Senate initiated legislative action designed to increase the minimum wage but not provide for a youth differential. Spearheaded by Senator Edward Kennedy, chairman of the Senate Labor and Human Resources Committee, and Congressman Augustus Hawkins, chairman of the House Education and Labor Committee, Congress attempted to refocus the debate from the one dimensional youth differential to a series of changes in the law including an overall phased-in increase in the minimum wage. Senator Kennedy started the process by stressing his commitment to the "old Democratic values" that included a "living wage" for all Americans. The senator attacked the administration's youth subminimum wage initiative by arguing that "we already have a subminimum wage—for everyone."[32] Secretary Brock countered by suggesting that what was needed was "to concentrate on how we get our kids into the work force, rather than on new ways to keep them out."[33]

Testimony in the Senate Labor Committee produced witnesses diametrically opposed to one another on the impact of increases in the minimum wage. F. Gerard Adams of the University of Pennsylvania argued that "estimates of large job losses and dire consequences to the economy as a result of raising the minimum wage do not stand up to scrutiny."[34] Two other witnesses, John Glennie, vice president of a Washington consulting firm, and Finis Welch, University of California Los Angles economics professor, both argued that the proposed increases would produce high levels of job loss and accelerate inflationary pressures. Both Adams and Welch are highly respected economic forecasters, and the diametrically opposed positions on this issue are indicative of the state of the art related to economic projecting of legislative change impacts. Congressional leaders have been particularly frustrated with this seemingly intractable situation, particularly in relation to changes in the FLSA.

As the debate intensified on both sides of Capitol Hill, the solid Democratic front began to show signs of cracking. House leaders wanted to raise the minimum wage to $4.65 an hour over a three-year period and index the wage rate after the three-year escalation to average wages in the private sector. Congressman Austin Murphy favored a wage increase but strongly opposed the indexation scheme. His Subcommittee on Labor Standards would not report out a bill containing both a $4.65 an hour minimum wage and indexing. Therefore, union lobbyists decided to abandon the indexing provision and attempt to keep the $4.65 wage rate in the bill. The tactic worked, and the subcommittee voted a bill out with the wage rate sought by House leaders. Most important was a provision to raise the small business sales exemption level from $362,500 a year to $500,000 a year. Congressman Hawkins hoped that an amendment could be made on the House floor that would reinsert indexing into the bill, but subcommittee chairman Austin Murphy argued that if indexing were restored, the bill would be doomed.

Full committee consideration of the bill produced several surprises. Most significant was the passage of a minimum wage of $5.05 an hour rather than the subcommittee provision of $4.65 an hour. Second, the committee voted to extend the FLSA to congressional employees who were not on the personal staff of a member of Congress. Most important was the application of FLSA overtime provisions to these employees. Third, the committee adopted a 50 percent tip credit in place of the existing 40 percent tip credit.

Committee Republicans attempted to amend the bill in committee to create a "training wage" for youth and exempt motorcycle dealers from FLSA protection, among others. The Democratic majority swept aside these amendments and voted out a bill on March 16, 1988, that contained the $5.05 minimum wage, an increased tip credit, an increased small firm sales test level, and a congressional employee coverage provision. Apparently, the House leadership wanted to use the $5.05 minimum wage as a "bargaining chip" because the indexing scheme had been eliminated earlier in the process. However, the transparency of this bargaining ploy made its overall effectiveness minimal.

Over the last ten years, there has been sporadic attention to a scheme other than the minimum wage or, more precisely, a scheme in conjunction with the minimum wage that would address problems of poverty, disemployment, and other vagaries attributed to the minimum wage. Again, in mid-1988, two congressmen, Tim Penny, a Democrat, and Thomas Petri, a Republican, argued that what was needed to address the needs of low-income workers was a two-pronged scheme involving the minimum wage and legislation entitled Job Enhancement for Families Act (JEFFA). The latter bill was one of several that had as its operable function a tax credit provision that was linked to family size. A low-wage worker could receive a tax credit ("reverse withholding") to a maximum of $2,500 per year. These congressmen argued that the JEFFA combined with a $4.00 minimum wage would provide much more needed assistance to low-skilled workers than a $4.65 or $5.05 an hour minimum wage and would produce fewer negative side effects.[35] While these arguments drew considerable attention and positive editorial comment, the Congress moved ahead with a bill focusing primarily on a higher minimum wage.

In late June, it appeared that the proposed minimum wage levels in both the Senate and House bills were going nowhere. Therefore, a compromise was worked out with organized labor that provided for a maximum increase to $4.55 an hour. The small business exemption related to annual sales was raised to $500,000, and the tip credit was increased from 40 percent to 50 percent for those employed in the restaurant industry. With little fanfare and little discussion, the Senate Labor and Human Resources Committee approved the compromise bill on June 29. Two Republicans joined the Democratic majority to pass the measure on an eleven to five vote. Senator Kennedy told the committee, "For 50 years, the minimum wage has been a promise by America that if you work for a living, you won't have to live in poverty. Reaganomics broke that promise, and it's time for Congress to fix it."[36] Republicans on the committee opposed the bill in most dimensions, and Senator Orrin Hatch promised a "donnybrook" on the Senate floor when the bill was debated.

With the Senate bill heading for rough waters on the floor, the Center on Budget and Policy Priorities released a study showing that the job-destroying potential of the bill was much less than most expected. The nonprofit organization argued that rather than potentially millions of jobs being destroyed, as some analysts had suggested, the impact was in the 70,000 jobs range. The U.S. Chamber of Commerce had estimated about 1.9 million fewer jobs over a six-or seven year-period, while Robert R. Nathan Associates estimated a loss of about 882,000 fewer jobs over the next two years, 1989 and 1990. The analysis supporting the center's findings was directed by Charles Brown, a former economist with the Minimum Wage Study Commission. The basic explanation provided by the center for the wide disparity in estimates was that most of the other studies used data that were a decade or more old rather than more current data. While not wanting to recognize job loss in any form, the Senate supporters of the committee bill found the center's findings much more palatable.

Late in the summer of 1988, the political rhetoric began to heat up. Democratic candidate Michael Dukakis spoke out strongly in favor of increasing the minimum wage, while Vice President George Bush and running mate Senator Dan Quayle were generally opposed to further increases. Senator Quayle led the fight against the Senate bill that would have raised the minimum wage and indexed it to a wage series. On the campaign trail, the senator modified his position, however, and argued that he was in favor of a gradual increase in the minimum wage to $4.00 an hour if it was coupled with a training wage. Secretary Ann McLaughlin indicated that she and Quayle were on the "same wavelength." The secretary indicated, "We're sort of talking about the same thing. There is an interest in increasing the minimum wage, but there's a greater interest in having some kind of a training wage."[37] Not to be outdone by his running mate and the sitting labor secretary, Vice President Bush shifted positions and indicated that he would propose "some adjustment" in the minimum wage if elected president. The vice president would not indicate the magnitude or level of a minimum wage he would support.

To deflect the initiative by the Republican candidate, Senator Kennedy launched a scathing attack on the Bush/Quayle/McLaughlin proposal. The senator called it a "hire 'em and fire 'em" wage proposal that if enacted would provide a "Bush push into the unemployment lines." Senator Kennedy introduced an alternative proposal based on the expansion of an existing provision in the FLSA that permits employers flexibility in hiring a limited number of full-time students at less than the minimum wage. The Kennedy proposal would permit employers to hire twelve full-time students, rather than the current six students, at 85 percent of the minimum wage as long as the number employed at the subminimum wage contributed no more than 10 percent of the firm's working hours. Republican opponents saw little in the Kennedy proposal that would address the critical problems of central city youth unemployment and low family income.

The Democrats were eager to pass a minimum wage bill before the fall elections. The Republicans were equally eager to ensure that President Reagan's judicial nominations received favorable Senate action before the president left office. Key Senate Republicans indicated that unless there was action on the judicial nominations, there would be no action on the minimum wage bill or several other pieces of legislation important to the Democratic leadership. Democrats immediately charged Senate Republicans of holding the minimum wage bill hostage in an attempt to get what Senator Ted Kennedy labeled "jobs for justices." The Senate Judiciary Committee, chaired by Senator Joseph Biden, was considering twenty-five judicial nominations. In an exchange between Senators Robert Dole and Kennedy, about the encouragement that Senator Dole had received from many Republicans to halt Senate action until the Judiciary Committee moved on the nominations, Senator Kennedy vehemently argued, "Now we know the real reason [for the reluctance of Republicans to support the minimum wage bill], . . . jobs for judges." Senator Dole retorted that "good people are dying on the vine in the Judiciary Committee . . . because they're Republicans." "But," Senator Kennedy argued, "none of them are living on the minimum wage."[38] Senate Republicans initiated debate on the minimum wage bill that prevented a floor vote. Efforts by Democrats to invoke cloture and cut off the debate failed, and the process was stymied.

George Bush became the new president of the United States. The nominees for judicial positions that President Reagan supported did not obtain Senate confirmation, and the low-income people of the United States did not obtain a mandated wage increase. The official fiftieth anniversary of the FLSA occurred on October 24, 1988, two weeks before the presidential election. This auspicious event passed with little attention from the nation's power brokers. The tug of war between Democrats and Republicans resulted in 5 million workers being denied a mandated wage increase, and twenty-five judicial nominations evaporated from the Judiciary Committee's hearing calendar. Whether the trade-off was in the national interest only history will determine.

ENFORCEMENT ACTIVITIES IN THE 1980S

There is a direct relationship between changes in the minimum wage and violations of the law. It is not surprising, then, to see the numbers of employees underpaid minimum wages escalate in the second half of the 1970s, peak in 1979, and decline monotonically throughout the 1980s. The increase in the minimum wage in the 1980s occurred on January 1, 1981.

In 1980, 348,000 workers were underpaid about $44 million. The findings increased to 397,000 workers and about $53 million in 1981, but then decreased dramatically over the next eight years. In 1988, 154,000 workers were found to be underpaid about $29.8 million.

The other half of wage investigations, that is, overtime compensation, showed uncanny stability during the decade in terms of the numbers of workers found underpaid but a rising amount of underpayment. In 1980, 276,000 workers were underpaid about $76 million in overtime compensation. In 1988, about 324,000 workers were underpaid about $113.7 million.

To place these activities in perspective, the reader may want to review the data relating to Wage and Hour investigative staff provided later in this chapter. In general, the numbers of COs grew throughout the program until a peak was reached in 1978. The staffing high point produced 1,343 COs. Reductions occurred from 1979 to 1982, involving a change of about 414 investigative staff. There were 929 COs in 1982, 1983, 1984, 1985, and 1987. There were about 940 COs in 1986. Staff expansion to almost 1,000 COs occurred in 1988.

A final point is needed to provide perspective about these changes. Wage and Hour COs do not have the luxury of simply enforcing the traditional programs, for example, FLSA, Davis-Bacon Act, Service Contract Act, and so forth. Their enforcement responsibilities expand and contract as public policy, legislation, and court decisions mandate. Returning over 7 million state and local employees to FLSA coverage in response to the *Garcia* decision expanded the division's workload. Requiring COs to examine payroll records and employment activities under the Immigration Reform and Control Act (IRCA), the Polygraph Act, and several others also spreads the time and resources available even thinner. In addition, special initiatives such as strike forces in certain industries and regions, the utilization of COs for research and study purposes, and a variety of increased training activities all lead, at least initially, to less time for direct FLSA investigations. A complete enumeration of these types of ancillary demands on Wage and Hour Division COs may partially explain some changes in investigation findings during the 1980s.

FIVE DECADES OF PROGRAM OPERATION

The FLSA enforcement program identified and recovered billions of dollars of back wages for millions of workers, established conditions for the safe employment of children, and provided standards for health and safety in the workplace. To understand the dimensions of the FLSA enforcement program, a brief summary of the numerical changes in FLSA coverage is needed. The general picture one receives is that the *absolute* number of nonsupervisory wage and salary workers subject to the FLSA minimum wage provisions has increased steadily throughout the five decades, but more important, the *percentage* of the workforce subject to the minimum wage provisions of the FLSA has also grown steadily (see Appendix Table A.1).

The numbers of nonsupervisory wage and salary employees subject to the *overtime* provisions of the FLSA have been lower in recent years than those subject to the *minimum wage* provisions. In FY 1986, for example, 74,680,000 employees were subject to the minimum wage provisions, and 69,630,000 were subject to the overtime provisions. The primary differences between the estimates stem from the differing exemptions applying to overtime payments. Seasonal agricultural workers, firefighters, policemen, other public protection service employees, and several industrial segments with particular overtime needs are excluded from the FLSA overtime provisions.

There are reasonably good data showing the number of compliance actions that have occurred, the number of workers found due back wages, the amounts of back wages due, and so forth. These data will be discussed below. What must be kept in mind in the interpretation of these data is what would have happened in the absence of the program. No one knows for sure what would have happened had the program never been implemented, but it is a safe guess that some employers who paid the statutory minimum wage and overtime requirements would have paid something less. In this sense, the estimates described below are the lower bound impact estimates. In addition, the estimates below relating to employees found due back wages and the amount of back wages found due are the amounts determined in the investigation process. A relatively small and decreasing percentage of covered establishments are investigated each year. In the early years of the FLSA, about 10 percent of covered establishments were investigated each year. In 1987, about 2 percent of covered establishments were investigated.

The summary data relating to FLSA activities over the five decades are as follows:

1. Between 1938 and 1987, there were more than 2.6 million compliance actions by the Wage and Hour Division. Compliance actions are primarily on-site investigations by a compliance officer, but some compliance actions take the form of conciliations by telephone. Conciliations have become more widely used in the last four to five years of program enforcement effort. (See "Staffing of the Wage and Hour Division" below.)
2. Between 1951 and 1987, more than 6.6 million employees were found to be due back pay as a result of minimum wage violations. The data for the twelve years prior to 1951 are not complete enough to permit inclusion in this summary. It might be appropriate, however, to add another 400,000 to 500,000 employees to the total for these twelve years, which would bring the five-decade total to about 7 million employees.
3. Between 1951 and 1987, about 8.5 million employees were found to be due back pay as a result of overtime violations. Some of these employees may also have been counted in the minimum wage estimates above if they experienced both types of violations. Here, too, the data are incomplete for the years prior to 1951, but an estimate of about 9 million employees found due back pay related to overtime violations would be a reasonable estimate for the five-decade period.
4. Employees involved in overtime and minimum wage violations were found to be due over $2.5 billion in back wages between 1946 and 1987. Data related to the dollar volume of back wages due were available for five additional years. Therefore, it may be appropriate to adjust this estimate upward by $100 to $200 million. The dollar volume of back wages found due was in the $2.5 to $2.7 billion range for the fifty years of program operation.

The summary impacts of the FLSA described above have occurred through enforcement actions. There are other "impacts" that occurred through voluntary compliance with the law that are also extremely important. The vast majority of employers voluntarily comply with FLSA provisions. A study in 1980 showed that about 5 percent of employers subject to FLSA provisions do not comply. By inference, 95 percent do comply. Therefore, the FLSA impacts must include the actions taken by these employers to improve the working conditions of their employees in response to statutory mandates. As noted elsewhere in this report, without effective enforcement, employers do not take the law seriously and compliance becomes problematical, at best.

Besides the basic minimum wage and overtime activities, there were also extensive child labor and FLSA Section 14 enforcement actions. Before discussing these activities, it is important to recognize that the actions identified above are approximations due to the commingling of reviews. An investigation or conciliation may occur for one of two reasons—a complaint was received or the action was "targeted." In general, all conciliations are complaint driven. However, often, an investigation of, say, a minimum wage complaint may end up with overtime and child labor violations as well. In fact, when the Wage and Hour Division COs investigate an enterprise, they are alert to not only possible FLSA violations but also Davis–Bacon Act, Service Contract Act, Walsh–Healey Act, Migrant and Seasonal Farmworker Protection Act,

Immigration Reform and Control Act, and other legislatively covered activities related to the Wage and Hour Division's organizational jurisdiction. In this sense, a single investigation related to one aspect of the FLSA can expand into an extensive investigation of the enterprise's overall labor standards experience. Consequently, to avoid gross double counting, the enforcement action is typically aligned with the major category of violations for statistical reporting purposes.

MINIMUM WAGE WORKERS IN 1988

Data from the first year of the FLSA—1938—do not provide demographic or industrial characteristics of workers paid the minimum wage. The data for 1988 provide a wealth of detailed characteristics of these workers, but care is needed in the interpretation of the data. In a general sense, the numbers of minimum wage or sub-minimum wage workers have declined over the last ten years. The Bureau of Labor Statistics (BLS) publishes wage distribution data drawn from the *Current Population Survey (CPS)*. The CPS is a representative monthly household survey of more than 60,000 units. The data from the *CPS* that are most applicable here were tabulated in response to two questions: "Is (*Worker's name*) paid by the hour on this job?" and "How much does (*Worker's name*) earn per hour?" In 1988, there were about 125 million workers in the labor force, about 101 million received wage and salary compensation, and about 61 million were paid at hourly rates. In the latter category, about 3.9 million were paid at or below the prevailing minimum wage.

The difficulties with the interpretation of these data are several. First, there are low-wage workers paid on a piece-rate basis or receiving a salary. They are not included in the *CPS* data. Second, tipped workers, of which there are about 2 million, may or may not be in the survey data, depending upon how they designated the form of compensation. Third, there is no direct relationship between the *CPS* data and minimum wage data consistent with FLSA coverage definitions. About 30 percent of the labor force is not subject to the FLSA provisions. Large proportions of the not-subject labor force are undoubtedly in the upper segments of the wage/income distribution. In particular, executives, administrative, and professional employees and a significant proportion of outside sales workers are high-wage-income workers. However, segments of the labor force in agriculture, services, and the trade industries that are not subject to the law earn low wages.

The point is that the data relating to "minimum wage workers" are ambiguous. There is no ambiguity about the number of hourly paid workers receiving the minimum wage. However, piece-rate and salaried workers also receive minimum wage income, and it is unclear in the data how many of them there are or what economic or demographic characteristics they possess.

However, the BLS data described below are based on a consistent set of definitions and survey methodology and will be used here to provide insights into the characteristics of low-wage workers. Table 8.2 provides a summary of the total numbers of these workers from 1979 to 1988.

Table 8.2
Workers Paid at Hourly Rates, 1979–1988 (000)

Year	Total Wage and Salary Workers	Paid at Hourly Rate	Paid at Prevailing Minimum Wage	Paid Below Prevailing Minimum Wage
1979	85,773	50,637	3,907	2,846
1980	85,780	50,210	4,581	3,017
1981	86,651	50,770	4,201	3,440 (70 weights)
1981	88,516	51,869	4,311	3,515 (80 weights)
1982	87,368	50,846	4,148	2,348
1983	88,290	51,820	4,261	2,077
1984	92,194	54,143	4,125	1,838
1985	94,521	55,762	3,899	1,639
1986	96,903	57,529	3,461	1,599
1987	99,303	59,552	3,229	1,468
1988	101,407	60,878	2,608	1,319

Source: Bureau of Labor Statistics.

Increases in the prevailing minimum wage in 1979, 1980, and 1981 in response to the 1977 FLSA amendments increased the absolute and relative number of workers at or below the minimum wage. During the remainder of decade of the 1980s, there were no further increases in the federal minimum wage. Therefore, as the overall wage structure moved up, there were fewer and fewer workers at or below the prevailing minimum wage.

Most workers working at or below the minimum wage are women. Table 8.3 shows this relationship from 1979 to 1988.

The *Report of the Minimum Wage Study Commission in 1981* provided data on the characteristics of minimum wage workers in the earlier years of the program.[39] The interested reader can review the commission's *Report* for these data. What follows is a summary description of low-wage worker characteristics in the fiftieth year of the FLSA.

If one were to select a minimum wage worker randomly from the total population of these workers, this individual would probably be female, white,

Table 8.3

Hourly Paid Workers At or Below the Minimum Wage,
by Sex, 1979–1988 (000)

Year	Total	Men	Women	% Women
1979	6,753	2,138	4,615	68%
1980	7,598	2,611	4,987	66
1981	7,640	2,579	5,061 (70 weights)	66
1981	7,824	2,652	5,172 (80 weights)	66
1982	6,496	2,284	4,212	65
1983	6,338	2,243	4,095	65
1984	5,963	2,116	3,847	65
1985	5,538	1,984	3,554	64
1986	5,061	1,744	3,317	66
1987	4,698	1,647	3,051	65
1988	3,927	1,377	2,550	65

Source: Bureau of Labor Statistics.

working part-time, living in the South or Midwest, working in a service occupation, working in the retail trade industry, and be under twenty-five years of
age. This profile is not particularly important in an analytical sense because
few workers would meet all or even most of these characteristics. However, it
does suggest several dimensions of this population that have given rise to controversy in recent years.

   Minimum wage workers are predominantly young, and they are concentrated in two industrial sectors—service and trade. In 1988, more than 58
percent of minimum wage workers were under twenty-five years of age.
Thirty-six percent were between the ages of sixteen and ninteen years. Slightly
more than 3 percent were aged sixty-five years and over. While substantially
fewer men worked at or below the minimum wage, relatively more of the working men were under the age of twenty-five years. As Table 8.4 shows, almost
three-fourths of the men working at the prevailing wage in 1988 were under
twenty-five years of age. About 55 percent of women working at the prevailing
wage were under twenty-five years of age.

Table 8.4
Workers at the Prevailing Minimum Wage, by Age and Sex, 1988 (000)

Age	Male	Female
Total—all ages	1066	1542
Under 25	759	853
16–19	501	534

Source: Bureau of Labor Statistics.

White workers represented 2.047 million out of a total of 2.608 million workers working at the minimum wage in 1988. Minimum wage workers by race and sex are shown in Table 8.5. White workers represented over 90 percent of all workers working at less than the minimum wage. White female workers are disproportionately represented in the category of "paid under prevailing minimum wage" with 925,000 workers out of a total of 1,319,000 workers in this group.

Table 8.5
Minimum Wage Workers Paid at Hourly Rates, by Race and Sex, 1988 (000)

Sex and Race	Paid Under Prevailing Minimum Wage	Paid at Prevailing Minimum Wage
Total	1,319	2,608
Male	311	1,066
Female	1,008	1,542
White	1,189	2,047
Male	264	821
Female	925	1,225
Black	100	499
Male	33	209
Female	67	290
Hispanic	44	278
Male	13	117
Female	31	162

Source: Bureau of Labor Statistics.

The number of part-time workers (less than thirty-five hours per week) dominates the minimum wage and less-than-minimum wage workforce. In 1988, about 2,615,000 workers in these two categories out of a total of 3,927,000 worked part-time schedules. White women were again the dominant group, with a total of 1,487,000 workers working in the two categories.

Besides being young, most minimum wage and less-than-minimum wage workers have never been married. In 1988, over 60 percent of the workers in these categories were classified as "never married." In the "never married" category, workers between the ages of sixteen and twenty-four were about 86 percent of the workers in the minimum wage and less-than-minimum wage classifications. Slightly more than 1 million workers in the minimum wage and less-than-minimum wage classifications were married with a spouse present.

Geographically, minimum wage workers lived in the South and central regions of the country. Table 8.6 shows the regional distribution by four major divisions.

Table 8.6
Regional Location of Hourly Paid Workers, 1988 (000)

Region	Less than Prevailing Minimum Wage	At Prevailing Minimum Wage
Total United States	1,319	2,608
Northeast	264	278
North Central	435	711
South	452	1,238
West	168	380

Source: Bureau of Labor Statistics.

The state with the largest number of workers in these two wage classifications was Texas, with about 369,000 workers in 1988. Three large industrial states—California, Pennsylvania, and Ohio—each had over 200,000 workers in these two wage classifications.

Finally, the industrial and occupational affiliations of minimum wage and less-than-minimum wage workers has settled into a well-known pattern over the last two decades. These workers are primarily located in the service, sales, and clerical occupations. Within these classifications, food service occupations are the dominant subgroup. These observations are consistent with the rapid rise in the fast-food industry over the last two or three decades.

Industrially, these workers are primarily located in the "service-producing industries." The wholesale and retail trade classifications and the service industry dominate the total sector. Out of 3,207,000 workers in the service-producing industries, 3,134,000 workers were in the trade and service industry classifications in 1988.

These descriptive statistics produce a consistent and well-known picture. All of these data are presented in absolute terms. A somewhat different, but not inconsistent, picture emerges if the data are analyzed in relation to the labor force participation of the various demographic and industrial categories. This is particularly true in relation to the several race, age, and education classifications.

STAFFING OF THE WAGE AND HOUR DIVISION

The level of personnel budgeted for FLSA investigations was approximately 985 FTEs (full-time equivalents) in FY 1988. The largest number of budgeted personnel for the division was 1,343 in FY 1978. As Table 8.7 shows, the Wage and Hour Division staffed up very quickly for the national implementation effort. From September 1938 (the month before the FLSA was implemented) to the end of December 1938, field staff increased from 0 to 51 staff. During the next twelve months, field staff increased from 51 to 669 personnel.

Fiscal year 1965 was the first time that budgeted investigation positions exceeded 1,000 staff. From FY 1974 to FY 1978, budgeted investigator positions increased from 1,003 to 1,343—33.9 percent. Over the next five years (FY 1978 to FY 1982) budgeted investigator positions decreased from 1,343 to 929—a 30.8 percent decrease. Throughout most of the 1980s, budgeted investigator positions remained in the low to mid-900 range. Table 8.8 shows the number of budgeted investigator positions for the Wage and Hour Division from 1938 to 1989. It is important to note that these investigative staff worked on a variety of investigative activities including FLSA enforcement. There were investigations of government contract cases (Davis-Bacon Act, Service Contract Act, and Walsh-Healey Act), Equal Pay Act and Age Discrimination

Table 8.7

Personnel of the Wage and Hour Division Classified by Departmental or Field Service, by Month, September 1938–December 1939

Month		Total	Departmental	Field
August	1938	3	3	0
September	1938	44	44	0
October	1938	140	119	21
November	1938	186	156	30
December	1938	264	213	51
January	1939	374	292	82
February	1939	464	344	120
March	1939	523	373	150
April	1939	531	362	169
May	1939	570	380	190
June	1939	570	380	190
July	1939	575	404	171
August	1939	709	423	286
September	1939	786	433	353
October	1939	942	442	500
November	1939	1,115	468	647
December	1939	1,147	478	669

Source: U.S. Department of Labor, Wage and Hour Division, *First Annual Report of the Administrator for Calendar Year 1939*, submitted to the Congress of the United States on January 8, 1940, Washington, D.C.: USGPO, p. 63.

Table 8.8
Number of Compliance Officer (Investigator) Positions Budgeted for the Wage
and Hour and Public Contracts Divisions, 1938–1989

Fiscal Year	Number of Positions
1938 (October)	21
1938 (December)	51
1939 (December)	669
1940	453(E)
1941	464(E)
1942	529(E)
1943	736(E)
1944	560
1945	504
1946	517
1947	571
1948	513
1949	513
1950	527
1951	852
1952	740
1953	612
1954	493
1955	481
1956	747
1957	749
1958	683
1959	656
1960	659
1961	659
1962	959
1963	959
1964	980
1965	1,024
1966	1,024
1967	1,024
1968	1,147
1969	1,198
1970	1,026
1971	1,025
1972	1,027
1973	984
1974	1,003
1975	1,088
1976	1,135
1977	1,205
1978	1,343
1979	1,173
1980	1,107
1981	1,107
1982	929
1983	929
1984	929
1985	929
1986	940
1987	929
1988	985(E)
1989	1,028(E)

Source: U.S. Department of Labor, Employment Standards Administration, Office of Management,
Administration, and Planning, E=Estimated.

in Employment Act cases, farmworker investigations, and so forth. While some effort was made to determine the amounts of investigative effort spent on each category of enforcement, it was not possible to reconstruct a meaningful comparative series over the five-decade period.

Illustrative of the levels of enforcement effort expended on the several major categories of investigative activity in the 1980s is shown in Table 8.9.

Table 8.9
Compliance Actions Related to the
FLSA and the Government Contract Labor Standards, FY 1980–1989

Fiscal Year (A)	CO FTEs (Ceiling) (B)	COs (On-board) (C)	FLSA Compliance Actions (D)	Government Contract Compliance Act (E)	E/D
1980	1,107	1,059	65,110	3,986	6.1%
1981	1,107	953	60,248	5,252	8.7
1982	929	914	64,844	4,658	7.2
1983	929	928	64,214	3,863	6.0
1984	929	916	64,155	4,117	6.4
1985	929	950	66,943	4,423	6.6
1986	940	908	72,641	4,690	6.5
1987	929	951	72,028	4,749	6.6
1988	985	971	72,800e	4,600e	6.3
1989	1,028	—	75,700e	4,700e	6.2

Source: U.S. Department of Labor, Employment Standards Administration, Division of Financial Management, E=Estimated.

For most years in the 1980s, the Wage and Hour Division conducted about fifteen FLSA compliance actions for each government contracts compliance action. Interestingly, as shown in Table 8.10, the division receives about fifteen times as many FLSA complaints as it does government contract complaints. It is not surprising that a roughly similar distribution of compliance actions occurs.

From approximately FY 1984, there was a shift in the type of investigation activity related to FLSA complaints. For most of the program's history, the primary investigative vehicle was an on-site investigation of the firm. Occasionally, a complaint could be resolved by a less formal process involving a telephone call to the firm. This process was labeled a "conciliation." In FY 1984 and subsequent years, the division has placed increasing reliance on conciliations rather than on-site investigations. Some regions use relatively few conciliations—less than 10 percent—while other regions use them extensively

—in excess of 50 percent. The Agency initiated an internal study to determine the impact of the use of conciliations and to determine what the appropriate mix of investigations and conciliations will be most effective in the enforcement process. The study findings were inconclusive.

Table 8.10
Complaints Received under the FLSA and the
Government Contracts Programs, FY 1980–1989

Fiscal Year (A)	FLSA Complaints Received (B)	Government Contracts Complaints Received (C)	C/B
1980	45,366	2,159	4.8%
1981	46,020	2,752	6.0
1982	46,582	2,623	5.6
1983	44,869	3,037	6.8
1984	50,037	3,462	6.9
1985	57,314	3,997	7.0
1986	59,988	3,850	6.4
1987	58,936	3,811	6.5
1988	61,400E	3,800E	6.2
1989	62,000E	3,800E	6.1

Source: U.S. Department of Labor, Employment Standards Administration, Wage and Hour Division, E=Estimated.

CONCLUSION

This chapter has attempted to summarize the character of the federal minimum wage program. Besides the description of the activities of the program in the last decade, several elements in the program were separated out for particular attention. These data and information, in conjunction with the data in the appendix, can provide a launching point for understanding the character and scope of the federal program. There is much misinformation about minimum wage workers and their relative role in the economy. Their numbers are relatively small in relation to the total labor force, but this fact alone should not determine the attention they receive in the federal policy process.

NOTES

1. *Economic Report of the President*, transmitted to the Congress in February 1988 (Washington, D.C.: U.S. Government Printing Office, 1988), p. 357.

2. Jerry Knight, "U.S. Minimum Wage to Rise by 20 Cents an Hour Today," *Washington Post*, January 1, 1980, p. D-7.

3. Minimum Wage Study Commission, *Final Report*, Vol. I (Washington, D.C.: U.S. Government Printing Office, 1980), pp. 6–7.

4. James G. O'Hara, Letter to President Ronald Reagan, The Honorable Thomas P. O'Neill, and the Honorable George Bush, Washington, D.C., May 24, 1981, n.p.

5. Minimum Wage Study Commission, 1080, pp. 179–240.

6. Ibid., p. 163.

7. Ibid., p. 165.

8. Ibid., p. 166.

9. Ibid., pp. 137–138.

10. Ibid., p. 21.

11. Ibid., p. 126.

12. Ibid., p. 125.

13. Ibid., p. 123.

14. Ibid., pp. 107–138.

15. U.S. Department of Labor, Employment Standards Administration, *Minimum Wage and Maximum Hours Standards under the Fair Labor Standards Act*, transmitted to the Congress on January 19, 1981 (Washington, D.C.: Government Printing Office, 1981), p. 32.

16. U.S. Department of Labor, *Minimum Wage and Maximum Hours Standards Under the Fair Labor Standards Act—1982 Report*, transmitted to the Congress on April 22, 1983, Washington,D.C.: Government Printing Office, 1983), p. 23.

17. Ibid., p. 1.

18. William Raspberry, "It Won't Pay," *Washington Post*, November 14, 1980, p. A-23.

19. George Lardner, Jr., "Business Gets Cold Feet on Subminimum Wage," *Washington Post*, March 20, 1981, p. A-1.

20. Warren Brown, "Administration Fudges on Subminimum Wage," *Washington Post*, March 25, 1981, p. A-7.

21. *Washington Post*, March 20, 1981, p. A-5.

22. U.S. Department of Labor, *Minimum Wage and Maximum Hours Standards Under the Fair Labor Standards Act—1984 Report*, transmitted to the Congress on April 26, 1985, (Washington, D.C.: Government Printing Office, 1985), p. 1.

23. Ibid.

24. Ibid., p. 2.

25. Margaret Shapiro, "President Criticizes Minimum Wage, Indicates Push for Lower Youth Rate," *Washington Post*, December 16, 1983, p. A-11.

26. Ellen Goodman, "Son of Minimum Wage," *Washington Post*, May 22, 1984, p. A-15.

27. William Raspberry, "A Lower Wage—For Blacks Only," *Washington Post*, June 11, 1984, p. A-15.

28. U.S. Department of Labor, *Minimum Wage and Maximum Hours Standards Under the Fair Labor Standards Act*, Transmitted to the Congress on April 17, 1986, (Washington, D.C.: Government Printing Office, 1986), p. 2.

29. Juan Williams, "Brock Backs Youth-Wage Trial," *Washington Post*, May 7, 1985, p. A-3.

30. U.S. Department of Labor, 1986, p. 6.

31. U.S. Department of Labor, *Minimum Wage and Maximum Hours Standards Under the Fair Labor Standards Act*, transmitted to the Congress on June 30, 1988 (Washington, D.C.: Government Printing Office, 1988), p. 2.

32. Helen Dewar, "Democrats Try to Lift Wage Floor," *Washington Post*, March 26, 1987, p. A-3.

33. Ibid.

34. Mark Lawrence, "Higher Minimum Wage Would Not Damage Economy, Hill Told," Washington Post, July 18, 1987, p. A-8.

35. Tim Penny and Thomas Petri, "A Decent Minimum Wage," *Washington Post*, June 13, 1988, p. A-10.

36. Chris Adams, "Senate Panel Votes $4.55 Minimum Wage," *Washington Post*, June 30, 1988, p. A-28.

37. "McLaughlin Opposes Higher Minimum Wage," *Washington Post*, September 6, 1988, p. D-2.

38. Helen Dewar, "Senate Locked in Partisan Tug of War over Minimum Wage, Judgeships," *Washington Post*, September 23,1988, p. A-4.

39. Minimum Wage Study Commission, *Report of the Minimum Wage Study Commission*, transmitted to President Ronald Reagan, President of the Senate George Bush, and Speaker of the House of Representatives Thomas P. O'Neill, Jr., on May 24, 1981, Washington, D.C., 1981, *passim*.

Chapter 9

Conclusion

The golden anniversary of a major federal policy and program warrants a retrospective examination of the roots of the initiative and what it has accomplished. The federal minimum wage program has been an integral part of the nation's worker standards program for all of the fifty years and remains so today. However, it is not a program devoid of controversy. Except for the trauma of the early legal challenges, the program was under closer scrutiny and direct attack in its golden anniversary year and the beginning of the 1990s than at any time in its history.

This study was initiated as an examination of the roots of minimum wage programs and their use as tools of economic and social policy. The title of the book, *The Quest for a Living Wage*, begs the question, Has the "Quest" been successful? Unfortunately, an unambiguous answer is not possible. The reasons for ambiguity are several. First, at different times throughout the five decades, the level of the minimum wage may have approached a "living wage" —in other words, a full-time minimum wage worker earning sufficient income to acquire the basic necessities of life. Second, the minimum *wage* is quite different from minimum *income* in terms of standard of living. A young worker, possibly living at home, may function fairly effectively on minimum wage remuneration. A worker attempting to maintain an independent household on minimum wage–based income will be much less successful. Third, when the FLSA was initiated in 1938, about 40 percent of nonsupervisory wage and salary workers were protected by minimum wage and overtime provisions. Today, about 80 percent of workers in the same category are covered.

One cannot say with certainty what the structure of wages would be today without FLSA protection. It may be reasonable to postulate that wage rates for some categories of workers would be lower. The concept of a living wage relates to the real purchasing power of wages or income earned. The minimum wage in 1988 had about twice the purchasing power that it had in 1938. Whether a doubling of real purchasing power over a five-decade period is meaningful in comparison to other changes in the economy is a judgment the reader can make.

A different and arguably better perspective on the consequences of the minimum wage program would relate to its impacts on American workers. One would have to assert that the "impacts" have been both positive and negative. Some workers undoubtedly earn higher wages than they would have received without the program, but other workers may have been displaced from their jobs. Nevertheless, the hard program data suggest that millions of workers have received billions of dollars in back wages as a result of compliance activity by the Wage and Hour Division. Most of this restitution would probably not have occurred without the FLSA. Whether the number of workers benefited or the amount of back wage restoration should have been greater is an intriguing question. It was not the purpose of this study to make those judgments. After all, every program operates within resource constraints, administrative procedures, and operating rules that define and delimit the outcome of its activities.

Much more compliance targeting is used today in comparison with the early years of the program. The targeting mechanism may or may not make enforcement more effective or efficient. About 2 percent of establishments subject to the provisions of the FLSA are investigated each year. Over 10 percent of establishments subject to the law were investigated annually in the early years of the program. Of some importance has been the shift in recent years from on–site investigations to telephone "conciliations." Whether or not covered workers receive equal and as effective treatment through this alternative compliance process is also an open question. There is some evidence that violations of the law are "missed" through the conciliation process, but there is disagreement about the magnitude and character of these violations. In spite of all of these open questions and unresolved issues, one must not lose sight of the program's objectives. The minimum wage has not been, and is not today, the panacea for all economic or labor market problems. In fact, there are those who suggest that the minimum wage is the *cause* of many labor market problems today.

First and foremost it was designed to set a floor under the structure of wages. It has accomplished that goal. More than 80 percent of nonsupervisory wage and salary workers are protected by the FLSA minimum wage provisions. However, it is significant that only about 3 or 4 percent of all wage and salary employees work at or below the existing minimum wage level whether or not they are covered by the FLSA minimum wage provisions. Therefore, the floor directly affects a relatively small number of workers. Other objectives such as equity and efficiency are less easily quantified. It is less clear that either of these global objectives has been achieved.

The FLSA is the law of the land. It provides a powerful economic and political statement about which many disagree. What is critically important is that the federal minimum wage law and program is a political rather than an economic statement. Certainly, there are important economic relationships within and around this program. However, when all of the analyses are completed, there is sufficient ambiguity in the interpretation of these results to prevent either side from "proving" their case. Since this is true and since it is likely to be the case far into the future, continual disagreement will surround this program.

These disagreements evolve into heated intellectual and emotional debates that have done little—and will do little—to clarify the multitude of questions underlying the program. This may not be all bad. After all, minimum wage programs are statements of policy and purpose that presumably reflect the values and goals of a society. There can be, and usually is, profound and changing viewpoints about the reflection of these values and goals in the policy and program machinery. The Fair Labor Standards Act is a perfect example of how these types of debates develop and are sustained.

Epilogue

The Fair Labor Standards Act was not amended during 1988 to increase the minimum wage or expand coverage. There was intense congressional debate that resulted in the passage of a bill providing for an increase from the current level of $3.35 an hour to $4.55 an hour over a three-year period. President George Bush had promised during the campaign that he supported an increase in the minimum wage to $4.25 an hour and the provision of a "training wage" for young workers. Therefore, since the bill sent to the president in early 1989 contained a higher minimum wage and no training wage, it was vetoed.

After the president vetoed the bill containing a $4.55 an hour minimum wage, he signaled the Congress that he would support the $4.25 an hour wage if phased in over a three-year period. House supporters were less than enthusiastic about both the lower wage and the inclusion of the youth differential. As the compromise bill moved through the Congress, Representative Pat Williams noted, "There are no smiles about this bill." However, he went on to observe that "because it's all we've got, I'm going to vote for it."[1] Opponents of the bill argued that it would have a devastating effect on small business and would destroy jobs for those most needing them. In spite of these prognostications, on November 1, 1989, the House passed a bill by an overwhelming margin of 382 to 37.

The Senate took up the legislative package on November 6 with assurances from the White House that the House bill was generally acceptable. To the surprise of Majority Leader George Mitchell, Senator Simms blocked Senate consideration by attempting to tie the bill to other legislation involving taxes on capital gains. While the Simms initiative was defeated, Senate supporters of the earlier bill expressed dissatisfaction with the compromise bill. Senator Ted Kennedy was particularly unhappy with the compromise bill, but he realized that it was the best that could be achieved in the current environment. He argued, "This is a back door, back-of-the-hand increase. The compromise is a modest victory for the working poor, but it owes more to the ideological embarrassment of those seeking tax relief for capital gains than it does to any real commitment to the minimum wage."[2] As a leading advocate of a higher minimum wage, Senator Kennedy observed that the minimum wage compromise was a measure of how the Congress had failed the test of fairness to the working poor. While there were apparently "no smiles" in the Senate either, on November 8, 1989, the Upper House passed a minimum wage bill by a vote of eighty-nine to eight. Since the bill was identical to the House bill, it was sent immediately to the president for signature. The Fair Labor Standards Amendments of 1989 (Public Law 101–157) became law on November 17, 1989.

The new law contained both the lower minimum wage supported by the president and the training wage provision. In addition to these provisions, the bill increased the sales volume test for the small retail and service establishment exemption from $362,500 to $500,000. Establishments subject to the $3.35 minimum wage but exempted from the minimum wage provisions of the new law were "grandfathered" in and were not to be permitted to pay their employees less than $3.35 an hour. The tip credit was phased back up to 45 percent of the minimum wage on April 1, 1990, and to 50 percent of the minimum wage on April 1, 1991. The specific provisions of the new law provided for an increase in the minimum wage to $3.80 an hour on April 1, 1990, and to $4.25 an hour on April 1, 1991. The law provided for a youth training wage of $3.35 an hour for a ninety-day period after the $3.80 minimum wage went into effect. When the $4.25 minimum wage became effective, the training wage was increased to $3.61 an hour. Employees could be employed for an additional ninety days at the training wage if a bona-fide on-the-job-training program was provided by the employer. The training wage provision had a sunset requirement that would lead to its elimination in 1993 unless specifically reauthorized by the Congress. The law provided for a study of the impact of the training wage which was to be submitted to the Congress in early 1993.

The response to the new legislation was predictable. Once it became clear that the president was going to sign the bill into law, many of the dire consequences purportedly emanating from the change seemed to evaporate into mid–air. There were still those who opposed the program on philosophical grounds, but much of the information in the media sounded an optimistic and more positive tone. Representative of those sentiments was an article in the *Wall Street Journal* entitled "Effects of Minimum Wage Increase Seen as Manageable." Staff reporter Barbara Marsh noted that the new $500,000 sales volume exemption would exempt thousands of small businesses.[3] Construction and laundry/dry cleaning enterprises became subject to the $500,000 sales volume test. However, an important change in the law resulted in a provision called "individual coverage." In brief, any employee of a firm that did not meet the sales volume test could still be covered if the employee was engaged in covered activity. The upward movement of the overall wage structure resulted in about 3.9 million workers out of a labor force of over 127 million earning the minimum wage.

The youth training wage was seen as a vehicle to moderate the impacts on small business and the economy.[4] Opponents of the training wage had argued that there were few impacts and therefore relatively few workers would gain from this initiative. Even the fast-food industry did not seem to be affected materially by the increases. In *Fortune*, it was noted that while fast-food chains were believed to be the big losers when the minimum wage increases, most of the large chains were paying substantially in excess of the mandated wage level. McDonald's was paying an average of $4.65 an hour and Wendy's International was paying $4.25 an hour. A spokesperson for McDonald's suggested that "Contrary to what people think, McDonald's is not a minimum-wage employer. In an industry as competitive as ours in finding employees, we can't afford to be."[5]

In any event, the most important aspect of the new minimum wage law was the initiation of the training wage. It was clearly a defeat for organized labor and Congressional supporters who had vigorously opposed this proposal for decades. The mandated study ultimately vindicated the opponents of the subminimum wage for youth.

The optimistic assessment by Lane Kirkland, President of the AFL–CIO, that "We believe the provision for a training wage contains adequate safeguards so the youth are not exploited and older workers are not displaced" seemed consistent with the findings of the mandated Study. In a Report to the Congress in 1994, the Department of Labor provided survey information that showed negligible use of the youth minimum wage by American industry. There was considerable evidence that the reservation wage of workers was higher than what the youth training wage provided. The Report noted that "In the 27 states allowing full use of the training wage, . . . just one percent [of employers] actually utilized the training wage provision."[6] While the law permitted employers to use the training wage in two 90-day segments, *if the employer had a bona-fide training program in effect in the second 90-day interval,* the study found that "No employers, in any state, indicated they had paid workers the training wage during the second 90 days of eligibility."[7] Apparently, employers that used the training wage only used it when they could reduce their wage bill but chose not to use it to provide *training,* as the proponents had intended. The conclusions from the study were sufficiently convincing to prevent extension of the training wage provision, and it expired on March 31, 1993.

A FINAL NOTE

As this book moved toward press, President Bill Clinton proposed an increase in the Federal minimum wage in his 1995 State of the Union message. The general outline seems to be a two-year escalation of the minimum wage of

$.45 per year. This would lead to a $5.15 minimum wage at the end of the escalation process. In his weekly radio address on March 30, 1996, President Clinton said, "it's hard to raise a family on $4.25 an hour. We must make sure that the minimum wage is a living wage."[8] Taking the challenge directly to the U.S. Senate, the president argued that over the last five years, "while the minimum wage has been stuck at $4.25 an hour, a senator's salary has gone up by a third," from $101,900 to $133,600[9]

To date, while the traditional rumblings of dire consequences are heard in the background, there has been relatively little discussion about the president's proposal. With the last mandated increase occurring in 1991, the relative position of America's lowest-paid workers continues to deteriorate. There are those who will continue to resist any efforts to raise the wage of low-wage workers, but as this study has shown, they cannot definitively or even proximally demonstrate that the increases will have the predicted adverse economic or social effects. The president noted that the minimum wage *in real purchasing power* will fall to a 40-year low this year if an increase does not occur.[10]

On the other hand, while increases in the minimum wage do not materially affect the incidence of poverty, there is substantial evidence that individual workers benefit from higher minimum wages and extended coverage. The nation is in the advanced stages of a robust economic growth process in which profits have substantially increased. Inflation is relatively stable, and modest wage increases have occurred. Many workers have thus experienced a growth in their monetary and real income during this process. Minimum wage workers have not experienced these gains.

During the first week of August of 1996, as the Congress moved toward its August Recess, two major pieces of Federal legislation suddenly emerged. The twice-vetoed Welfare Reform legislation took on new life, was passed by both houses of Congress, and prepared for Presidential signature.

The second piece of legislation concerned increases in the Federal minimum wage. After beating back attempts by House republicans to reduce coverage by exempting certain categories of small businesses, a new clean bill was under consideration by the House and Senate. As predicted, the proposed bill contains two forty-five cent increases in the Federal minimum wage that will bring it to the level of $5.15 per hour in January 1998. The bill is also heading for Presidential signature, but so far, he has not signed either the Welfare Reform or Minimum Wage measures.

Presidential signature is predicted on both bills. If these bills become law, they will represent fulfillment of two promises the President made early in his term of Office—reforming the Nation's Welfare System and increasing the Federal minimum wage. In both cases, the bills provide the framework for addressing pressing economic and social needs that have gone unattended. We should not expect either bill to fully resolve every question related to low wage rates or welfare dependency. However, if they become law, they will continue the nation's quest for economic and social justice.

Policymakers can continue to quibble about this federal program and refuse to address the needs of those least able to participate in the American Dream. The American economy is the strongest economic system in the world. The creative entrepreneurship of American business relies on a strong, productive workforce that has sufficient income to enjoy the benefits of productive work and the maintenance of the American family. There will always be lower-wage workers in a competitive market system, but this realization does not lead to the conclusion that those at the lowest wage levels should be forgotten. The nation must begin a reasoned dialogue about these workers that comports with a more balanced perspective about impacts and needs. The federal minimum wage program provides a statement to society and to the world about the values and attitudes of this nation's political and policy leaders. Whether the president's recommendations in his State of the Union message are the best for the nation's low-wage workers is a debatable question. What should not be in question is whether the most advanced nation on earth should improve the economic position of its lowest-paid workers. There may be several policy tools that can move workers in that direction, but clearly, a minimum wage that is commensurate with the state of the economy and the overall structure of wages and salaries should be a leading tool in that change process.

NOTES

1. *Wall Street Journal*, November 2, 1989, p. A-4.

2. Michael Krenish, "Minimum Wage Bill Awaits Bush Signature," *Boston Globe*, Thursday, November 1, 1989, p. B-1.

3. *Wall Street Journal*, November 8, 1989, p. B-2.

4. *Fortune*, December 4, 1989, p. 11.

5. U.S. Department of Labor, *Report to the Congress on the Training Wage Provisions of the Fair Labor Standards Act Amendments of 1989 From the Secretary of Labor* (Washington, D.C.: Government Printing Office, n.d.), p. 3.

6. Ibid.

7. Lawrence L. Knutsen, "Clinton Presses for Vote on Raising Minimum Wage," *Register Herald* (Beckley, West Virginia), March 31, 1996, p. 1C.

8. Ibid.

9. Ibid.

10. Ibid.

Appendix

Table A.1

**Estimated Number of Employed Nonsupervisory Employees
by Status under the Minimum Wage
Provisions of the FLSA, by Industry Division,
Selected Years, 1939-1988**

Industry and Minimum Wage Coverage Status	Nonsupervisory Employees (000)				
	April 1939	Sept. 1947	August 1950	Sept. 1953	August 1957
All industries					
• Subject	12,291	22,601	20,933	23,976	24,301
• Not subject	-	-	-	-	-
Private sector	-	-	-	43,754	43,926
• Subject	12,291	22,601	20.933	23,776	24,301
• Not subject	-	-	-	19,978	19,625
Agriculture, forestry, and fisheries	-	-		3,066	1,816
• Subject	-	19	14	14	5
• Not subject	-	-	-	3,052	1,811
Mining	-	-	-	768	722
• Subject	796	875	877	747	712
• Not subject	-	-	-	21	10
Contract construction	-	-	-	2,565	2,909
• Subject	-	707	590	614	1,293
• Not subject	-	-	-	1,951	1,616
Manufacturing	-	-	-	16,131	15,341
• Subject	7,658	14,612	13,081	15,448	14,601
• Not subject	-	-	-	683	740
Transportation, communications, and public utilities	-	-	-	3,956	3,877

Table A.1 (continued)

Industry and Minimum Wage Coverage Status	Nonsupervisory Employees (000)				
	April 1939	Sept. 1947	August 1950	Sept. 1953	August 1957
• Subject	2,325	3,273	3,286	3,441	3,362
• Not subject	-	-	-	515	515
Wholesale trade	-	-	-	2,539	2,660
• Subject	1,183	1,349	-	1,693	1,863
• Not subject	-	-	-	846	797
Retail trade	-	-	-	6,928	7,163
•Subject	41	395	-	230	243
•Not subject	-	-	-	6,698	6,920
Finance, insurance and real estate	-	-	-	1,792	2,001
• Subject	288	709	899	1,048	1,360
• Not subject	-	-	-	744	641
Service industry (except private household)	-	-	-	4,188	5,100
• Subject	-	-	-	741	862
• Not subject	-	-	-	3,447	4,238
Private household	-	-	-	2,021	2,337
• Subject	-	-	-	-	-
• Not subject	-	-	-	2,021	2,337
Public sector	-	-	-	-	-
• Subject	-	-	-	-	-
• Not subject	-	-	-	-	-
Federal government	-	-	-	-	-
• Subject	-	-	-	-	-
• Not subject	-	-	-	-	-
State/local government	-	-	-	-	-
• Subject	-	-	-	-	-
• Not subject	-	-	-	-	-

Table A.1 (continued)

Industry and Minimum Wage Coverage	Nonsupervisory Employees (000)				
	Feb. 1959	Feb. 1960	Feb. 1962	Feb. 1964	Feb. 1967
Misc. industry					
(not elsewhere classified)	-	662	499	-	-
• Subject	-	662	499	-	-
• Not subject	-	-	-	-	-
All industries	-	-	-	-	-
• Subject	23,723	23,857	28,496	29,593	41,428
• Not subject	-	-	-	-	-
Private sector	43,760	44,220	45,577	46,000	50,429
• Subject	23,723	23,857	28,496	29,000	38,992
• Not subject	20,037	20,363	17,081	17,000	11,437
Agriculture, forestry, and					
fisheries	1,883	1,928	2,045	1,882	1,517
• Subject	2	2	-	-	477
• Not subject	1,881	1,926	2,045	1,882	1,040
Mining	637	616	567	559	560
• Subject	626	606	562	554	554
• Not subject	11	10	5	5	6
Contract construction	2,897	2,897	2,880	3,029	3,236
• Subject	1,273	1,273	2,294	2,413	3,201
• Not subject	1,624	1,624	586	616	35
Manufacturing	15,071	15,077	15,362	15,851	17,481
• Subject	14,238	14,238	14,737	15,207	16,903
• Not subject	833	839	625	644	578
Transportation, communications,					
and public utilities	3,675	3,679	3,566	3,664	3,823
• Subject	3,208	3,224	3,380	3,474	3,751
• Not subject	467	455	186	190	72

Table A.1 (continued)

Industry and Minimum Wage Coverage Status	Nonsupervisory Employees (000)				
	Feb. 1959	Feb. 1960	Feb. 1962	Feb. 1964	Feb. 1967
Wholesale trade	2,561	2,639	2,866	3,013	3,133
• Subject	1,784	1,834	1,989	2,090	2,368
• Not subject	777	805	877	923	765
Retail trade	7,349	7,537	7,594	7,986	8,690
• Subject	229	241	2,466	2,591	5,060
• Not subject	7,120	7,296	5,128	5,395	3,630
Finance, insurance, and real estate	2,126	2,193	2,391	2,515	2,687
• Subject	1,413	1,472	1,777	1,869	1,998
• Not subject	713	721	614	646	689
Service industry (except private household)	5,100	5,160	5,812	6,253	6,861
• Subject	950	967	1,291	1,391	4,680
• Not subject	4,150	4,193	4,521	4,862	2,181
Private household	2,461	2,494	2,494	2,504	2,441
• Subject	-	-	-	-	-
• Not subject	2,461	2,494	2,494	2,504	2,441
Public Sector	-	-	-	-	-
• Subject	-	-	-	-	2,436
• Not Subject	-	-	-	-	-
Federal government	-	-	-	-	-
• Subject	-	-	-	-	-
• Not subject	-	-	-	-	-
State/local government	-	-	-	-	-
• Subject	-	-	-	-	-
• Not subject	-	-	-	-	-

Table A.1 (continued)

Industry and Minimum Wage Coverage Status	Nonsupervisory Employees (000)				
	Feb. 1968	Feb. 1969	Feb. 1970	Sept. 1970	Sept. 1971
All industries	-	-	62,763	61,904	62,111
• Subject	42,778	44,569	46,255	45,511	45,383
• Not subject	-	-	16,508	16,393	16,728
Private sector	51,866	53,506	54,897	53,807	53,857
• Subject	40,097	41,827	43,114	42,163	42,056
• Not subject	11,769	11,679	11,783	11,644	11,801
Agriculture, forestry and fisheries	1,513	1,327	1,273	1,190	1,236
• Subject	466	617	620	535	495
• Not subject	1,047	710	653	655	741
Mining	533	558	570	559	557
• Subject	529	553	565	554	552
• Not subject	4	5	5	5	5
Contract construction	3,292	3,312	3,444	3,219	3,192
• Subject	3,257	3,277	3,409	3,202	3,175
• Not subject	35	35	35	17	17
Manufacturing	17,517	18,081	18,381	17,549	16,945
• Subject	16,942	17,495	17,793	16,987	16,389
• Not subject	575	586	588	562	556
Transportation, communications, and public utilities	3,917	4,026	4,164	4,092	4,045
• Subject	3,842	3,952	4,095	4,018	3,962
• Not subject	75	74	69	74	83
Wholesale trade	3,275	3,392	3,524	3,307	3,317
• Subject	2,487	2,576	2,686	2,513	2,522
• Not subject	788	816	838	794	795
Retail trade	9,150	9,574	9,948	10,054	10,322
• Subject	5,372	5,566	5,803	5,886	6,222
• Not subject	3,778	4,008	4,145	4,168	4,100

Table A.1 (continued)

Industry and Minimum Wage Coverage Status	Nonsupervisory Employees (000)				
	Feb. 1968	Feb. 1969	Feb. 1970	Sept. 1970	Sept. 1971
Finance, insurance and real estate	2,877	2,963	3,119	3,170	3,285
• Subject	2,153	2,215	2,349	2,400	2,490
• Not subject	724	748	770	770	795
Service Industry (except private household)	7,589	7,893	8,289	8,542	8,844
• Subject	5,069	5,576	5,794	6,068	6,249
• Not subject	2,520	2,317	2,495	2,474	2,595
Private household	2,223	2,380	2,185	2,125	2,114
• Subject	-	-	-	-	-
• Not subject	2,223	2,380	2,185	2,125	2,114
Public sector	-	-	7,866	8,097	8,254
• Subject	2,861	2,742	3,141	3,348	3,327
• Not subject	-	-	4,725	4,749	4,927
Federal government	-	-	2,440	2,365	2,367
• Subject	-	-	729	693	641
• Not subject	-	-	1,711	1,672	1,726
State/local government	-	-	5,426	5,732	5,887
• Subject	-	-	2,412	2,655	2,686
• Not subject	-	-	3,014	3,077	3,201

Table A.1 (continued)

Industry and Minimum Wage Coverage Status	Nonsupervisory Employees (000)				
	Sept. 1972	Sept. 1973	Sept. 1974	Sept. 1975	Sept. 1976
All Industries	63,889	66,199	67,788	66,317	68,054
• Subject	46,950	49,427	57,965	56,648	51,875
• Not subject	16,939	16,772	9,823	9,669	16,179
Private sector	55,406	57,591	58,823	57,038	58,887
• Subject	43,497	45,898	49,000	47,369	49,327
• Not subject	11,909	11,693	9,823	9,669	9,560
Agriculture, forestry and fisheries	1,199	1,232	1,373	1,375	1,409
• Subject	485	513	587	597	640
• Not subject	714	719	786	778	769
Mining	547	573	612	674	714
• Subject	542	568	608	670	710
• Not subject	5	5	4	4	4
Contract construction	3,481	3,627	3,771	3,293	3,206
• Subject	3,462	3,608	3,751	3,273	3,186
• Not subject	19	19	20	20	20
Manufacturing	17,356	18,107	17,980	16,517	17,148
• Subject	16,788	17,524	17,509	16,083	16,698
• Not subject	568	583	471	434	450
Transportation, communications, and public utilities	4,080	4,190	4,185	3,991	4,042
• Subject	3,991	4,104	4,110	3,921	3,971
• Not subject	89	86	75	70	71
Wholesale trade	3,387	3,528	3,679	3,598	3,689
• Subject	2,576	2,683	2,943	2,878	2,951
• Not subject	811	845	736	720	738
Retail trade	10,731	11,120	11,594	11,614	12,034
• Subject	6,611	7,149	7,992	8,227	9,100
• Not Subject	4,120	3,971	3,602	3,387	2,934

Table A.1 (continued)

Industry and Minimum Wage Coverage Status	Nonsupervisory Employees (000)				
	Sept. 1972	Sept. 1973	Sept. 1974	Sept. 1975	Sept. 1976
Finance, insurance and real estate	3,395	3,502	3,576	3,630	3,719
• Subject	2,577	2,662	2,726	2,766	2,834
• Not subject	818	840	850	864	885
Service industry (except private household)	9,167	9,652	10,223	10,567	11,087
• Subject	6,465	7,087	7,438	7,680	8,063
• Not subject	2,702	2,565	2,785	2,887	3,024
Private household	2,063	2,060	1,830	1,779	1,839
• Subject	-	-	1,336	1,274	1,174(8)
• Not subject	2,063	2,060	494	505	665
Public sector	8,483	8,608	8,965	9,279	9,167
• Subject	3,453	3,529	8,965	9,279	2,548
• Not subject	5,030	5,079	-	-	6,619
Federal government	2,333	2,308	2,295	2,304	2,211
• Subject	636	615	2,295	2,304	2,211
• Not subject	1,697	1,693	-	-	-
State/local government	6,150	6,300	6,670	6,975	6,956
• Subject	2,817	2,914	6,670	6,975	337
• Not subject	3,333	3,386	-	-	6,619

Table A.1 (continued)

Industry and Minimum Wage Coverage Status	Nonsupervisory Employees (000)				
	Sept. 1977	Sept. 1978	Sept. 1979	Sept. 1980	Sept. 1981
All industries	70,801	74,038	76,838	76,735	77,903
• Subject	54,446	57,572	60,129	60,191	61,316
• Not subject	16,355	16,466	16,709	16,544	16,587
Private sector	61,510	64,611	67,317	66,875	68,223
• Subject	51,893	54,998	57,538	57,575	58,702
• Not subject	9,617	9,613	9,779	9,300	9,521
Agriculture, forestry and fisheries	1,431	1,518	1,472	1,438	1,468
• Subject	565	553	540	586	566
• Not subject	866	965	932	852	902
Mining	763	792	866	908	1,016
• Subject	759	788	861	904	1,012
• Not subject	4	4	5	4	4
Contract construction	3,740	4,126	4,482	4,213	4,059
• Subject	3,720	4,105	4,461	4,192	4,037
• Not subject	20	21	21	21	22
Manufacturing	17,618	18,246	18,723	17,916	18,207
• Subject	17,146	17,744	18,208	17,422	17,706
• Not subject	472	502	515	494	501
Transportation, communications, and public utilities	4,124	4,350	4,646	4,580	4,633
• Subject	4,052	4,317	4,611	4,547	4,600
• Not subject	72	33	35	33	33
Wholesale trade	3,799	4,231	4,466	4,538	4,606
• Subject	3,039	3,372	3,559	3,618	3,672
• Not subject	760	859	907	920	934

Table A.1 (continued)

Industry and Minimum Wage Coverage Status	Nonsupervisory Employees (000)				
	Sept. 1977	Sept. 1978	Sept. 1979	Sept. 1980	Sept. 1981
Retail trade	12,645	13,246	13,560	13,866	14,010
• Subject	9,871	10,551	10,938	11,519	11,651
• Not subject	2,774	2,695	2,622	2,347	2,359
Finance, insurance and real estate	3,896	4,041	4,151	4,438	4,579
• Subject	2,969	3,066	3,117	3,366	3,473
• Not subject	927	975	1,034	1,072	1,106
Service industry (except private household)	11,600	12,216	13,055	13,553	14,278
• Subject	8,557	9,322	9,958	10,458	11,077
• Not subject	3,043	2,894	3,097	3,095	3,201
Private household	1,894	1,845	1,768	1,425	1,367
• Subject	1,215	1,180	1,157	963	908
• Not subject	679	665	611	462	459
Public sector	9,291	9,427	9,521	9,860	9,680
• Subject	2,553	2,574	2,591	2,616	2,614
• Not subject	6,738	6,853	6,930	7,244	7,066
Federal government	2,208	2,226	2,232	2,232	2,222
• Subject	2,208	2,226	2,232	2,232	2,222
• Not subject	-	-	-	-	-
State/local government	7,083	7,201	7,289	7,628	7,458
• Subject	345	348	359	384	392
• Not subject	6,738	6,853	6,930	7,244	7,066

Table A.1 (continued)

Industry and Minimum Wage Coverage Status	Nonsupervisory Employees (000)				
	Sept. 1982	Sept. 1983	Sept. 1984	Sept. 1985	Sept. 1986
All industries	75,779	77,321	80,750	83,564	85,417
• Subject	59,208	60,461	63,438	73,046	74,680
• Not subject	16,571	16,860	17,312	10,518	10,737
Private sector	66,185	67,731	70,975	73,539	75,134
• Subject	56,617	57,868	60,802	63,021	64,397
• Not subject	9,568	9,863	10,173	10,518	10,737
Agriculture, forestry, and fisheries	1,539	1,620	1,590	1,570	1,564
• Subject	593	623	612	604	602
• Not subject	946	997	978	966	962
Mining	941	896	889	842	655
• Subject	937	892	885	838	651
• Not subject	4	4	4	4	4
Contract construction	3,698	3,853	4,187	4,517	4,787
• Subject	3,677	3,831	4,165	4,495	4,765
• Not subject	21	22	22	22	22
Manufacturing	16,611	16,916	17,583	17,238	17,053
• Subject	16,151	16,448	17,098	16,762	16,581
• Not subject	460	468	485	476	472
Transportation, communications, and public utilities	4,499	4,499	4,664	4,766	4,758
• Subject	4,468	4,468	4,633	4,734	4,727
• Not subject	31	31	31	32	31
Wholesale trade	4,521	4,532	4,805	4,994	5,044
• Subject	3,604	3,613	3,831	3,982	4,023
• Not subject	917	919	974	1,012	1,021

Table A.1 (continued)

Industry and Minimum Wage Coverage Status	Nonsupervisory Employees (000)				
	Sept. 1982	Sept. 1983	Sept. 1984	Sept. 1985	Sept. 1986
Retail trade	13,762	13,920	14,839	15,911	16,357
• Subject	11,475	11,587	12,419	13,439	13,931
• Not subject	2,287	2,333	2,420	2,472	2,426
Finance, insurance, and real estate	4,593	4,705	4,881	5,127	5,473
• Subject	3,483	3,567	3,701	3,887	4,150
• Not subject	1,110	1,138	1,180	1,240	1,323
Service industry (except private household)	14,498	15,163	15,973	16,995	17,899
• Subject	11,239	11,790	12,419	13,204	13,942
• Not subject	3,259	3,373	3,554	3,791	3,957
Private household	1,523	1,627	1,564	1,579	1,544
• Subject	990	1,049	1,039	1,076	1,025
• Not subject	533	578	525	503	519
Public sector	9,594	9,590	9,775	10,025	10,283
• Subject	2,591	2,593	2,636	10,025	10,283
• Not subject	7,003	6,997	7,139	-	-
Federal government	2,195	2,197	2,235	2,330	2,345
• Subject	2,195	2,197	2,235	2,330	2,345
• Not subject	-	-	-	-	-
State/local government	7,399	7,393	7,540	7,695	7,938
• Subject	396	396	401	7,695	7,938
• Not subject	7,003	6,997	7,139	-	-

Table A.1 (continued)

Industry and Minimum Wage Coverage Status	Nonsupervisory Employees (000)	
	Sept. 1987	Sept. 1988
All industries	86,886	90,193
• Subject	76,023	79,150
• Not subject	10,863	11,043
Private sector	76,390	79,495
• Subject	65,527	68,452
• Not aubject	10,863	11,043
Agriculture, forestry, and fisheries	1,670	1,635
• Subject	642	628
• Not subject	1,028	1,007
Mining	664	646
• Subject	660	642
• Not subject	4	4
Contract construction	4,771	5,092
• Subject	4,749	5,069
• Not subject	22	23
Manufacturing	17,093	17,426
• Subject	16,620	16,945
• Not subject	473	481
Transportation, communications, and public utilities	4,844	5,013
• Subject	4,813	4,988
• Not subject	31	32
Wholesale trade	5,007	5,353
• Subject	3,993	4,270
• Not subject	1,014	1,083
Retail trade	16,566	17,498
• Subject	14,254	15,157
• Not subject	2,312	2,291

Table A.1 (continued)

Industry and Minimum Wage Coverage Status	Nonsupervisory Employees (000)	
	Sept. 1987	Sept. 1988
Finance, insurance, and real estate	5,683	5,735
• Subject	4,309	4,349
• Not subject	1,374	1,386
Service industry (except private household)	18,696	19,754
• Subject	14,564	15,474
• Not subject	4,132	4,280
Private household	1,396	1,386
• Subject	923	930
• Not subject	473	456
Public sector	10,283	10,698
• Subject	10,283	10,698
• Not subject	-	-
Federal Government	2,345	2,412
• Subject	2,345	2,412
• Not subject	-	-
State/local government	7,938	8,286
• Subject	7,938	8,286
• Not subject	-	-

Source: Compiled from *Minimum Wage and Maximum House Standards Under the Fair Labor Standards Act* and related *Annual Reports to the Congress* between 1939-1988.

Table A.2

**Minimum Wage and Overtime Standards Established
Under the Fair Labor Standards Act, 1938-1988**

Act or Amendment	Minimum Wage Standards		Maximum Hours Standards	
	Rate	Effective Date	Time and One-half the Regular Rate of Pay for Weekly Hours Over	Effective Date
FLSA of 1938	$.25	10/24/38	44	10/24/38
	.30	10/24/39	42	10/24/39
	.40	10/24/45	40	10/24/40
FLSA Amendments of 1949	.75	10/25/50	-	-
FLSA Amendments of 1955	1.00	3/1/56	-	-
FLSA Amendments of 1961 Employees covered prior to the 1961 amendments	1.15	09/3/61	-	-
Employees covered as a result of the 1961 amendments	1.00	9/3/61	-	-
	1.15	9/3/64	-	-
	1.25	9/3/65	-	-
FLSA Amendments of 1966 Employees covered prior to the 1966 amendments	1.40	2/1/67	-	-
	1.60	2/1/68		-
Nonfarm employees covered as a result of the 1966 amendments [a]	1.00	2/1/67	44	2/1/67

Table A.2 (continued)

Act or Amendment	Minimum Wage Standards		Maximum Hours Standards	
	Rate	Effective Date	Time and One-half the Regular Rate of Pay for Weekly Hours Over	Effective Date
Nonfarm employees covered as a result of the 1966 amendments [a]	1.15	2/1/68	42	2/1/68
	1.30	2/1/69	40	2/1/69
	1.45	2/1/70	-	-
	1.60	2/1/71	-	-
Hired farmworkers	1.00	2/1/67	none	
	1.15	2/1/68	none	
	1.30	2/1/69	none	
FLSA Amendments of 1974				
Employees covered prior to the 1966 amendments	2.00	5/1/74	[b]	
	2.10	1/1/75	[b]	
	2.30	1/1/76	[b]	
Nonfarm employees covered as a result of the 1966 or 1974 amendments	1.90	5/1/74	[b]	
	2.00	1/1/75	[b]	
	2.20	1/1/76	[b]	
	2.30	1/1/77	[b]	
Hired farmworkers	1.60	5/1/74	none	
	1.80	1/1/75	none	

Table A.2 (continued)

Act or Amendment	Minimum Wage Standards		Maximum Hours Standards	
	Rate	Effective Date	Time and One-half the Regular Rate of Pay for Weekly Hours Over	Effective Date
FLSA Amendments of 1977				
All employees	2.65	1/1/78	c	
	2.90	1/1/79	c	
	3.10	1/1/80	c	
	3.35	1/1/81	c	

a.   Newly covered employees in restaurants, hotels, and motels were exempt from overtime provisions.

b.   Overtime exemption eliminated for many previously covered or newly covered nonfarm workers on 5/1/74 and phased out or modified over a period of years for many others.

c.   Several overtime exemptions were repealed, phased out, or modified. The most significant was the overtime exemption for employees of hotels, motels, and restaurants (maids and custodial employees of hotels and motels were not exempt).

Source: U.S. Department of Labor, Employment Standards Administration. Compiled from various issues of the *Minimum Wage and Maximum Hours Standards Under the Fair Labor Standards Act* and various *Annual Reports to the Congress* between 193 -1988.

Table A.3

Estimated Number of Nonsupervisory Employees Paid Less
Than the Minimum Wage Rates Specified in the FLSA of 1938
and Its Subsequent Amendments, and Estimated Direct
Cost of Raising Their Wages to Those Rates,
October 1938-January 1981

Act or Amendment			Covered Employees		Estimated	
Effective Date of Minimum Wage Change and Coverage	*Minimum Wage Rate*	*Estimated Number of Covered Employees*	*Paid Less Than Minimum Wage*		*Annual Wage Bill Increase*	
		(000)	*(000)*	*(%)*	*(000,000)*	*(%)*
FLSA of 1938						
10/24/38	$ .25	11,000	300	2.7	a	a
10/24/39	.30	12,548	650	5.2	a	a
10/24/45	.40	20,000	1,600	8.0	a	a
1949 Amendments						
1/25/50	.75	20,933	1,300	6.2	a	a
1955 Amendments						
3/1/56	1.00	23,976	2,000	8.3	$560	0.7
1961 Amendments						
9/3/61		27,478	2,569	9.3	536	0.4
Covered prior to 1961 amendments	1.15	23,854	1,906	8.0	336	0.3
Newly covered by 1961 amendments 9/3/63	1.00	2,624	663	18.3	200	1.5
Covered prior to 1961 amendments 9/4/64	1.25	23,900	2,600	10.8	365	0.3
Newly covered by 1961 amendments 9/3/65	1.15	3,600	565	15.7	115	0.8
Newly covered by 1961 amendments	1.25	3,600	810	22.5	162	1.1

Table A.3 (continued)

Act or Amendment — Effective Date of Minimum Wage Change and Coverage	Minimum Wage Rate	Estimated Number of Covered Employees (000)	Covered Employees Paid Less Than Minimum Wage (000)	(%)	Estimated Annual Wage Bill Increase (000,000)	(%)
1966 Amendments 2/1/67		40,434	4,553	11.3	1,080	0.5
Covered prior to 1966 amendments	1.40	32,307	3,715	11.5	800	0.5
Newly covered nonfarm and farm [b]	1.00	8,127b	838	10.3	280	0.9
2/1/68		41,562	7,260	17.5	2,285	1.1
Covered prior to 1966 amendments	1.60	33,052	5,958	18.0	1,960	1.1
Newly covered nonfarm and farm [b]	1.15	8,510	1,302	15.3	325	0.9
2/1/69		44,569	2,089	4.7	505	0.2
Newly covered nonfarm and farm	1.30	10,356	2,089	20.2	505	1.1
2/1/70		46,255	2,143	4.6	486	0.2
Newly covered nonfarm only	1.45	10,889	2,143	19.7	486	1.0
2/1/71		45,511	1,599	3.5	324	0.1
Newly covered nonfarm only	1.60	11,261	1,599	14.2	324	0.6
1974 Amendments 5/1/74		56,112	4,230	7.5	1,915	0.5
Nonfarm covered prior to 1966 amendments	2.00	37,124	1,382	3.7	511	0.2
Covered as a result of the 1966 amendments	1.90	11,790	1,563	13.3	552	0.8

Table A.3 (continued)

Act or Amendment Effective Date of Minimum Wage Change and Coverage	Minimum Wage Rate	Estimated Number of Covered Employees (000)	Covered Employees Paid Less Than Minimum Wage		Estimated Annual Wage Bill Increase	
			(000)	(%)	(000,000)	(%)
Covered as a result of the 1974 amendments [c]	1.90	6,660	1,197	18.0	827	1.8
Farm	1.60	53	888	16.4	25	1.4
1/1/75		57,342[d]	4,517	7.9	739	0.2
Nonfarm						
Covered prior to 1966 amendments	2.10	37,650	1,490	4.0	268	0.1
Covered as a result of the 1966 amendments	2.00	12,345	1,751	14.2	303	0.4
Covered as a result of the 1974 amendments	2.00	6,670	1,137	16.8	135	0.3
Farm	1.80	587	139	23.7	33	1.6
1/1/76		56,121	3,877	6.9	1,201	0.2
Nonfarm						
Covered prior to 1966 amendments	2.30	35,677	1,199	3.4	431	0.1
Covered as a result of the 1966 amendments	2.20	12,806	1,492	11.7	501	0.6
Covered as a result of the 1974 amendments [e]	2.20	7,041	1,098	15.6	239	0.4

Table A.3 (continued)

Act or Amendment			Covered Employees				
Effective Date of Minimum Wage Change and Coverage	Minimum Wage Rate	Estimated Number of Covered Employees	Paid Less Than Minimum Wage		Estimated Annual Wage Bill Increase		
		(000)	(000)	(%)	(000,000)	(%)
Farm		597	88	14.7	30	0.9
1/1/77		51,875	2,266	4.4	515	0.1
Nonfarm						
Covered as a result of the 1966 amendments [f]	2.30	10,472	1,267	12.9	247	0.4
Covered as a result of the 1974 amendments [f]	2.30	3,830	881	23.0	229	0.7
Farm	2.20	640	118	18.4	39	1.0
1977 Amendments						
1/1/78 [f]	2.65	54,446	24,581	8.4	1,975	0.4
1/1/79 [f]	2.90	57,343[g]	5,080	8.9	1,916	0.3
1/1/80 [f]	3.10	60,129	5,345	8.9	1,814	0.3
1/1/81 [f]	3.35	59,566[h]	5,501	9.2	2,193	0.3

[a.] Not available.

[b.] Excludes retail and service employees added to coverage by the 1966 amendments who became subject to the minimum wage provisions of the FLSA on February 1, 1969.

[c.] Number covered totals 57,965,000 when employees who became subject at a later date as a result of the phaseout of the minimum wage exemption under Section 13(a)(2) are included. Employment reference period is September 1975.

[d.] Excludes retail and service workers in multi-unit enterprises who became subject at a later date as a result of the phaseout of the minimum wage exemption under Section 13(a)(2).

[e.] Number covered totals 56,648,000 (see noted). Employment reference period is September 1975.

Table A.3 (continued)

f.   Excludes state and local government employees engaged in activities that are an integral part of traditional government functions that the Supreme Court ruled, in *National League of Cities*, to be outside the scope of the minimum wage and overtime provisions of the FLSA. In the *Garcia* decision (February 18, 1985) the Supreme Court reestablished coverage, and the wage impact was estimated to be $396 million accruing to 260,000 employees.

g.   Number covered totals 57,572,000 when workers affected by the increase in the annual sales volume test under Section 3(s) from $250,000 to $275,000 are included. Employment reference period is September 1978.

h.   Number covered totals 60,191,000 when workers affected by the increase in the annual sales volume test under Section 3(s) from $275,000 to $325,000 are included. Employment reference period is September 1980.

Source: U.S. Department of Labor, Employment Standards Administration. Compiled from various issues of the *Minimum Wage and Maximum Hours Standards Under the Fair Labor Standards Act* and various *Annual Reports to the Congress* between 1938 - 1988.

Table A.4

Investigation Findings under the FLSA, 1941-1988

Fiscal Year	Employees Underpaid		Amount of Underpayment	
	Minimum Wage[a]	Overtime Compensation[b]	Minimum Wage[c]	Overtime Compensation
1941	51,006	110,922	$879,800	$3,892,021
1942	56,972	208,781	$1,070,357	--
1943				
1944				
1945				
1946	38,034	233,444		
1947	37,307	174,949		
1948	12,232	90,566		
1949	15,888	170,422		
1950	11,899	128,793		
1951	42,642	96,396	$2,105,799	
1952	72,157	135,921	$3,891,918	
1953	62,266	156,843	$3,712,200	
1954	40,138	118,533	$2,716,376	$11,057,872
1955	36,894	108,006	$2,135,731	$12,015,346
1956	27,617	97,082	$1,612,902	$9,473,050
1957	77,463	138,803	$5,289,873	$13,544,861
1958	63,349	130,792	$6,145,385	$13,509,914
1959	70,467	137,640	$6,937,265	$15,465,851
1960	62,253	155,746	$8,663,703	$19,369,703
1961	75,051	164,758	$9,252,992	$21,689,539
1962	89,130	162,571	$10,255,086	$28,749,252
1963	165,350	210,768	$18,910,822	$30,899,804
1964	203,513	237,180	$24,209,632	$35,499,852
1965	209,930	295,789	$28,104,994	$46,191,263
1966	191,332	327,168	$28,370,932	$59,460,982
1967	139,533	288,105	$18,839,742	$53,737,920
1968	169,344	296,037	$20,437,008	$54,507,347
1969	205,269	304,740	$27,127,308	$54,653,115
1970	207,881	284,542	$29,410,934	$53,921,420
1971	208,193	253,868	$28,893,460	$50,742,736
1972	220,839	265,627	$28,887,908	$53,099,776
1973	152,784	200,410	$21,288,874	$41,973,823
1974	119,561	207,629	$18,251,688	$46,304,358

Table A.4 (continued)

Fiscal Year	Employees Underpaid		Amount of Underpayment	
	Minimum Wage [a]	Overtime Compensation [b]	Minimum Wage [c]	Overtime Compensation
1975	216,886	250,388	$27,462,451	$45,118,303
1976	296,324	261,892	$37,889,306	$51,171,641
1977	371,041	265,744	$37,180,291	$51,249,841
1978	378,000	264,000	$40,000,000	$51,700,000
1979	426,000	287,000	$54,000,000	$70,000,000
1980	348,000	276,000	$43,800,000	$76,200,000
1981	397,000	292,000	$52,900,000	$74,600,000
1982	295,000	288,000	$49,500,000	$80,700,000
1983	218,000	268,000	$40,400,000	$74,800,000
1984	187,500	260,700	$33,000,000	$74,000,000
1985	166,700	268,100	$29,600,000	$79,700,000
1986	167,000	317,000	$29,000,000	$93,000,000
1987	155,100	328,600	$28,400,000	$98,000,000
1988	154,000	324,000	$29,800,000	$113,700,000

[a] Includes disclosures under the FLSA and Public Contracts Act to 1964; 1964-1979 disclosures under the Equal Pay Act, Government Contract Discrimination in Employment Act, and Title III of The Consumer Credit Protection Act. After 1979, Age Discrimination in Employment Act disclosures not included in the estimates.

[b] Estimated.

[c] Includes disclosures under the FLSA and Public Contracts up to 1964; 1971-1986, disclosures under FLSA only.

Source: U. S. Department of Labor Employment Standards Administration. Compiled from various issues of the *Minimum Wage and Maximum Hours Standards Under the Fair Labor Standards Act* and various *Annual Reports to the Congress* between 1939-1988.

Table A.5

Employer Agreements to Pay Minimum Wages and Overtime Compensation Found Due under the Provisions of the FLSA, FY 1939-1988

Fiscal Year	Unduplicated Count	Minimum Wage	Overtime Compensation	Total	Minimum Wage	Overtime Compensation
	Number of Employees Affected:				*Amount Agreed To:* [a]	
1939				$51,828		
1940	70,233			$1,714,494		
1941	379,984			$11,540,889		
1942	578,545			$20,920,956		
1943	389,467			$16,824,021		
1944	534,422			$18,620,369		
1945	442,516			$15,824,377		
1946	271,478			$13,360,826		
1947	212,256			$8,864,186		
1948	102,794			$4,256,761		
1949	104,333			$4,279,085		
1950	80,297			$4,081,193		
1951	95,604			$6,666,995		
1952	144,792			$8,467,668		
1953	114,770			$8,282,043		
1954	85,049			$6,485,545		
1955	81,330			$6,165,117		
1956	74,762			$6,051,909		
1957	110,379			$9,211,286		
1958	116,797			$10,953,896		
1959	124,046			$12,885,921		
1960	119,373			$13,895,377		
1961	121,558			$14,477,883		
1962	136,558			$16,174,884		
1963	176,260			$20,170,103		
1964	189,048			$22,733,910		
1965 to 1972 [b]						
1973		95,872	153,945	$33,775,804	$9,595,056	$24,180,748
1974		87,723	158,100	$37,6548,810	$10,205,905	$27,448,905
1975		170,109	208,361	$46,689,436	$16,247,210	$30,442,226

Table A.5 (continued)

Fiscal Year	Number of Employees Affected:			Total	Amount Agreed To: [a]	
	Unduplicated Count	Minimum Wage	Overtime Compensation		Minimum Wage	Overtime Compensation
1976		226,295	212,790	$55,626,791	$22,595,244	$33,031,547
TQ [c]		40,130	40,006	$8,303,089	$2,712,191	$5,590,898
1977		265,510	215,037	$53,035,257	$20,209,272	$32,825,985
1978		316,482	222,837	$59,135,672	$24,397,256	$34,738,416
1979		308,628	233,491	$73,396,356	$28,260,395	$45,135,961
1980		250,910	225,466	$69,652,642	$25,026,851	$44,625,791
1981		325,172	250,652	$83,586,437	$31,912,354	$51,674,083
1982		252,078	246,076	$86,927,974	$32,718,898	$54,209,076
1983	369,544	172,698	232,272	$83,260,041	$26,855,406	$56,404,635
1984	341,752	150,182	223,310	$78,846,140	$21,860,163	$56,985,977
1985	347,713	139,707	239,862	$80,667,623	$19,069,020	$61,598,603
1986	397,459	150,597	274,943	$93,319,152	$21,931,101	$71,542,742
1987	399,553	135,865	293,255	$99,704,733	$20,138,835	$79,565,898
1988	391,600	137,900	283,300	$108,400,000	$22,500,000	$85,900,000

[a] From October 1942 through FY 1970, data include employer agreements to pay under PCA as well as FLSA. For FY 1973 to FY 1987, data include employer agreements to pay only under FLSA.

[b] Data comparable to that shown for earlier or later years not available.

[c] Transition quarter.

Source: U. S. Department of Labor Employment Standards Administration. Compiled from various issues of the *Minimum Wage and Maximum Hours Standards Under the Fair Labor Standards Act* and various *Annual Reports to the Congress* between 1939-1988.

Table A.6

**Real Value of the Federal Minimum Wage
in Constant Dollars, October 1938-January 1988**

Effective Date	Old Coverage		New Nonfarm Coverage		Farmworkers	
	Minimum Wage Rate	Value in Constant Dollars*	Minimum Wage Rate	Value in Constant Dollars	Minimum Wage Rate	Value in Constant Dollars*
10/38	$.25	$.25	-	-	-	-
10/39	.30	.30	-	-	-	-
10/45	.40	.31	-	-	-	-
01/50	.75	.45	-	-	-	-
03/56	1.00	.52	-	-	-	-
09/61	1.15	.54	$1.00	$.47	-	-
09/63	1.25	.57	-	-	-	-
09/64	-	-	1.15	.52	-	-
09/65	-	-	1.25	.55	-	-
02/67	1.40	.60	1.00	.43	$1.00	.43
02/68	1.60	.66	1.15	.47	1.15	.47
02/69	-	-	1.30	.51	1.30	.51
02/70	-	-	1.45	.53	-	-
02/71	-	-	1.60	.56	-	-
05/74	2.00	.58	1.90	.55	1.60	.46
01/75	2.10	.56	2.00	.54	1.80	.48
01/76	2.30	.58	2.20	.55	2.00	.50
01/77	-	-	2.30	.55	2.20	.53
01/78	2.65	.59	2.65	.59	2.65	.59
01/79	2.90	.59	2.90	.59	2.90	.59
01/80	3.10	.56	3.10	.56	3.10	.56
01/81	3.35	.54	3.35	.54	3.35	.54
01/82	3.35	.50	3.35	.50	3.35	.50
01/83	3.35	.48	3.35	.48	3.35	.48
01/84	3.35	.46	3.35	.46	3.35	.46
01/85	3.35	.45	3.35	.45	3.35	.45
01/86	3.35	.43	3.35	.43	3.35	.43
01/87	3.35	.43	3.35	.43	3.35	.43
01/88	3.35	.41	3.35	.41	3.35	.41

* 10/38 = 100.

Source: U. S. Department of Labor Employment Standards Administration. Compiled from various issues of the *Minimum Wage and Maximum Hours Standards Under the Fair Labor Standards Act* and various *Annual Reports to the Congress* between 1939-1988.

Table A.7

Ratio of Minimum Wage Worker Income to Poverty Level
Threshold for a Four-Person Family, 1959-1988 [a]

| | *Poverty Level for* [a] *Four-Person Family* | | *Ratio of Minimum Wage to Poverty Level Threshold (in percent)* | | |
| | | | Old | New Nonfarm | |
Year	*Nonfarm*	*Farm*	*Coverage*	*Coverage*	*Farmworkers* [b]
1959	$2,973	$2,539	70%	-	-
1960	3,022	2,576	69	-	-
1961	3,054	2,602	78	68%	-
1962	3,089	2,632	77	67	-
1963	3,128	2,664	83	66	-
1964	3,169	2,701	82	75	-
1965	3,223	2,750	81	81	-
1966	3,317	2,831	78	78	-
1967	3,410	2,906	85	61	72%
1968	3,553	3,034	94	67	79
1969	3,743	3,195	89	72	85
1970	3,968	3,385	84	76	80
1971	4,137	3,527	80	80	77
1972	4,275	3,643	78	78	74
1973	4,450	3,871	73	73	70
1974	5,038	4,302	83	78	77
1975	5,500	4,695	79	76	80
1976	5,815	4,930	83	79	84
1977	6,191	5,273	77	77	87
1978	6,662	5,681	82	82	97
1979	7,412	6,320	81	81	95
1980	8,414	7,151	77	77	90
1981	9,287	c	75	75	75
1982	9,862	c	71	71	71
1983	10,178	c	68	68	68
1984	10,609	c	66	66	66
1985	10,989	c	63	63	63
1986	11,200	c	62	62	62
1987	11,612	c	60	60	60
1988	--				

[a] Minimum wage earnings reflect the earnings of a full-time year round worker (2,080 hours) at the minimum wage.
[b] Ratio of annual earnings of a farmworker to the poverty threshold for families living on farms.
[c] Modification of the poverty concept included the elimination of separate thresholds for farm families.

Source: U. S. Department of Labor Employment Standards Administration. Compiled from various issues of the *Minimum Wage and Maximum Hours Standards Under the Fair Labor Standards Act* and various *Annual Reports to the Congress* between 1939-1988.

Table A.8

Number of Student-Worker Certificates Issued under Section 14 of the FLSA and Estimated Number of Workers Authorized to Be Employed under These Certificates, United States, FY 1956–1980

Fiscal Year	Certificates	Workers
1956	31	
1957	33	
1958	--	
1959	39	
1960	38	1,412
1961	33	1,320
1962	31	1,343
1963	29	1,382
1964	26	1,336
1965	27	1,353
1966	24	1,342
1967	23	1,169
1968	23	1,146
1969	21	1,414
1970	19	1,293
1971	17	1,050
1972	13	933
1973	10	755
1974	10	729
1975	1	3
1976-1980	0	0

Source: U. S. Department of Labor Employment Standards Administration.   Compiled from various issues of the *Minimum Wage and Maximum Hours Standards Under the Fair Labor Standards Act* and various *Annual Reports to the Congress* between 1939-1988.

Table A.9

Number of Apprentice Certificates Issued under Section 14 of the FLSA, United States and the Caribbean, FY 1950–1988

Fiscal Year	Total	Mainland	Caribbean
1950	564		
1951	1,042		
1952	423		
1953	228		
1954	--		
1955	--		
1956	241	60	181
1957	453	272	181
1958	320	107	213
1959	337	184	153
1960	450	103	347
1961	343	62	281
1962	372	130	242
1963	479	145	334
1964	633	161	472
1965	541	86	455
1966	774	98	676
1967	902	64	838
1968	474	48	426
1969	355	12	343
1970	295	0	295
1971	379	5	374
1972	355	3	352
1973	402	0	402
1974	252	0	252
1975	144	0	144
1976	101	0	101
1977	73	0	73
1978	93	0	93
1979	86	0	86
1980	17	0	17
1981	15	0	15
1982	27	0	27
1983	13	0	13
1984	10	0	10
1985	1	0	1
1986	0	0	0
1987	1	0	1
1988	0	0	0

Source: U. S. Department of Labor Employment Standards Administration.   Compiled from various issues of the *Minimum Wage and Maximum Hours Standards Under the Fair Labor Standards Act* and various *Annual Reports to the Congress* between 1939-1988.

Table A.10

Number of Institutions with Patient-Worker Certificates in Effect at the End of the FY 1975-1988

Fiscal Year	Institutions with Certificates in Effect on September 20		Total	Certified Workers
	Public	Private		
1975	--	--	331	26,422
1976	306	108	414	24,770
1977	0	110	110	2,064
1978	0	133	133	2,531
1979	0	144	144	1,677
1980	0	132	132	2,662
1981	0	133	133	3,372
1982	0	147	147	3,456
1983	0	145	145	3,169
1984	0	155	155	3,273
1985	0	190	190	4,726
1986	109	108	217	5,467
1987	114	119	233	6,108
1988	--	--	253	7,543

Source: U. S. Department of Labor Employment Standards Administration. Compiled from various issues of the *Minimum Wage and Maximum Hours Standards Under the Fair Labor Standards Act* and various *Annual Reports to the Congress* between 1939-1988.

Table A.11

Number of Student-Learner Certificates Issued under Section 14
of the FLSA, United States and the Caribbean, FY 1950–1988

Fiscal Year	Total	Mainland	Caribbean
1950	1,078		
1951	1,313		
1952	638		
1953	474		
1954	379		
1955	305		
1956	625		
1957	1,091		
1958	790		
1959	824		
1960	782		
1961	793	744	49
1962	4,577	4,390	187
1963	3,053	2,814	239
1964	3,302	3,070	232
1965	4,182	3,983	199
1966	4,630	4,379	251
1967	6,598	6,293	305
1968	9,460	9,074	386
1969	10,548	10,035	513
1970	10,740	10,174	566
1971	12,289	11,733	556
1972	14,136	13,582	554
1973	17,677	17,278	399
1974	14,293	13,726	567
1975	17,206	16,574	632
1976	11,984	11,456	528
1977	6,530	6,086	444
1978	5,956	5,463	493
1979	4,448	3,983	465
1980	4,436	3,856	580
1981	3,025	2,460	565
1982	2,936	2,422	514
1983	2,454	1,977	477
1984	2,462	1,646	816
1985	1,861	1,374	487
1986	1,704	1,254	450
1987	1,564	1,192	372
1988	1,064	--	--

Source: U. S. Department of Labor Employment Standards Administration. Compiled from various
issues of the *Minimum Wage and Maximum Hours Standards Under the Fair Labor Standards Act*
and various *Annual Reports to the Congress* between 1939-1988.

Table A.12

Number of Certificates Granted Handicapped Workers in Competitive Industry and Number of Temporary Trainee Certificates Granted by State Divisions of Vocational Rehabilitation and Veterans Administration under Section 14 of the FLSA, United States, FY 1939-1988

	Type of Certificate	
Fiscal Year	*Handicapped Worker in Competitive Industry Other Than Trainee*	*Trainee*
1939	2,385	
1940	3,953	
1941	5,304	
1942	4,886	
1943	3,399	
1944	1,881	
1945	1,183	
1946	423	
1947	389	
1948	231	
1949	158	
1950	6,349	
1951	4,699	
1952	3,660	
1953	2,826	
1954	2,253	
1955	1,865	
1956	4,513	
1957	4,252	
1958	3,708	
1959	433	
1960	--	--
1961	2,252	149
1962	12,292[a]	242
1963	6,424[a]	354
1964	3,839	490
1965	3,234	584
1966	2,916	678
1967	5,252	1,776
1968	6,993	3,457
1969	4,950	3,611
1970	6,390	4,135
1971	7,419	3,503
1972	10,222	4,316

Table A.12 (continued)

| Fiscal Year | Type of Certificate | |
	Handicapped Worker in Competitive Industry Other Than Trainee	Trainee
1973	11,887	3,766
1974	13,071	4,675
1975	14,862	3,748
1976	11,843	3,748
1977	7,899	1,953
1978	6,520	1,730
1979	6,301	1,543
1980	6,452	968
1981	6,017	696
1982	6,708	692
1983	6,386	847
1984	7,750	1,002
1985	7,116	1,282
1986	7,985	1,191
1987	7,234	1,286
1988	7,974	--

[a]   In 1962 and 1963, temporary special standards were established for issuing handicapped worker certificates to workers with impaired productivity in the newly-covered shellfish industry.

Source: U. S. Department of Labor Employment Standards Administration. Compiled from various issues of the *Minimum Wage and Maximum Hours Standards Under the Fair Labor Standards Act* and various *Annual Reports to the Congress* between 1939-1988.

Table A.13

**Number of Sheltered Workshops Holding Certificates in Effect at the End of the
Fiscal Year and Estimated Number of Workers Authorized to
Be Employed under These Certificates, United States, FY 1949–1988**

Fiscal Year	Number of Workshops	Number of Workers
1949	90	
1950	149	
1951	181	
1952	201	
1953	231	
1954	247	
1955	262	
1956	308	
1957	349	
1958	397	
1959	433	23,635
1960	483	28,361
1961	541	29,122
1962	582	32,871
1963	619	34,441
1964	674	37,636
1965	799	43,412
1966	885	47,412
1967	978	49,645
1968	1,078	47,900
1969	1,168	51,882
1970	1,420	63,154
1971	1,623	70,298
1972	1,863	80,450
1973	2,062	87,348
1974	2,392	104,791
1975	2,835	120,452
1976	2,998	143,552
1977	3,323	156,475
1978	3,431	164,709
1979	3,879	174,746
1980	4,150	185,916
1981	4,397	191,894
1982	4,702	195,445
1983	4,631	216,030
1984	4,814	225,017
1985	5,120	245,043
1986	5,401	259,178
1987	5,165	275,358
1988	5,413	289,125

Source: U. S. Department of Labor Employment Standards Administration. Compiled from various
issues of the *Minimum Wage and Maximum Hours Standards Under the Fair Labor Standards Act*
and various *Annual Reports to the Congress* between 1939-1988.

Table A.14

**FLSA Child Labor Enforcement Activities
for Selected Years, 1942-1988**

Year	Establishments in Violation of HO [a]	Establishments Investigated	Firms in Violation of FLSA Child Labor Provisions	Minors Employed in Violation of FLSA Child Labor Provision		CMP Assessment [b]
				Nonagricultural	Agricultural	
1942		74,676	--	--	--	
1943		16,301	3,000	4,567	NA	
1944		54,224	NA	8,436	NA	
1945		44,271	NA	NA	NA	
1946		43,832	2,717	NA	NA	
1947		40,350	2,061	NA	NA	
1948		29,024	1,443	4,628	NA	
1949		32,012	1,807	4,438	NA	
1950		26,164	1,621	4,702	NA	
1951		33,479	2,973	7,310	NA	
1952		41,860	5,284	6,232	5,385	
1953		38,634	3,369	6,439	NA	
1954		39,412	3,265	6,506	NA	
1955		39,312	3,545	6,095	NA	
1956		33,136	2,953	4,831	NA	
1957	3,923	48,482	3,599	5,867	5,477	
1958		53,796		7,214	4,491	
1959		54,916		5,853	NA	
1960		45,729		5,429	NA	
1961	4,902	44,268		7,005	5,727	
1962	3,364	44,115		6,204	4,236	
1963						
1969	NA	NA	NA	NA	NA	
1970	4,412	68,787		11,570	NA	
1971			20,000	NA		
1972		68,000				
1973				12,461		
1974				14,201	497	
1975	2,849	55,212	2,466	16,115	851	
1976	2,999		1,919	10,142	599	$0.5M
1977	3,152		2,129	15,385	663	1.3
1978	3,674	61,239		13,830	773	1.9
1979	4,123		2,838	12,426	563	1.9

Table A.14 (continued)

Year	Establishments in Violation of HO [a]	Establishments Investigated	Firms in Violation of FLSA Child Labor Provisions	Minors Employed in Violation of FLSA Child Labor Provision		CMP Assessment [b]
				Nonagricultural	Agricultural	
1980	3,721		2,418	9,558	410	1.7
1981	3,781		2,493	13,150	675	1.5
1982	3,385		2,328	9,720	246	1.0
1983	--	64,227	2,330	8,572	422	0.8
1984	3,791	64,155	2,406	8,354	523	1.0
1985	4,083	66,943	--	9,321	515	1.0
1986	4,671	72,641	2,706	12,361	301	1.5
1987				10,160		1.5
1988				13,838		2.1

[a]   Hazardous Occupations Order
[b]   Civil Money Penalties

Source: U.S. Department of Labor, Employment Standards Administration.   Compiled from various issues of the *Minimum Wage and Maximum Hours Standards Under the Fair Labor Standards Act* and various *Annual Reports to the Congress* between 1930 - 1988.

Bibliography

Abel, Elis. "Urban League Hits 'Politics' on Rights." *New York Times,* September 6, 1952.

Adams, Chris. "Senate Panel Votes $4.55 Minimum Wage." *Washington Post,* June 30, 1988.

Adie, Douglas K. "Teen-Age Unemployment and Real Federal Minimum Wages." *Journal of Political Economy*, Vol. 81, No. 2., Part 1, March–April 1973.

Adie, Douglas K., and Gene L. Chapin. "Teenage Unemployment Effects of Federal Minimum Wages." *Proceedings of the 23rd Winter Meeting*, Industrial Relations Research Association, December 28–29, 1970.

Adie, Douglas K., and Lowell Gallaway. "The Minimum Wage and Teenage Unemployment: A Comment." *Western Economic Journal*, Vol. XI, No. 4, December 1973.

Adkins v. Children's Hospital of the District of Columbia, 261 U.S. 525 (1923).

Allen, S.P. "Taxes, Redistribution, and the Minimum Wage: A Theoretical Analysis." *Quarterly Journal of Economics*, CII No. 3, August 1987.

American Federation of Labor. *Report of Proceedings*. Fifty-third Annual Convention, Washington, D.C., October 2–13, 1933.

American Federation of Labor. *Report of Proceedings*. Fifty-eighth Annual Convention, Houston, Texas, October 3–12, 1938.

American Federation of Labor. *Report of Proceedings*. Fifty-ninth Annual Convention, Cincinnati, Ohio, October 2–13, 1939.

American Manufacturers Association. *Men, Methods, and Machines in Automobile Manufacturing*, Adapted from a study by Andrew T. Court. New York: 1939.

American Retail Federation. "The District of Columbia Minimum Wage for Women in the Retail Trade: How the $17 Minimum was Established." Washington, D.C., May 1938. Mimeographed.

Andrews, Elmer F. "Making the Wage-Hour Law Work." *American Labor Legislation Review*, Vol. XXIX, No. 2, June 1939.

Andrews, Elmer F. "The Administration of the Fair Labor Standards Act in the United States." *International Labour Review*, Vol. XL, No. 5, November 1939.

Andrews, Elmer F. "Tribulations of a Wage-Hour Administrator." *Public Opinion Quarterly*, Vol. 4, No. 1, March 1946.

Andrews, Irene O. "Minimum Wage Comes Back!" *American Labor Legislation Review*, Vol. XXIII, No. 2, June 1933.

Andrews, John B. "Legislation for Women in Industry: Minimum Wage." *American Labor Legislation Review*, Vol VI, No. 4, December 1916.

Andrews, John B. "Beginnings of International Labor Standards." *American Labor Legislation Review*, Vol. XXV, No. 3, September 1935.

Apple, R.W. "President Signs Rise in Pay Base to $2.30 an Hour." *New York Times*, April 9, 1974.

Arkansas Department of Labor. *Annual Report 1987*. Little Rock, Arkansas.

Arles, J.P. "Minimum Wages in the Congo (Kinshasa)." *International Labour Review*, Vol. 96, No. 4, October 1967.

Ashenfelter, Orley, and Robert S. Smith. "Compliance with the Minimum Wage Law." *Journal of Political Economy*, Vol. 87, No. 2, April 1979.

"Asks Labor Act Change." *New York Times*, March 9, 1957.

"Associated Press Note." *New York Times*, January 17, 1969.

Badenhoop, Louis E. "Effects of the $1 Minimum Wage in Seven Areas." *Monthly Labor Review*, Vol. 81, No. 7, July 1958.

Baker, Russell. "Democrats Call Congress Recess for Conventions." *New York Times*, June 30, 1960.

Baker, Russell. "Nixon and Kennedy Clash in TV Debate on Spending, Farms, and Social Issues." *New York Times*, September 9, 1960.

Barkin, Solomon. "Toward Fairer Federal Labor Standards" (Questions and Answers on Improving the Fair Labor Standards Act of 1938). Washington, D.C.: Congress of Industrial Organizations Committee on the Revision of the Fair Labor Standards Act, 1948.

Barth, Peter S. "The Minimum Wage and Teen-Age Unemployment." *Proceedings of the 22nd Annual Winter Meeting*, Industrial Relations Research Association, December 29–30, 1969.

Barton, Dorothea M. "Women's Minimum Wages." *Journal of the Royal Statistical Society*, Vol. LXXXIV, No. 4, July 1921.

Behrman, Jere R., Robin C. Sickles, and Paul Tambman, "The Impact of Minimum Wages on the Distribution of Earnings for Major Race-Sex Groups: A Dynamic Analysis." *American Economic Review*, Vol. 83, No. 4, September 1983.

Belair, Felix, Jr. "Roosevelt Deal with South Wins Support of Wage Bill; Rail Rate Basis Is Involved." *New York Times*, January 8, 1938.

Belair, Felix, Jr. "Roosevelt Favors Only Public Works that Pay Own Way." *New York Times*, February 2, 1938.

Belair, Felix, Jr. "Kennedy Presses $1.25 Minimum Pay with Wider Scope." *New York Times*, February 8, 1961.

Benewitz, Maurice, and Robert E. Weintraub. "Employment Effects of a Local Minimum Wage." *Industrial and Labor Relations Review*, Vol. 17, No. 2, January 1964.

Beney, M. Ada. *Wages, Hours and Employment in the United States, 1914–1936*, No. 229. New York: National Industrial Conference Board, 1937.

Bernstein, Irving. *The Lean Years: A History of the American Worker, 1920–1933*. Boston: Houghton Mifflin Co., 1960.

Bernstein, Irving. *Turbulent Years: A History of the American Worker, 1933–1941*. Boston: Houghton Mifflin Company, 1970.

Bernstein, Irving. "Public Policy and the American Worker, 1933–1945," *Monthly Labor Review*, Vol. 99, No. 10, October 1976.

Bernstein, Irving. "The Historical Significance of the CIO," *Labor Law Journal*, Vol. 36, No. 8, August 1985.

Beyer, Clara M. "State Wage and Hour Legislation: Which Way Ahead?" Address before the Forty-first Annual Meeting of the National Consumers' League, New York City, January 11, 1941.

Blum, Fred H. "The Social and Economic Implications of the Fair Labor Standards Act: An Interpretation in Terms of Social Cost." *Proceedings*, Industrial Relations Research Association, 1956.

Boles, Walter E., Jr. "Some Aspects of the Fair Labor Standards Act." *Southern Economic Journal*, Vol. VI, No. 4, April 1940.

Bowlby, Roger L. "Union Policy toward Minimum Wage Legislation in Post-War Britain." *Industrial and Labor Relations Review*, Vol. 11, No. 1, October 1957.

Brandeis, Louis D. "The Constitution and the Minimum Wage: Defense of the Oregon Minimum Wage Law before the United States Supreme Court." Reprinted from *Survey*, December 26, 1917.

Brock, William E. "The Application of the FLSA to State and Local Governments." *Labor Law Journal*, Vol. 36, No. 10, October 1985.

Brock, William E. "They're Not 'McJobs.'" *Washington Post*, June 11, 1987.

Broda, Rudolf. "Minimum Wage Legislation in the United States." *International Labour Review*, Vol. XVII, No. 1, January 1920.

Brogan, Denis W. *The Era of Franklin D. Roosevelt: A Chronicle of the New Deal and Global War*. New Haven: Yale University Press, 1950.

Brooke, E. *Factory Laws of European Countries*. London: Grant Richards, 1898.

Broom, Jack. "Poll Shows Strong Support for Raising Minimum Wage." *Seattle Times*, February 29, 1988.

Brown, Charles, *et. al.* "Time-Series Evidence of the Effect of the Minimum Wage on Youth Employment and Unemployment." *Journal of Human Resources*, Vol. XVIII, No. 1, 1983.

Brown, H.L. "Massachusetts and the Minimum Wage." *Annals*, Vol. XLVIII, July 1913.

Brown, Warren. "Administration Fudges on Subminimum Wage." *Washington Post*, March 25, 1981.

Brozen, Yale. "Minimum Wage Rates and Household Workers." *Journal of Law and Economics*, Vol. V, October 1962.

Brozen, Yale. "The Effect of Statutory Minimum Wage Increases on Teen-Age Employment." *Journal of Law and Economics*, Vol. XII, No. 1, April 1969.

Bruere, R.W., "Meaning of the Minimum Wage." Reprinted from *Harper's Magazine*, January 1916.

Bureau of Labor Statistics. *Handbook of Labor Statistics* Washington, D.C.: U.S. Government Printing Office, 1947. Government Printing Office, May 1921.

Bureau of Labor Statistics. *Minimum-Wage Laws of the United States: Construction and Operation*. Washington, D.C.: U.S. Government Printing Office, 1964.

Bureau of Labor Statistics. *Handbook of Labor Statistics* (Washington, D.C.: Government Printing Office, 1971), tables 60 and 63.

California Department of Industrial Relations. *1983 Annual Report: Centennial Issue*. Sacramento, California: Department of Industrial Relations, 1983.

"Ceiling Unlimited." *New York Times*, September 22, 1973.

Chang, Yang-Ming and Isaac Ehrlich. "On the Economics of Compliance with the Minimum Wage Law." *Journal of Political Economy*, Vol. 93, No. 1, February 1985.

Chesworth, D.P. "Statutory Minimum Wage Fixing in the Sugar Industry of Mauritius." *International Labour Review*, Vol. 96, No. 3, September 1965.

Cheyney, Alice S. "The Course of Minimum Wage Legislation in the United States." *International Labour Review*, Vol. XXXVIII, No. 1, July 1938.

Chilton Company. *Automotive Industry*, Vol. 116, No. 6, March 1957.

Clark, Kim B., and Richard B. Freeman. "How Elastic Is the Demand for Labor?" *Review of Economics and Statistics*, Vol. LXII, No. 4, November 1980.

Cobble, Dorothy Sue. "A Self-Possessed Woman: A View of FDR's Secretary of Labor, Madame Perkins." *Labor History*, Vol. 29, No. 2, spring 1988.

Colberg, Marshall R. "Minimum Wage Effects on Florida's Economic Development." *Journal of Law and Economics*, Vol. III, October 1960.

Cole, G.D.H. "The Minimum Wage: Why Not a National Wages Commission?" *Socialist Review*, Vol. XXIII, No. 125, February 1924.

Cole, G.D.H. *Living Wages: The Case for a New Minimum Wage Act*. London: Victor Gollancz Ltd., September 1938.

"Commitment Denied." *New York Times*, April 16, 1965.

"Common Sense Is Key to the Minimum Wage." *Spokane Chronicle*, June 8, 1988.

Congressional Record. November 15, 1937, to December 21, 1937, Vol. 82, pt. 3.

Congressional Record. February 24, 1938, to March 16, 1938, Vol. 83, pt. 3.

Congressional Record. April 28, 1938 to May 19, 1938, Vol. 83, pt. 3.

Cotterill, Philip G., and Walter J. Wadycki. "Teenagers and the Minimum Wage in Retail Trade." *Journal of Human Resources,* Vol. XI, No. 1, Winter 1976.

Cowan, Edward. "Washington and Business: Battle Looms on Minimum Wage 'Indexation,'" *New York Times,* May 7, 1976.

Cummins, E.E., and Frank T. DeVyver. *The Labor Problem in the United States.* New York: D. Van Nostrand Company, 1947.

"Current U.S. Minimum Wage Too Far Below Living Standard." *Salt Lake Tribune,* June 8, 1988.

Dale, Edwin L. "Economic Aide to Nixon Scores Sentimentality and Prejudice on Major Issues." *New York Times,* February 15, 1973.

Dale, Edwin L., Jr. "Researchers Conclude that Raising the Wage Floor Causes Loss of Jobs." *New York Times,* November 8, 1969.

Delaney, Paul. "Minimum Wage Cut for Youths Studied." *New York Times,* September 8, 1969.

Delaney, Paul. "Shultz Opposes a Youth Wage Rate." *New York Times,* November 18, 1969.

Delaney, Paul. "Rise in Blacks' Income Is Easing." *New York Times,* March 3, 1973.

Devine, Edward T. "The Harm of Low Wages." Reprinted from *Survey,* October 2, 1915.

Dewar, Helen. "Democrats Try to Lift Wage Floor." *Washington Post,* March 26, 1987.

Dewar, Helen. "Senate Locked in Partisan Tug of War over Minimum Wage, Judgeships." *Washington Post,* September 23, 1988.

"Dirksen Sees Delay on Minimum Wage." *New York Times,* May 15, 1960.

Douglas, Dorothy W. "Wages and Hours Legislation and the Child Labor Problem." Address before the Annual Meeting of the National Consumers' League on "Labor Standards Legislation: A Bulwark for Democracy," New York City, December 8, 1939.

Douty, H.M. "Minimum Wage Regulation in the Seamless Hosiery Industry." *Southern Economic Journal,* Vol. VIII, No. 2, October 1941.

Douty, H.M. "Some Effects of Wage Orders under the Fair Labor Standards Act." *American Labor Legislation Review,* Vol. XXXII, No. 4, December 1942.

Douty, H.M. "Some Effects of the $1.00 Minimum Wage in the United States" *Economica,* Vol. XXVII, No. 106, May 1960.

Du Pre Lumpkin, Katharine. "The Child Labor Provisions of the Fair Labor Standards Act." *Law and Contemporary Problems,* summer 1939, Duke University Law School, Durham, North Carolina.

Dyer, Ellen. "Congress to Renew Fight over Minimum Wage," *Albuquerque Journal*, February 1, 1988.

Economic Report of the President. January 20, 1955. Washington, D.C.: Government Printing Office, 1955.

Economic Report of the President. January 23, 1957. Washington, D.C.: Government Printing Office, 1958.

Economic Report of the President. Transmitted to the Congress in February 1970. Washington, D.C.: U.S. Government Printing Office, 1970.

Economic Report of the President. Transmitted to the Congress in February 1986. Washington, D.C.: U.S. Government Printing Office, 1986.

Economic Report of the President. Transmitted to the Congress in February 1988. Washington, D.C.: U.S. Government Printing Office, 1988.

"Economists Urge Minimum-Wage Increase." *Rocky Mountain News*, February 21, 1988.

Edelman, Marian Wright, and Clifford M. Johnson. "To Save Young Families, Raise Minimum Wage." *Los Angeles Times*, April 4, 1988.

Edgren, Gus. "Fair Labor Standards and Trade Liberalisation." *International Labour Review*, Vol. 118, No. 5, September–October 1979, pp. 523–535.

"Effects of Minimum Wage Rise Seen with Glee, Gloom." *San Diego Union*, March 28, 1988.

Egan, Leo. "Democrats Give '60 Plan Scoring G.O.P. Fiscal Aim." *New York Times*, December 7, 1959.

Ehrenberg, Ronald G., and Paul L. Schumann, "Compliance with the Overtime Pay Provisions of the Fair Labor Standards Act." *Journal of Law and Economics*, Vol. XXV No. 1, April 1982.

"Eisenhower Hears Union Wage Plea." *New York Times*, March 8, 1955, p. 21.

"Eisenhower's Economic Report to Congress." *New York Times*, January 25, 1956.

"Eisenhower's Message to Congress on His Programs." *New York Times*, May 4, 1960.

Elder, Peyton. "The 1974 Amendments to the Federal Minimum Wage Law" *Monthly Labor Review*, Vol. 97, No. 7, July 1974.

"Ellender Cautions on Encroachments." *New York Times*, March 30, 1959.

Elward, Elizabeth. "Information on Fair Labor Standards Act and Major Amendments." The Library of Congress, Legislative Reference Service, American Law Division, Washington, D.C., January 10, 1958. Mimeographed.

Employment and Training Report of the President. Transmitted to the Congress in 1982. Washington, D.C.: U.S. Government Printing Office, 1982.

"Employment Standards." *New York Times*, August 27, 1968.

Eubank, Laile. "Reception of the Fair Labor Standards Act of 1938." National Institute of Public Affairs, Washington, D.C. 1949. Mimeographed.

"Executives Back Minimum-Pay Rise," *New York Times*, March 17, 1960.

Falconer, Robert T. "The Minimum Wage: A Perspective." *Quarterly Review* (Federal Reserve Bank of New York), autumn 1978.

"Farm Group Responds." *New York Times*, May 10, 1955.

"Federal Minimum Wage Increase Unlikely to Cause Local Job Cuts." *Washington Post*, June 6, 1988.

Feldman, Herman. "Possible Effects of the Wage–Hour Law on Employment Opportunities and Status." Reprinted from *Occupations, the Vocational Guidance Magazine*, May 1939.

Filene, Edward A. "The Minimum Wage and Efficiency." *American Economic Review*, Vol. XIII, No. 3, September 1923.

Fisher, Alan A. "The Minimum Wage and Teenage Unemployment: A Comment on the Literature." *Western Economic Journal*, Vol. XI, No. 4, December 1973.

Fisher, Alan A. "Adult Disemployment Effects of a Youth Minimum Wage Differential." Report prepared for the Assistant Secretary of Labor for Policy, Washington, D.C., June 1975. Mimeographed.

Fleming, Philip B. "Relation of the Fair Labor Standards Act to Defense Production." Address before the Forty-first Annual Meeting of the National Consumers' League, New York City, January 11, 1941.

Flug, Karnit, and Oded Galor. "Minimum Wage in a General Equilibrium Model of International Trade and Human Capital." *International Economic Review*, Vol. 27, No. 1, February 1986.

Forster, C. "Unemployment and Minimum Wages in Australia, 1900–1930." *Journal of Economic History*, Vol. XLV, No. 2, June 1985.

Fourcans, Andre. "The Minimum Wage and Unemployment: A French View." *Wall Street Journal*, November 12, 1980.

Frankel, Max. "President Signs Minimum Pay Bill." *New York Times*, September 24, 1966.

Furman, Bess. "Labor Urges Rise in Minimum Wage." *New York Times*, December 5, 1958.

Gallagher, Michael, and Richard Kazis. *The Real Subminimum Wage Program*. Washington, D.C.: National Center for Jobs and Justice, February 25, 1981.

Gallasch, H.F., Jr. "Minimum Wages and the Farm Labor Market." *Southern Economic Journal*, Vol. 41, No. 3, January 1975.

Gallasch, H.F., Jr., and Bruce L. Gardner. "Schooling and the Agricultural Minimum Wage." *American Journal of Agricultural Economics*, Vol. 60, No. 2, May 1978.

Gallup, George. "Pay Differential Favored in Survey." *New York Times*, June 1, 1938.

Gallup, George. "Trend Today Seen to Conservatism." *New York Times*, August 28, 1938.

Garcia v. San Antonio Metropolitan Transit Authority, 105S.Ct.1005 (1985).

Gardner, Bruce. "Minimum Wages and the Farm Labor Market." *American Journal of Agricultural Economics*, Vol. 54, No. 3, August 1972.

Gavett, Thomas W. "Youth Unemployment and Minimum Wages: An Overview." *Proceedings of the 23rd Winter Meeting*, Industrial Relations Research Association, December 28–29, 1970.

Georgia Department of Labor. *Annual Report 1981*. Albany, Georgia: Georgia Department of Labor 1981.

Germanis, Peter G. "The Minimum Wage: Restructuring Jobs for Youth," Washington D.C.: The Heritage Foundation, July 1, 1981.

"Goldberg Hails Raise." *New York Times*, February 3, 1962.

Goldfarb, Robert S. "Quantitative Research on the Minimum Wage." *Monthly Labor Review*, Vol. 98, No. 4, April 1975.

Golding, Elroy D. "The Industry Committee Provisions of the Fair Labor Standards Act." *Yale Law Journal*, Vol. 50, No. 7, May 1941.

Goldmark, Josephine. "Minimum Wage in Practice." *New Republic*, Vol. V, No. 60, December 25, 1915.

Gompers, Samuel. *Labor and the Employer*. Compiled and edited by Hayes Robbins. New York: E.P. Dutton and Company, 1920.

Goodman, Ellen. "Son of Minimum Wage." *Washington Post*, May 22, 1984.

"G.O.P. Pay Bill Offered." *New York Times*, January 10, 1961.

Gramlich, Edward M. "Impact of Minimum Wages on Other Wages, Employment, and Family Incomes," *Brookings Papers on Economic Activity*, Vol. 2: 1976.

"Green Pledges Aid for the Wage Bill." *New York Times*, March 17, 1938.

Grossman, Jean Baldwin. "The Impact of the Minimum Wage on Other Wages." Staff Paper 80E–02, Mathematica Policy Research, Princeton, New Jersey, rev. September 1980. Mimeographed.

Grossman, Jean Baldwin. "The Impact of the Minimum Wage on Other Wages." *Journal of Human Resources*, Vol. XVIII, No. 3, 1983.

Grossman, Jonathan. "Fair Labor Standards Act of 1938: Maximum Struggle for a Minimum Wage." *Monthly Labor Review*, June 1978..

Haake, A.P. *A "Model Code" for Self-Governing Industries under the National Industrial Recovery Act* (Now Pending in Congress) Washington , D.C.: May 31, 1933.

Hacker, Louis M. *A Short History of the New Deal*. New York: F.S. Crofts and Company, 1934.

Hammer v. Dagenhart 247U.S.251(1918).

Hammermesh, D.S. "Minimum Wages and the Demand for Labor." *Economic Inquiry*, Vol. XX, No. 3, July 1982.

Hammond, Matthew B. "Judicial Interpretation of the Minimum Wage in Australia." *American Economic Review*, Vol. III, No. 2, June 1913.

Hammond, Matthew B. "The Minimum Wage in Great Britain and Australia." *Annals*, Vol. XLVIII, July 1913.

Hammond, Matthew B. "Where Life Is More Than Meat: The Australian Experience with Wages Boards." Reprinted from *The Survey*, October 2, 1915.

Hand, Learned. "The Hope of the Minimum Wage." *New Republic*, Vol. X, No. 55, November 1915.

Hanna, H.S., Editor. "Minimum Wage: Minimum-Wage Law of Washington State Held Constitutional." *Monthly Labor Review*, Vol. 44, No. 5, May 1937.

Hapgood, Norman. "Why We Should Have a Minimum Wage." *Industrial Outlook*, February 1915.

Hashimoto, Masanori. "Minimum Wage Effects on Training on the Job." *American Economic Review*, Vol. 72, No. 5, December 1982.

Hashimoto, Masanori. "The Minimum Wage Law and Youth Crimes: Time-Series Evidence." *Journal of Law and Economics*, Vol. XXX, No. 2, October 1987.

Herbers, John. "Clash between President and Congress Intensifies." *New York Times*, September 7, 1973.

Higgins, Henry Bournes. "A New Province for Law and Order: Industrial Peace through Minimum Wages and Arbitration." *Harvard Business Review*, Vol. XXIX, No. 1, November 1915.

Hince, K. "Wage Fixing in a Period of Change: The New Zealand Case." *International Labour Review*, Vol. 125, No. 4, July–August 1986.

Hobson, John A. "The State and the Minimum Wage in England." Reprinted from *The Survey*, October 2, 1915.

Holcombe, A.N. "The Effects of the Legal Minimum Wage for Women." *Annals*, Vol. LXIX, January 1917.

Holly, Fred. "Federal Minimum Wage Determinations in Puerto Rico." Washington, D.C., n.d., Mimeographed.

Holt, Pat. "The Sweatshop Defined." *New Republic*, May 9, 1949.

Hopkins, Mary D. "Do Wages Buy Health? The Oregon Minimum Wage Case Re-Argued." Reprinted from *The Survey*, February 3, 1917.

"House Unit Votes $1.75 Pay Base and Adds 7.2 Million to Rolls." *New York Times*, August 19, 1965.

"Humphrey Asks Aid to Depressed Areas." *New York Times*, January 26, 1960.

Hunt, George W.P. "Ridiculous Reasoning," *Survey*, Vol. L, No. 4, May 15, 1923.

Hunter, Marjorie. "Kennedy Praises Congress Record." *New York Times*, October 11, 1962.

Hunter, Marjorie. "G.O.P. Fails to Bar New Poverty Unit." *New York Times*, May 13, 1964.

Hunter, Marjorie. "Johnson's Plan to Delay $1.60 Base Wage Till '68 Gains in House; Meany Vows Fight." *New York Times*, February 25, 1966.

Hunter, Marjorie. "Colmer to Allow Wage Bill Action." *New York Times*, March 15, 1972.

Hunter, Marjorie. "Plains, Ga., Farmer Puts His Feelings in Nutshell." *New York Times*, May 18, 1977.

Hutchinson, Emilie J. *Women's Wages*. New York: Columbia University, Longmans, Green and Company, Agents, 1919.

Iman, M.H., and J. Whalley. "Incidence Analysis of a Sector-Specific Mini-
    mum Wage in a Two-Sector Harris-Todaro Model." *Quarterly Journal of
    Economics*, Vol. C, No. 1, February 1985.
"The Impact of Minimum Wages on Young People's Jobs." *OECD* Observer,
    No. 118, September 1982.
"Increase Urged in Minimum Pay." *New York Times*, December 3, 1958.
International Labour Office. *The Law and Women's Work: A Contribution to
    the Study of the Status of Women.* Series I (Employment of Women and
    Children), No. 4. Geneva: ILO, 1939.
International Labour Office. *The Minimum-Wage: An International Survey.*
    Series D (Wages and Hours of Work), No. 22. Geneva: ILO, 1939.
"Jobless Aid Bill Pressed in House." *New York Times*, January 18, 1961.
"Joblessness Tied to Economic Gain." *New York Times*, May 23, 1964.
Johnson, Alvin S. "Beclouding the Minimum Wage." *New Republic*, Vol. VII,
    No. 90, July 22, 1916.
Johnson, Ethel M. "Interstate Compacts on Labour Legislation in the United
    States." *International Labour Review*, Vol. XXXIII, No. 6, June 1936.
Johnson, Ethel M. "The Administration of Minimum Wage Laws in the United
    States." *International Labour Review*, Vol. XXXIX, No. 2, February 1939.
Johnson, Robert W. "Proposed: $30 a Week Minimum Pay" *Labor and Nation*,
    Vol. 1, No. 3, December 1945.
Johnson, William R., and Edgar K. Browning. "The Distributional and Effi-
    ciency Effects of Increasing the Minimum Wage: A Simulation." *Ameri-
    can Economic Review*, Vol. 73, No. 1, March 1983.
Jones, Lamar B., and Loren C. Scott. "Minimum Wages and Black Employ-
    ment in the Louisiana Sugarcane Industry." *Proceedings of the 24th An-
    nual Meeting*, Industrial Relations Research Association, December 27–29,
    1971.
Kaufman, R.T. "Nepotism and the Minimum-Wage." *Journal of Labor Re-
    search*, Vol. IV, No. 1, winter 1983.
Kaun, David E. "Minimum Wages, Factor Substitution and the Marginal Pro-
    ducer." *Quarterly Journal of Economics*, Vol. LXXIX, No. 3, August 1965.
Kelley, Florence. "Status of Legislation in the United States." Reprinted from
    The Survey, February 1915.
Kelley, Florence. "The Inescapable Dilemma," *The Survey*, March 22, 1919.
Kellogg, Paul U. "Immigration and the Minimum Wage." *Annals*, Vol. XLVII,
    July 1913.
Kennedy, John F. "Remarks upon Signing the Minimum Wage Bill." In *Public
    Papers of the Presidents of the United States, January 20 to December 31,
    1961*, Washington, D. C.: U. S. Government Printing Office, 1962.
"Kennedy Plan Opposed." *New York Times*, January 29, 1961.
"Kennedy Signs Wage-Floor Bill, 3.6 Million More Get Coverage." *New York
    Times*, May 6, 1961.

Kilpatrick, James J. "Minimum-Wage Bill Will Hurt the People It Aims to Help." *Atlanta Journal and Constitution*, April 3, 1988.

King, Allan G. "Minimum Wages and the Secondary Labor Market." *Southern Economic Journal*, Vol. 41, No. 2, October 1974.

Knight, Jerry. "U.S. Minimum Wage to Rise by 20 Cents an Hour Today." *Washington Post*, January 1, 1980.

Kolehmainen, John I. and John C. Shinn. "Labor and Public Representation on Industry Committees." *American Labor Legislation Review*, Vol. XXXI, No. 4, December 1941.

Kosters, Marvin, and Finis Welch. "The Effects of Minimum Wages on the Distribution of Changes in Aggregate Employment." *American Economic Review*, Vol. LXII, No. 3, June 1972.

Kruger, Daniel H. "Minimum Wages and Youth Employment." *Proceedings of the 23rd Winter Meeting*, Industrial Relations Research Association, December 28–29, 1970.

"Labor and Manpower." *New York Times*, January 17, 1956.

"Labor's Push to Boost Minimum Wage Draws Unexpected Opposition from Some Democrats." *Wall Street Journal*, June 3, 1988.

Landes, E.M., "The Effect of State Maximum-Hours Laws on the Employment of Women in 1920." *Journal of Political Economy*, Vol. 88, No. 3, June 1980.

Lardner, George, Jr. "Business Gets Cold Feet on Subminimum Wage." *Washington Post*, March 20, 1981.

Lauck, Jett W. "Require a Two-thirds Vote," *Survey,* Vol. L, No. 4, May 15, 1923.

Laughlin, Clara E. *The Work-a-Day Girl*. New York: Fleming H. Revell Company, 1913.

Lawrence, Mark. "Higher Minimum Wage Would Not Damage Economy, Hill Told." *Washington Post*, July 18, 1987.

Layton, Mike. "Henry Ford Knew It was Smart to Raise Minimum Pay." *Seattle Post-Intelligencer*, February 2, 1988.

Leffler, Keith B. "Minimum Wages, Welfare, and Wealth Transfers to the Poor." *Journal of Law and Economics*, Vol. XXI, No. 2, October 1978.

Lester, Richard A. "Employment Effects of Minimum Wages." *Industrial and Labor Relations Review*, Vol. 13, No. 2, January 1960.

Levitan, Sar A. "Proposed 1960 Amendments to the Fair Labor Standards Act." The Library of Congress, Legislative Reference Service, Washington, D.C., June 14, 1960. Mimeographed.

Lianos, Theodore P. "Impact of Minimum Wages upon the Level and Composition of Agricultural Employment." *American Journal of Agricultural Economics*, Vol. 54, No. 3, August 1972.

Lindley, Ernest K. *The Roosevelt Revolution: First Phase*. New York: Viking Press, 1933.

Linneman, P. "The Economic Impacts of Minimum Wages Laws: A New Look at an Old Question." *Journal of Political Economy*, Vol. 90, No. 3, June 1982.

Lissner, Will. "3 Candidates for Senator Give Prescriptions to Cure Poverty." *New York Times*, October 27, 1968.

Loftus, Joseph. "75-Cent Pay Floor Is Voted by House," *New York Times*, August 11, 1949.

Loftus, Joseph. "75-Cents Base Pay Voted by House, 361 to 35." *New York Times*, August 12, 1949.

Loftus, Joseph A. "Message Causes Labor to Frown." *New York Times*, January 7, 1955.

Loftus, Joseph A. "Farm-Labor Bloc Upsets the G.O.P.," *New York Times*, April 11, 1955.

Loftus, Joseph A. "Union Heads Urge $1.25 Pay Minimum." *New York Times*, April 20, 1955.

Loftus, Joseph A. "Eisenhower Urges Wage Law Spread." *New York Times*, April 28, 1955.

Loftus, Joseph A. "10-Point Legislative Plan Offered by A.F.L.–C.I.O." *New York Times*, November 8, 1958.

Loftus, Joseph A. "Labor Urges Rise in Minimum Wage." *New York Times*, May 8, 1959.

Loftus, Joseph A. "$1.25 Wage Voted by Senate Group." *New York Times*, July 11, 1959.

Loftus, Joseph A. "2 Disputes Likely on Minimum Wage." *New York Times*, February 6, 1960.

Loftus, Joseph A. "Mitchell Favors Minimum-Pay Rise." *New York Times*, February 19, 1960.

Loftus, Joseph A. "Congress Nearing Action on Wages." *New York Times*, June 12, 1960.

Lom, H., and E.F. Lizano, "The National Wage Board and Minimum Wage Policy in Costa Rica." *International Labour Review*, Vol. 114, No. 1, July–August 1976.

Lovell, Michael C. "The Minimum Wage, Teenage Unemployment, and the Business Cycle." *Western Economic Journal*, Vol. X, No. 4, December 1972.

Lovell, Michael C. "The Minimum Wage Reconsidered." *Western Economic Journal*, Vol XI, No. 4, December 1973.

"A Lower Wage Base Urged for Unskilled." *New York Times*, June 12, 1964.

Lubin, Isador, and Charles A. Pearce. "New York's Minimum Wage Law: The First Twenty Years." *Industrial and Labor Relations Review*, Vol. 11, No. 2, January 1958.

Macesich, George, and Charles T. Stewart, Jr. "Recent Department of Labor Studies of Minimum Wage Effects." *Southern Economic Journal*, Vol. XXVI, No. 4, April 1960.

MacKenzie, Frederick W. "Minimum Wage for Women and Children." *American Labor Legislation Review*, Vol. XIII, No. 4, December 1923.

Madden, Richard L. "Republicans Fail to Cut Wage Bill." *New York Times*, July 18, 1973.

Majure, Janet. "Results of Higher Minimum Wage Far from Certain." *Kansas City Star*, February 21, 1988.

Marks, Marcus M. "Objections to a Compulsory Minimum Wage."*Industrial Outlook*, March 1915.

Maryland, State of. Division of Labor and Industry. *Annual Report*. Annapolis: Division of Labor and Industry, 1986.

Massachusetts, The Commonwealth of. *Report of the Commission on Minimum Wage Boards*. Boston: Wright and Potter Printing Company, State Printers, 1912.

Massachusetts, The Commonwealth of. Department of Labor and Industries. *Law Regarding the Establishment of Minimum Wages for Women and Minors*. Boston: Wright and Potter Printing Company, State Printers, November 1920.

Matthews, W.H. "The Muckers." Reprinted from *The Survey*, October 1915.

Mattila, Peter J. "The Effect of Extending Minimum Wages to Cover Household Maids." *Journal of Human Resources*, Vol. VIII, No. 3, summer 1973.

Mattila, Peter J. "Youth Labor Markets, Enrollments, and Minimum Wages." *Proceedings of the 31st Annual Meeting*, Industrial Relations Research Association, August 29–31, 1978.

McAdoo, W.G. "'Living Wage' Essential to Industrial Stability." *The American Labor Legislation Review*, Vol. XIII, No. 2, June 1923.

McGee, M., and E.G. West. "Minimum Wage Effects on Part-Time Employment," *Economic Inquiry*, Vol. XXII, No. 3, July 1984.

McKenzie, Richard B. "Minimum Wage: A Weaker Case Both For and Against." *Challenge*, Vol. 30, No. 4, September–October 1987.

"McLaughlin Opposes Higher Minimum Wage." *Washington Post*, September 6, 1988.

"Meany Denounces Wage Floor Plan." *New York Times*, March 5, 1957.

"Meany Seeks Rise to $2 in Pay Floor." *New York Times*, July 30, 1970.

"Meany Sees Room for Big Wage Gain." *New York Times*, February 21, 1964.

Mellor, E.F. "Workers at the Minimum Wage or Less: Who Are They and the Jobs They Hold." *Monthly Labor Review*, Vol. 110, No. 7, July 1987.

Mendelsohn, Sigmund. *Labor's Crisis: An Employer's View of Labor Problems*. New York: MacMillan Company, 1920.

Millis, Harry A. "Some Aspects of the Minimum Wage." *Journal of Political Economy*, Vol. XXII, No. 2, February 1914.

Mincer, Jacob. "Unemployment Effects of Minimum Wages." *Journal of Political Economy*, Vol. 84, No. 4, Part 2, August 1976.

"The Minimally Useful Minimum Wage." *New York Times*, March 21, 1977.

"Minimum Wage Bill Debated in House." *New York Times*, August 9, 1949.

"Minimum Wage Increase Appears Likely." *Providence Journal–Bulletin*, May 27, 1988.

"Minimum Wage: Interstate Compact for Establishing Uniform Minimum Wages." *Monthly Labor Review*, Vol. 39, No. 1, July 1934.

"Minimum Wage Legislation in the United States." *American Labor Legislation Review*, Vol. VIII, No. 4, December 1918.

"Minimum Wage, Minimal Sense." *Plain Dealer* (Cleveland) March 28, 1988.

"Minimum Wage Stability Affects Shirt and Nightwear Industry Pay." *Monthly Labor Review*, Vol. 109, No. 3, March 1986.

Minimum Wage Study Commission. *Final Report*. Vol. I. Washington, D.C.: U.S. Government Printing Office, 1980.

"Minimum Wages and Recovery." *New Republic*, Vol. LXXXXV, No. 1227, June 8, 1938.

Mitchell, A.A.. *The Breakdown of Minimum Wages and a Memorandum on Unemployment*. Glasgow: MacLehose, Jackson and Co., 1922.

Moloney, John M. "Some Effects of the Federal Fair Labor Standards Act upon Southern Industry." *Southern Economic Journal*, Vol. IX, No. 1, July 1942.

Moore, Thomas Gale. "The Effect of Minimum Wages on Teenage Unemployment Rates." *Journal of Political Economy*, Vol. 79, No. 4, July–August 1971.

Morehead v. *Tipaldo* 298 U.S. 587 (1936).

Morris, John D. "Kennedy Will Press School Aid and Wages Bills, Powell Reports." *New York Times*, December 1, 1960.

Morris, John D. "Wage Bill's Fate Lies with Senate." *New York Times*, March 26, 1961.

National Consumers' League. *Earnings of Women in Factories and a Legal Living Wage*. New York: National Consumers League, January 1921.

National Industrial Conference Board. *Salary and Wage Policy in the Depression*. New York: 1932.

National Industrial Recovery Act. Public Law 67, 73rd Cong., Section 7(a)(3).

National League of Cities v. Usery, 426 U.S. 833 (1976).

Naughton, James M. "Nixon, in Challenge to Congress, Will Submit 'Bipartisan' Plans; He Will Veto Minimum-Wage Bill." *New York Times*, September 6, 1973.

Neary, J.P. "International Factor Mobility, Minimum Wage Rates, and Factor-Price Equalization: A Synthesis." *Quarterly Journal of Economics*, Vol. C, No. 3, August 1985.

Nelson, Richard R. "State Labor Laws: Changes during 1987." *Monthly Labor Review*, January 1988.

Nevins, Arthur W. *The Federal Wage and Hour Law*. New York: National Foreman's Institute, Inc., 1941.

"The New Deal: An Analysis and Appraisal." *The Economist*. October 3, 1936.

New York State Department of Labor. "Statistics on Operation." *Supplement to the Annual Report 1980.* Vol. 33. Albany: New York State Department of Labor 1981.

"Nixon Aide Is Sure of Phase 4 Stability." *New York Times,* July 23, 1973.

Nordlund, Willis J. "Minimum Wage Programs in Developing Countries: A Framework for Analysis." Washington, D.C., 1986. Mimeographed.

Nordlund, Willis J. "Sultanate of Oman: Minimum Wage Study." Report prepared for the World Bank. Washington, D.C., 1986. Mimeographed.

Nordlund, Willis J. "A Brief History of the Fair Labor Standards Act." *Labor Law Journal,* Vol. 39, No. 11, November 1988.

Norton, Mary T. "The Defense of the Federal Wages and Hours Law from Attack." Address before the Annual Meeting of the National Consumers' League on "Labor Standards Legislation: A Bulwark for Democracy," New York City, December 8, 1939.

Oelsner, Lesley. "High Court Frees States and Cities from U.S. Pay Laws." *New York Times,* June 25, 1976, p. D-13.

O'Hara, Edwin V. *A Living Wage by Legislation: The Oregon Experience.* Salem: State Printing Department, 1916.

O'Hara, James G. Letter to President Ronald Reagan, The Honorable Thomas P. O'Neill, and the Honorable George Bush, Washington, D.C., May 24, 1981.

Papert, Kate. "Experience from a State Administrator's Standpoint." Address before the Forty-first Annual Meeting of the National Consumers' League, New York City, January 11, 1941.

Parkinson, Thomas I. "Minimum Wage and the Constitution." *American Labor Legislation Review,* Vol. XIII, No. 2, June 1923.

Parsons, Donald O. *Poverty and the Minimum Wage.* Washington, D.C.: American Enterprise Institute, 1980.

Penny, Tim, and Thomas Petri. "A Decent Minimum Wage." *Washington Post,* June 13, 1988.

Perkins, Frances. "A National Labor Policy." *Annals,* Vol. 184, March 1936.

Perkins, Frances. "Minimum-Wage Standards Must Be Preserved." *Labor Information Bulletin,* Vol. III, No. 7, July 1936.

Persons, C.E. "Women's Work and Wages in the United State" *Quarterly Journal of Economics,* Vol. XXIX, 1913.

Peterson, John M. "Employment Effects of Minimum Wages, 1938–50," *Journal of Political Economy,* Vol. LXV, No. 5, October 1957.

Peterson, John M. "Employment Effects of State Minimum Wages for Women: Three Historical Cases Re-Examined." *Industrial and Labor Relations Review,* Vol. 12, No. 3, April 1959.

Peterson, John M. "Employment Effects of Minimum Wages." *Industrial and Labor Relations Review,* Vol. 13, No. 2, January 1960.

Peterson, John M. "Reply," *Industrial and Labor Relations Review*, Vol. 13, No. 2, January 1960.

Phelps, Orme W. "The Legislative Background of the Fair Labor Standards Act." *Journal of Business*, Vol. XII, April 1939.

Piore, Michael J. "Of 'Target Earners,' Aliens, and Wages." *New York Times*, April 4, 1977.

Pomfret, John D. "President Urges Congress to Kill Union Shop Curb." *New York Times*, May 19, 1965.

Powell, Thomas Reed. "The Oregon Minimum-Wage Cases." *Political Science Quarterly*, Vol. XXXII, No. 2, June 1917.

Powell, Thomas Reed. "The Constitutional Issue in Minimum-Wage Legisla-tion." *Minnesota Law Review*, Vol. II, No. 1, December 1917.

"The President's Press Conference on Foreign and Domestic Issues." *New York Times*, October 29, 1953.

"President Truman's Address to the Jefferson-Jackson Dinner." *New York Times*, February 25, 1949.

Ragan, James F., Jr. "Minimum Wages and the Youth Labor Market" *Review of Economics and Statistics*, Vol. LIX, No. 2, May 1977.

Raskin, A.H. "Steel Workers Back Stevenson." *New York Times*," September 20, 1956.

Raskin, A.H. "Hoffa Will Urge $1.50 Pay Floor." *New York Times*, March 13, 1960.

Raspberry, William. "It Won't Pay." *Washington Post*, November 14, 1980.

Raspberry, William. "A Lower Wage—for Blacks Only." *Washington Post*, June 11, 1984.

Ratner, Ronnie Steinberg. "The Paradox of Protection: Maximum Hours Legis-lation in the United States." *International Labour Review*, Vol. 119, No. 2, March–April 1980.

"Report Cautions on Minimum Wage." *New York Times*, January 29, 1954.

"Report Lists Farm Aid and 'Human Concerns' as Pressing Problems for the Session." *New York Times*, January 6, 1956.

"Report Roosevelt Changing Strategy." *New York Times*, April 3, 1938.

Richmond, William L., and Daniel L. Reynolds. "The Fair Labor Standards Act: A Potential Legal Constraint upon Quality Circles and Other Em-ployee Participation Programs." *Labor Law Journal*, Vol. 37, No. 4, April 1986.

"Rise in Minimum Wage Hinted by Humphrey." *New York Times*, April 14, 1965.

Roosevelt, Franklin D. *The Year of Crisis*. Public Papers and Addresses, 1933 vol. New York: Random House, 1938.

Roosevelt, Franklin D. *The Advance of Recovery and Reform*. Public Papers and Addresses, 1934 vol., New York: Random House, 1938.

Roosevelt, Franklin D. *The Court Disapproves*. Public Papers and Addresses, 1935 vol., New York: Random House, 1938.

Roosevelt, Franklin D. *The Constitution Prevails*. Public Papers and Addresses, 1937 vol., New York: Macmillan, 1941.

Roosevelt, Franklin D. *The Continuing Struggle for Liberalism*. Public Papers and Addresses, 1938 vol. New York: Macmillan, 1941.

"Roosevelt Program Is Facing Stiff Opposition." *New York Times*, January 9, 1938.

"Roosevelt's Message Opening the Second Regular Session of the 75th Congress: Declares People Favor Industrial Legislation." *New York Times*, January 4, 1938.

Rorty, Malcom Churchill. *A Practical Study of the Minimum Wage Theory*, Washington, D.C.:American Statistical Association, n.d.

Rosenbaum, David. "House Bars Move on Minimum Wage." *New York Times*, October 4, 1972.

Rosenbaum, David. "House Holds Up Wage Base Rise." *New York Times*, October 4, 1972.

Rottenberg, Simon. "Economic Estimation in Minimum Wage Administration." *Industrial and Labor Relations Review*, Vol. 7, No. 1, October 1953.

Rowntree, B.S. "The Effect of Minimum Wage Legislation upon British Industry." *Financial Reviews of Review*, July 1914.

Ryan, Franklin W. "The Wage Bargain and the Minimum Wage Decision," *Harvard Business Review*, Vol. II, No. 2, January 1924.

Ryan, John A. *The Supreme Court and the Minimum Wage*. New York: Paulist Press, 1923.

Samuels, Norman J. "Plant Adjustments of the $1 Minimum Wage." *Monthly Labor Review*, Vol. 81, No. 10, October 1958.

Sayre, Frances Bowes. "The Minimum Wage Decision: How the Supreme Court Becomes Virtually a House of Lords." *The Survey*, Vol. L, No. 3, May 1, 1923.

Schechter v. *United States*, 295 U.S. 495 (1935).

Seager, Henry R. "The Minimum Wage as Part of a Program for Social Reform." *Annals*, Vol. XLVIII, July 1913.

Seager, Henry R. "The Theory of the Minimum Wage." *The American Labor Legislation Review*, Vol. III, 1913.

Seager, Henry R. "The Minimum Wage–What Next?" *The Survey*, Vol. L, No. 4, May 15, 1923.

Sellekaerts, Brigitte. "The Case for Indexing the Minimum Wage." *Proceedings of the 34th Annual Meeting*, Industrial Relations Research Association, December 28–30, 1981.

"Senate Rejects Substitute for Wage Bill." *New York Times*, July 19, 1973.

Shabecoff, Philip. "$2.30 Wage Base by '76 Proposed." *New York Times*, April 11, 1973.

Shabecoff, Philip. "Labor and the Minimum Wage." *New York Times*, September 16, 1973.

Shabecoff, Philip. "Meany Says Labor Will Need 10% Pay Increase This Year." *New York Times*, February 21, 1974.

Shabecoff, Philip. "Compromise Seen on Minimum Wage." *New York Times*, February 28, 1974.

Shabecoff, Philip. "$2.30 Minimum Wage Proposed by Carter in Setback to Labor. *New York Times*, March 25, 1977.

Shanahan, Eileen. "Albert Bids Democrat Lead a Drive to End Slump" *New York Times*, April 9, 1971.

Shapiro, Margaret. "President Criticizes Minimum Wage, Indicates Push for Lower Youth Rate." *Washington Post*, December 16, 1983.

Sharkey, Charles F. "Secord of the Discussion before the Congress of the United States on the Fair Labor Standards Act of 1938." U.S. Bureau of Labor Statistics, Labor Law Information Division. Washington, D.C., October 1, 1938. Mimeographed.

Sheinkman, Jack. "Today's Minimum Wage was a Living — in 1955." *Newsday*, February 29, 1988.

Sherwood, Robert E. *Roosevelt and Hopkins*. New York: Universal Library, Grosset and Dunlap, 1950.

Shishkin, Boris. "Wage-Hour Law Administration from Labor's Viewpoint." *American Labor Legislation Review*, Vol. XXIX, No. 2, June 1939.

Shkurti, William J., and Belton M. Fleisher. "Employment and Wage Rates in Retail Trade Subsequent to the 1961 Amendments of the Fair Labor Standards Act." *Southern Economic Journal*, Vol. XXXV, No. 1, July 1968.

Silberman, Jonathan I., and Garey C. Durden. "Determining Legislative Preferences on the Minimum Wage: An Economic Approach." *Journal of Political Economy*, Vol. 84, No. 2, April 1976.

Simplex, S. *The "Minimum Wage" Stunt*. Keighley: Ogden and Sieuttleworth, London 1918.

Siskind, Frederic B. "Minimum Wage Legislation in the United States: Comment." *Economic Inquiry*, Vol. XV, No. 1, January 1977.

Smith, Jane Norman. "The Background of the Interstate Minimum Wage Compact." *Equal Rights*, Vol. XX, No. 32, September 8, 1934.

Smith, Lewis H. "The Role of Minimum Wages in the Rural South." *Proceedings of the 34th Annual Meeting*, Industrial Relations Research Association, December 28–30, 1981.

Smith, R.E., and B. Vavrichek. "The Minimum Wage: Its Relation to Income and Poverty," *Monthly Labor Review*, Vol. 110, No. 6, June 1987.

Solon, Gary. "The Minimum Wage and Teenage Employment: A Reanalysis with Attention to Serial Correlation and Seasonality." *Journal of Human Resources*, Vol. XX, No. 2, 1985.

Sowell, Thomas. "Raising the Minimum Wage for Selfish Reasons," *Indianapolis Star*, June 29, 1988.

Starr, Gerald. *Minimum Wage Fixing*. Geneva: International Labour Office, 1981.

Starr, Gerald. "Minimum Wage Fixing: International Experience with Alternative Roles." *International Labour Review*, Vol. 129, No. 5, September–October 1981.

Stetson, Damon. "A.F.L.–C.I.O. to Seek $2 Minimum Wage and 35–Hour Week." *New York Times*, February 21, 1965.

Stetson, Damon. "I.L.G.W.U. Urges Repeal of Law." *New York Times*, May 14, 1965.

Stigler, George. "The Economics of Minimum Wage Legislation." *American Economic Review*, Vol. 36, June 1946.

Stitt, Louise. "Minimum-Wage Legislation in the United States," *Labor Information Bulletin*, Vol. II, No. 11, November 1935.

Supreme Court of the United States. *Minimum Wage Cases*. October Term, 1914: No. 507, *Stettler* v. *O'Hara*, and No. 508, *Simpson* v. *O'Hara*, "Brief and Arguments for Plaintiffs in Error." Minneapolis: Review Publishing Company, 1914.

Supreme Court of the United States. *Oregon Minimum Wage Cases*, October Term, 1916: Nos. 25 and 26, *Stettler* v. *O'Hara* and *Simpson* v. *O'Hara*, "Brief for Defendants in Error upon Re-Argument," Reprinted by the National Consumers' League.

Supreme Court of the United States. October Term, 1922: Nos. 795 and 796 Justice Sutherland Writing for the Court, Affirmed Decision in *Adkins* v. *Children's Hospital*, April 9, 1923.

Supreme Court of the United States. October Term, 1936: No. 293, *West Coast Hotel Company* v. *Parrish*, March 29, 1937, (57 Sup Ct. 578).

"Supreme Court Reversal Validates Minimum Wage Laws." *American Labor Legislation Review*, Vol. XXVII, No. 2, June 1937.

Swenson, Rinehart J. *Public Regulation of the Rate of Wages*. New York: H.H. Wilson Company, 1917.

Taussig, F.W. "Minimum Wages for Women." *Quarterly Journal of Economics*, Vol. XV, May 1916.

"Tobin Pushes Plan to Raise Pay Scale." *New York Times*, January 28, 1949.

Tolchin, Martin. "Mrs. Chisholm Led Fight for Domestics Base Pay." *New York Times*, June 21, 1973.

Truman, Harry S. *Public Papers of the Presidents of the United States*, January 1 to December 31, 1946. Washington, D.C.: U.S. Government Printing Office, 1962.

Truman, Harry S. *Public Papers of the Presidents of the United States*, January 1 to December 31, 1947. Washington, D.C.: U S. Government Printing Office, 1963.

Truman, Harry S. *Public Papers of the Presidents of the United States*, January 1 to December 31, 1949. Washington, D.C.: U.S. Government Printing Office, 1964.

Truman, Harry S. *Public Papers of the Presidents of the United States*, January 1 to December 31, 1950. Washington, D.C.: U.S. Government Printing Office, 1965.

"Unemployment Rate Off to 7.3% in March." *New York Times*, April 2, 1977.

"Uniform Pay Base Urged." *New York Times*, October 7, 1937.

"Unionists and Nixon Discuss Pay Floor," *New York Times*, April 8, 1960.

"Urge Budget Basis for Women's Wage." *New York Times*, October 22, 1937.

Uri, Noel D., and J. Wilson Mixon, Jr. "An Economic Analysis of the Determinants of Minimum Wage Voting Behavior." *Journal of Law and Economics*, Vol. XXIII, No. 1, April 1980.

U.S. Congress, House of Representatives. *Fair Labor Standards Act of 1938*, Report No. 2182, 75th Cong., 3rd sess., April 21, 1938.

U.S. Congress, House of Representatives. *Fair Labor Standards Act of 1938*. Conference Report No. 2738 to Accompany S. 2475, 75th Cong., 3rd sess., June 11, 1938.

U.S. Congress, House of Representatives. *Minimum Wage Standards and Other Parts of the Fair Labor Standards Act of 1938: Hearings before Subcommittee No. 4 of the Committee on Education and Labor*, Vol. 3. 80th Cong., 1st sess., November 5–8, 10–15, 1947.

U.S. Congress, House of Representatives. *Report*, No. 267. Washington, D.C.: Government Printing Office, March 16, 1949.

U.S. Congress, Senate. *Minimum Wages for Women*. Document No. 46, "Opinion of the U.S. Supreme Court of the United States," 75th Cong., 1st sess., March 29, 1937.

U.S. Congress, Senate. *Fair Labor Standards Act*. Report No. 884 to Accompany S. 2475, 75th Cong., 1st sess., July 6, 1937.

U.S. Congress, Senate Committee on Education and Labor and House Committee on Labor, *Fair Labor Standards Act of 1937*, Part 1, Joint Hearings on S. 2475 and H.R. 7200, 75th Cong., 1st sess., June 2–5, 1937.

U.S. Congress, Senate Committee on Education and Labor and House Committee on Labor, *Fair Labor Standards Act of 1937*, Part 2, Joint Hearings on S. 2475 and H.R. 7200, 75th Cong., 1st sess., June 7–15, 1937.

U.S. Department of Labor. *Report to the Congress on the Training Wage Provisions of the Fair Labor Standards Act Amendments of 1989 from the Secretary of Labor* (Washington, D.C.: n.d.).

U.S. Department of Labor. "Proceedings of the Seventh Minimum Wage Conference." Washington, D.C., October 21–22, 1937. Mimeographed.

U.S. Department of Labor. "Proceedings of the Tenth Minimum–Wage Conference." Washington, D.C., January 17–18, 1941. Mimeographed.

U.S. Department of Labor. "Supplemental Statement of the Administrator of the Wage and Hour and Public Contracts Divisions, U.S. Department of Labor." Washington, D.C., December 1947. Mimeographed.

U.S. Department of Labor. "Proceedings of the Seventeenth Annual Conference of State Minimum-Wage Administrators," Washington, D.C., September 18–19, 1952. Mimeographed.

U.S. Department of Labor. *Annual Report*, Fiscal Year 1959. Washington, D.C.: Government Printing Office, 1960.

U.S. Department of Labor. "Report Submitted to the Congress in Accordance with the Requirements of Section 4(d) of the Fair Labor Standards Act, 1960." Washington, D.C. 1960. Mimeographed.

U.S. Department of Labor. "Report Submitted to the Congress in Accordance with the Requirements of Section 4(d) of the Fair Labor Standards Act, 1962." Washington, D.C., 1962. Mimeographed.

U.S. Department of Labor. *Fifty-ninth Annual Report, Fiscal Year 1971*. Washington, D.C.: Government Printing Office, 1972.

U.S. Department of Labor. *Annual Report*, Fiscal Year 1974. Washington, D.C.: Government Printing Office, 1975.

U.S. Department of Labor. *First Section 4(d)(3) Report to Congress.* Washington D.C.: Government Printing Office, 1975.

U.S. Department of Labor, Employment Standards Administration. *Minimum Wage and Maximum Hours Standards under the Fair Labor Standards Act—1984 Report.* Transmitted to the Congress on April 26, 1985 Washington, D.C.: Government Printing Office, 1985.

U.S. Department of Labor, Employment Standards Administration. *Minimum Wage and Maximum Hours Standards under the Fair Labor Standards Act.* Transmitted to the Congress on January 31, 1972. Washington, D.C.: Government Printing Office, 1972.

U.S. Department of Labor, Employment Standards Administration. *Minimum Wage and Maximum Hours Standards under the Fair Labor Standards Act.* Transmitted to the Congress on January 19, 1973. Washington, D.C.: Government Printing Office 1973.

U.S. Department of Labor, Employment Standards Administration. *Minimum Wage and Maximum Hours Standards under the Fair Labor Standards Act.* Transmitted to the Congress on January 31, 1974. Washington, D.C.: Government Printing Office, 1974.

U.S. Department of Labor, Employment Standards Administration. *Groups with Historically High Incidences of Unemployment.* First Biennial Report to the Congress as Required by Section 4(d)(3) of the Fair Labor Standards Act. Washington, D.C.: Government Printing Office, May 1975.

U.S. Department of Labor, Employment Standards Administration. *Minimum Wage and Maximum Hours Standards under the Fair Labor Standards Act.* Transmitted to the Congress on January 31, 1975. Washington, D.C.: Government Printing Office, 1975.

U.S. Department of Labor, Employment Standards Administration. *Minimum Wage and Maximum Hours Standards under the Fair Labor Standards Act.* Transmitted to the Congress on January 30, 1976. Washington, D.C.: Government Printing Office, 1976.

U.S. Department of Labor, Employment Standards Administration. *Worker Certificates under Section 14 of the Fair Labor Standards Act: A Report of Certificates of Learners, Apprentices, Students, and Handicapped Workers.* Washington, D.C.: Government Printing Office, 1976.

U.S. Department of Labor, Employment Standards Administration. *Minimum Wage and Maximum Hours Standards under the Fair Labor Standards Act.* Transmitted to the Congress on January 19, 1977. Washington, D.C.: Government Printing Office, 1977.

U.S. Department of Labor, Employment Standards Administration. *Minimum Wage and Maximum Hours Standards under the Fair Labor Standards Act.* Transmitted to the Congress on August 9, 1978. Washington, D.C.: Government Printing Office, 1978.

U.S. Department of Labor, Employment Standards Administration. *Minimum Wage and Maximum Hours Standards under the Fair Labor Standards Act.* Transmitted to the Congress on August 15, 1979. Washington, D.C.: Government Printing Office, 1979.

U.S. Department of Labor, Employment Standards Administration. *Nonsupervisory Fire Protection and Law Enforcement Employees in State and Local Government.* Washington, D.C.: Government Printing Office, 1979.

U.S. Department of Labor, Employment Standards Administration. *Minimum Wage and Maximum Hours Standards under the Fair Labor Standards Act.* Transmitted to the Congress on January 19, 1981. Washington, D.C.: Government Printing Office, 1981.

U.S. Department of Labor, Employment Standards Administration. *Minimum Wage and Maximum Hours Standards under the Fair Labor Standards Act —1982 Report.* Transmitted to the Congress on April 22, 1983. Washington, D.C.: Government Printing Office, 1983.

U.S. Department of Labor, Employment Standards Administration. *Minimum Wage and Maximum Hours Standards under the Fair Labor Standards Act.* Transmitted to the Congress on April 17, 1986. Washington, D.C.: Government Printing Office, 1986.

U.S. Department of Labor, Employment Standards Administration. *Minimum Wage and Maximum Hours Standards under the Fair Labor Standards Act.* Transmitted to the Congress on June 30, 1988. Washington, D.C.: Government Printing Office, 1988.

U.S. Department of Labor, Office of the Solicitor. "Child Labor Law in the United States." Washington, D.C., n.d. Mimeographed.

U.S. Department of Labor, Wage and Hour and Public Contracts Divisions. *Interim Report to Congress.* Transmitted to the Congress on January 14, 1939. Washington, D.C.: Government Printing Office, 1939.

U.S. Department of Labor, Wage and Hour and Public Contracts Divisions. *Annual Report,* Fiscal Year 1939. Transmitted to the Congress on January 8, 1940. Washington, D.C.: Government Printing Office, 1940.

U.S. Department of Labor, Wage and Hour and Public Contracts Divisions. *First Annual Report of the Administrator for Calendar Year 1939.* Submitted to the Congress of the United States on January 8, 1940. Washington, D.C.: Government Printing Office, 1940.

U.S. Department of Labor, Wage and Hour and Public Contracts Division. *Annual Report,* Fiscal Year 1940. Transmitted to the Congress on January 2, 1941. Washington, D.C.: Government Printing Office, 1941.

U.S. Department of Labor, Wage and Hour and Public Contracts Division. *Annual Report* Fiscal Year 1942. Transmitted to the Congress on January 4, 1943. Washington, D.C. 1943. Mimeographed.

U.S. Department of Labor, Wage and Hour and Public Contracts Divisions. *Annual Report,* Fiscal Year 1943. Transmitted to the Congress on January 15, 1944. Washington, D.C., 1944. Mimeographed.

U.S. Department of Labor, Wage and Hour and Public Contracts Divisions. *Annual Report,* Fiscal Year 1944. Transmitted to the Congress on January 3, 1945. Washington, D.C., 1945. Mimeographed.

U.S. Department of Labor, Wage and Hour and Public Contracts Divisions. *Annual Report,* Fiscal Year 1946. Washington, D.C.: Government Printing Office, 1947.

U.S. Department of Labor, Wage and Hour and Public Contracts Divisions. *Annual Report,* Fiscal Year 1947. Transmitted to the Congress on January 2, 1948. Washington, D.C.: Government Printing Office.

U.S. Department of Labor, Wage and Hour and Public Contracts Divisions. *Annual Report,* Fiscal Year 1948. Transmitted to the Congress on January 3, 1949. Washington, D.C.: Government Printing Office, 1949.

U.S. Department of Labor, Wage and Hour and Public Contracts Divisions. *Annual Report,* Fiscal Year 1949. Transmitted to the Congress on January 3, 1950. Washington, D.C.: Government Printing Office, 1950.

U.S. Department of Labor, Wage and Hour and Public Contracts Divisions. *Annual Report,* Fiscal Year 1950. Reprinted from the 38th *Annual Report of the Secretary of Labor.* Washington, D.C.: Government Printing Office, 1951.

U.S. Department of Labor, Wage and Hour and Public Contracts Divisions. *Annual Report,* Fiscal Year 1951. Washington, D.C.: Government Printing Office, 1952.

U.S. Department of Labor, Wage and Hour and Public Contracts Divisions. *Annual Report*, Fiscal Year 1952. Transmitted to the Congress on December 31, 1952. Washington, D.C.: Government Printing Office, 1953.

U.S. Department of Labor, Wage and Hour and Public Contracts Divisions. *Annual Report*, Fiscal Year 1953. Washington, D.C.: Government Printing Office, 1954.

U.S. Department of Labor, Wage and Hour and Public Contracts Divisions. *Annual Report*, Fiscal Year 1954, Washington, D.C.: Government Printing Office, 1955.

U.S. Department of Labor, Wage and Hour and Public Contracts Divisions. *Annual Report*, Fiscal Year 1955. Washington, D.C.: Government Printing Office, 1956.

U.S. Department of Labor, Wage and Hour and Public Contracts Divisions. *1956 Annual Report*. Reprinted from the Secretary of Labor's *Annual Report for 1956*. Washington, D.C.: Government Printing Office, 1957.

U.S. Department of Labor, Wage and Hour and Public Contracts Divisions. *Studies of the Economic Effects of the $1 Minimum Wage: Interim Report.* Washington, D.C.: Government Printing Office, March 1957.

U.S. Department of Labor, Wage and Hour and Public Contracts Divisions. *1957 Annual Report*. Reprinted from the Secretary of Labor's *Annual Report for 1957*. Washington, D.C.: Government Printing Office, 1958.

U.S. Department of Labor, Wage and Hour and Public Contracts Divisions. "Wage Order Program for Puerto Rico, the Virgin Islands, and American Samoa." Washington, D.C., January 1959. Mimeographed.

U.S. Department of Labor, Wage and Hour and Public Contracts Divisions. *Annual Report*, Fiscal Year 1959. Reprinted from the 1959 *Annual Report of the Secretary of Labor* Washington, D.C.: Government Printing Office, 1960.

U.S. Department of Labor, Wage and Hour and Public Contracts Divisions. *Annual Report*, Fiscal Year 1961. Washington, D.C.: Government Printing Office, 1962.

U.S. Department of Labor, Wage and Hour and Public Contracts Divisions. *Annual Report*, Fiscal Year 1962. Reprinted from the 1962 *Annual Report of the Secretary of Labor.* Washington, D.C.: Government Printing Office, 1963.

U.S. Department of Labor, Wage and Hour and Public Contracts Divisions. *Report Submitted to the Congress in Accordance with the Requirements of Section 4(d) of the Fair Labor Standards Act.* Transmitted to the Congress on January 31, 1963. Washington, D.C.: Government Printing Office, 1963.

U.S. Department of Labor, Wage and Hour and Public Contracts Divisions. *Report Submitted to the Congress in Accordance with the Requirements of Section 4(d) of the Fair Labor Standards Act.* Transmitted to the Congress in January 1964. Washington, D.C.: Government Printing Office, 1964.

U.S. Department of Labor, Wage and Hour and Public Contracts Divisions. *Report Submitted to the Congress in Accordance with the Requirements of Section 4(d) of the Fair Labor Standards Act.* Transmitted to the Congress on January 29, 1965. Washington, D.C.: Government Printing Office, 1965.

U.S. Department of Labor, Wage and Hour and Public Contracts Divisions. *Annual Report,* Fiscal Year 1966. Transmitted to the Congress on January 31, 1966. Washington, D.C.: Government Printing Office, 1966.

U.S. Department of Labor, Wage and Hour and Public Contracts Divisions. *Minimum Wage and Maximum Hours Standards under the Fair Labor Standards Act.* Transmitted to the Congress on January 31, 1966. Washington, D.C.: Government Printing Office, 1966.

U.S. Department of Labor, Wage and Hour and Public Contracts Divisions. *Minimum Wage and Maximum Hours Standards under the Fair Labor Standards Act.* Transmitted to the Congress on January 14, 1967. Washington, D.C.: Government Printing Office, 1967.

U.S. Department of Labor, Wage and Hour and Public Contracts Division. *Annual Report,* Fiscal Year 1968. Transmitted to the Congress on January 3, 1968. Washington, D.C.: Government Printing Office, 1968.

U.S. Department of Labor, Wage and Hour and Public Contracts Divisions. *Minimum Wage and Maximum Hours Standards under the Fair Labor Standards Act.* Transmitted to the Congress on January 31, 1968. Washington, D.C.: Government Printing Office, 1968.

U.S. Department of Labor, Wage and Hour and Public Contracts Divisions. *Annual Report,* Fiscal Year 1969. Transmitted to the Congress on January 14, 1969. Washington, D.C.: Government Printing Office, 1969.

U.S. Department of Labor, Wage and Hour and Public Contracts Divisions. *Minimum Wage and Maximum Hours Standards under the Fair Labor Standards Act.* Transmitted to the Congress on January 14, 1969. Washington, D.C.: Government Printing Office, 1969.

U.S. Department of Labor, Wage and Hour and Public Contracts Divisions, *Annual Report,* Fiscal Year 1970, transmitted to the Congress on January 30, 1970. Washington, D.C.: Government Printing Office, 1970.

U.S. Department of Labor, Wage and Hour and Public Contracts Divisions. *Minimum Wage and Maximum Hours Standards under the Fair Labor Standards Act.* Transmitted to the Congress on January 30, 1970. Washington, D.C.: Government Printing Office, 1970.

U.S. Department of Labor, Wage and Hour Division. "History of the Fair Labor Standards Act." Washington, D.C., December 1938. Mimeographed.

U.S. Department of Labor, Wage and Hour Division. "Basis for Field Discussions of the Wage and Hour Law." No. 1, rev. Washington, D.C., November 17, 1939. Mimeographed.

U.S. Department of Labor, Wage and Hour Division. *Interim Report of the Administrator of the Wage and Hour Division: For the Period August 15 to December 31, 1938.* Washington, D.C.: Government Printing Office, 1939.

U.S. Department of Labor, Wage and Hour Division. "Wartime Policies on Wages, Hours, and Other Labor Standards in the United States, 1917–1918." Washington, D.C., May 1942. Mimeographed.

U.S. Department of Labor, Women's Bureau. "Proceedings of the Washington Conference of New Minimum Wage States." Washington, D.C., July 19, 1933. Mimeographed.

U.S. Department of Labor, Women's Bureau. "Report of the Fifth Minimum Wage Conference." Washington, D.C., November 25, 1935. Mimeographed.

U.S. Department of Labor, Women's Bureau. "Report of the Minimum Wage Conference Called by Secretary of Labor Frances Perkins." Washington, D.C., June 16, 1936. Mimeographed.

U.S. Department of Labor. Women's Bureau, "Proceedings of the Seventh Minimum Wage Conference." Washington, D.C., October 21–22, 1937. Mimeographed.

U.S. Department of Labor, Workplace Standards Administration. *Minimum Wage and Maximum Hours Standards under the Fair Labor Standards Act*. Transmitted to the Congress on January 29, 1971. Washington, D.C.: Government Printing Office, 1971.

U.S. General Accounting Office. "Enforcement of the Fair Labor Standards Act." GAO/HRD–87–68FS, Draft, March 1987.

U.S. Library of Congress. Legislative Reference Service. "Pros and Cons re Amendments to Fair Labor Standards Act." Based on Hearings before Senate Committee on Education and Labor. Washington, D.C., September 25–October 10, 1945. Mimeographed.

Van Sickle, John V. "Geographical Aspects of a Minimum Wage." *Harvard Business Review*, Vol. XXIV, No. 3, spring 1946.

Vanderbrink, D.C. "The Minimum Wage: No Minor Matter for Teens." *Economic Perspectives* (Federal Reserve Bank of Chicago), March–April 1987.

Verrill, Chas. H. "Minimum-Wage Legislation in the United States and Foreign Countries." *Bulletin of the U.S. Bureau of Labor Statistics*. Whole No. 167. Washington, D.C.: Government Printing Office, April 1915.

"Wage Bill Changes Sought by Labor." *New York Times*, June 16, 1938.

"Wage Bill Reintroduced." *New York Times*, February 3, 1961.

"Wage-Floor Bill Passed in Senate by 62–to–28 Vote." *Wall Street Journal*, August 3, 1973.

"Wage-Hour Plan of G.O.P. Scored." *New York Times*, March 16, 1957.

"Wage-Price Policies." *New York Times*, February 3, 1961.

"Wage Rise Opposed by Cotton Council." *New York Times*, February 8, 1949.

"Wage Violations Mount." *New York Times*, March 18, 1957.

"Washington: For the Record." *New York Times*, April 12, 1972.

Watanabe, S. "Minimum Wages in Developing Countries: Myth and Reality." *International Labour Review*. Vol. 113, No. 3, May–June 1976.

Weaver, Warren Jr. "Long Is Rebuffed on Welfare Idea." *New York Times*, August 7, 1970.

Webb, Beatrice (Potter). *The Wages of Men and Women: Should They be Equal?* London: Fabian Society, n.d.

Weinstock, Harris. "Justifying the Minimum Wage." *Industrial Outlook*, January 1915.

Weiss, Harry. "Minimum Wage Fixing under the United States Fair Labor Standards Act." *International Labour Review*, Vol. LI, No. 1, January 1945.

Welch, Finis. "Minimum Wage Legislation in the United States." *Economic Inquiry*, Vol. XII, No. 3, September 1974.

Welch, Finis. "Reply to Minimum Wage Legislation in the United States: Comment." *Economic Inquiry*, Vol. XV, No. 1, January 1977.

Welch, Finis, and James Cunningham. "Effects of Minimum Wages on the Level and Age Composition of Youth Employment." *Review of Economics and Statistics*, Vol. LX, No. 2, February 1978.

Wessels, Walter J. "The Effect of Minimum Wages in the Presence of Fringe Benefits: An Expanded Model." *Economic Inquiry*, Vol. XVIII, No. 2, April 1980.

West, E.G. and Michael McKee "Monopsony and 'Shock' Arguments for Minimum Wages." *Southern Economic Journal*, Vol. 46, No. 3, January 1980.

West Coast Hotel Co. v. Parrish, 57 Sup. Ct. 578 (1937).

"What Pete's Pizza Will Do with Higher Minimum Wage." *Bismarck Tribune*, April 2, 1988.

White, C.B. "Brief History of the U.S. Child Labor Laws in Nonagricultural Employment and Child Labor Regulation 3." Washington, D.C., n.d. Mimeographed.

White, William S. "75 Cent Minimum Wage Set for House Vote." *New York Times*, January 19, 1949.

Whittaker, William. "Youth Unemployment and the Federal Minimum Wage." *Issue Brief.* The Library of Congress, Congressional Research Service, Washington, D.C., February 26, 1980.

"Wider Wage Bills Dying in Congress." *New York Times*, July 7, 1957.

"Wider Wage Law Backed by Wirtz." *New York Times*, July 7, 1965.

Williams, Juan. "Brock Backs Youth-Wage Trial." *Washington Post*, May 7, 1985.

"Wirtz Asks Minimum Wage for 2.6 Million Workers." *New York Times*, February 8, 1964.

"Wirtz Says Young Face a Job Crisis." *New York Times*, May 16, 1965.

Wolman, Leo. "Economic Justification of the Legal Minimum Wage." *American Labor Legislation Review*, Vol. XIV, No. 3, September 1924.

Wolman, Leo. "Minimum Wage Laws Are for States—But Any Legislation of This Character Is Regarded as Bar to Trade Revival and Reemployment." *Congressional Record*, Vol. 83, Part 10, March 28, 1938, to June 1, 1938.

Women's Industrial Council. *The Case for and Against a Legal Minimum Wage for Sweated Workers.* London: Women's Industrial Council 1909.

Woolston, H.B. "Wages in New York." Reprinted from *The Survey*, October 1915.

"Wrong End Squeeze." *New York Times*, September 7, 1973.

Zell, Steven P. "The Minimum Wage and Youth Unemployment." *Economic Review* (Federal Reserve Bank of Kansas City), January 1978.

Zuchoff, Mitchell. "$4.65 Is Aim on Minimum Wage's 50th." *Boston Sunday Globe*, January 17, 1988.

Zucker, Albert. "Minimum Wages and the Long-Run Elasticity of Demand for Low-Wage Labor." *Quarterly Journal of Economics*, Vol. LXXXVII, No. 2, May 1973.

Index

About the Author

WILLIS J. NORDLUND is Dean, School of Business at the College of West Virginia. He is former Regional Director of the Office of Worker's Compensation Programs and was the Executive and Special Assistant to the Under Secretary of Labor from 1976 to 1980. Dr. Nordlund has been a life-long observer of the nation's minimum wage program.

ISBN 0-313-26412-0

EAN

90000>

9 780313 264122

HARDCOVER BAR CODE